D1500228

Foraging in the Past

Foraging
IN THE Past

ARCHAEOLOGICAL STUDIES OF
HUNTER-GATHERER DIVERSITY

EDITED BY

ASHLEY K. LEMKE

UNIVERSITY PRESS OF COLORADO
Louisville

© 2018 by University Press of Colorado

Published by University Press of Colorado
245 Century Circle, Suite 202
Louisville, Colorado 80027

 The University Press of Colorado is a proud member of
the Association of University Presses.

The University Press of Colorado is a cooperative publishing enterprise supported, in part, by Adams State University, Colorado State University, Fort Lewis College, Metropolitan State University of Denver, Regis University, University of Colorado, University of Northern Colorado, Utah State University, and Western State Colorado University.

∞ This paper meets the requirements of the ANSI/NISO Z39.48-1992 (Permanence of Paper).

ISBN: 978-1-60732-773-8 (cloth)
ISBN: 978-1-60732-774-5 (ebook)
DOI: https://doi.org/10.5876/9781607327745

Library of Congress Cataloging-in-Publication Data

Names: Lemke, Ashley K., 1985– editor.
Title: Foraging in the past : archaeological studies of hunter-gatherer diversity / edited by Ashley K. Lemke.
Description: Boulder : University Press of Colorado, [2018] | Includes bibliographical references and index.
Identifiers: LCCN 2018014002| ISBN 9781607327738 (cloth) | ISBN 9781607327745 (ebook)
Subjects: LCSH: Hunting and gathering societies. | Archaeology. | Prehistoric peoples. | Antiquities, Prehistoric.
Classification: LCC GN388 .F67 2018 | DDC 306.3/64—dc23
LC record available at https://lccn.loc.gov/2018014002

Cover photograph of Panel VIII of Agawa Rock (Lake Superior Provincial Park, Ontario, Canada), by D. Gordon E. Robertson. From Wikimedia Commons.

Contents

DOI: 10.5876/9781607327745.c000

Foreword

ROBERT L. KELLY

In 2016, I participated in a meeting about hunter-gatherers at the University of Cambridge. There I gave a keynote on work we have been doing with radiocarbon dates as a measure of human population (Kelly et al. 2013; Zahid et al. 2016). I presented what I thought were some striking relationships between climate change and human population. Afterwards, someone in the audience challenged me, claiming that I had no evidence for any such relationships. At a loss for words, all I could do was point to a slide in which the correlations—between population, site spacing, groundstone frequency, and other variables—were obvious, at least in my opinion. "Yes," my critic replied, "but such correlations cannot explain what is going on now; for example, neither climate nor population explains what is happening in Russia today." I was taken aback because I had been discussing the prehistoric sequence of Wyoming; I admit I had not taken modern Russia into account.

A year earlier, I gave a talk at Dartmouth about hunter-gatherer warfare that aimed to test the contention of Hill et al. that high rates of homicide and warfare had held the population growth rates of hunter-gatherer in check for millennia (Hill et al. 2007; Zahid et al. [2016] point out that the long-term hunter-gatherer growth rate is only ~0.04 percent). Quoting Sahlins, I pointed out that individual hunter-gatherers go to war for different reasons than those driving societies to war. People may fight because of insults, witchcraft, the loss of a song duel, a perceived threat to "our way of life," or a belief in the domino theory. People fight, and come up with a culturally logical reason to fight, when they have no other choice. I pointed out that our data showed that regardless of the specific reasons, which for prehistoric cases we cannot know, the Wyoming record only contains evidence of warfare during the Late Prehistoric period, when population density and population pressure were at their highest. Warfare was not a constant condition of the past and therefore could not account for prehistory's low long-term population growth rate.

Again, there was a critic: "you can't cast aside individual motivations because they are real to those individuals; they are not merely secondary factors." I agreed with the critic: after all, people have to be motivated to take the life of another human, or to put themselves in harm's way. But I pointed out that my interest was with the frequency of warfare at the scale of thousands of years, not with the immediate cause of any particular war. I was interested in why societies fight, not why individuals participate in warfare. "Oh, well, if that's what you're interested in," my critic concluded. Clearly, we didn't find the same things to be interesting.

Cultural anthropologists and archaeologists think differently. This is partly a product of our different sources of data—interviews and observations of daily life on the one hand as opposed to materials objects mostly left behind as trash. It's also a product of a difference in scale: ethnographers can observe behavior moment-by-moment, and a long-term study might go on for 50 years. On the other hand, by looking at material culture, archaeologists "see" behavior in large chunks of time—decades if we're lucky, but usually centuries, millennia, or, for Paleolithic archaeologists, longer. This ability to see long-term history is, in fact, the strength of archaeology. Ask archaeologists to do something else and you might as well ask them to not do archaeology.

But there is another, cultural, difference between the two fields. Cultural anthropologists take seemingly "small" behaviors and show them to be a portal into a very complex world. These are Marcel Mauss's "total social facts" (Mauss 1966). Archaeologists, on the other hand, take disparate data drawn from sequences covering (often vast) stretches of time and seek the primary factors that lie behind whatever pattern the data present. This is why comparative ethnographic studies (e.g., Ember and Ember 1992) often draw archaeologists' attention. Cultural anthropologists seek complexity; archaeologists seek simplicity. Both are valid paths of anthropological inquiry.

But these two paths can clash when archaeologists use ethnographic data. Many cultural anthropologists focus (and must focus) on the particular history, context, and cultural logic of one society, and avoid any sort of cross-cultural generalizations. They may have little patience when their field data are added to that of other cases and used to produce a graph showing relationships between one variable and another. "It's more complex than that," they might say. In the early 1990s, a reader of my *Foraging Spectrum* manuscript submitted a single paragraph as a review to the Smithsonian Institution Press, saying that the book's approach was so wrong that there was no need to write a more thorough review (fortunately, the press went with Eric Smith's long, detailed, and useful review).

Ethnographers would also cringe at the idea of projecting ethnographic data onto the past, a tactic that requires ripping those data from their historical context and essentializes a society's culture and behavior. Martin Wobst long ago detailed all the bad that can come when the ethnographic record tyrannizes archaeology (Wobst 1978). The ethnographic present is rarely "just like" the archaeological past. Archaeologists make a grave error when they simply rummage around in the ethnographic attic until they find a case that shows their interpretation of an archaeological dataset is "not impossible." Just because the alleged behavior occurred somewhere doesn't make it a statistically likely interpretation of the prehistoric case.

These manuscripts don't make these errors. They don't warrant their arguments by appealing to ethnographic analogy, cross-cultural generalizations, or attic rummaging. Instead, the authors use relationships established by cross-cultural data as a background against which to bounce the empirical patterns of prehistory in order to learn something new. Many might still feel that the nuance of ethnography is lost, and that's true, but that's also the tradeoff archaeology makes: we lose detail in favor of understanding the relationships between variables that produce the long-term history of humanity. This is what we do to bring to the anthropological table what archaeology and only archaeology can bring.

And what it brings would not excite my critics at Cambridge and Dartmouth. Beginning in the 1960s and continuing into the 1980s, archaeology focused on material factors as the driving forces of human evolutionary change, notably population and subsistence. By the 1990s many had become bored with this approach, or thought it was impoverished as more and more archaeologists read postmodern ethnographies and realized that much more besides population density and food mattered to human societies. Or they abandoned archaeology's professed interest in explanation in favor of interpretation.

This isn't the place for a discussion of post-processual archaeology, but I do want to point out that these chapters show the importance of things that mattered to processual archaeology: population and environment (e.g., Binford's

[1968] classic "Post-Pleistocene Adaptations"). And one can't help but notice that the old-fashioned but never fully resolved issues of processual archaeology matter in a world expected to reach 11 billion by the end of the century and to undergo massive climate change at the same time.

As so often happens in science, ideas about how things work precede our ability to test those ideas. Although processual archaeology focused on the effects of population and environment, it never produced very convincing results because it couldn't measure population and environment in sufficient detail. We sometimes compared site frequencies, grouped in temporal phases that covered hundreds if not thousands of years against simplistic climate intervals, usually cool/wet versus warm/dry. These didn't, and couldn't, convince anyone, not even the field's most stalwart practitioners. What we needed were more accurate and detailed measures of both climate and population.

Fortunately, climate scientists worked out new approaches to various climate data (e.g., pollen, lake levels) that, aided by age-depth models, provide quantitative measures of temperature and moisture in small increments of time, 50 years or less. And, beginning in the late 1980s (Rick 1987), processual archaeologists discovered that large databases of radiocarbon dates can provide detailed measures of human population change over time. Although few could capitalize upon this approach until the databases were constructed and the analytical capacity created, archaeological measures have now breached those barriers (e.g., Kelly et al. 2013; Tallavaara et al. 2015; Zahid et al. 2016, among many others).

The chapters in this volume fulfill some of the promise of processual archaeology by demonstrating what many processual archaeologists long suspected: environment and population matter, so much so that *at the long-term scale that is archaeology's strength* they might be the two primary variables conditioning hunter-gatherer behavior around the globe. Sometimes science moves very slowly, but I suspect that new tools and approaches, along with more detailed data from the four corners of the globe, will allow us now to move rapidly. If this volume is any sign, we can all look forward to the next few decades with excitement.

REFERENCES CITED

Binford, L. R. 1968. "Post-Pleistocene Adaptations." In *New Perspectives in Archaeology*, ed. Sally Binford and Lewis R. Binford, 313–341. Chicago, IL: Aldine.

Ember, Carol, and Melvin Ember. 1992. "Resource Unpredictability, Mistrust, and War: A Cross-Cultural Study." *Journal of Conflict Resolution* 36(2):242–262. https://doi.org/10.1177/0022002792036002002.

Hill, Kim, A. Magdalena Hurtado, and Robert S. Walker. 2007. "High Adult Mortality among Hiwi Hunter-Gatherers: Implications for Human Evolution." *Journal of Human Evolution* 52(4):443–454. https://doi.org/10.1016/j.jhevol.2006.11.003.

Kelly, Robert L., Todd Surovell, Bryan Shuman, and Geoff Smith. 2013. "A Continuous Climatic Impact on Holocene Human Population in the Rocky Mountains." *Proceedings of the National Academy of of the United States of America* 110:443–447. https://doi.org/10.1073/pnas.1201341110.

Mauss, Marcel. 1966. *The Gift: Forms and Functions of Exchange in Archaic Societies.* London: Cohen & West.

Rick, J. W. 1987. "Dates as Data: An Examination of the Peruvian Preceramic Radiocarbon Record." *American Antiquity* 52(1):55–73. https://doi.org/10.2307/281060.

Tallavaara, M., M. Luoto, N. Korhonen, H. Järvinen, and H. Seppä. 2015. "Human Population Dynamics in Europe over the Last Glacial Maximum." *Proceedings of the National Academy of Sciences of the United States of America* 112(27):8232–8237. https://doi.org/10.1073/pnas.1503784112.

Wobst, H. M. 1978. "The Archaeo-Ethnology of Hunter-Gatherers or the Tyranny of the Ethnographic Record in Archaeology." *American Antiquity* 43(2):303–309. https://doi.org/10.2307/279256.

Zahid, H. Jabran, Erick Robinson, and Robert L. Kelly. 2016. "Agriculture, Population Growth and Statistical Analysis of the Radiocarbon Record." *Proceedings of the National Academy of Sciences of the United States of America* 113(4):931–935. https://doi.org/10.1073/pnas.1517650112.

This volume would not be possible without the tireless work of each contributor—it is they, first, who deserve thanks. The majority of these authors as well as several others participated in a Society for American Archaeology symposium in San Francisco in 2015. That conference marked the 25th anniversary of the original printing of Robert Kelly's seminal work, *The Foraging Spectrum: Diversity in Hunter-Gatherer Lifeways*. This book is often referred to as the "hunter-gatherer bible" as archaeologists and anthropologists interested in forager societies have incorporated its central message into their scholarship and teaching—hunter-gatherers are far more diverse than we tend to imagine. This message is an important one, particularly given the fact that the vast amount of data presented in *Foraging Spectrum* is ethnographic, collected within the last 200 or so years. Imagine the variability within hunter-gatherers as far back as 10,000 years ago, or 100,000 years ago, or even to our earliest human ancestors, who were the first hunters and gatherers. Ethnographic data depicts just the tip of the iceberg, and this volume is a first attempt to explore forager diversity in the past. Each contributor has worked towards this goal and together these chapters contribute new approaches to age old questions. To Nicholas Conard, Raven Garvey, Keiko Kitagawa, John Krigbaum, Petra Krönneck, Steven Kuhn, Julia Lee-Thorp, Peter Mitchell, Katherine Moore, Susanne Münzel, Kurt Rademaker, Patrick Roberts, Britt Starkovich, Brian Stewart, Mary Stiner, and of course, Robert Kelly—I give thanks. I consider myself extremely fortunate to have had the opportunity to wrangle such a brilliant group of friends, colleagues, mentors, and scholars.

It was Jessica d'Arbonne, the acquisitions editor at University Press of Colorado who first suggested turning our symposium into a book—and I thank her for her foresight and guidance. The entire staff at University Press of Colorado has my deep gratitude, as well as Karl Yambert for his detailed and insightful copyediting.

Joyce Marcus and John O'Shea have my sincere thanks for their encouragement and advice throughout this project. To my numerous friends and family members who have supported each stage—thanks to you!

Foraging in the Past

Hunter-Gatherers and Archaeology

Ashley K. Lemke

Hunter-gatherer societies have played a pivotal role in anthropology as a discipline. Early anthropologists including Émile Durkheim, A. R. Radcliffe-Brown, Julian Steward, and Claude Lévi-Strauss used hunter-gatherer data to address broad anthropological topics such as kinship, division of labor, and the origins of religion (Kelly 2013). In fact, hunter-gatherers have been so foundational to anthropology that the entire history of the discipline could be viewed in terms of hunter-gatherer ethnography (Yengoyan 1979). Foragers can be seen as the *quintessential* topic of anthropology (Bettinger et al. 2015). After more than a century of study, hunter-gatherer societies are now well documented and known to be extremely diverse.

Given the central role of hunter-gatherers in creating foundational theories and principles of anthropology, ethnographic studies of these living groups were common. Thus, hunter-gatherer diversity is primarily known from ethnographic data. These ethnographic cases, however, provide only a small sample of the extensive variability in hunter-gatherer adaptations.

The central problem facing anthropologists interested in documenting the entire range of human behavior, and archaeologists interested in hunter-gatherer diversity in the past, is that most of our pictures of prehistoric hunter-gatherers are based on ethnographic analogy rather than archaeological evidence. Given the tremendous range of variability present among ethnographic foragers explored by Robert Kelly (1995,

DOI: 10.5876/9781607327745.c001

2013), Lewis Binford (e.g., 2001), and others, such diversity must have been even greater in the past when foraging was the most common (or only) mode of subsistence. Over the course of foraging lifeways on the planet, there are vast amounts of time and space available to the archaeologist that are not represented in the ethnographic record. Therefore, in contrast to ethnography, archaeology has access to a greater range of hunter-gatherer phenomena in the recent and remote past. Robert Kelly (1995, 2013) has highlighted diversity in the ethnographic record, has championed human behavioral ecology as a method for understanding foraging adaptations, and has identified the problem of trying to explore and appreciate diversity among hunter-gatherers in the past.

The goal of this book is to address this problem explicitly—to discuss how to explore diversity in the past—and essentially move the *Foraging Spectrum*, Robert Kelly's seminal work, back in time. In order to take the first steps toward recognizing and documenting forager variability in prehistory, this volume covers a wide range of time and space as well as theoretical perspectives and methodological approaches. It is our belief that such a diverse theoretical and methodological toolkit is essential for exploring variability in past human behavior.

NORMATIVE VIEWS OF HUNTER-GATHERERS IN ANTHROPOLOGY

The term *hunter-gatherer* most often refers to a mode of subsistence, but disparate cultures fitting these economic criteria have traditionally been grouped together despite variation in demography, mobility, foraging behavior, and sociopolitical organization. Because of this, there is considerable debate concerning who actually *is* a hunter-gatherer (Ames 2004). There are two primary definitions. The first is economic, referring to people without domesticated plants and animals (except dogs) and incorporates a number of different social forms (Kelly 1995, 2013). The second is social, referring to band societies or small groups who are egalitarian, with flexible membership, and with differences among individuals based primarily on age, gender, and charisma. This social definition encompasses a variety of economies (Lee 1992). The existence of two distinct definitions makes of *hunter-gatherers* a broad analytical category that masks significant sociocultural and economic variability. Anthropological archaeologists continue to struggle with this variability.

Contemporary, historic, and ethnographic hunter-gatherers are extremely diverse in all aspects of life—from economy, to social organization, kinship, and ritual (e.g., Ames 2004; Binford 2001; Kelly 1995, 2013; Kent 1996; Panter-Brick, Layton, and Rowley-Conwy 2001). Variability was presumably even greater in the past. However, due to the wealth of ethnographic data, and the inherent problems of poor preservation of hunter-gatherer remains in the archaeological record, the issue remains: most reconstructions of prehistoric hunter-gatherers conform to a single normative view:

> We have built up remarkably detailed pictures of early human society complete with family bands of twenty-five people who share food, trace kin relations bilaterally, reside bilocally, and eat a generalized diet with women gathering plant food and men hunting . . . But this detailed picture comes not from archaeological evidence as much as from ethnographic analogy . . . *If prehistoric hunter-gatherers all look the same, it is because we supposed them to be that way from the outset.* (Kelly 1995:339, emphasis added)

The central problem concerning prehistoric hunter-gatherer archaeology is surpassing the limited view of foragers drawn from the ethnographic record and the resulting normative characterization of simple, highly mobile, acephalous bands with limited property. Ethnographic cases that do not fit this model are referred to as "complex" hunter-gatherers, as they are influenced by historical contingency or a unique resource suite. These restricted views of forager lifeways are largely due to inherent biases in the ethnographic record. The picture drawn from ethnographic data is incomplete, limited, and (out of necessity) considers only modern humans.

LIMITATIONS OF THE ETHNOGRAPHIC RECORD

The ethnographic record of foraging societies is an incomplete and biased sample, as certain groups have been overrepresented and others underrepresented, and yet others are left out of more general hunter-gatherer studies completely. As different forager groups wax and wane in popularity, their particular behaviors and view of the world have become the general model of hunter-gatherers (Kelly 1995). Historically, Kalahari groups, Arctic groups (specifically the Nunamiut), and more recently the Hadza, have come to dominate archaeological interpretations of foragers. This handful of ethnographic cases has been overrepresented in models of hunter-gatherers and used to characterize foraging style as egalitarian, highly mobile, and with few material wants. Other ethnographic groups have been historically underrepresented, such as South American foragers living in tropical rainforests. While these groups are generally thought to be too reliant on cultivation to be true foragers (Politis 2015), archaeological evidence demonstrates that hunter-gatherers have a long prehistory of occupying similar environments (Roberts et al., chapter 5, this volume).

Furthermore, other societies have been left out of more general studies and are relegated to other categories, such as "complex" hunter-gatherers. In many classic anthropological works concerning foragers, certain ethnographic cases that did not conform to general models were left out. For example, Service (1966) did not include Native Americans of the Northwest Coast in *The Hunters*, and many other societies—including the Tlingit and Nootka, the Calusa of Florida, and the horse-riding groups of Native Americans from the Great Plains—were excluded from *Man the Hunter* (1968). The rationale behind these analytical choices was that these were extreme cases of either environment (e.g., concentrated resources in both time and space, such as salmon runs on the Pacific Coast) or historical contingency (e.g., the importation of Spanish colonial horses) (see Garvey and Bettinger 2014 on unique local circumstances versus diffusion). Historical contingency is often linked to contact with state societies, but it must be stressed that *all* ethnographic foragers were in contact with states, and *all* ethnographic foragers were subject to their own unique historical contingencies. Significantly, archaeological evidence has demonstrated that many traits believed to be the result of culture exchange, such as social complexity, social inequality, and complex economies, in fact *predate* colonial contact (e.g., Prentiss et al. 2007; Zedeño et al. 2014). These traits are perhaps more characteristic of prehistoric hunter-gatherers than traditionally assumed (Lemke 2016).

In addition to these biases, ethnographic data are inherently limited by the small amounts of both time and space in which ethnographers have been working with foraging groups. Historic ethnographic research with hunter-gatherers was often considered "salvage ethnography" as these cultures and economies were rapidly changing (see the frontispiece from *Man the Hunter*, Lee and DeVore 1968). The time and space available to ethnographers is particularly narrow when compared to the broad stretches available in the archaeological record. Not only were prehistoric foraging populations more numerous but over the great stretch of time when humans were hunting and gathering, massive environmental changes took place. Among the most significant are global fluctuations in both ice sheets and sea level, which submerged and reexposed large portions of the prehistoric landscape over the last 2 million years. These coastlines, particularly on the continental shelf and in many inland lakes and karstic features, were likely some of the most attractive habitats for hunter-gatherers. These sites, and the evidence of prehistoric foraging lifeways they preserve, are now underwater and are only available through submerged archaeological research (see Lemke, chapter 3, this volume). These processes in the past resulted in unique environments that have no modern analog, and it is likely that such environments supported novel hunter-gatherer lifeways unlike any known from the ethnographic record.

Finally, the ethnographic record is limited to biologically and culturally modern humans. Prior to modern human culture, our early human ancestors, such as Neanderthals, *Homo erectus*, and Australopithecines were likely very different kinds of hunter-gatherers (see Kitagawa et al., chapter 7, this volume; Kuhn and Stiner 2001, chapter 8, this volume; Roberts et al., chapter 5, this volume).

Significantly, even within the biased and limited ethnographic record, diversity is clear. Ethnographic data demonstrate that even within small regions, such as the Kalahari Desert or Southeast Asia, a variety of hunter-gatherer lifeways are observed (e.g., Kelly 2013; Kusimba 2005; Stewart and Mitchell, chapter 6, this volume). Some hunter-gatherer groups are highly mobile, others more sedentary, many are band societies whereas others have different social systems. Hunted animals are sometimes a large part of the diet in some geographic regions, such as the Arctic, and gathering plant foods and smaller animals are more important in other areas, or at different times of year. In certain groups, hunting is done exclusively by men, while in others women do the hunting, (e.g., Bird and Bird 2008; Kelly 2013). Given this diversity in the ethnographic record with limited time and space parameters, it can be expected that variability in the past was much greater, and certainly extends beyond the limited view of foragers still pervasive in anthropology. With a limited range of groups and adaptations, the ethnographic present is just the tip of the iceberg; the archaeological record preserves the rest of the iceberg.

ENTER ARCHAEOLOGY

In marked contrast to the ethnographic record, archaeology has access to a broader range of contexts, including time, space, and environments, and likewise a greater range of hunter-gatherer lifeways. Archaeology's greatest contribution to general anthropology is the vast time scale at its disposal (Jochim 1991; Marcus 2008). It is the only method available for anthropologists to view all the variable aspects of behavior in both space and time, from the individual to groups, from the small settlements to large regions, from single events to patterns over millennia (Wobst 1978:307)—and to see evidence of behaviors that predates colonial contact. For these reasons, archaeologists should not be limited by the range of behaviors known from the ethnographic record and the resulting biased characterization of hunter-gatherers. Furthermore, archaeology is the approach best suited for investigating forager diversity since it is the only discipline that explicitly and directly deals with prehistoric hunter-gatherers and the remnants of their actual behavior.

Archaeologists are in an ideal position to push forager theory forward. To date, the primary goal for anthropologists concerning hunter-gatherers has been to characterize the 99 percent of human history when foraging lifeways were dominant; while this 99 percent still represents a significant stage in human prehistory, it is far from homogeneous (Kuhn and Stiner, chapter 8, this volume). The long-term perspective available to archaeologists provides a window into changing patterns of human behavior, and an incomplete but accurate record of hunter-gatherer diversity and adaptations. In this way, archaeology will always serve as the definitive test for hunter-gatherer variability.

Given the vast range of time, space, and unique environments at its disposal, the archaeological record provides evidence of novel forms of social and economic organization that are only available in the deep past. The creative and challenging role for archaeologists is to produce new portraits of hunter-gatherer diversity in the past, de novo, drawing on but not reproducing the ethnographic present.

RECOGNIZING VARIABILITY IN THE PAST

While contemporary studies of hunter-gatherers acknowledge that ethnographic hunter-gatherers are not living a prehistoric lifestyle, and that forager lifeways are extremely diverse (e.g., Ames 2004; Binford 2001; Kent 1996; Panter-Brick, Layton, and Rowley-Conwy 2001), documenting diversity within *prehistoric* foraging societies remains elusive. How do archaeologists recognize novel forager adaptations in the deep past? To achieve this goal, archaeological investigations must move away from the normative characterization of hunter-gatherers, and work instead with models and hypotheses that are explicitly designed to capture variability.

This volume presents seven distinct geographic and temporal case studies that examine forager diversity. It moves back through time from ethnographic to historic contact periods to considerations of Pleistocene foraging and our early human ancestors. Each case study focuses on a particular geographic region, including the North American Arctic; southern South America; the North American Great Lakes; the Andean highlands of Peru, Bolivia, Chile, and Argentina; tropical rainforests in Sri Lanka; southern Africa; Central Europe; the Mediterranean; and the Near East. Many chapters also track change through time in these areas (see herein Rademaker and Moore, chapter 4; Roberts et al., chapter 5; Stewart and Mitchell, chapter 6; Kitagawa et al., chapter 7; Kuhn and Stiner, chapter 8).

Two central, related questions connect the diverse case studies presented in each chapter: How should ethnographic data be used in the archaeological study of hunter-gatherers? How can we discover novel foraging lifeways in the past?

On the Use of Ethnography

> There is no alternative to using our knowledge of modern peoples to help us penetrate the past. Abandoning the ethnographic record makes archaeology like a paleontology cut off from the biology of living organisms. The real issue is not whether we do it, but *how* we do it.
>
> KEN AMES (2004:366, EMPHASIS ADDED)

The archaeology of prehistoric hunter-gatherers is deeply rooted in ethnographic analogy—and while ethnographic data are helpful in providing generalizations, creating models, and exploring human lifeways, those analogies may limit archaeological discoveries of novel human behavior. Archaeologists should not expect to see "whole" societies from the ethnographic record represented in the past, but rather be prepared to recognize some familiar elements that may be put together in novel ways.

For example, Garvey (chapter 2, this volume) presents a critical use of ethnographic data to establish first-order predictions concerning sources of hunter-gatherer diversity. Similarly, I (Lemke, chapter 3, this volume) use ethnographic data to examine variability in ethnographic and archaeological hunting strategies. Both case studies explicitly acknowledge the limitations of the ethnographic data but still find ways to use such data either to identify sources of diversity (see also Garvey and Bettinger 2014) or to document diversity (Lemke 2016). As Garvey outlines, ethnographic data can be used to explore potential sources of diversity, where a greater level of detail is available to identify such sources as environmental, ecological, technological, or social mechanisms, as well as their interconnections. Furthermore, ethnographic data can be used to build models of hunting behavior to form predictions concerning the nature of hunting sites to aid in the identification of such sites in difficult contexts (e.g., underwater; Lemke, chapter 3, this volume). In the first case study, the environment is held constant to understand cultural diversity between two groups living in similar climates. In the second case, animal behavior is held constant to address hunting strategies over time.

Along these lines, ethnographic data are useful for identifying uniformitarian assumptions that can be made to guide archaeological research. Certain patterns of behavior or phenomena seen in ethnographic accounts were likely the same or similar to phenomena operating in the past, such as the observation that caloric contributions of vegetables to forager diets decline with latitude, for obvious ecological reasons (see Garvey, chapter 2, this volume; Kuhn and Stiner, chapter 8, this volume), or that certain patterns of animal behavior which can be observed today were similar in the past, ultimately conditioning aspects of human hunting strategy and behavior (Lemke, chapter 3, this volume). In both cases, ethnographic data serve as a hypothesis-generating tool within an integrative research design that ultimately tests theory with empirical archaeological data rather than applying a direct ethnographic analogy (*sensu* Kelly 2013).

While ethnographically documented foragers look like prehistoric foragers in many important ways, there are also anomalies (Kuhn and Stiner, chapter 8, this volume). As illustrated in Stewart and Mitchell (chapter 6, this volume), ethnographic and prehistoric foragers differ when considered either at regional or global scales, as southernmost African hunter-gatherers differ from Kalahari groups within Africa and from the broad range of other foragers observed ethnographically around the globe as well. For example, Stewart and Mitchell test Binford's predictions for foragers inhabiting environments within a certain "effective temperature" derived from ethnographic data (from Binford 2001). The expectations are only partially met with archaeological data, with the prehistoric case providing evidence for different behaviors. However, this should not be surprising, because we should not *a priori* expect prehistoric hunter-gatherers to always conform to generalizations drawn from ethnographic cases.

Broad comparative ethnographic comparisons like Kelly's (1995, 2013) and Binford's (2001) are significant first steps toward documenting forager variability. Cases in this volume further demonstrate that comparisons between the ethnographic and archaeological records are important, as prehistoric deviations from the expected pattern of behavior derived from more recent accounts give archaeologists something to explain. However, given historical circumstance, environmental fluctuations, the rates and nature of technological innovation, population growth, and increasing world connectivity and globalization, ethnographic foragers operate in vastly different social, environmental, and cultural contexts than did prehistoric foragers. The next step involves similar studies of *archaeological* data. These comparisons are instrumental for detecting diversity in foraging adaptations over time and space across different contexts, and are essential for discovering novel social forms in the past.

On Discovering Novel Foraging Lifeways:
Environment and Ecology

Indeed, many environments and geographic regions have a limited or absent ethnographic record to draw upon, making archaeological studies especially important. For example, high-altitude areas in general and the Andean puna specifically, as well as tropical rainforests, are often viewed as formidable barriers to hunter-gatherers. Therefore, prehistoric hunter-gatherer populations were not expected to live in either of these environments, or, if they did, their use of them would be fleeting, characterized by logistical forays, short-term occupation, or diets supplemented by other resources. However, contrary to expectations drawn solely from the ethnographic record, evidence of prehistoric hunter-gatherer groups has been found in both places—puna and rainforests—to a much greater extent than traditionally assumed (Rademaker and Moore, chapter 4, this volume; Roberts et al., chapter 5, this volume). Indeed, rather than being "marginal," these zones often have greater resource abundance than adjacent areas. This evidence points to pull (e.g., access to a broader range of resources) rather than push (e.g., population pressure) factors to explain early human occupation of these areas.

What both of these case studies highlight is a source of diversity, the environmental and ecological background. While it has long been acknowledged that these factors are related to diversity in foraging groups (i.e., human behavioral ecology), the picture drawn exclusively from ethnography is limited. Archaeological evidence, on the other hand, shows that people had access to a greater range of environments. These case studies reveal that environmental *flexibility* is a hallmark of humanity (Roberts et al., chapter 5, this volume, and references therein), and more specifically, a hallmark of hunter-gatherers. For example, humans are the only hominin thus far to demonstrate reliance on closed-canopy rainforest resources. In contrast to ethnographic foragers, who were often territorially circumscribed at contact, the archaeological record preserves evidence of foragers who utilized diverse environments and ecologies in the past. These societies peopled every continent on the planet expect for Antarctica, and in so doing encountered every possible environment, all the while demonstrating tremendous flexibility in food-getting strategies. Prehistoric foragers occupied a wider range of environments than their ethnographic counterparts, and within these environments they displayed variable patterns of settlement and mobility strategies.

Rather than environmental determinism, the analysis of such flexibility can be referred to as *environmental possibilism*, the understanding that while the resource structure (including access to freshwater, primary production, and so on) may limit how intensely some areas can be used, foragers make choices to avoid or limit use in more marginal areas (see Rademaker and Moore, chapter 4, this volume). It is not that high altitudes, rainforests, or other environments could not support human populations or that people could not live there; rather, foragers made active choices between more or less marginal areas, and these patterns of landscape use and settlement change over time. As pulses of environmental change shifted areas of primary productivity, forage for animals, the animals themselves, and other critical resources (e.g., firewood/ fuel), people shifted as well. Such alterations in mobility regimes and landscape use can be documented diachronically in the Andean puna (Rademaker and Moore, chapter 4, this volume), southern Africa (Stewart and Mitchell, chapter 6, this volume), and tropical rainforests (Roberts et al., chapter 5, this volume). In these cases, and likely others, forager decision-making and environmental flexibility can be documented in great detail. Such diverse settlement and mobility patterns are not due to foragers' incapacity for long-term or permanent residence; instead, these patterns ultimately correspond with those documented for so many foragers—that mobility was adaptive (Kelly 1995; Rademaker and Moore, chapter 4, this volume) and that foraging lifeways characterized by mobility provide nearly infinite flexibility in their ability to exploit different environments.

This focus on the environment, particularly the concept of environmental possibilism—that all environments were open to hunter-gatherer exploitation and that diverse landscape use results in diverse archaeological records—is significant both theoretically and methodologically. Evidence of prehistoric forager occupation of "marginal" or barrier environments provides new ideas into how flexible these societies were, and analysis of such behavior can draw on one of archaeology's greatest strengths.

Whereas many anomalies between ethnographic and archaeological records of foragers are due largely to inherent differences in context, archaeology has the ability to reconstruct the ancient context, especially in terms of the environment. Paleoenvironmental analyses are increasingly more sophisticated, and such data are crucial for understanding different types of local and regional landscapes. Paleoenvironmental contexts can be reconstructed in great detail; particularly when aided by underwater preservation (see Lemke, chapter 3, this volume), but also in more challenging preservation contexts, such as tropical rainforests (Roberts et al., chapter 5, this volume). There are clear, documented cases of radically different environments in the past, not just in terms of broad characterizations such as cold Pleistocene and warm Holocene, but down to smaller details of resource structure. For instance, there were greater numbers of animals and exploitable resources in the past and these larger populations resulted in different food-getting strategies in prehistory than those documented either historically or ethnographically (see Lemke 2016; Stewart and Mitchell, chapter 6, this volume).

Examples of detailed paleoenvironmental studies are found throughout this volume (for example, Rademaker and Moore, chapter 4; Roberts et al., chapter 5; Stewart and Mitchell, chapter 6), as are calls for finer grained data and studies to aid future research (Garvey, chapter 2 and Bettinger 2014). Because indirect comparisons between archaeological sites and sometimes poorly dated "off-site" lake or marine cores can mask significant spatial and local/regional variability, finer grained, "on-site" paleoenvironmental studies are needed to support analyses such as Garvey's (chapter 2, this volume; Garvey and Bettinger 2014) for prehistoric cases, especially as characterizations of certain environments as "favorable" or "unfavorable" can change with the scale of the analysis (Rademaker and Moore, chapter 4, this volume). One proposed method to improve paleoenviromental studies is additional long-term, multispecies, stable isotope studies, particularly as these analyses provide *direct* measures of resource exploitation (Roberts et al., chapter 5, this volume).

Ideally, future research will provide studies similar to Garvey's, using archaeological data, holding the environment as a constant variable, and comparing cultural adaptations. For example, new analyses could compare the use of tropical rainforests in Sri Lanka, southeast Asia, and Africa. While there are hints that foragers use these similar environments in different ways (Roberts et al., chapter 5, this volume), future studies could move beyond simple detection to systematically document variability in the past. Traditionally, hunter-gatherer anthropologists and archaeologists have often proceeded from the known to the unknown (ethnographic present to prehistoric foragers) in their interpretations, but new studies indicate that we may be able to reverse this trend and use methods derived from archaeological studies (e.g., stable isotopes) and apply them to increasingly younger phenomena, such as protohistoric foragers, perhaps to track the gradual incorporation of agricultural foods into forager populations near tropical rainforests.

As is often the case for ethnographic foragers, variability in one factor is linked to variability in others. This is significant because the same kind of local variability that we document in environments is likely to generate corresponding variability in local cultural adaptations—particularly given the demonstrated relationships among resource structure, mobility patterns, reproductive costs, demographic growth, and intra- and intergroup connectivity, for example. Within such broad categories as the Pleistocene or the Holocene, we have documented local variations on a theme across time and space—a similar solution is needed for the extensive category "prehistoric hunter-gatherers."

On Discovering Novel Foraging Lifeways: Demography and Cultural Transmission

Exploring diversity in the past is easier said than done, particularly in the deep past when sites and behaviors of foraging societies are particularly ephemeral. In documenting modern human behavior, simple trait lists have been the traditional method for describing aspects of prehistoric hunter-gatherers. However, it is now clear that this method has limited analytical utility (Kitagawa et al., chapter 7, this volume; Kuhn and Stiner, chapter 8, this volume; see also McBrearty and Brooks 2000; Shea 2011).

The hallmarks of "modern" human behavior are found increasingly farther back in time. Instead of simple presence-or-absence trait lists, the frequency and flexibility of behaviors can be documented and compared (Kitagawa et al., chapter 7, this volume; Kuhn and Stiner, chapter 8, this volume; Shea 2011). Simple presence or absence of certain traits does little to explain the cognitive and/or cultural capacities of Neanderthals—for example, while items of personal adornment are present, they are far from ubiquitous. Furthermore, the frequency of these items (and the social and cognitive mechanisms behind them) are still notably different between the Middle Paleolithic and the early Upper Paleolithic (Kitagawa et al., chapter 7, this volume; Kuhn and Stiner, chapter 8, this volume). Kuhn and Stiner attribute this and other differences to demography, more specifically the size and nature of social groups of Neanderthals and anatomically modern humans. They relate the homogeneity of Middle Paleolithic technology to smaller social groups—small and locally unstable populations that are spatially dispersed. Kuhn, Stiner, and others (e.g., see Gilligan 2007 for discussion of clothing and cold stress) have argued that it was the demographic and reproductive capacities of modern humans that may have given them the edge over our Neanderthal relatives.

These arguments find parallels with cultural transmission theory as shown by Garvey (chapter 2, this volume). Garvey outlines archaeological expectations for cultural and behavioral mechanisms that mediate the negative effects of cold stress and resource shortfall on health, longevity, and reproduction. These expectations include visible diversity either directly as evidence of larger populations and the social dynamics they involve, or indirectly though the material culture outcomes of larger populations. Rates of cultural transmission, either of ideas or tangible technologies, are drastically influenced by the size and connectivity between populations. For example, small populations with limited connectivity (i.e., intra- and intergroup interaction) often result in low technological diversity (Garvey and Bettinger 2014). In their reevaluation of the Middle Paleolithic record, Kuhn and Stiner find that Neanderthals demonstrate technological homogeneity across significant spans of both time and space, likely indicating smaller, less-connected populations (Kuhn and Stiner 2001). This in turn suggests that Middle Paleolithic Neanderthals did not have the culturally mediated behaviors to offset reproduction costs, such as large populations and social connections between these populations, in contrast to ethnographic foragers, who are essentially hard wired for density (Hamilton et al. 2007).

It has long been acknowledged that these variables—environment, ecology, and demography—are critical for a general understanding of hunter-gatherers and the diversity inherent within this category. While these new insights gleaned from the archaeological record do not radically alter our understanding of such variables and their relationships, they do amplify it. In addition, social ties and collaborative strategies (e.g., hunting in groups, working to share food, creating fictive kin to buffer times of shortfall, etc.) are powerful ways to explain the diversity of hunter-gatherers, ultimately demonstrating that some familiar elements identified during the ethnographic study of foragers were put together in novel ways in the past.

On Discovering Novel Foraging Lifeways: Moving Forward

Simple trait lists, similar to other typological categories used to classify hunter-gatherers, are incapable of dealing with such complex relationships. Both methods are limited in their analytical power, and more often serve to mask important variability. Certain binary oppositions common in conceptualizing hunter-gatherer behavior—forager versus collector, simple versus complex, specialist versus generalist, mobile versus sedentary, etc.—disguise significant variation. One of the primary goals for future studies should be to move away from such typological categories. Instead, hypotheses and models of hunter-gatherer behavior need to be designed to capture variability—not dismiss or underemphasize it.

This volume makes a first explicit attempt to explore diversity among prehistoric hunter-gatherers. It pulls together geographic and temporal case studies to demonstrate that hunter-gatherers in the ethnographic record are not nearly as diverse as those that preceded them. The contributors show the importance of employing integrative and interdisciplinary approaches for explaining novel lifeways and diversity among prehistoric foragers. Exploring cultural diversity is a central goal of archaeology and of anthropology more generally, because we cannot truly understand what is shared among humanity without understanding what is different (Kelly 1995, 2013). We hope to contribute to this ongoing investigation.

REFERENCES CITED

Ames, Kenneth M. 2004. "Review: Supposing Hunter-Gatherer Variability." *American Antiquity* 69(2):364–374. https://doi.org/10.2307/4128427.

Bettinger, Robert L., Raven Garvey, and Shannon Tushingham. 2015. *Hunter-Gatherers: Archaeological and Evolutionary Theory*. New York: Springer. https://doi.org/10.1007/978-1-4899-7581-2.

Binford, Lewis R. 2001. *Constructing Frames of Reference: An Analytical Method for Archaeological Theory Building and Using Ethnographic and Environmental Data Sets*. Berkeley: University of California Press.

Bird, Rebecca Bliege, and Douglas W. Bird. 2008. "Why Women Hunt: Risk and Contemporary Foraging in a Western Desert Aboriginal Community." *Current Anthropology* 49(4):655–693. https://doi.org/10.2307/20142695.

Garvey, Raven, and Robert L. Bettinger. 2014. "Adaptive and Ecological Approaches to the Study of Hunter-Gatherers." In *The Oxford Handbook of Archaeology and Anthropology of Hunter-Gatherers*, ed. Vicki Cummings, Jordan Peter, and Marek Zvelebil, 69–91. Oxford, UK: Oxford University Press.

Gilligan, Ian. 2007. "Neanderthal Extinction and Modern Human Behaviour: The Role of Climate Change and Clothing." *World Archaeology* 39(4):499–514. https://doi.org/10.1080/00438240701680492.

Hamilton, M. J., B. T. Milne, R. S. Walker, and J. H. Brown. 2007. "Nonlinear Scaling of Space Use in Human Hunter-Gatherers." *Proceedings of the National Academy of Sciences of the United States of America* 104(11):4765–4769. https://doi.org/10.1073/pnas.0611197104.

Jochim, Michael A. 1991. "Archaeology as Long-Term Ethnography." *American Anthropologist* 93(2):308–321. https://doi.org/10.1525/aa.1991.93.2.02a00020.

Kelly, Robert L. 1995. *The Foraging Spectrum: Diversity in Hunter-Gatherer Lifeways*. Washington, DC: Smithsonian Institution Press.

Kelly, Robert L. 2013. *The Lifeways of Hunter-Gatherers: The Foraging Spectrum*. Cambridge, UK: Cambridge University Press. https://doi.org/10.1017/CBO9781139176132.

Kent, Susan, ed. 1996. *Cultural Diversity among Twentieth-Century Foragers: An African Perspective*. Cambridge, UK: Cambridge University Press.

Kuhn, Steven L., and Mary C. Stiner. 2001. "The Antiquity of Hunter-Gatherers." In *Hunter-Gatherers: An Interdisciplinary Perspective*, ed. Catherine Panter-Brick, Robert H. Layton, and Peter Rowley-Conwy, 99–129. Cambridge, UK: Cambridge University Press.

Kusimba, Sibel B. 2005. "What Is a Hunter-Gatherer? Variation in the Archaeological Record of Eastern and Southern Africa." *Journal of Archaeological Research* 13(4):337–366. https://doi.org/10.1007/s10814-005-5111-y.

Lee, Richard B. 1992. "Art, Science, or Politics? The Crises in Hunter-Gatherer Studies." *American Anthropologist* 94(1):31–54. https://doi.org/10.1525/aa.1992.94.1.02a00030.

Lee, Richard B., and Irven DeVore, eds. 1968. *Man the Hunter*. Chicago: Aldine Press.

Lemke, Ashley K. 2016. "Anthropological Archaeology Underwater: Hunting Architecture and Foraging Lifeways beneath the Great Lakes." PhD dissertation, Department of Anthropology, University of Michigan, Ann Arbor.

Marcus, Joyce. 2008. "The Archaeological Evidence for Social Evolution." *Annual Review of Anthropology* 37(1):251–266. https://doi.org/10.1146/annurev.anthro.37.081407.085246.

McBrearty, S., and A. S. Brooks. 2000. "The Revolution That Wasn't: A New Interpretation of the Origin of Modern Human Behavior." *Journal of Human Evolution* 39(5):453–563. https://doi.org/10.1006/jhev.2000.0435.

Panter-Brick, Catherine, Robert H. Layton, and Peter Rowley-Conwy, eds. 2001. *Hunter-Gatherers: An Interdisciplinary Perspective*. Cambridge, UK: Cambridge University Press.

Politis, Gustavo. 2015 *Myths about Tropical Rainforest Hunter-Gatherers: A Reappraisal from South America*. Paper presented at the 18th Annual Meeting of the Society for American Archaeology, San Francisco, CA.

Prentiss, Anna Marie, Natasha Lyons, Lucille E. Harris, Melisse R. P. Burns, and Terrence M. Godin. 2007. "The Emergence of Status Inequality in Intermediate Scale Societies: A Demographic and Socio-Economic History of the Keatley Creek Site, British Columbia." *Journal of Anthropological Archaeology* 26(2):299–327. https://doi.org/10.1016/j.jaa.2006.11.006.

Service, Elman. 1966. *The Hunters*. Englewood Cliffs, NJ: Prentice-Hall.

Shea, J. J. 2011. "*Homo sapiens* Is as *Homo sapiens* Was." *Current Anthropology* 52(1):1–35. https://doi.org/10.1086/658067.

Wobst, Martin. 1978. "The Archaeo-Ethnology of Hunter-Gatherers or the Tyranny of the Ethnographic Record in Archaeology." *American Antiquity* 43(2):303–309. https://doi.org/10.2307/279256.

Yengoyan, Aram A. 1979. "Economy, Society, and Myth in Aboriginal Australia." *Annual Review of Anthropology* 8(1):393–415. https://doi.org/10.1146/annurev.an.08 .100179.002141.

Zedeño, María Nieves, Jesse A. M. Ballenger, and John R. Murray. 2014. "Landscape Engineering and Organizational Complexity among Late Prehistoric Bison Hunters of the Northwestern Plains." *Current Anthropology* 55(1):23–58. https://doi .org/10.1086/674535.

2

Among the enduring contributions of Robert Kelly's (1995) *The Foraging Spectrum* is a compelling elaboration of Wobst's (1978) warning: archaeologists should not be content to rely on the ethnographic record, but should endeavor to identify behavioral diversity unique to the prehistoric past—that is, diversity without ethnographic analog. The charge is as difficult as it is important. One potentially constructive approach to illuminating that shadowy portion of the behavioral spectrum is to identify and analyze *sources* of diversity; understanding causal relationships and mechanisms of change (or stasis) is key to interpreting archaeological records in their own terms. Here I examine environmental, ecological, and cultural sources of diversity—and interactions among them—and explore their potential effects on technological complexity.

Understanding diversity is by definition a comparative endeavor, the present approach to sources of diversity is illustrated through a comparison of two groups of maritime foragers living in very similar environments at opposite ends of the globe: the Unangan (Aleut) of Alaska's Aleutian Islands and the Yámana (Yaghan) of Tierra del Fuego, the southern tip of South America. Environmental similarities between the groups' respective archipelagos might account for certain basic cultural resemblances, but striking contrasts in their technological complexity require alternative explanations. This chapter explores the hypothesis that ecological constraints on and/or cultural attitudes

Cultural Transmission and Sources of Diversity

A Comparison of Temperate Maritime Foragers of the Northern and Southern Hemispheres

RAVEN GARVEY

DOI: 10.5876/9781607327745.c002

toward group size and connectivity, culturally mediated differences in fertility, and feedback between demographic variables and technological innovation led to more and less favorable conditions for cumulative cultural evolution among the Unangan and Yámana, respectively. I argue further that archaeological data are not only well suited to examining sources of diversity and mechanisms of cultural change, they are essential.

ACCOUNTING: POTENTIAL SOURCES OF DIVERSITY

Mechanisms functioning in different domains can help account for differences between the contact-period Unangan and Yámana and perhaps foraging diversity more generally, including that of the remote past. Such mechanisms can usefully be classed as environmental, ecological, or social.

Environmental Mechanisms

In this context, I use *environmental* to refer to Earth systems that affect the abundance, timing, and dispersion of resources. Environmental effects often correlate with latitude and include variables that define resources biomes—which can be meaningful categories in geographic studies of trait distributions—such as amount and timing of precipitation, annual average and seasonal temperature extremes, length of growing season, and so forth. Interest in relationships between environmental variables and cultural attributes has a long history in anthropology and Steward's explicit, cross-cultural analyses (e.g., Steward 1936, 1955) brought them to the fore of science-minded anthropological research. The study of environment–culture relationships was eventually formalized (approached quantitatively) by Binford (e.g., Binford 1980, 2001), Keeley (1988, 1995), Kelly (1995, 2013), and others, which has helped to clarify the role of environmental factors in instances of cultural change, and to identify groups that deviate from expectations derived from broad, quantitatively defined patterns.

Biogeographical studies of non-human animals indicate that environmental factors often account for a substantial portion of the variation observed in species distributions (cf. Hubbell 2001). A phenomenon Harcourt (2012) refers to as the *Forster effect* (after Johann Forster [1778], who noted the phenomenon in the late 1700s) describes a latitudinal gradient in diversity; on average, there is more biological diversity at low latitudes than at high. A similar relationship has been reported for human cultural diversity. For example, Collard and Foley (2002:375) analyzed a sample of 3,814 cultures drawn from Price's (1990)

Atlas of World Cultures and found a significant relationship between latitude and human cultural density (i.e., diversity; $r = 0.93$, $p < 0.001$).

A variety of hypotheses have been advanced to explain the geographical pattern of species diversity described by the Forster effect (e.g., Lomolino et al. 2010). Harcourt (2012) explored the applicability of several of these to the distribution of human cultural diversity and identified a handful of plausible explanations: greater (1) environmental heterogeneity and (2) stability (i.e., reduced seasonality) promote cultural diversification at low latitudes; and (3) geographic range size tends to increase with latitude (the *Rapoport effect*; Rapoport 1982) while culturally distinct human groups' ranges tend not to overlap, which, in conjunction, leads to a negative correlation between diversity and latitude. The Rapoport effect, while not universally accepted as an ecological rule (e.g., Gaston et al. 1998), finds best empirical support at latitudes above 40° and may be explained by a variety of factors, including increased seasonality, decreased productivity, and deceased competition at higher latitudes (Grove et al. 2012; Nettle 1999; Pearce 2014). Among human groups, range size is positively correlated with latitude (Binford 2001; Collard and Foley 2002; Harcourt 2012; Mace and Pagel 1995), likely as a result of seasonality and productivity; where plant resources are relatively scarce, animals must range farther to meet their caloric needs, and humans must range farther in response.

Latitude is, of course, a proxy for the suite of environmental variables that affects the abundance, timing, and dispersion of resources. In some instances, the proxy is preferable because it obviates a detailed accounting of spatial and temporal variations in individual variables and the sometimes unpredictable interactions among them. Analyses based on latitude are correspondingly gross, though, and some authors have favored finer-grained comparisons based on individual variables. Cashdan (2001), for example, noted a negative correlation between cold month mean daily minimum temperatures and cultural diversity, suggesting that high-latitude winters constrain cultural outcomes, just as they appear to constrain biological diversity (Harcourt 2012). Collard and colleagues (2005) likewise prefer variables they believe directly affect resource availability (and, therefore, human behavior), including effective temperature (a composite variable that reflects growing season; Bailey 1960) and above ground net productivity; a summary of their analysis of toolkit variation appears in the following section. Either approach (analyses based on latitude or particular environmental variables) can be used to generate hypotheses regarding human groups' mobility, range size, and relative isolation, which have implications for other aspects of culture and can therefore inform interpretations of prehistoric behavior and cultural diversity.

Ecological Mechanisms

Ecological mechanisms influence the degree to which environmental energy is available to organisms and can usefully be thought of in terms of constraints commonly applied in optimization (e.g., optimal foraging) models. Among humans, these include a variety of intrinsic and extrinsic factors such as foraging skills and strategies, ecological knowledge, and technology (Smith and Winterhalder 1992; Stephens and Krebs 1986). As with the environmental relationships described in the previous section, interest in ecological mechanisms has a long history in anthropology. Steward (1936, 1955), for example, was fundamentally concerned with the *techno-economics* of humans' extraction of environmental energy. Indeed, he distinguished the physical environment from the *effective environment*, or that portion of the physical environment potentiated by technology and the organization of work such that two foragers equipped with different technologies or strategies (e.g., communal hunting) experience the same physical environment differently. Holding environment constant, individuals (or groups) with distinct toolkits potentially differ in their ability to access resources: projectile technologies facilitate hunting small-bodied, arboreal species that might otherwise be forgone; transportation technologies effectively reduce travel costs, making distant resources patches accessible; permanent dwellings offer increased security and protection from the elements, but often preclude residential mobility as a subsistence strategy. This sort of techno-economic accounting is relevant to the present analysis of sources of cultural diversity.

Technology

Technological complexity, as the term is used here, was not an explicit focus of Steward's work, but his examination of technology's role in shaping the effective environment influenced subsequent studies of complexity. Wendell Oswalt (1973, 1976), for example, drew on Steward's (1955:37) description of technology as central to the *culture core* (that "constellation of features which are most closely related to subsistence activities and economic arrangements") when he established the *subsistant* (a tool that supports subsistence) as a major taxonomic unit in his artifact classification scheme. Oswalt was interested in the evolution of technology and sought a principled means of comparing technological complexity between cultural groups. To do so, he defined *technounits* as "different kinds of parts in a finished artifact" and measured technological complexity in terms of technounits per subsistant (Oswalt 1976:45; Torrence 1989). This metric has since been combined with various others, including toolkit *diversity*, or the number of tools per kit (Shott 1986; Torrence 1989), to assess technological sophistication and its global distribution.

Factors affecting tool complexity, toolkit diversity, and technological evolution have been a subject of recent debate (Clark 2011; Collard et al. 2005; Henrich 2004, 2006; Kline and Boyd 2010; Kolodny et al. 2015; Read 2006; Shennan 2015). For example, Oswalt (1976) made a cross-cultural comparison of toolkit complexity and noted a correlation with prey species' mobility. He argued that groups who rely on aquatic resources should have relatively complex toolkits because such resources have larger ranges than terrestrial ones. Robin Torrence (1983, 1989), Peter Bleed (1986), and others (e.g., Eerkens 1998) have built on this idea, putting a finer point on the relationship between resource characteristics and technological complexity. Specifically, they cite the timing of key resources and risk associated with resources shortfall as primary factors affecting toolkit composition. According to these studies, tools are often made to be *reliable*—designed to minimize the likelihood of failure in high-risk situations through redundancies and over-designing (e.g., making tools stronger than necessary)—when failure (of the tool or subsistence activity to which it is put) would be costly. We might then reasonably expect for technological sophistication to track seasonality (and, therefore, latitude), and indeed this seems to be borne out. Torrence (1983) found a significant positive correlation between toolkit complexity and latitude among the groups summarized by Oswalt (1976) and hypothesized that this owes to decreased plant biomass with increased latitude and humans' increased reliance on animal resources at higher latitudes. Henrich (2004) has also demonstrated a strong positive correlation between tool complexity and latitude, as did Collard and colleagues (2005), who compared four competing hypotheses for toolkit complexity (characteristics of food resources, risk of shortfall, mobility, and population size) and found risk of resource failure to be the best predictor.

ENERGY BUDGETS

Many recent approaches to archaeological records have looked to optimal foraging theory for insights into spatial and temporal differences in subsistence strategies. While the effects of technology are seldom explicitly included in foraging models, tools can profoundly affect optimal decision-making. In the diet breadth model, for example, resources are ranked according to their post-encounter handling times, which can change dramatically based on tool availability. That is, different subsistence tools are associated with different handling costs and caloric yields such that, holding environment constant, two otherwise identical foragers might have very different optimal diets when equipped with different tools (Bettinger et al. 2015:113; Winterhalder and Bettinger 2010). Similarly, foragers equipped with identical technologies might have very different caloric needs—*energy budgets*—which could lead to different long-term foraging strategies (e.g., heightened risk sensitivity in foragers with lower starvation thresholds). Yet energy budgets, when considered at all, are often glossed as static, universal, or inconsequential. That is, many ecological studies (e.g., of feeding ecology in evolutionary biology and foraging studies in human behavioral ecology) focus on "supply-side" dynamics, or how prey availability and forager efficiency affect net returns. "Demand" is often overlooked, but is also key to understanding ecological relationships and potential sources of behavioral and cultural diversity.

Basal metabolic rate (BMR)—or the energy required to maintain the essential body functions (e.g., brain activity, respiration, circulation, immune function, thermoregulation) of an individual at rest—is a useful metric for assessing and comparing energy budgets because BMR typically constitutes a large majority of total caloric expenditure and can be thought of as a threshold, below which health and longevity are increasingly threatened (Leonard et al. 2007). BMR varies by individual according to age, sex, body proportions, percent lean body mass, and other factors. Particularly relevant to this study are variations in BMR according to latitude, season, and reproductive state (e.g., gestation, lactation).

Controlling for body size and composition, high-latitude populations tend to have elevated BMRs relative to low-latitude populations (Galloway et al. 2000; Leonard et al. 2002; Snodgrass et al. 2008), suggesting an adaptation to chronic cold stress. Moreover, a recent study among the Yukat (Sakha) of northern Siberia suggests that this effect may be amplified seasonally among prime-aged adults, likely as a result of changes in both thyroid hormone activity (associated with decreased temperature and photoperiod) and physical activity (Leonard et al. 2014). Ethnographically and very likely prehistorically, food availability also fluctuated seasonally often even among groups that relied on storage, such that populations living in cold climates may have experienced significant periods of negative energy balance.

Like all budgets, energy budgets are characterized by the zero-sum property: energy allocated to BMR, subsistence activities, and other aspects of somatic maintenance is unavailable for other functions, including reproduction (Ellison 2003). Women in negative energy balance (experiencing frequent episodes of resource shortfall) may have compromised reproductive function (Rosetta 1993:71) for at least two reasons. Human pregnancy is energetically costly and results in an elevated BMR, due in part to (1) "increased oxygen consumption because of enhanced work with respect to maternal circulation, respiration, and renal function and to the increased tissue mass," as well as to (2) increased cardiac work and serum concentrations of thyroid hormone (Lof et al. 2005). Meeting these higher energy requirements can be difficult, particularly during seasons of restricted resource availability. Moreover, ovarian function is directly affected by energetic state (Ellison 2001; Ellison et al. 2005) and women in negative energy balance may have reduced fertility. Cultural or behavioral apparatuses that mediate the negative effects of cold stress and resource shortfall on health, longevity, and reproduction can lead to archaeologically visible diversity either directly as evidence of larger populations and the changed social dynamics they may necessitate, or indirectly through material cultural outcomes of larger populations. The latter is the topic of the following section.

Social Mechanisms

Mechanisms of cultural transmission (e.g., learning norms) and demographic variables (e.g., population size) can affect cultural diversity. I group these under the heading "social mechanisms" both for convenience and because interactions among them influence rates of cumulative cultural evolution. Understanding the dynamics of these interactions is a primary agenda of the emerging multidisciplinary field of cultural evolution (e.g., Boyd and Richerson 1985; McElreath and Henrich 2007; Richerson and Boyd 2005), and recent studies relevant to the present analysis investigate relationships between technological complexity and group size and/or connectivity (Baldini 2015; Henrich 2004; Kline and Boyd 2010; Shennan 2015).

As Kline and Boyd (2010:2559) succinctly state, human cultural adaptation "depends on the gradual accumulation of culturally transmitted knowledge and technology . . . [in which process] demography plays an important role." They go on to explain that, according to models of cultural evolution, technological complexity (tool complexity and toolkit diversity) should covary with population size: large populations' toolkits should surpass those of small, isolated populations in both dimensions. The models that predict these trends are effectively illustrated by Henrich's (2004) examination of Tasmanian material culture.

At European contact, the Tasmanian toolkit comprised an exceedingly small number of items (est. 24; Henrich 2004). Archaeological evidence indicates that after Tasmania was cut off from Australia at the end of the last ice age (ca. 12–10 kya) the toolkit became increasingly less complex, and critical technologies including cold-weather clothing, barbed spears, and bone tools were apparently lost. Henrich attributes these losses to interactions between population size and two important aspects of human social learning: selective choice of cultural models and imperfect imitation. People tend to model their behaviors on those of particularly skilled or successful individuals (Henrich and Gil-White 2001), so Henrich explored the Tasmanian case using a model in which novice individuals attempt to copy the behaviors/tools of the most skilled individual in a population. However, due to imperfect imitation (e.g., variations in perception or ability), on average learners will be unable to match the skill level of the behavioral model (the most skilled individual), particularly when behaviors/tools are hard to imitate or replicate. This force constrains the rate of technological evolution in a population. Moreover, since highly skilled individuals are, ostensibly, a minority in most populations, certain behaviors and tools may be lost if behavioral models are removed from the population by chance. Statistically, this type of random loss of behaviors/tools has a greater effect in smaller populations. The negative effects of biased learning and imperfect copying were further exacerbated in the Tasmanian case by the fact that innovation rates are generally lower in smaller populations (Diamond 1997; Richerson et al. 2009), and by Tasmania's isolation from other populations (e.g., Australia), which are sources of both skilled individuals and new ideas/technologies.

Of course, the same dynamics that led to the Tasmanian loss of culture can also be generative. Through occasional "lucky guesses or errors," some learners' behaviors/tools are *superior* to the behavioral model's and these individuals are then preferentially copied by subsequent learning generations, leading to cultural evolution (Henrich 2004:201). As groups of interacting social learners grow, rates of cumulative technological evolution can increase since larger groups are more likely to produce rare, superior behaviors/tools. Indeed Kline and Boyd (2010) conclude that population size is the best predictor of technological complexity among the variables they considered: larger populations' toolkits comprise a much higher mean number of technounits than smaller populations' kits.

It is important to note that, in addition to population size, *connectivity*—or the degree of interaction between individuals or segments of a population, sometimes referred to as *network size*–has become an increasingly important variable in studies of demographic effects on cultural evolution (Baldini 2015; Henrich 2004; Powell et al. 2009; Shennan 2015). Recently, Baldini (2015) used a model similar to Henrich's (2004) to explore the relative effects of population size and connectivity on cultural evolution. His model is distinct from Henrich's, though, in that it does not assume every novice individual has access to the single most skilled behavioral model (i.e., that novices' social networks comprise the total population), but establishes network size as a separate variable and observes its effects given different population sizes. He finds that connectivity indeed has significant effects on cumulative cultural evolution under certain circumstances, as when innovation rates are low, since connectivity through migration or trade effectively increases population size.

It is also important to note that demography—particularly population size—is not universally accepted as an explanation for differences in cultural complexity (Collard, Buchanan et al. 2005, 2013; Read 2008, 2012). Still, it would be unwise to dismiss demographic variables without further testing, given the strength of their effect in some studies.

CASE STUDY: THE UNANGAN AND YÁMANA

It takes little reflection to see that the environmental, ecological, and social variables described in the previous section are inextricably and causally linked. So, while understanding mechanisms functioning in each of these realms is itself a worthwhile challenge, confronting the still greater challenge of identifying interactions among mechanisms will be key to understanding prehistoric cultural diversity. The goal of the present essay is to explore such interactions informally; mathematical modeling and simulations similar to those exemplified by Henrich (2004) and Baldini (2015) are the logical next steps.

The following case study explores the hypothesis that stark differences in cultural complexity between two groups of maritime foragers living in very similar environments—the Unangan of Alaska's Aleutian Islands and the Yámana of Tierra del Fuego (figure 2.1; table 2.1)—arose through differences in (1) ecological constraints on and/or cultural attitudes toward group size and connectivity, (2) culturally mediated fertility, and (3) feedback between demographic variables and technological innovation. An exploration of this hypothesis follows a brief description of each group' habitat and history.

The Unangan of the Aleutian Islands

The Aluetian Islands are located between 51° and 55° N, extend roughly 1,200 km west from the Alaska Peninsula, and comprise a total land area of approximately 17,700 km². The region is fairly cold (mean annual temperature ≈3°C; effective temperature, ET = 10.28°C) but temperature seasonality

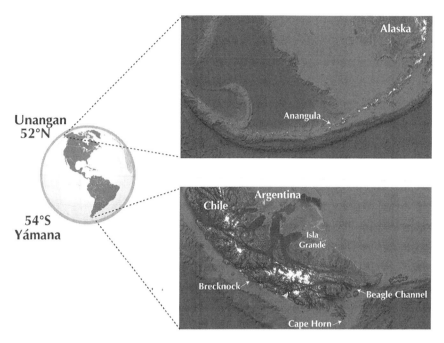

FIGURE 2.1. *The Aleutian Islands (top) and Tierra del Fuego (bottom). The Yámana occupied the southern coast of Isla Grande de Tierra del Fuego and numerous islands south of Isla Grande, from Brecknock Peninsula to the eastern end of the Beagle Channel and south to Cape Horn. (Image credits: globe: PAT ©2013 Ian Macky; satellite images: (Aluetians) Google Earth, IBCAO; data LDEO-Columbia, NSF, NOAA; image Landsat / Copernicus; data SIO, NOAA, US. Navy, NGA, GEBCO). (Tierra del Fuego) Google Earth, LDEO-Columbia, NSF, NOAA; image Landsat / Copernicus; data SIO, NOAA, US. Navy, NGA, GEBCO).*

is moderated by the marine environment (coldest/warmest month mean = −2°C/11°C; Binford 2001). Regardless, the Aleutian Low pressure system generates intense winter storms (Rodionov et al. 2007) and the region is characterized by frequent high winds and dense cloud cover most of the year. Rain and mist are likewise frequent although annual average precipitation is modest (~120 cm).

The region is incredibly rich in marine resources due in part to upwelling from the deep Aleutian Trench (Johnson and Winslow 1991). Resources important to the contact-period Unangan included (resident) sea lions (*Eumetopias jubatus*), harbor seals (*Phoca vitulina*), otter (*Enhydra lutris kenyoni*), cod (*Gadus*

TABLE 2.1. General characteristics of the Unangan and Yámana.

	Unangan	Yámana
Effective temperature	10.3°C	9.6°C
Initial occupation	8500 BP	10,500 BP
Toolkit	complex	relatively simple
Mobility	sedentary	high, residential
Houses	permanent	temporary
Storage	heavy reliance	virtually none
Boats	oceangoing	near-shore only
Clothing	tailored, water-tight	untailored skins
Social group size	relatively large	relatively small

sp.) and halibut (*Hippoglossus stenolepis*); (migratory) humpback (*Megaptera novaeangliae*) and baleen whales (*Eubalaena glacialis*), fur seals (*Callorhinus ursinus*), salmon (*Salmo* sp.), and a wide variety of sea birds (McCartney and Veltre 1999). Seaweeds, marine invertebrates, and some terrestrial berries and tubers were also harvested (Laughlin 1980). The only terrestrial mammals on the Aleutians are foxes and lemmings, and the Unangan subsisted almost exclusively on marine resources (McCartney and Veltre 1999).

The archipelago appears to have been occupied initially ca. 8500 BP. This date roughly coincides with the post-Pleistocene stabilization of global sea levels, however, and earlier occupations are not beyond reason. The Anangula site (Ananiuliak Island, near Umnak Island) is characterized by cores and blades of various sizes, burins, scrapers, and fishing-line weights, among other stone tools, and oval, semisubterranean houses; soils are acidic and no subsistence refuse or organic artifacts were recovered. The site's location and composition suggest a well-established early Holocene maritime adaption that included boat technology (Gómez Coutouly 2015; McCartney and Veltre 1996). Gómez Coutouly (2015) recently presented previously unpublished lithic data that suggest Anangula is an important microblade site with possible technological affinities to interior Alaska's Denali Complex (an early microblade tradition in northwestern North America).

Middle Holocene–aged sites in the Aleutians generally lack the blades and blade cores typical of earlier occupations and are characterized instead by bifacial chipped stone tools, bone harpoon heads, and fishhooks that suggest a subsistence focus on ocean fish and sea mammals. Subsequently, the so-called Aleutian Tradition—characterized by semisubterranean houses with interior storage, and an extensive and specialized toolkit (e.g., toggling harpoons, atlatls, fishhooks, basketry; McCartney and Veltre 1999)—appeared ca. 4500 BP and is marked throughout the Aleutians by large shell middens on coastal terraces and near the mouths of streams.

The Yámana of Tierra del Fuego

The Yámana occupied the southern coast of Isla Grande de Tierra del Fuego and numerous islands south of Isla Grande, from Brecknock Peninsula to the eastern end of the Beagle Channel and south to Cape Horn (figure 2.1). These islands extend approximately 350 km northwest by southeast between 54° and 56° S, and comprise a land area of roughly 11,000 km². The climate in this most southerly part of South America is very similar to that of the Aleutian Islands: relatively cold (mean annual temperature ≈6°C; ET = 9.6°C) with only modest seasonal variation in temperature (coldest/warmest month mean = 2°C/9°C; Binford 2001). Precipitation is evenly distributed throughout the year and snows are frequent, even in summer. Volatility is the norm and "violent squalls and strong gales are common" (Cooper 1946:81).

The interiors of Fuegian islands are difficult to navigate due to both topography and the fact that they are heavily wooded with dense understories. Like the Unangan, the Yámana, therefore, made little use of islands' interiors or their resources, focusing instead on coastlines and marine resources. Cooper (1946) reports that the dietary item of primary importance was mussels (*Mytilus* sp.), and that pinnipeds (*Otaria flavescens*, *Arctocephalus australis*) and fish were also staples. In addition, though in lesser amounts, the Yámana consumed limpets (Nacellidae), birds' eggs, various avian species, whales (*Eubalaena australis*), and a variety of berries, fungi, and wild plants.

Archaeological evidence indicates initial occupation of Tierra del Fuego ca. 10,500 BP (northern Isla Grande; Massone et al. 1999), and for roughly 2,500 years Fuegian groups may have maintained contact with larger populations to the north. By 8000 BP, postglacial sea levels had risen sufficiently to cut Tierra del Fuego off from mainland Patagonia (McCulloch et al. 2005), after which time contact may have been more limited and Fuegian populations themselves may have begun to diverge (Charlin et al. 2013).

There is some debate regarding the emergence of the cultural pattern observed at contact, which was characterized by impermanent settlements, limited subsistence technology, heavy reliance on shellfish, and a lack of storage. Orquera and colleagues (2011) suggest that the subsistence focus and residential pattern had developed by 6000 BP, while Yesner (1990) has argued that the pattern developed relatively late—after 500 BP—and that between ca. 1000 and 500 BP, small groups may have serially occupied semisubterranean houses, perhaps for as long as a season, and subsisted on a more diverse set of resources. This issue is revisited in the Discussion section below.

Environmental Factors Relevant to the Unangan-Yámana Comparison

Global-scale patterns discussed in the Accounting section above permit first-order predictions of Unangan and Yámana mobility and technological complexity. Specifically, the positive correlation between latitude and range size (the Rapoport effect) suggests that both groups should have had relatively large ranges and been highly mobile, while the negative correlation between latitude and cultural diversity (the Forster effect) predicts they should have shared their particular latitudes with relatively few other groups (i.e., cultural diversity should be low near both 52° N and 52° S). In fact, the Unangan and Yámana violated these expectations in interesting ways.

Contact-period Unangan and Yámana ranges do not conform to expectations. "Range size" has been defined as "the total area of land over which a group moves and procures resources" (MacDonell 1995–1996:33; Stanner 1965). True range sizes can be difficult to assess, and they are neither reported universally nor assessed in a standard way (e.g., annual versus lifetime range; MacDonell 1995–1996; Sampson 1988), for which reasons some authors use territory size as a proxy for range (e.g., Harcourt 2012). By this measure, the Unangan range (24,700 km²; Binford 2001) was slightly larger than predicted by the Rapoport effect (predicted range = 19,156 km², based on a regression between latitude and $\log_{10}$ area), while the Yámana range was considerably smaller than predicted (8,800 km²; Binford 2001; figure 2.2). One possible explanation for the deviations is that the Rapoport effect has been attributed to relatively low aboveground biomass at higher latitudes and humans' increased reliance on prey species that themselves have correspondingly large ranges; the Unangan and Yámana relied almost exclusively on marine resources, which are not constrained by terrestrial biomass.

Clearly assessments of range size require refinement. In the present instance, territory size is likely to be an overestimate of range size, in the case of the groups under consideration as well as those used to calculate the regression equation. Moreover, territory size may reflect properties of the physical environment in some cases, and historical or social factors in others. Nonetheless, the Rapoport effect and other global-scale phenomena can help to clarify the

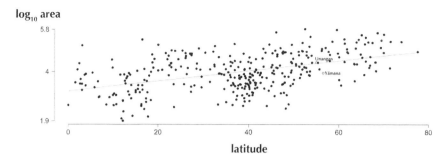

FIGURE 2.2. *The Rapoport effect illustrated using data from Binford (2001; Unangan and Yámana indicated with open circles). The Unangan range (24,700 km²) is slightly larger than predicted by the Rapoport effect (19,156 km²), while the Yámana range is considerably smaller than predicted (8,800 km²; Groups = 339; R² = 0.23).*

role of environmental factors in instances of cultural change, and to identify groups that deviate from expectations derived from broad, quantitatively defined patterns. In the present comparison, a deviation from the predictions of the Forster effect is particularly informative.

The Forster effect describes a negative relationship between cultural diversity and latitude, based in part on the fact that groups' range size requirements tend to increase with latitude to meet resource needs (Rapoport effect). The amount of cultural diversity (groups per 10^6 km²) reported between 52° and 56° northern latitude more or less conforms to expectations; no area, including the Aleutian Islands, exhibits unusual diversity (Collard and Foley 2002). The corresponding southern latitudes, however, show a surprising amount of cultural diversity in Collard and Foley's (2002) analysis of over 3,800 cultures. Tierra del Fuego is a clear outlier: there are far more cultural groups than predicted by the Forster effect.

These results are both ambiguous and intriguing. First, the unexpected diversity between 52° and 56° southern latitude requires explanation. With the exception of Antarctica and a handful of small islands (including the Falklands, which appear not to have been inhabited before 1764; Goebel 1971), Tierra del Fuego is the only landmass south of 52° S. This makes Southern Hemisphere high-latitude diversity all the more surprising, since cultural groups are concentrated in a very small geographical area, made smaller still where islands' interiors are uninhabitable (see above).

Low cultural diversity between 52° and 55° N might also require explanation, though it is as predicted by the Forster effect. Collard and Foley (2002:376) note that "high cultural densities in the higher latitudes of the southern hemisphere are the product of the islands of the southern Atlantic. Islands are outliers in these distributions as they usually have only one cultural unit regardless of the size of the island." By this logic, we might reasonably expect more cultural diversity than observed on the Aleutian Islands. It is presently unclear whether this odd distribution of diversity owes to ecological constraints on or cultural attitudes toward group size and connectivity, but its outcome is explored below.

ECOLOGICAL EFFECTS ON DIVERSITY

The present comparison of northern and southern hemisphere maritime foragers attempts to hold environment relatively constant to explore ecological and social sources of cultural diversity. The groups' respective deviations from predictions based on global-scale environmental trends, demonstrated in the previous section, suggest that such alternative mechanisms may have indeed been in play. In archaeological records, the most accessible aspect of ecological relationships is technology, which clearly differed between the Unangan and Yámana, both at European contact and previously.

According to the ecological hypotheses explored in the Accounting section, both the Unangan and Yámana should have had fairly complex toolkits. In fact, only the Unangan did (see below). By contact, the differences between the two groups were so stark that an exact accounting of tool complexity or toolkit diversity is unnecessary to appreciate that Unangan technological sophistication far surpassed that of the Yámana.

SUBSISTENCE TECHNOLOGY

The contact-period Unangans' hunting toolkit was extensive and specialized, with technologies well designed for efficient procurement of a wide variety of marine and littoral resources (e.g., toggling harpoons, atlatls, fishhooks, basketry). They made lightweight, seaworthy kayaks of skins over wooden frames that facilitated hunting of both fish and sea mammals on the open ocean, as well as sea lions and other animals on offshore rocky outcrops. Storage was an important component of the subsistence routine ("major investment in storage and in the duration of anticipated use" [Binford 2001:258, 394]; see also McCartney and Veltre 1999).

Conversely, the Yámana subsistence toolkit was relatively small and simple. It consisted of spears and clubs for seals; wooden gore hooks, pole snares, and clubs for birds; and pronged forks for urchins. Mussels were gathered by hand, as were fish, often, though women sometimes baited kelp stems or sinew lines to draw fish to the surface and scooped them up in baskets. Unmodified sticks were used for extracting clams and limpets; unmodified stones were used opportunistically in place of clubs or manufactured projectiles when necessary; unmodified mussel shells were frequently used as expedient tools (Oswalt 1973). The Yámana lacked fishhooks, rarely worked stone with the exception of crudely made projectile points and scrapers, and did not rely on storage except for small amounts of dried fungi and oil (Cooper 1946).

The Yámana traveled almost exclusively by boat, but their sewn bark canoes "leaked much" (Cooper 1946:88) and were generally used for moving from camp to camp and in near-shore subsistence activities rather than open-water navigation or hunting. Notably, while whale meat was prized, whales "were not hunted in the usual sense of the word," but rather dispatched if wounded and run into shallow waters by marine predators (Oswalt 1973:102). The Yámana would occasionally follow flocks of seabirds to a sick or wounded baleen whale in the open water, but they were most often seen as an unanticipated windfall when beached (Cooper 1946).

It is reasonable to think that both the Unangan and Yámana were foraging efficiently according to the technologies each possessed. However, the fact that the Yámana either never developed or else lost the capability for offshore hunting and fishing kept carrying capacity much lower in Tierra del Fuego than in the Aleutians (Steager 1963; Yesner et al. 2003), and, more generally, the Unangans' large assemblage of specialized tools allowed them to access a greater portion of the available energy than that of the Yámana. Moreover, the Unangans' reliance on storage likely alleviated seasonal or periodic resource shortfalls.

Temperature Regulation

Difference in the groups' respective abilities to mitigate negative effects of chronic cold (e.g., elevated BMR, compromised fertility, see above) might also have contributed to cultural differences between them. Clothing may have played an especially important role in this regard. Gilligan (2007) has suggested that small differences in ambient temperature inside tailored clothing make a significant difference in basal metabolic rates and overall energy budgets, and that this may have been a contributing factor in the differential survival of anatomically modern humans relative to Neanderthals. Clothing may likewise have been a significant factor in the technological disparity between the Unangan and Yámana.

At contact, the Unangan made and wore expertly tailored bird- and sea-mammal-skin clothing and water-tight outerwear. Yámana clothing, on the other hand, was not tailored and consisted only of seal, sea otter, or fox pelts draped over the shoulders, pubic coverings, and, occasionally, leggings; they smeared their bodies with fat to further protect against snow, rain, and temperatures that were routinely below freezing. Gilligan (2007:501) indicates that tailored clothing is two to five times more thermally resistant than simple, draped clothing, "reducing the thermal gradient between the body and the external environment," such that the Unangan's wardrobe may have afforded them a considerable advantage in the cold climate. Tailored clothing would have reduced adult and infant mortality due to direct cold stress, and decreased metabolic upregulation (i.e., held BMR more or less constant), thereby limiting episodes of negative energy balance and compromised female fertility. In addition, warm and watertight clothing might have facilitated Unangan mobility, particularly offshore hunting, while the lack of such garments might have further limited the Yámana's ability to navigate and hunt on the open water (Gilligan 2007).

Housing can perform a similar function to clothing, providing a relatively stable climate despite daily and seasonal temperature fluctuations. At contact, the Unangan lived in variously sized settlements consisting of semisubterranean, sod-covered whalebone or driftwood houses, the largest of which "housed well over one hundred related persons" (McCartney and Veltre 1999:505). McCartney and Veltre (1999) suggest that this particular house construction maintained a relatively constant indoor temperature and was effective against high winds and frequent, driving rain. Among the Yámana, on the other hand, single-family units constructed temporary dome- or cone-shaped, grass- or bark-covered structures of bent branches that were largely ineffectual against the elements (Cooper 1946; Oswalt 1973). Both forms of temperature regulation (clothing and houses) likely promoted greater health and fertility—and, therefore, larger populations—among the Unangan relative to the Yámana. This difference may have, in turn, have fostered cumulative cultural evolution through the effects of social mechanisms.

Social Effects on Diversity

Larger and more connected populations are better able to preserve existing technological complexity and more likely to produce innovations, which in turn raise local carrying capacities and improve survivorship and fertility, thereby further increasing innovation rates. At contact with Russian fur traders in the mid-eighteenth century, the Unangan numbered roughly

15,000 (Lantis 1984). In contrast, the Yámana population was one-fifth that size (approximately 3,000) when the first estimates were made the 1830s (Europeans initially encountered the Yámana in the early sixteenth century but no census was taken until the nineteenth century; see Discussion). The groups' respective population densities—54.7 people per 100 km² for the Unangan and 28.4 per 100 km² for the Yámana (Binford 2001)—do put the groups' populations in perspective, but it is a second major component of recent cultural transmission models, connectivity, that may better account for the pronounced technological disparity between the Unangan and Yámana. Specifically, the Yámana were decidedly less connected than the Unangan and this social isolation likely exacerbated the effect of small population size (Henrich's 2004).

The contact-period Unangan lived in longhouses that accommodated multiple family groups within large, permanent villages. Technological similarities suggest cultural continuity and contact both among the islands of the chain and between the chain and the Alaskan mainland (Turner 2008), despite there having been a number of different dialects and tribes across the islands. Tierra del Fuego, on the other hand, is characterized by exceptional cultural diversity, particularly given its relatively small geographic area (Collard and Foley 2002). At contact, there were four named cultural groups in Tierra del Fuego—the Yámana, Selk'nam (Ona), Manek'enk (Haush), and Kawéskar (Alacaluf)—that spoke mutually unintelligible languages, each of which was further subdivided into dialect groups and social units that were smaller still. The Yámana alone were divided into five territories where groups spoke mutually intelligible but distinct dialects. Within each territory, Yámana lived in small, independent family groups that were relatively isolated from one another. Social gatherings of any size were rare and occurred primarily to observe initiation rites or partition a beached whale. Cooper (1946) indicates that Yámana expressed a deep sense of individual independence.

These generalizations are supported by Binford's (2001:246) data on the aggregated and dispersed group sizes of the world's hunting and gathering groups. The Yámana average aggregated group size was 24 people, and dispersed groups contained 13 on average; occasional aggregations of 250 people were infrequent, as described by Cooper (1946). Unangan aggregated groups were more than twice as large (average = 55 people); no data are provided regarding dispersed group size, likely because the Unangan were largely sedentary by contact. For reference, among Binford's sample (N = 311), dispersed groups range from one to 70 people (Luiseño and Blackfeet, respectively), and aggregated groups from 20.5 to 346 (Chulanaickan and Blackfeet, respectively).

The causes of these differences in group size and connectivity could as easily be ecological as cultural, and resolution of the issue is beyond the scope of the current essay. Nonetheless, since "cultures that better facilitate sociality, information sharing, and effective teaching will be better able to maintain complex technologies and skills" (Baldini 2015:330; Henrich 2010; Pearce 2014), the Unangan's relatively large and well-connected groups may have led to more rapid cultural evolution among them, and to their superior cultural sophistication relative to the Yámana.

DISCUSSION

The primary aim of this exploratory chapter, which was initiated by an invitation to the symposium *Foraging Spectra: Hunter-Gatherer Diversity in Prehistory* (80th Annual Meeting of the Society for American Archaeology, San Francisco, CA, April 16, 2015), was to identify potential sources of cultural diversity that may help us discern behaviors unique to the prehistoric past. Three broad source categories formed the basis of this preliminary assessment—environmental, ecological, and social—each of which offers a variety of first-order predictions regarding basic cultural characteristics. In the archaeological literature, each has been associated with cultural diversity and change through time. Often, one or another is taken to be a "prime mover," or singular cause, whose relationship to a particular cultural phenomenon is direct and unambiguous. But, as with any complex phenomenon, it is reasonable to think—in fact we should expect—that causes of cultural diversity are usually multivariate. In the case of the Unangan and Yámana, for example, it is clear that environmental factors and adaptive behaviors cannot alone account for stark differences between the two groups at European contact. A comparison of relevant data to the first-order predictions generated by the framework outlined here indicates that the small but important differences in mortality and fertility among the Unangan afforded by tailored clothing led to larger populations that were therefore better able to preserve existing technological complexity and produce innovations, which in turn raised local carrying capacities and led to a complex cycle of feedback between demography, technology, and carrying capacity. The next phase of this project centers on development of formal models of the mechanisms' singular and aggregate effects, and tests of their predictions using ethnographic and archaeological data.

To conclude the present exercise, I note two caveats pertaining to the foregoing case study, and offer two alternative hypotheses for the absence of tailored clothing in Tierra del Fuego.

Consistent with Kelly's (1995) warning, and Wobst's before him (1978), it is possible that the contact period is an inappropriate point of departure for the exploration of predictions generated by the models presented here. For example, Yesner (1990:19; Yesner et al. 2003) has argued that the prehistoric Yámana lifeway was so disrupted by European contact that the subsistence and settlement patterns described in the ethnographic literature should be considered an artifact of "murder, disease, and resource competition" rather than cultural "devolution" or a failure to develop more sophisticated technologies and strategies. Furthermore, it is not clear whether the population sizes reported for the groups' respective contact periods accurately reflect precontact numbers. Furthermore, for all of their physical similarities, the Aleutian and Fuegian environments may not, in fact, be functionally equivalent. For example, McCartney (1975; see also Yesner 2004) suggested that subtle but important environmental differences may have led to larger populations in the Aleutians. Specifically, he cites larger sea lion colonies and a considerably larger tidal range in the Aleutians than in the Beagle Channel of Tierra del Fuego. Here, resolution requires more and finer-grained paleoenvironmental data. Still, it seems likely that population size was consistently smaller and technological complexity correspondingly lower in prehistoric Tierra del Fuego, though our understanding of the degree to which this was true will surely be improved as new data come to light. Important work is ongoing in both regions.

ALTERNATIVE HYPOTHESES FOR THE ABSENCE OF YÁMANA TAILORED CLOTHING

Whether the Yámana lost or never had tailored clothing has important implications for our understanding of broader issues of human adaptability and cultural evolution. A few of these are explored here.

Loss of technology

It is possible that Fuegian groups had but lost the knowledge and tools necessary to produce tailored clothing, perhaps for reasons similar to those in the Tasmanian case. As a previous section describes, Tierra del Fuego was cut off from mainland Patagonia circa 8000 BP, at which time the distinct ethnic groups documented at contact may have begun to diversify (Charlin et al. 2013). This social fragmentation and isolation may have restricted the flow of people and ideas between groups, holding innovation rates low, as described in Henrich's (2004) model. This effect may have been exacerbated—and tailored clothing and other technologies lost—if chance events such as natural disasters removed cultural models from populations.

Both the Aleutians and Fuegian islands are subject to periodic, potentially devastating natural events. As part of the Pacific "Ring of Fire," the Aleutians are both seismically and volcanically active. Archaeological site distributions suggest that camps and settlements were rarely positioned at the bases of hills or cliffs, perhaps to avoid earthquake-induced landslides and avalanches (McCartney and Veltre 1999; though it is possible this reflects a preservation bias caused by the landslides themselves). Earthquake-generated tsunamis likely also presented real dangers, particularly since most camps and settlements were located along the coast, just above high-tide lines; losses of life and property (e.g., dwellings, boats, cached food) may have been fairly regular occurrences (McCartney and Veltre 1999). Volcanic eruptions may have had a greater impact still. The region's volcanoes are explosive and can produce devastating ashfalls with long-lasting effects on both humans and their key resources, including salmon streams, plants, and intertidal zones (McCartney and Veltre 1999:510).

Tierra del Fuego is likewise seismically and volcanically active. Although modern seismicity is relatively low (Lodolo et al. 2003), earthquakes may have caused periodic landslides and avalanches, and sediment geomorphology on the east coast of Isla Grande suggests that a subduction zone east of Tierra del Fuego may have produced occasional tsunamis (Bujalesky 2012). Volcanoes in the immediate area likely produced ash and pyroclastic material periodically (D'Orazio et al. 2000), but volcanoes farther north may have had the most significant impact on prehistoric people and their resources. In particular, a middle Holocene eruption of the Volcán Hudson (Aysén, Chile, roughly 1,100 km northwest of Yámana territory) may have led to a dramatic decline in human populations in central Patagonia (Cardich 1985; Prieto et al. 2013). In sum, ancestral Unangans and Yámana were both prone to periodic natural disasters, so perhaps the populations in Tierra del Fuego were more susceptible to losses of culture during these events due to their generally smaller populations and greater social isolation.

In light of the mechanisms Henrich (2004) cites as potentially responsible for the impoverished Tasmanian toolkit observed at contact, it is relevant that Tierra del Fuego is isolated in a more general sense. That is, the total land area between 50° and 55° southern latitude is vanishingly small relative to that of the same latitudinal range north of the equator; Tierra del Fuego is a peninsula of sorts. The northern Hemisphere subarctic, on the other hand, is vast and developments in one part of the region could easily have spread to others even if groups had little direct contact with one another. That is, it was simply a larger effective population of people experiencing similar environmental conditions; a larger effective "idea pool" where the potential for beneficial innovations was greater.

Failure to develop clothing technology

There is currently no archaeological evidence to suggest tailored clothing was ever produced by the ancestral Yámana, as would be indicated by needles, awls, and microblades. Conversely, the earliest sites on the Aleutians are microblade sites and it is likely that the islands were first colonized by people who already had tailored cold-weather clothing. Genetic evidence suggests that all Native Americans descended from Siberian populations (Goebel et al. 2008) that almost certainly had tailored clothing (Hoffecker 2005). It is possible, then, that the tropics, and perhaps the lower midlatitudes, may have been an ecological barrier to the production of tailored clothing. This hypothesis has further implications for the timing and speed of the initial colonization of the New World, particularly in light of new data indicating early (ca. 18,500–15,000 cal BP) occupation of cold parkland and boreal environments in Chile (Dillehay et al. 2015). Clothing would certainly have been advantageous under such conditions and, if migration to that part of the world from Siberia was as rapid as some suggest, early Fuegians' having had clothing is more plausible. Conversely, if the early occupants of the Monte Verde area did not have clothing, it might have been because migration from Siberia was relatively slow. Limited evidence suggests the Alacaluf (the Yámana's western neighbors) had a physiological adaptation to the cold (Hammel et al. 1960), which might further support an extended period in far southern South America without tailored cold-weather clothing.

Final considerations

The foregoing discussion is far from a definitive statement regarding cultural evolution in the Aleutians and Tierra del Fuego. It is an exploration of preliminary hypotheses that now form the basis of more rigorous formal modeling. Certainly, every case of cultural evolution is distinct, but observing general trends and quantitative patterns in various domains can help identify and understand prehistoric behaviors that may not have an ethnographic analog.

I conclude by noting that archaeology is uniquely positioned to inform our understanding of these mechanisms and interactions. The record, granting its shortcomings, can help us estimate past humans' energy budgets, which in turn can inform interpretations of basal metabolism and fertility. We can also identify moments of increased or decreased population size and density and to track the tempo of cultural change through time. By these means and with careful attention to sources of diversity, we may be better able to identify diversity unique to the prehistoric past.

REFERENCES CITED

Bailey, Harry. 1960. "A Method of Determining the Warmth and Temperateness of Climate." *Geografiska Annaler* 43:1–16.

Baldini, Ryan. 2015. "Revisiting the Effect of Population Size on Cumulative Cultural Evolution." *Journal of Cognition and Culture* 15(3–4):320–336. https://doi.org/10.1163/15685373-12342153.

Bettinger, Robert, Raven Garvey, and Shannon Tushingham. 2015. *Hunter-Gatherers: Archaeological and Evolutionary Theory.* 2nd ed. New York: Springer. https://doi.org/10.1007/978-1-4899-7581-2.

Binford, Lewis. 1980. "Willow Smoke and Dog's Tails: Hunter-Gatherer Settlement Systems and Archaeological Site Formation." *American Antiquity* 45(01):4–20. https://doi.org/10.2307/279653.

Binford, Lewis. 2001. *Constructing Frames of Reference: An Analytical Method for Archaeological Theory Building Using Hunter-Gatherer and Environmental Data Sets.* Berkeley: University of California Press.

Bleed, Peter. 1986. "The Optimal Design of Hunting Weapons: Maintainability or Reliability." *American Antiquity* 51(04):737–747. https://doi.org/10.2307/280862.

Boyd, Robert, and Peter Richerson. 1985. *Culture and the Evolutionary Process.* Chicago: Chicago University Press.

Bujalesky, Gustavo. 2012. "Tsunami Overtopping Fan and Erosive Scarps at Atlantic Coast of Tierra del Fuego." *Journal of Coastal Research* 28:442–456. https://doi.org/10.2112/JCOASTRES-D-11-00037.1.

Cardich, Augusto. 1985. "Una Fecha Radiocarbónica Más de la Cueva 3 de Los Toldos (Santa Cruz, Argentina)." *Relaciones de la Sociedad Argentina de Antropología* 16:269–275.

Cashdan, Elizabeth. 2001. "Ethnic Diversity and Its Environmental Determinants: Effects of Climate, Pathogens, and Habitat Diversity." *American Anthropologist* 103(4):968–991. https://doi.org/10.1525/aa.2001.103.4.968.

Charlin, Judith, Karen Borrazzo, and Marcelo Cardillo. 2013. "Exploring Size and Shape Variations in Late Holocene Projectile Points from Northern and Southern Coasts of Magellan Strait (South America)." In *Understanding Landscapes, from Land Discovery to their Spatial Organization,* vol. 2541. ed. F. Djinjian and S. Robert, 39–50. BAR International Series. Oxford, UK: Archaeopress.

Clark, Jamie. 2011. "The Evolution of Human Culture During the Later Pleistocene: Using Fauna to Test Models on the Emergence and Nature of 'Modern' Human Behavior." *Journal of Anthropological Archaeology* 30(3):273–291. https://doi.org/10.1016/j.jaa.2011.04.002.

Collard, Mark, Briggs Buchanan, Michael O'Brien, and Jonathan Scholnick. 2013. "Risk, Mobility or Population Size? Drivers of Technological Richness among Contact-Period Western North American Hunter-Gatherers." *Philosophical Transactions of the Royal Society of London. Series B, Biological Sciences* 368(1630):20120412. https://doi.org/10.1098/rstb.2012.0412.

Collard, Mark, and Robert Foley. 2002. "Latitudinal Patterns and Environmental Determinants of Recent Human Cultural Diversity: Do Humans Follow Biogeographical Rules?" *Evolutionary Ecology Research* 4:371–383.

Collard, Mark, Michael Kemery, and Samantha Banks. 2005. "Causes of Tool Kit Variation Among Hunter-Gatherers: A Test of Four Competing Hypotheses." *Canadian Journal of Archaeology* 29:1–19.

Cooper, John. 1946. "The Yahgan." In *Handbook of South American Indians*, Volume 1: *The Marginal Tribes*, ed. Julian Steward, 81–106. Washington, DC: Smithsonian Institution.

D'Orazio, Massimo, Samuele Agostini, Francesco Mazzarini, Fabrizio Innocenti, Piero Manetti, Miguel J Haller, and Alfredo Lahsen. 2000. "The Pali Aike Volcanic Field, Patagonia: Slab-Window Magmatism Near the Tip of South America." *Tectonophysics* 321(4):407–427. https://doi.org/10.1016/S0040-1951(00)00082-2.

Diamond, Jared. 1997. *Guns, Germs, and Steel: The Fates of Human Societies*. New York: W. W. Norton and Company.

Dillehay, Tom, Carlos Ocampo, José Saavedra, Andre Oliveira Sawakuchi, Rodrigo Vega, Mario Pino, Michael Collins, Linda Scott Cummings, Iván Arregui, Ximena Villagran, et al. 2015. "New Archaeological Evidence for an Early Human Presence at Monte Verde, Chile." *PLoS One* 10(11):e0141923. https://doi.org/10.1371/journal.pone.0141923.

Eerkens, Jelmer. 1998. "Reliable and Maintainable Technologies: Artifact Standardization and the Early to Later Mesolithic Transition in Northern England." *Lithic Technology* 23(1):42–53. https://doi.org/10.1080/01977261.1998.11720937.

Ellison, Peter. 2001. *On Fertile Ground*. Harvard, MA: Harvard University Press.

Ellison, Peter. 2003. "Energetics and Reproductive Effort." *American Journal of Human Biology* 15(3):342–351. https://doi.org/10.1002/ajhb.10152.

Ellison, Peter, Claudia Valeggia, and Diana Sherry. 2005. "Human Birth Seasonality." In *Seasonality in Primates: Studies of Living and Extinct Human and Non-Human Primates*, ed. Diane Brockman and Carel van Schaik, 379–399. Cambridge, UK: Cambridge University Press. https://doi.org/10.1017/CBO9780511542343.014.

Forster, Johann. 1778. "Excerpts from Remarks on the Organic Bodies, Observations Made During a Voyage Around the World." In *Foundations of Biogeography*, ed. M. V. Lomolino, D. F. Sax, and J. H. Brown, 19–27. Chicago, IL: University of Chicago Press.

Galloway, Victoria, William Leonard, and Evgueny Ivakine. 2000. "Basal Metabolic Adaptation of the Evenki Reindeer Herders of Central Siberia." *American Journal of Human Biology* 12(1):75–87. https://doi.org/10.1002/(SICI)1520-6300(200001/02)12:1<75::AID-AJHB9>3.0.CO;2-G.

Gaston, Kevin, Tim Blackburn, and John Spicer. 1998. "Rapoport's Rule: Time for an Epitaph?" *Trends in Ecology and Evolution* 13(2):70–74. https://doi.org/10.1016/S0169-5347(97)01236-6.

Gilligan, Ian. 2007. "Neanderthal Extinction and Modern Human Behaviour: The Role of Climate Change and Clothing." *World Archaeology* 39(4):499–514. https://doi.org/10.1080/00438240701680492.

Goebel, Julius. 1971. *The Struggle for the Falkland Islands: A Study in Legal and Diplomatic History*. Port Washington, NY: Kennikat Press.

Goebel, Ted, Michael Waters, and Dennis O'Rourke. 2008. "The Late Pleistocene Dispersal of Modern Humans in the Americas." *Science* 319(5869):1497–1502. https://doi.org/10.1126/science.1153569.

Gómez Coutouly, Yan Axel. 2015. "Anangula—A Major Pressure-Microblade Site in the Aleutian Islands, Alaska: Reevaluating Its Lithic Component." *Arctic Anthropology* 52(1):23–59. https://doi.org/10.3368/aa.52.1.23.

Grove, Matt, Eiluned Pearce, and Robin I. M. Dunbar. 2012. "Fission-Fusion and the Evolution of Hominin Social Systems." *Journal of Human Evolution* 62(2):191–200. https://doi.org/10.1016/j.jhevol.2011.10.012.

Hammel H. T., R. W. Elsner, K. L. Andersen, P. F. Scholander, C. S. Coon, A. Medina, L. Strozzi, F. A. Milan, and R. J. Hock. 1960. "Thermal and Metabolic Responses of the Alacaluf Indians to Moderate Cold Exposure." *WADD Technical Report*: 60–633.

Harcourt, Alexander. 2012. *Human Biogeography*. Berkeley: University of California Press. https://doi.org/10.1525/california/9780520272118.001.0001.

Henrich, Joseph. 2004. "Demography and Cultural Evolution: How Adaptive Cultural Processes Can Produce Maladaptive Losses—The Tasmanian Case." *American Antiquity* 69(02):197–214. https://doi.org/10.2307/4128416.

Henrich, Joseph. 2006. "Understand Cultural Evolutionary Models: A Reply to Read's Critique." *American Antiquity* 71(04):771–782. https://doi.org/10.2307/40035890.

Henrich, Joseph. 2010. "The Evolution of Innovation-Enhancing Institutions." In *Innovation in Cultural Systems: Contributions from Evolutionary Anthropology*, ed. Michael O'Brien and Stephen Shennan, 99–120. Cambridge, MA: MIT Press.

Henrich, Joseph, and Francisco Gil-White. 2001. "The Evolution of Prestige: Freely
 Conferred Deference as a Mechanism for Enhancing the Benefits of Cultural
 Transmission." *Evolution and Human Behavior* 22(3):165–196. https://doi.org/10
 .1016/S1090-5138(00)00071-4.
Hoffecker, John. 2005. "Innovation and Technological Knowledge in the Upper
 Paleolithic of Northern Eurasia." *Evolutionary Anthropology* 14(5):186–198. https://
 doi.org/10.1002/evan.20066.
Hubbell, Stephen. 2001. *The Unified Neutral Theory of Biodiversity and Biogeography.*
 Princeton, NJ: Princeton University Press.
Johnson, Lucille Lewis, and Margaret Winslow. 1991. "Paleoshorelines and Prehis-
 toric Settlement on Simeonof and Churnabura Islands, Outer Shumagin Islands,
 Alaska." In *Paleoshorelines and Prehistory: An Investigation of Method*, ed. Lucille
 Lewis Johnson and Melanie Straight, 171–186. Boca Raton, FL: CRC Press.
Keeley, Lawrence. 1988. "Hunter-Gatherer Economic Complexity and 'Popula-
 tion Pressure': A Cross-Cultural Analysis." *Journal of Anthropological Archaeology*
 7(4):373–411. https://doi.org/10.1016/0278-4165(88)90003-7.
Keeley, Lawrence. 1995. "Proto-Agricultural Practices among Hunter-Gatherers: A
 Cross Cultural Survey." In *Last Hunters, First Farmers: New Perspectives on the
 Prehistoric Transition to Agriculture*, ed. T. Douglas Price and Ann Gebauer, 243–272.
 Santa Fe, NM: School of American Research Press.
Kelly, Robert. 1995. *The Foraging Spectrum: Diversity in Hunter-Gatherer Lifeways.*
 Washington, DC: Smithsonian Institution Press.
Kelly, Robert. 2013. *The Lifeways of Hunter-Gatherers: The Foraging Spectrum.* Cam-
 bridge, UK: Cambridge University Press. https://doi.org/10.1017/CBO9781139176132.
Kline, Michelle, and Robert Boyd. 2010. "Population Size Predicts Technologi-
 cal Complexity in Oceania." *Proceedings of the Royal Society B: Biological Sciences*
 277(1693):2559–2564. https://doi.org/10.1098/rspb.2010.0452.
Kolodny, Oren, Nicole Creanza, and Marcus Feldman. 2015. "Evolution in Leaps:
 The Punctuated Accumulation and Loss of Cultural Innovations." *Proceedings of
 the National Academy of Sciences of the United States of America* 112(49):E6762–E6769.
 https://doi.org/10.1073/pnas.1520492112.
Lantis, Margaret. 1984. "Aleut." In *Handbook of North American Indians*, Volume 5,
 Arctic, ed. David Damas, 161–184. Washington, DC: Smithsonian Institution Press.
Laughlin, W.S. 1980. *Aleuts: Survivors of the Bering Land Bridge.* New York: Holt,
 Rinehart and Winston.
Leonard, William, Stephanie Levy, Larissa Tarskaia, Tatiana Klimova, Valentina
 Fedorova, Marina Baltakhinova, Vadim Krivoshapkin, and J. Josh Snodgrass.
 2014. "Seasonal Variation in Basal Metabolic Rates Among the Yakut (Sakha) of

Northeastern Siberia." *American Journal of Human Biology* 26(4):437–445. https://doi.org/10.1002/ajhb.22524.

Leonard, William, Marcia Robertson, and J. Josh Snodgrass. 2007. "Energetic Models of Human Nutritional Evolution." In *Evolution of the Human Diet: The Known, the Unknown, and the Unknowable*, ed. Peter Ungar, 344–359. Oxford, UK: Oxford University Press.

Leonard, William, Mark Sorensen, Victoria Galloway, Gary Spencer, M. J. Mosher, Ludmilla Osipova, and Victor Spitsyn. 2002. "Climatic Influences on Basal Metabolic Rates among Circumpolar Populations." *American Journal of Human Biology* 14(5):609–620. https://doi.org/10.1002/ajhb.10072.

Lodolo, Emanuele, Marco Menichetti, Roberto Bartole, Zvi Ben-Avraham, Alejandro Tassone, and Horacio Lippai. 2003. "Magallanes-Fagnano Continental Transform Fault (Tierra del Fuego, Southernmost South America)." *Tectonics* 22(6):. https://doi.org/10.1029/2003TC001500.

Lof, Marie, Hanna Olausson, Karin Bostrom, Birgitta Janerot-Sjöberg, Annica Sohlstrom, and Elisabet Forsum. 2005. "Changes in Basal Metabolic Rate during Pregnancy in Relation to Changes in Body Weight and Composition, Cardiac Output, Insulin-Like Growth Factor I, and Thyroid Hormones in Relation to Fetal Growth." *American Journal of Clinical Nutrition* 81(3):678–685. https://doi.org/10.1093/ajcn/81.3.678.

Lomolino, Mark, Brett Riddle, Robert Whittaker, and James H. Brown. 2010. *Biogeography*. 4th ed. Sunderland, MA: Sinauer Associates.

MacDonell, George. 1995–1996. "Environmental Resources and Range Size: A Study of Modern and Ancient Hunter Gatherers." *Nebraska Anthropologist* 12:31–45.

Mace, Ruth, and Mark Pagel. 1995. "A Latitudinal Gradient in the Density of Human Languages in North America." *Proceedings of the Royal Society B: Biological Sciences* 261(1360):117–121. https://doi.org/10.1098/rspb.1995.0125.

Massone, Mauricio, Alfredo Prieto, Donald Jackson, G. Cardenas, M. Arroyo, and Pedro Cardenas. 1999. "Los Cazadores Tempranos y sus Fogatas: Una Nueva Historia para la Cueva Tres Arroyos 1, Tierra del Fuego." *Boletín de la Sociedad Chilena de Arqueología* 26:11–18.

McCartney, Allen. 1975. "Maritime Adaptations in Cold Archipelagos." In *Prehistoric Maritime Adaptations of the Circumpolar Zone*, ed. William Fitzhugh, 281–338. The Hague, Netherlands: Mouton.

McCartney, Allen, and Douglas Veltre. 1996. "Anangula Core and Blade Site." In *American Beginnings: The Prehistory and Paleoecology of Beringia*, ed. Frederick West, 443–450. Chicago, IL: University of Chicago Press.

McCartney, Allen, and Douglas Veltre. 1999. "Aleutian Island Prehistory: Living in Insular Extremes." *World Archaeology* 30(3):503–515. https://doi.org/10.1080/004382 43.1999.9980426.

McCulloch, R., M. J. Bentley, R. M. Tipping, and C. Clapperton. 2005. "Evidence for Late-Glacial Ice Dammed Lakes in the Central Strait of Magellan and Bahía Inútil, Southernmost South America." *Geografiska Annaler* 87A(2):335–362. https://doi.org/10.1111/j.0435-3676.2005.00262.x.

McElreath, Richard, and Joseph Henrich. 2007. "Dual Inheritance Theory: The Evolution of Human Cultural Capacities and Cultural Evolution." In *Oxford Handbook of Evolutionary Psychology*, ed. Robin Dunbar and Louise Barrett, 555–570. Oxford, UK: Oxford University Press.

Nettle, Daniel. 1999. *Linguistic Diversity*. Oxford, UK: Oxford University Press.

Orquera, Luis, Dominique Legoupil, and Ernesto Piana. 2011. "Littoral Adaptation at the Southern End of South America." *Quaternary International* 239(1-2):61–69. –https://doi.org/10.1016/j.quaint.2011.02.032.

Oswalt, Wendell. 1973. *Habitat and Ecology: The Evolution of Hunting*. New York: Holt, Rinehart and Winston.

Oswalt, Wendell. 1976. *An Anthropological Analysis of Food-Getting Technology*. New York: Wiley-Interscience.

Pearce, Eiluned. 2014. "Modelling Mechanisms of Social Network Maintenance in Hunter-Gatherers." *Journal of Archaeological Science* 50:403–413. https://doi.org/10.1016/j.jas.2014.08.004.

Powell, Adam, Stephen Shennan, and Mark Thomas. 2009. "Late Pleistocene Demography and the Appearance of Modern Human Behavior." *Science* 324(5932):1298–1301. https://doi.org/10.1126/science.1170165.

Price, David. 1990. *Atlas of World Cultures*. London: Sage Publications.

Prieto, Alfredo, Charles Stern, and Jordi Estévez. 2013. "The Peopling of the Fuego-Patagonia Fjords by Littoral Hunter-Gatherers after the Mid-Holocene H1 Eruption of Hudson Volcano." *Quaternary International* 317:3–13. https://doi.org/10.1016/j.quaint.2013.06.024.

Rapoport, Eduardo. 1982. *Areography: Geographical Strategies of Species*. New York: Pergamon Press.

Read, Dwight. 2006. "Tasmanian Knowledge and Skill: Maladaptive Imitation or Adequate Technology?" *American Antiquity* 71(01):164–184. https://doi.org/10.2307/40035327.

Read, Dwight. 2008. "An Interaction Model for Resource Implement Complexity Based on Risk and Number of Annual Moves." *American Antiquity* 73(04):599–625. https://doi.org/10.1017/S0002731600047326.

Read, Dwight. 2012. "Population Size Does Not Predict Artifact Complexity: Analysis of Data from Tasmania, Arctic Hunter-Gatherers, and Oceania Fishing Groups." *UC Los Angeles: Human Complex Systems* 2012.

Richerson, Peter, and Robert Boyd. 2005. *Not by Genes Alone: How Culture Transformed Human Evolution.* Chicago, IL: University of Chicago Press.

Richerson, Peter, Robert Boyd, and Robert Bettinger. 2009. "Cultural Innovations and Demographic Change." *Human Biology* 81(2–3):211–235. https://doi.org/10.3378/027.081.0306.

Rodionov, S. N., N. A. Bond, and J. E. Overland. 2007. "The Aleutian Low, Storm Tracks, and Winter Climate Variability in the Bering Sea." *Deep-Sea Research*, Part II, *Topical Studies in Oceanography* 54(23–26):2560–2577. https://doi.org/10.1016/j.dsr2.2007.08.002.

Rosetta, L. 1993. "Seasonality and Fertility." In *Seasonality and Human Ecology*, ed. S. J. Ulijaszek and S. S. Strickland, 65–75. Cambridge, UK: Cambridge University Press. https://doi.org/10.1017/CBO9780511600517.006.

Sampson, C. G. 1988. *Stylistic Boundaries among Mobile Hunter-Foragers.* Washington, DC: Smithsonian Institution Press.

Shennan, Stephen. 2015. "Demography and Cultural Evolution." In *Emerging Trends in the Social and Behavioral Sciences: An Interdisciplinary, Searchable, and Linkable Resource*, ed. Robert Scott and Stephan Kosslyn, 1–14. Hoboken, NJ: John Wiley & Sons; https://doi.org/10.1002/9781118900772.etrds0073.

Shott, Michael. 1986. "Technological Organization and Settlement Mobility: An Ethnographic Examination." *Journal of Anthropological Research* 42(1):15–51. https://doi.org/10.1086/jar.42.1.3630378.

Smith, Eric A., and Bruce Winterhalder. 1992. "Natural Selection and Decision-Making: Some Fundamental Principles." In *Evolutionary Ecology and Human Behavior*, ed. Eric A. Smith and Bruce Winterhalder, 24–60. New York: Aldine de Gruyter.

Snodgrass, J. Josh, William Leonard, Mark Sorensen, Larissa Tarskaia, and M. J. Mosher. 2008. "The Influence of Basal Metabolic Rate on Blood Pressure among Indigenous Siberians." *American Journal of Physical Anthropology* 137(2):145–155. https://doi.org/10.1002/ajpa.20851.

Stanner, William E. H. 1965. "Aboriginal Territorial Organization: Estate, Range, Domain and Regime." *Oceania* 36(1):1–26. https://doi.org/10.1002/j.1834-4461.1965.tb00275.x.

Steager, Peter. 1963. "Yahgan and Alacaluf: An Ecological Description." *Kroeber Anthropological Society Papers* 32:69–76.

Stephens, David W., and John R. Krebs. 1986. *Foraging Theory.* Princeton, NJ: Princeton University Press.

Steward, Julian. 1936. "The Economic and Social Basis of Primitive Bands." In *Essays in Anthropology Presented to Alfred L. Kroeber*, ed. Robert Lowie, 331–350. Berkeley: University of California Press.

Steward, Julian. 1955. *Theory of Culture Change: The Methodology of Multilinear Evolution*. Urbana: University of Illinois Press.

Torrence, Robin. 1983. "Time Budgeting and Hunter-Gatherer Technology." In *Hunter-Gatherer Economy and Stone Tools*, ed. Robin Torrence, 57–66. Cambridge, UK: Cambridge University Press.

Torrence, Robin. 1989. "Retooling: Towards a Behavioral Theory of Stone Tools." In *Time, Energy and Stone Tools*, ed. Robin Torrence, 57–66. Cambridge, UK: Cambridge University Press.

Turner, Lucien. 2008. *An Aleutian Ethnography*. Ed. Raymond Hudson. Fairbanks: University of Alaska Press.

Winterhalder, Bruce, and Robert Bettinger. 2010. "Nutritional and Social Benefits of Foraging in Ancient California." *California Archaeology* 2(1):93–110. https://doi.org/10.1179/cal.2010.2.1.93.

Wobst, Martin. 1978. "The Archaeo-Ethnology of Hunter-Gatherers or the Tyranny of the Ethnographic Record in Archaeology." *American Antiquity* 43(2):303–309. https://doi.org/10.2307/279256.

Yesner, David. 1990. "Fuegians and Other Hunter-Gatherers of the Subantarctic Region: 'Cultural Devolution' Reconsidered." In *Hunter Gatherer Demography: Past and Present*, ed. Betty Meehan and Neville White, 1–21. Sydney: University of Sydney.

Yesner, David. 2004. "Prehistoric Maritime Adaptations of the Subarctic and Subantarctic Zones: The Aleutian/Fuegian Connection Considered." *Arctic Anthropology* 41(2):76–97. https://doi.org/10.1353/arc.2011.0097.

Yesner, David, Maria Jose Figuerero Torres, Ricardo Guichon, and Luis Borrero. 2003. "Stable Isotope Analysis of Human Bone and Ethnohisotric Subsistence Patterns in Tierra del Fuego." *Journal of Anthropological Archaeology* 22(3):279–291. https://doi.org/10.1016/S0278-4165(03)00040-0.

3

Archaeologists are the only anthropologists whose data contain information about behavioral variance in all of its dimensions . . . Long after the ethnographic era of hunter-gatherer research will have passed into history, archaeologists will be busy removing the ethnographically imposed form and structure from their data and retrodicting both the ethnographic and archaeological record. (Wobst 1978:307)

Much of our understanding of hunter-gatherer societies and the diversity inherent in them is generated from ethnographic accounts. However, it is clear that the ethnographic picture is limited in time and space, particularly in contrast to archaeological data. In searching for explanations concerning hunter-gatherer behavior, archaeologists should not expect to see "whole" foraging societies from the ethnographic record represented in the past but rather some familiar elements that may be put together in novel ways (see Lemke, chapter 1, this volume). Prehistoric hunter-gatherers lived in dramatically different social and environmental contexts than ethnographic or historic foragers—including drastic fluctuations in human and animal populations and environmental changes.

Throughout the long span of human prehistory global environmental shifts have radically changed the world in which hunter-gatherers were living. Of these changes, sea-level fluctuations are among the most dramatic, and had lasting effects on the landscape.

Underwater Archaeology and the Archaeo-Ethnology of Prehistoric Hunter-Gatherers

Examining the Role of Ethnography in Prehistoric Forager Research beneath the North American Great Lakes

ASHLEY K. LEMKE

DOI: 10.5876/9781607327745.c003

Over the last two million years large areas of the continental shelf as well as inland lakes and waterways were exposed and available for habitation and then subsequently submerged. These areas would have been prime habitat for hunter-gatherers due to abundant littoral and coastal resources, and contain archaeological records critical for understanding the emergence of modern human culture, early seafaring, and a long record of foraging adaptations. Underwater investigations are therefore critical for understanding global human expansion and the variable lifeways of prehistoric hunter-gatherers.

As this volume illustrates, archaeology is the only method for discovering and documenting hunter-gatherer diversity in the past. More specifically, *underwater* archaeology can play a critical role in documenting novel hunter-gatherer lifeways as entire prehistoric landscapes are preserved and offer unique data not available on land. One underwater case study documenting submerged caribou-hunting structures in the North American Great Lakes presents just such an example. Recent research in Lake Huron has documented a series of submerged prehistoric caribou-hunting sites and structures that rarely preserve in the terrestrial archaeological record.

While ethnographic data have been critical for identifying such hunting structures in an underwater context, the preserved archaeological record of an intact prehistoric hunting landscape and seasonal pattern of caribou exploitation differs significantly from ethnographic cases. Therefore, this case study can be used to investigate both the use of ethnographic data in archaeological research and how the unique preservation of submerged sites can reveal novel forager lifeways that extend beyond the ethnographic record.

PREHISTORIC CARIBOU HUNTING IN THE GREAT LAKES

THE STUDY CONTEXT

Global fluctuations in sea level and isostatic rebound over the past two million years are mirrored on a local level in the Great Lakes. With the withdrawal of the continental ice sheets at the end of the Pleistocene, the Great Lakes oscillated between higher and lower water levels before stabilizing at their modern elevations (Karrow 2004; Lewis et al. 2005, 2007). The most striking of these oscillations is the Lake Stanley lowstand in the Lake Huron basin, which lasted from ~11,200 to 8300 cal yr BP (9900–7500 ^{14}C yr BP). During this time water levels were more than 100 m lower than in modern day (Lewis and Anderson 1992; Lewis et al. 2005), and the Huron basin was divided into two distinct lakes separated by a rocky land bridge, the Alpena-Amberley Ridge (AAR) (figure 3.1). The AAR runs from northern Michigan to southern Ontario and is a

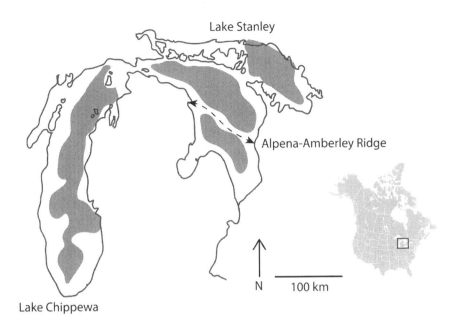

FIGURE 3.1. *Map of the Alpena-Amberley Ridge (AAR). Modern Great Lakes Michigan and Huron are indicated by the black outline. Lower water levels in these lake basins, the Chippewa and Lake Stanley lowstands are the shaded areas. The AAR is the narrow strip of dry land in Lake Huron at this time, indicated by the double-headed arrow.*

narrow (on average 15–20 km), limestone and dolomite formation that resisted glacial erosion; it is currently 12–45 m (~35–150 feet) underwater.

Underwater research on this submerged landform has identified a series of human-constructed stone features, lithic artifacts, faunal remains, and paleoenvironmental materials (e.g., rooted trees/wood, pollen, and testate amoeba) (Sonnenburg, Lemke, and O'Shea 2015). To date, over 60 stone constructions have been recorded on the lake bottom in depths between 80 and 120 feet (see Lemke 2016; O'Shea 2015a). These archaeological sites and structures date to the Lake Stanley lowstand when the water levels exposed vast stretches of land for human habitation that subsequently have become inundated. The Lake Stanley time period is little known from the terrestrial archaeological record, with overall poor preservation of organic materials due to acidic soils in the region, but also precisely because much of the prehistoric landscape is now underwater.

Research on the AAR serves as a case study for the importance of prehistoric submerged sites as it offers preservation unmatched on land, supplementing the particularly ephemeral archaeological records of hunter-gatherers. Submerged archaeological sites on this landform are both underwater and far away from shore, leaving them largely undistributed and relatively well protected. For example, while water level reconstructions in the Great Lakes are extremely difficult to absolute date and characterize, the transition from the Lake Stanley–stage lower water levels to higher water levels appears to have occurred fairly rapidly, but also gently—as intact rooted trees have been recorded on the AAR (Sonnenburg 2015). Furthermore, the primary research areas on the AAR landform are located far away from the mainland (35 and 50 miles offshore) and, as such, there is no source of modern sediment (O'Shea et al. 2014). All sediment preserved on the central AAR is therefore ancient and this submerged context has preserved not just archaeological sites but their background sediments and topography—essentially creating a Pompeii-like scenario. Finally, the submerged landscape beneath Lake Huron dates to a critical time period, in which massive cultural and environmental changes took place across the region at the end of the Pleistocene; much of the prehistoric landscape that presumably records the changes from this time is now underwater. Indeed, it appears the AAR served as a regional refugium, preserving an ice-age-like environment and cultural adaptations longer than the adjacent mainland (Lemke and O'Shea in press). Overall, the AAR offers a unique window into hunter-gatherer lifeways in the context of environmental fluctuations.

PRIOR RESEARCH

Terrestrial archaeological research in the Great Lake region has two long-held axioms. First, it is hypothesized that prehistoric archaeological sites dating to time periods of lower water levels are submerged beneath the Great Lakes. Lithic artifacts from many terrestrial sites are water rolled and display a distinct patination indicating that they were once submerged, which demonstrates that water levels across the Great Lakes have fluctuated significantly and affected archaeological sites (Deller 1976; Deller, Ellis, and Kenyon 1985; Ellis and Deller 1986). Therefore, systematic underwater research is critical for addressing questions about the early human occupation of the Great Lakes. Second, it has long been argued that prehistoric foragers in the region, particularly during the late Pleistocene/Early Holocene, were caribou hunters. Although few caribou bones have been found from terrestrial archaeological sites, indirect lines of evidence—site locations, raw-material use, and settlement patterns—have been used to support the inference of caribou hunting as a primary mode of subsistence (see Lemke 2015a and references therein). Historically, these two hypotheses have been difficult to evaluate, given the methodological challenges of underwater research and poor preservation of organic materials in the acidic soils of the region. Significantly, research on the AAR in Lake Huron provides direct evidence supporting both hypotheses in the form of prehistoric caribou-hunting structures preserved underwater.

Underwater research design on the AAR follows a layered strategy, using marine technology specifically adapted for locating prehistoric archaeological sites (O'Shea 2015b; O'Shea et al. 2013). Research began with large-scale regional surveys (e.g., 56 km²) using side-scan and multibeam sonars. On these early surveys, a long, narrow linear feature was recorded and subsequently investigated with scuba divers and a remote operated vehicle (see O'Shea and Meadows 2009). Through these initial investigations, it became clear that the feature was not the result of geologic processes but was human constructed. Underwater research has continued to identify, document, map, and sample this feature and other structures. This sustained research has resulted in the discovery of many different types of stone built features that have been independently confirmed as human constructions by the presence of lithic tools and debitage, charcoal, and a cervid tooth fragment (Lemke 2015a, 2015b).

The primary focus of research to date has been to document stone built architecture. Stone constructions on the AAR range from simple structures, such as a rectangular features, small V-shapes, and standing stones to more complex structures with interconnected linear and circular components. From the earliest investigations, it was noted that these structures bore striking resemblance to caribou drive lanes and other hunting features known on land (O'Shea and Meadows 2009) (figure 3.2). While similar structures are known from other parts of the world for targeting pronghorn and other ungulates (see Lemke 2015b), caribou are the most likely prey species of the Lake Huron structures for several reasons. As mentioned, preserved paleoenvironmental data characterize the AAR as a regional refugium that preserved an ice-age-like environment well into the Holocene, creating an ideal area for caribou with preferred forage, fresh water, and likely fewer insects (Lemke 2015a). In addition, an investigation of the terrestrial fossil record reveals a distinct gap in caribou remains during the Lake Stanley time period, with abundant fossils both before and after the lower water levels. The simple explanation for this apparent gap in the fossil record is that caribou remains from this time period are underwater, as those animals were most likely occupying the AAR and other exposed landscapes during that time (Lemke 2015a). These independent lines of evidence, as well as the lack of the other animals that would likely be

FIGURE 3.2. *Caribou drive-lane structures. (Left, top and bottom) Victoria Island, Canada; (top right) Dragon Drive lane beneath Lake Huron, visible on sonar: (A) drive lane, (B) hunting blind; and (bottom right) a remote operated vehicle photograph of the drive lane, courtesy of the Proceedings of the National Academy of Sciences. Arrows in the top-left photo indicate the start of each drive lane. (Adapted from O'Shea and Meadows 2009:figure 2.)*

hunted using drive lanes in the region at the time, indicate that caribou were the targeted prey species of the Lake Huron hunting structures.

MODELING CARIBOU BEHAVIOR AND HUMAN HUNTING STRATEGIES

Rangifer (caribou and reindeer) hunters have been studied extensively by anthropologists, as these animals were a critically important resource for many prehistoric and historic communities in the northern hemisphere (e.g., Anell 1969; Chard 1963; Gubser 1965; Hall 1989; Ingold 1980; Irimoto 1981; Krupnik 1993; Lips 1947; Lowie 1923; McClellan and Denniston 1981:337; Nellemann 1970; Rogers and Smith 1981:131–132; Simchenko 1976; Spencer 1959:29–30). There is a vast amount of diversity and complexity present in caribou exploitation strategies and extensive ethnographic documentation of these behaviors. Ethnographically, caribou were hunted using different technologies, employed by hunters ranging from individuals up to large groups of men, women, and children. Traps such as deadfalls and snares as well as trap lines were used alongside more active strategies such as stalking, simply running down the animal, and the use of structures such as hunting blinds or other shields. Despite this variability in ethnographically documented *Rangifer* hunting techniques (see Blehr 1990:315; Spiess 1979:103–137), strategies adopting hunting structures, primarily drive lanes, are by far the most common. These drives generally involved a large number of hunters and their families constructing linear stone, brush, and dirt structures with the goal of driving large numbers of caribou into the water, into narrow lanes or valleys, nets, or corrals (Gordon 1990; Riches 1982:33–39; Spiess 1979). Such communal hunts and features are akin to bison drives and other such structures (see Bar-Oz and Nadel 2013; Lemke 2016).

Hunting structures with drive lanes are common because they are dictated by animal behavior. Like other ungulates, caribou have innate curiosity and natural pattern recognition, and are attracted to linearity (e.g., Brink 2005; Spiess 1979:36). Hunting sites for targeting caribou are therefore often composed of long, linear drive lanes that are designed to channel the animals and are elaborated with hunting blinds, cairns, standing stones, and other features to attract the animals (e.g., Brink 2005; Gordon 1990; Riches 1982:33–39; Spiess 1979). Furthermore, caribou will often run alongside barriers rather than jump over or cross them (McCabe et al. 2004:14), even if they could easily step over them, resulting in drive lanes that do not need to be very tall. Animal behavior is therefore the critical variable affecting the physical nature and formal attributes of hunting sites. A uniformitarian assumption can be made that such behavior is not likely to change dramatically over time—from historic to prehistoric periods—resulting in consistent forms of hunting structures over that time.

Ethnographic and ethnohistoric examples of caribou-hunting structures across the arctic, dictated by animal behavior, can be used to identify their generalizable components and structural patterns—patterns that then can be compared to underwater sites and features. For example, such structures often include a drive lane constructed out of stone cairns, a shallow line of stones, or brush and pole fences. This first drive lane is usually associated with a second drive lane that creates convergence with the first to create a funnel. The second lane may be of a similar construction to the first, but oftentimes natural barriers such as lake margins, steep hills, cliffs, or rivers are used as the second side of the funneling feature. Within this funnel is an area of channeling before animals are directed through a small area of trapping and killing where awaiting hunters are stationed (Gordon 1990). Figure 3.3 is a generalized schematic of a caribou drive lane.

This understanding of the physical traits of hunting structures has been crucial for identifying such sites underwater. For example, several submerged sites

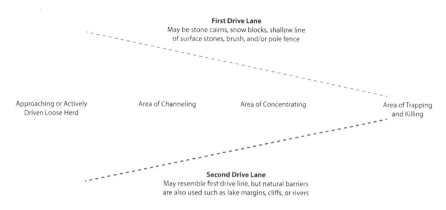

First Drive Lane
May be stone cairns, snow blocks, shallow line
of surface stones, brush, and/or pole fence

Approaching or Actively   Area of Channeling   Area of Concentrating   Area of Trapping
Driven Loose Herd   and Killing

Second Drive Lane
May resemble first drive line, but natural barriers
are also used such as lake margins, cliffs, or rivers

FIGURE 3.3. *Generalized caribou drive-lane schematic (after Gordon 1990:297).*

on the AAR fit within this generalization. While there are a variety of structure types, hunting features, and settings (see O'Shea 2015a), three of the largest and most complex hunting sites—Funnel, Dragon, and Drop 45—share
similar formal characteristics to those gleaned from the ethnohistoric record.
Each of these sites is comprised of at least one long, linear structure of stones
similar to the general pattern.

The Funnel Drive is in 25 m (82 feet) of water near a high limestone ridge.
The drive lane consists of a line of six stones on one side and a more complex
line opposite, creating the funnel shape. The opening of the funnel points to
the northwest and produces a gap of 5 m (figure 3.4) (see O'Shea 2015a). The
Dragon drive lane is also a long, linear feature formed of small rocks and
boulders to create a 365-m-long line. It rests in 31 m (100 feet) of water on a
level portion of the limestone bedrock of the AAR (see figure 3.2) (O'Shea
and Meadows 2009; O'Shea 2015a). Drop 45 is the most complex construction
recorded thus far. It is located in 37 m (120 feet) of water, is constructed on
level limestone bedrock, and is composed of a drive lane leading to a naturally
formed cul-de-sac created by a raised cobble pavement and a steeply rising
ridge. One drive lane is composed of human-moved stones, with an arm of the
natural cobble pavement serving as the second drive lane (figure 3.5) (O'Shea
et al. 2014; O'Shea 2015a).

These three sites serve as good examples of the variability in the second
drive line, as all three structures have a first drive line constructed out of stone,
paired with a second drive line of variable materials. Similar to ethnographic
cases, the secondary drive lines are either a built stone line similar to the first
drive line, as at the Funnel site, or the second line makes use of a natural

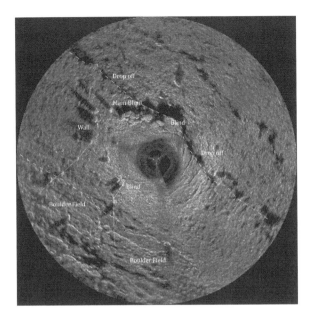

FIGURE 3.4. *Scanning sonar image of the Funnel site. This image looks straight down on the site, with a sonar view in a 360 degree circle. The main drive lane/wall is indicated along with associated hunting blinds. Radius is 25 m.*

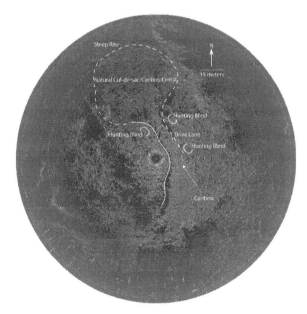

FIGURE 3.5. *Scanning sonar image of the Drop 45 site with major features labeled.*

feature, such as the steep rise near Dragon and the natural cobble pavement at Drop 45. Also similar to ethnographic and historic examples, each of these drive lane sites has smaller stone constructions associated with it, such as hunting blinds, or stone cairns.

In addition to drive-lane structures, there are a number of parallel features between the ethnohistoric and submerged archaeological records. For instance, standing stone *inuksuit*, which are known to be used for attracting caribou and as general landscape markers, have been identified under Lake Huron (see Lemke 2016:figures 7.33–7.34; and O'Shea 2015a:figure 10.12). Generally, historic/ethnographic caribou-hunting features and those under Lake Huron are strikingly similar, confirming the uniformitarian assumption that caribou *behavior* has changed very little throughout the Holocene. This is precisely why the general model derived from ethnohistoric sources (figure 3.3) can usefully be applied to a submerged archaeological context.

It is clear from ethnographic sources that animal behavior is the critical variable dictating the form of hunting structures, and that a general schematic of hunting structures can be made to help identify such features in challenging archaeological contexts (e.g., underwater). Beyond this, ethnographic data on caribou-hunting sites and descriptions of the operation of such structures can be used to inform models of how hunting may have operated in the past. For example, ethnographic data can be analyzed to identify relevant variables structuring caribou hunting, specifically group size (i.e., the labor force required to operate such structures) and seasonality.

It terms of group size, it is well documented ethnographically that hunts using constructed drive lanes are often communal, and involve the coordination of a large number of people to operate each stage of the drive. For example, several families of men, women, and children are known to cooperate through various tasks in large-scale drives (e.g., Binford 1991; Frison 2004; Gordon 1990; Hockett et al. 2013; Lemke 2016:60, table 3.2; Spiess 1979). In turn, the larger yields generated from the use of hunting structures can support these temporarily larger population aggregations (Binford 1991:35; Brink 2008; Carlson and Bement 2013; Frison 2004; Nadel et al. 2013; Smith 2013; Wilke 2013). Furthermore, it is historically documented that trapping ungulates such as pronghorn was viewed as both a ceremonial activity and a subsistence venture (Sundstrom 2000) and was often the largest social gathering of the year (Liljeblad 1986: 645). Therefore hunting structures often also serve as loci for social aggregation.

Seasonality is a critical variable as it determines the quality of the animals in terms of fat content, sinew/hide quality, and taste. Autumn is the primary time

TABLE 3.1. Relevant variables structuring human hunting of caribou and the resulting model derived from ethnographic and historic cases.

Relevant Variables	Expectation
Group size	The more elaborate a hunting structure is, the more people required to operate it.
Seasonality	Fall is the best time of year to hunt caribou, as animals are in prime condition.
Model	
Group size and seasonality	Large-group communal hunting in the fall

for hunting caribou: it is when the animals are in their prime, with maximum body weight and fat, and when their skins and sinews are at their most desirable (Blehr 1990:320; Enloe 1993:24; Reimers and Ringberg 1983; Stefansson 1951:337). Autumn migration routes also typically lead to relatively predictable winter ranges (Calef 1981:129). For all of these reasons, communal hunting in the autumn for furs and surplus meat for winter is a commonly documented activity among ethnographic and historic caribou hunters (e.g., Brink 2005:16). To continue with uniformitarian logic, we can assume that these documented biological traits can be applied to prehistoric caribou populations. A combination of the variables of group size and seasonality thus provides a model of large-group communal hunting in the fall as the expected behavior (table 3.1).

RESULTS

Ethnographic data served as a hypothesis-generating tool concerning the nature of caribou hunting. Ethnographic and ethnohistoric cases indicate that the patterns of caribou hunting are structured by group size and seasonality. Both of these variables can be tested explicitly with the underwater archaeological data. On the AAR, the prehistoric landscape is virtually intact, preserving much more of the settlement pattern than can be seen in terrestrial records. Numerous hunting structures can therefore be compared in terms of their complexity and required labor force.

Concerning group size, the ethnographic data reveal a connection between complex drive lanes and large social/hunting groups, and it can then be inferred that more complicated hunting structures beneath Lake Huron with interconnected lanes and hunting blinds should reflect larger group of cooperating individuals. All three of the drive lane features described above match the expectations for large groups. Such structures require a few hunters to be stationed in the hunting blinds, others along the drive lanes, and still others to keep caribou corralled at the end of the drive lanes. Vice versa, it is likely that smaller, individual structures and more simple hunting features, such as isolated hunting blinds, were used by smaller groups of individuals (see O'Shea et al. 2014). The interior space of these features could conceal only 1–2 hunters at a time. Therefore, expectations for group size are supported by the AAR data.

Season of use can be determined from the orientation of the hunting structures themselves. For example, if the prey animals are a migratory species, and if the hunters are targeting these animals during migrations, the season of use of hunting structures can be inferred from the orientation of funneling features, drive lanes, and in some cases, hunting blinds. Seasonality can be inferred by predicting the likely direction of movement of the prey animals during migrations and comparing this to the orientation of the hunting architecture. Since the general orientation of migrations is often known, the orientation of drive lanes can be used to infer the season of use with great accuracy (Morrison 1981:182). Therefore, orientation of hunting structures works particularly well for *Rangifer* or other species such as antelope that have predictable, semiannual migrations.

Again, the large sample of preserved structures underwater allows for an analysis of seasonal use. On the AAR, all three of drive lane complex structures are oriented for animals moving during their spring migration. In contrast, most of the simpler structures are oriented for hunting during fall migrations (see Lemke 2016; O'Shea et al. 2014). Overall, the majority of hunting structures on the AAR are simple constructions aligned for autumn hunting, which is consistent with uniformitarian logic that hunting in the fall is the best time of year (O'Shea, Lemke, and Reynolds 2013).

Significantly, when the variables of group size and seasonality are combined, the prehistoric data do not meet the expectations derived from ethnographic cases: on the AAR, most of the *simpler* sites are oriented for *fall* migration hunting, whereas all of the *complex* sites are oriented for *spring* hunting. This indicates that larger groups congregated on the AAR in the *spring* to participate in communal hunts using complex drive-lane structures, in marked contrast to ethnographic and historic accounts of caribou hunting in which large-group communal hunts take place in the *fall*.

DISCUSSION

The expectation derived from ethnohistoric cases suggests that large-scale communal hunting should take place in the fall, but in fact, on the AAR, all

TABLE 3.2. Testing expectations with archaeological data.

Relevant Variable(s)	Expectation	Supported with Underwater Data?
Group size	The more elaborate a hunting structure is, the more people required to operate it.	Yes
Seasonality	Fall is the best time of year to hunt caribou, as animals are in prime condition.	Yes
Model		
Group size and seasonality	Large-group communal hunting in the fall.	No

the complex structures requiring the most labor were oriented for spring hunting (table 3.2). This deviation is important, as we should not expect our a priori ethnographic expectations to be met in all cases in the past. In the instance of AAR prehistory, it is clear that the relevant variables of group size and seasonality were put together in different ways from our ethnographic expectations, which requires explanation. What likely accounts for this difference?

As this case study demonstrates, ethnographic data can be used to build generalized schematics of hunting structures, aid in the identification of such structures in an underwater context, and be used as a hypothesis-generating tool, specifically in this instance for creating models concerning the ways in which such structures may have been used in the past, including the number of people involved in the communal hunts, and the seasonal use of structures.

While ethnographic information is helpful in the AAR case for identifying shared patterns over time, it cannot be overlooked that prehistoric hunting took place in radically different social and economic contexts than the ethnographic present. Ethnographic data can never be used for wholesale interpretations of prehistoric sites. While expectations for individual variables are met, it is at the next scale up—concerning how these variables function together—where the ethnographic and archaeological data diverge. These differences are due to differences in context. Overall, while caribou behavior and biology remained consistent across the Holocene, caribou and human populations did not.

Strict analogies are limited because prehistoric caribou hunting took place in social and environmental contexts that have no modern analogs: for example, paleoenvironments of the Pleistocene/early Holocene were are characterized by disharmonious and diverse floral and faunal communities without modern equivalents during the late Glacial (e.g., Semken et al. 2010; Sommer and Nadachowski 2006). In addition, larges areas of the prehistoric landscape are now underwater, such as the AAR.

Furthermore, despite general similarities and uniformity in *Rangifer* behavior, prehistoric *Rangifer* herds were different: caribou populations and their geographic ranges were both much larger in the Pleistocene (Geist 1998:335; see also Wakelyn 1999:3). It is estimated that as many as 80,000 individuals aggregated in the late Pleistocene (Cohen 1997:246), but between 21,000 and 6000 cal yr BP caribou suffered a demographic decline in North America; while globally, the range of *Rangifer* declined by 84 percent (Lorenzen et al. 2011). Further depressing the overall caribou population were many specific regional declines, such as the caribou population crash in Greenland circa AD 1750 (Cuyler 2007:24; Grønnow et al. 1983:9; Meldgaard 1986:24; Nellemann 1970:150), the Fortymile caribou herd crash due to overhunting in the mid-1970s (Simeone 2007:318), and a substantial decline of caribou after the 1920s more generally (Bergerud et al. 2008:10, table 1). In addition, prehistoric herd composition and structure was different from modern herds. In contemporary populations there is at least one male for every five females (Nowak 1999), a lower proportion than in the fossil record, where there are often two males for every five females (Rivals et al. 2004:31).

Likewise, human demography is different, as there have been substantial changes in human population size, structure, density, and traditions of territoriality, as, for example, a doubling of Greenland's population from 6,000 in 1800 to 12,000 in 1900 (Hamilton and Rasmussen 2010:46), which significantly impacted subsistence practices. In addition to general growth and the associated subsistence demands, increasing populations would limit hunting territories by population in-filling, having a significant impact on hunting strategies and mobility regimes of prehistoric hunter-gatherers. Furthermore, colonial encounters significantly altered lifeways. Ethnographies and historic accounts in the arctic often deal with groups that had already suffered substantial devastation from contact with explorers, fur traders, whalers, and missionaries (Kenyon 1997:9; see also Cranz 1995:567, 769, 926; Gulløv 1985). The combination of trading posts in the interior of Canada and the smallpox epidemic of 1781–1782 significantly impacted Chipewyan lifeways and traditional hunting strategies (e.g., Gillespie 1975, 1976; Hearne 1958:115, footnote; Morrison 1981:183; Rich 1967:163–185). Furthermore, culture change after contact could occur very quickly (e.g., Kenyon 1997:9; Beck 2013). As early as the turn of the twentieth century, Steffansson documented that drastic changes had already taken place as hunter-gatherers occupying the Mackenzie River Delta no longer hunted using traditional drives (Stefansson 1919). "In fact, they thought it rather a tremendous effort because they possessed hunting rifles and could, in a more relaxed manner, shoot caribou from behind blinds, harvesting sufficient numbers with considerable less effort and at any time it was convenient" (Kenyon 1997:10).

Similarly, integration into the world system radically changed economies. While the historic Yukon Kutchin groups practiced caribou hunting using drive lanes and fences for subsistence, at the same time a large part of their economy was focused on the extraction of furs for market. Historical settlement patterns and communities are were largely determined by this dual economy (McFee 1981:161). Correspondingly, technological change significantly impacted hunting behavior. Technologies for capture and mobility changed dramatically in the historic era, impacting hunting strategies and *Rangifer* populations. The introduction of the flintlock gun in the second half of the eighteenth century, and the breech-loading rifle in the nineteenth century rapidly altered caribou hunting in Greenland and Canada from large communal hunts to individual stalking (Birket-Smith 1918:9; 1924:343; Dahl 2000:166; Grønnow et al. 1983:31; Nellemann 1970:151; McFee 1981; Petersen 2003:54, 141). Similarly, the combination of the flintlock gun and the fur trade altered caribou migration routes in Ungava (Elton 1942:16). The sudden and widespread use of firearms devastated caribou herds within 10 years during the late eighteenth and early nineteenth centuries in the central Canadian arctic, forcing Victoria Island Eskimo groups to move to the mainland (Manning 1960:8–10). Snowmobiles significantly altered mobility and hunting strategies (Pelto 1973). A classic example of these technological changes includes the use of planes by Nunamiut hunters to locate caribou herds (Binford 1978:141–142).

While there are certainly comparable aspects between the historic, ethnographic, and archaeological records of caribou hunters, such as the form of built hunting structures outlined above, the long prehistory of human interactions with the *Rangifer* species, including the nine-thousand-year-old caribou hunting structures underwater in Lake Huron, reveal prehistoric behaviors that differ from those of ethnographically known caribou hunters (O'Shea, Lemke, and Reynolds 2013). Many ethnographic accounts of caribou hunters document very large group communal hunts, but the much larger prehistoric herd sizes (prior to global population declines) significantly impacted past hunting strategies. Migrating herds on the AAR appear to have been so large that simple hunting structures along natural topographic feature could be used (See Lemke 2016; O'Shea, Lemke, and Reynolds 2013).

Furthermore, a general model of prehistoric caribou hunters—herd following—which is rooted in ethnographic analogy, finds no support in the AAR data. This example is presented to serve as cautionary tale, as herd following is a unique historical circumstance that has nonetheless run unbridled through archaeological interpretations. The model is based on a handful of post-European contact populations in the North America, including the Ethen-eldeli/Chipewyan caribou-eaters (Smith 1981), Gwich'in, and Caribou Inuit groups, and to a lesser extent, the Naskapi and Nunamiut. It has been suggested that groups attempt to follow caribou during their semiannual migrations and move with the herd rather than strategically intercept the fast-moving group of animals (e.g., Gordon 1988, 2003).

However, it is unlikely that any human group attempted to keep up with any group of animals. Instead some may have chosen to move to different seasonal locations to keep within broad ranges of a *Rangifer* population (Burch 1972; Burch and Blehr 1991; Heuer 2008; Thacker 1997:87). Indeed, it is physically impossible for humans without mechanized transport to keep up with a herd of long-distance-migrating caribou (Burch 1972). In addition, major population shifts—herds emigrating to new areas—may happen every 30 to 50 years, or one to two human generations (Spiess 1979:66), making the concept of herd following even more problematic, if not impossible. In fact, ethnographic hunter-gatherer groups claiming to follow herds did not qualitatively differ from other hunter-gatherers in their interaction with and exposure to prey species. Even the Chipewyan groups, who represent the closest candidate for "herd followers," did not consistently encounter caribou year round (Burch and Blehr 1991:444); rather, they sought the herds throughout their range but did not physically accompany them (Gordon 1990:298). Even in regions where prehistoric migrations were shorter, such as southwestern France (e.g., Spiess 1979), Magdalenian hunters situated themselves to intercept these herds and did not follow them. Indeed, herd following as a strategy is not represented in the archaeological record in either western or central Europe (Burch and Blehr 1991; Burke and Pike-Tay 1997; Thacker 1997; White et al. 1989) or the Great Lakes.

It is clear that behavior approximating herd following only happens under very specific conditions such as in areas where other resources are limited (offering little food to fall back on the rest of the year); between migrations; or among land-locked populations with no/limited access to marine resources (Gordon 1990:298). Examples of these historical occurances are known from the Canadian high arctic (Gorgon 1975) and Scandinavia before reindeer domestication (Blehr 1990). Under these conditions, ethnographic accounts have documented massive starvation of herd following groups (Mowat 1952; Tester and Kulchyski 1994). In addition, ethnographic groups that formed the ideal of herd followers only participated in this behavior due to territorial circumscription. Caribou Inuit groups, specifically the Harvaqtuurmiut and Ahiarmiut (Burch 1986:109), occupied inland areas year round, but this landlocked interior occupation did not happen until the mid-nineteenth century; prior to this, they occupied coastal regions at least part of the year (Freisen 2004:301). In the late eighteenth century, Chipewyan/Dene moved south, both as a response to epidemic diseases and to participate in the fur trade (Smith and Burch 1979:83). For all these reasons, this "adaptation" is a rare historical circumstance, not a generalizable model or a viable strategy that can be expected to be representative of prehistoric adaptations.

Overall, these differences between caribou hunting in the ethnographic present and in the past are due to differences in context—the social, environmental, and cultural contexts within which hunting took place. Ethnographically documented behaviors such as herd following happen only under the rarest of historical circumstances that just happen to be documented. It is therefore not surprising that there would be significant differences in caribou hunting through time on one hand, while there are some comparable, generalizable features dictated by animal behavior and biology on the other.

CONCLUSION

The AAR case study presented here reveals that uniformitarian assumptions about animal behavior can help us understand shared features of hunting sites. These shared features were known from ethnographic accounts, and were used to make a generalized model of physical characteristics to inform the search for such sites underwater. Beyond simple identification, additional features characterizing caribou hunting can be inferred from the formal attributes of hunting structures that find parallels in ethnographic accounts, including group size and seasonality.

In addition, the AAR case demonstrates that the archaeological record (particularly given the unique preservation underwater) can reveal significant differences between ethnographic and archaeological foragers. The specific example of caribou hunters—long dominated by ethnographic and ethnohistoric interpretations of prehistoric behavior—reveals that we should not expect prehistoric behavior to be replicated in ethnographic cases, most especially since prehistoric foragers were living in social and environmental contexts that have no modern analogs. For example, while there are parallels to ethnographic cases, the AAR archaeological record is unique. These are the earliest documented built structures for caribou hunting, and they demonstrate a sophisticated use of the natural landscape as well as unique patterns of fission-fusion in social groups during the early Holocene. Additional research is likely to reveal further ways these prehistoric foragers differ from ethnographically known groups, particularly given their context in an ice-age refugium (Lemke and O'Shea in press).

Overall, the AAR case aims to demonstrate how ethnographic data are still useful for archaeologists while also highlighting that such data cannot be used for wholesale interpretation or uncritical explanation (Wobst 1978). This is primarily due to radical differences in the social, environmental, and cultural contexts in which *Rangifer* hunting (and other types of foraging) took place over time.

Fortunately for prehistoric archaeologists, one of the archeological record's greatest strengths is that it can be used in tandem with paleoenvironmental, paleontological, geological, and other contemporary data sets to reconstruct ancient contexts. Furthermore, the investigation of submerged landscapes significantly improves our ability to do so. While underwater research provides unique challenges for the archaeologist, the preservation provided on submerged landscapes is often unparalleled on land. The cold, fresh waters of the Great Lakes preserve organic materials that are rarely recovered from contemporary terrestrial sites, and the rapid but gentle inundation has preserved an ancient landscape that has largely escaped subsequent post-depositional disturbances and modern development.

Underwater investigations, such as those on the AAR and on continental shelves throughout the globe, have an important role to play in modern archaeology, specifically for documenting the novel behaviors of prehistoric hunter-gatherers. While the archaeological remains of foragers tend to be particularly ephemeral, underwater preservation can supplement these records with additional data unlikely to survive in terrestrial settings. Submerged sites date to critical time periods in human evolution and prehistory, and such sites can be explored on a regional scale to reconstruct not only past human behavior but past environmental contexts, and fluctuations in both, over time. Significantly, absent underwater research, many models concerning hunter-gatherer mobility, landscape use, and peopling processes cannot be firmly evaluated. Underwater investigations can play an important role in documenting novel prehistoric hunter-gatherer behavior due to the preservation of intact prehistoric landscapes, with not only classes of data, but entire time periods that are not found in the terrestrial record. Despite obvious methodological hurdles, long-held critiques of underwater research are no longer viable (see Bailey 2011, 2014)—rather the investigation of submerged sites is essential, especially for addressing broader questions concerning hunter-gatherer variability.

REFERENCES CITED

Anell, B. 1969. *Running Down and Driving of Game in North America.* Studies Ethnographica Upsaliensia 30. Uppsala: Berlingska.

Arkush, Brooke S. 1986. "Aboriginal Exploitation of Pronghorn in the Great Basin." *Journal of Ethnobiology* 6(2):239–255.

Bailey, Geoffrey N. 2011. "Continental Shelf Archaeology: Where Next?" In *Submerged Prehistory*, ed. Jonathan Benjamin, Clive Bonsall, Catriona Pickard, and Anders Fischer, 311–331. Oxford, UK: Oxbow Books.

Bailey, Geoffrey N. 2014. "New Developments in Submerged Prehistoric Archaeology: An Overview." In *Prehistoric Archaeology on the Continental Shelf*, ed. Amanda M. Evans, Joe C. Flatman, and Nicholas C. Flemming, 291–300. New York: Springer. https://doi.org/10.1007/978-1-4614-9635-9_16.

Bar-Oz, G., and D. Nadel. 2013. "Worldwide Large-Scale Trapping and Hunting of Ungulates in Past Societies." *Quaternary International Guest Editorial* 297:1–7.

Beck, Robin. 2013. *Chiefdoms, Collapse, and Coalescence in the Early American South.* Cambridge: Cambridge University Press. https://doi.org/10.1017/CBO9781139135429.

Bergerud, A. T., and N. Stuart Luttich, and Lodewijk Camps. 2008. *The Return of Caribou to Ungava.* Montreal, QC: McGill-Queen's University Press.

Binford, Lewis R. 1978. *Nunamiut Enthoarchaeology.* New York: Academic Press.

Binford, Lewis R. 1991. "A Corporate Caribou Hunting: Documenting the Archaeology of Past Lifeways." *Expedition* 33(1):33–43.

Birket-Smith, Kaj. 1918. "The Greenland Bow." Meddelelser om Grønland 56. Copenhagen, Denmark: Bianco Lunos.

Birket-Smith, Kaj. 1924. "Ethnography of the Egedesminde District." Meddelelser om Grønland 66. Copenhagen, Denmark: Bianco Lunos.

Blehr, Otto. 1990. "Communal Hunting as a Prerequisite for Caribou (Wild Reindeer) as a Human Resource." In *Hunters of the Recent Past*, ed. L. B. Davis and B.O.K. Reeves, 304–326. London: Unwin Hyman.

Brink, J. W. 2005. "*Inukshuk*: Caribou Drive Lanes on Southern Victoria Island, Nunvut, Canada." *Arctic Anthropology* 42(1):1–28. https://doi.org/10.1353/arc.2011.0084.

Brink, J. W. 2008. *Imagining Head-Smashed-In: Aboriginal Buffalo Hunting on the Northern Plains.* Edmonton, AB: AU Press.

Burch, Ernest S., Jr. 1972. "The Caribou/Wild Reindeer as a Human Resource." *American Antiquity* 37(3):339–368. https://doi.org/10.2307/278435.

Burch, Ernest S., Jr. 1986. "The Caribou Inuit." In *Native Peoples: The Canadian Experience*, ed. R. B. Morrison and C. Roderick, 74–95. Toronto, ON: McLelland and Stewart.

Burch, E. S., Jr., and O. Blehr. 1991. "Herd Following Reconsidered." *Current Anthropology* 32(4):439–445. https://doi.org/10.1086/203980.

Burke, A., and A. Pike-Tay. 1997. "Reconstructing l'Age du Renne." In *Caribou and Reindeer Hunters of the Northern Hemisphere*, ed. L. J. Jackson and P. T. Thacker, 69–81. Burlington, VT: Ashgate Publishing.

Calef, George. 1981. *Caribou and the Barren-Lands*. Richmond Hill, ON: Firefly Books Limited.

Carlson, K., and L. Bement. 2013. "Organization of Bison Hunting at the Pleistocene/Holocene Transition on the Plains of North America." *Quaternary International* 297:93–99. https://doi.org/10.1016/j.quaint.2012.12.026.

Chard, C. S. 1963. "The Nganasan: Wild Reindeer Hunters of the Taimyr Peninsula." *Arctic Anthropology* 1(2):105.

Cohen, Vadim. 1997. "Reindeer Distribution in the Late Paleolithic of the Ukraine: Results of Research." In *Caribou and Reindeer Hunters of the Northern Hemisphere*, ed. L. J. Jackson and P. T. Thacker, 245–255. Burlington, VT: Ashgate Publishing.

Conkey, Margaret. 1991. "Context of Action, Context of Power: Material Culture and Gender in the Magdalenian." In *Engendering Archaeology: Women and Prehistory*, ed. J. Gero and M. Conkey, 57–92. Oxford, UK: Blackwell.

Cranz, David. 1995. "Historie von Gronland Teil I und II." In *Materialien und Dokumente* 26(1), by Nikolaus Ludwig von Zinzendorf. Ed. Erich Beyreuther. Hildesheim, Germany: Georg Olms.

Cuyler, Christine. 2007. "West Greenland Caribou Explosion: What Happened? What About the Future?" *Rangifer* 27(4):219–226. https://doi.org/10.7557/2.27.4.347.

Dahl, Jens. 2000. *Saqqaq: An Inuit Hunting Community in the Modern World*. Toronto, ON: University of Toronto.

Deller, D. Brian. 1976. "Paleo-Indian Locations on Late Pleistocene Shorelines, Middlesex County, Ontario." *Ontario Archaeology* 26:3–20.

Deller, D. Brian, Christopher J. Ellis, and I. T. Kenyon. 1985. *Archaeology of the Southeastern Huron Basin*. Paper presented in symposium: Archaeology of the Lake Huron Basin Area, organized by William Fox (Ontario Ministry of Citizenship and Culture). 12th Annual Meeting, Ontario Archaeological Society, London, ON.

Ellis, Christopher J., and D. Brian Deller. 1986. "Post-Glacial Lake Nipissing Waterworn Assemblages from the Southeastern Huron Basin Area." *Ontario Archaeology* 45:39–60.

Elton, C. 1942. *Voles, Mice, and Lemmings: Problems in Population Dynamics*. Oxford, UK: Clarendon Press.

Enloe, James G. 1993. "Subsistence Organization in the Early Upper Paleolithic: Reindeer Hunters of the Abri Du Flageolet, Couche V." In *Before Lascaux: The*

Complex Record of the Early Upper Paleolithic, ed. H. Knecht, A. Pike-Tay, R. White, and R. Boca Raton, 101–116. Boca Raton, FL: CRC Press.

Freisen, T. Max. 2004. "A Tale of Two Settlement Patterns: Environmental and Cultural Determinants of Inuit and Dene Site Distributions." In *Hunters and Gatherers in Theory and Archaeology*, ed. George M. Crothers, 299–315. Center for Archaeological Investigations, Occasional Paper No. 31. Carbondale: Southern Illinois University.

Frison, George C. 2004. *Survival by Hunting: Prehistoric Human Predation and Animal Prey*. Berkeley: University of California Press. https://doi.org/10.1525/california/9780520231900.001.0001.

Geist, Valerius. 1998. "Reindeer and Caribou." In *Deer of the World: Their Evolution, Behaviour, and Ecology*, 315–336. Mechanicsburg, MA: Stackpole Books.

Gillespie, Beryl C. 1975. "An Ethnohistory of the Yellowknives: A Northern Athapaskan Tribe." In *Contributions to Canadian Ethnology*, ed. D. B. Carlyle, 191–245. Ottawa, ON: National Museum of Man Mercury Series, Canadian Ethnology Service Paper 31.

Gillespie, Beryl C. 1976. "Changes in Territory and Technology of the Chipewyan." *Arctic Anthropology* 13:6–11.

Gordon, Bryan C. 1975. *Of Men and Herds in Barrenland Prehistory*. Ottawa, ON: National Museum of Man, Mercury Series, Archaeological Survey of Canada.

Gordon, Bryan C. 1988. *Of Men and Reindeer Herds in French Magdalenian Prehistory*. British Archaeological Reports. Oxford, UK: Archaeopress.

Gordon, Bryan C. 1990. "World *Rangifer* Communal Hunting." In *Hunters of the Recent Past*, ed. L. B. Davis and B.O.K. Reeves, 277–303. London: Unwin Hyman.

Gordon, Bryan C. 2003. "*Rangifer* and Man: An Ancient Relationship." *Rangifer* 23(5):15–28. https://doi.org/10.7557/2.23.5.1651.

Grønnow, B., M. Meldgaard, and J. Berglund Nielsen. 1983. *Aasivissuit: The Great Summer Camp. Archaeological, Ethnographical, and Zooarchaeological Studies of a Caribou-Hunting Site in West Greenland*. Meddelelser om Grønland (Man & Society) 5. Denmark: The Commission for Scientific Research in Greenland.

Gubser, N. J. 1965. *The Nunamiut Eskimos: Hunters of Caribou*. New Haven, CT: Yale University Press.

Gulløv, Hans Christian. 1985. "Whales, Whalers, and the Eskimos: The Impact of European Whaling on the Demography and Economy of Eskimo Society in West Greenland." In *Cultures in Contact*, ed. William W. Fitzhugh, 1–96. Washington, DC: Smithsonian Institution.

Hall, E.S.J., ed. 1989. *People and Caribou in the Northwest Territories*. Yellowknife: Department of Renewable Resources, Government of the Northwest Territories.

Hamilton, Lawrence C., and Rasmus O. Rasmussen. 2010. "Populations, Sex Ratios, and Development in Greenland." *Arctic Anthropology* 63(1):43–52.

Hearne, Samuel. 1958. *A Journal to the Northern Ocean*, ed. R. Glover. Toronto, ON: Macmillan.

Heuer, Karsten. 2008. *Being Caribou: Five Months on Foot with an Arctic Herd*. Seattle, WA: The Mountaineers Books.

Hockett, B., C. Creger, B. Smith, C. Young, J. Carter, E. Dillingham, R. Crews, and E. Pellegrini. 2013. "Large-Scale Trapping Features from the Great Basin, USA: The Significance of Leadership and Communal Gatherings in Ancient Foraging." *Quaternary International* 297:64–78. https://doi.org/10.1016/j.quaint.2012.12.027.

Ingold, T. 1980. *Hunters, Pastoralists, and Ranchers: Reindeer Economies and Their Transformations*. Cambridge, UK: Cambridge University Press. https://doi.org/10.1017/CBO9780511558047.

Irimoto, T. 1981. *Chipewyan Ecology: Group Structure and Caribou Hunting System*. Osaka Senri Ethnological Studies No. 8. Osaka, Japan: National Museum of Ethnology.

Karrow, Paul F. 2004. "Ontario Geological Events and Environmental Change in the Time of the Late Palaeo-Indian and Early Archaic Cultures (10,500 to 8,500 B.P.)." In *The Late Palaeo-Indian Great Lakes: Geological and Archaeological Investigations of Late Pleistocene and Early Holocene Environments*, ed. Lawrence J. Jackson and Andrew Hinshelwood, 1–23. Mercury Series, Archaeology Paper 165. Gatineau, QC: Canadian Museum of Civilization.

Kenyon, Dienje. 1997. "Large Kill Sites and the Potential for Illuminating Provisioning Behavior: Preliminary Thoughts and Expectations." In *Caribou and Reindeer Hunters of the Northern Hemisphere*, ed. L. J. Jackson and P. T. Thacker, 1–26. Burlington, VT: Ashgate Publishing.

Krupnik, I. 1993. *Arctic Adaptations: Native Whalers and Reindeer Herders of Northern Eurasia*. Hanover, NH: University Press of New England.

Lemke, Ashley K. 2015a. "Great Lakes *Rangifer* and Paleoindians: Archaeological and Paleontological Caribou Remains from Michigan." *PaleoAmerica* 1(3):276–283. https://doi.org/10.1179/2055557115Y.0000000003.

Lemke, Ashley K. 2015b. "Comparing Global Ungulate Hunting Strategies and Structures: General Patterns and Archaeological Expectations." In *Caribou Hunting in the Upper Great Lakes: Archaeological, Ethnographic, and Paleoenvironmental Perspectives*, ed. E. Sonnenburg, A. K. Lemke, and J. O'Shea, 73–99. University of Michigan Museum of Anthropology Memoirs, No. 57. Ann Arbor: University of Michigan.

Lemke, Ashley K. 2016. "Anthropological Archaeology Underwater: Hunting Architecture and Foraging Lifeways beneath the Great Lakes." PhD dissertation, Department of Anthropology, University of Michigan, Ann Arbor.

Lemke, Ashley K., and John M. O'Shea. In press. "The End of an Era? Early Holocene Paleoindian Caribou Hunting in a Great Lakes Glacial Refugium." In *People* and Culture in Ice Age Americas: New Discoveries in Paleoindian Archaeology, ed. R. Suarez and C. F. Ardelean. Salt Lake City: University of Utah Press.

Levine, Mary Ann. 1997. "The Tyranny Continues: Ethnographic Analogy and Eastern Paleo-Indians." In Caribou and Reindeer Hunters of the Northern Hemisphere, ed. L. J. Jackson and P. T. Thacker, 222–244. Burlington, VT: Ashgate Publishing.

Lewis, Christopher F. M., and T. W. Anderson. 1992. "Stable Isotope (O and C) and Pollen Trends in Eastern Lake Erie: Evidence for a Locally Induced Climatic Reversal of Younger Dryas Age in the Great Lakes Basins." Climate Dynamics 6(3–4):241–250. https://doi.org/10.1007/BF00193537.

Lewis, Christopher F. M., S. M. Blasco, and P. L. Gareau. 2005. "Glacial Isostatic Adjustment of the Laurentian Great Lakes Basin: Using the Empirical Record of Strandline Deformation for Reconstruction of Early Holocene Paleo-Lakes and Discovery of a Hydrologically Closed Phase." Géographie physique et Quaternaire 59(2–3):187–210. https://doi.org/10.7202/014754ar.

Lewis, Christopher F. M., Clifford W. Heil, Jr., J. Brad Hubeny, John W. King, Theodore C. Moore, Jr., and David K. Rea. 2007. "The Stanley Unconformity in Lake Huron Basin: Evidence for a Climate-Driven Closed Lowstand about 7900 ^{14}C BP, with Similar Implications for the Chippewa Lowstand in Lake Michigan Basin." Journal of Paleolimnology 37(3):435–452. https://doi.org/10.1007/s10933-006-9049-y.

Liljeblad, S. 1986. "Oral Tradition: Content and Style of Verbal Arts." In Handbook of North American Indians, vol. 11., Great Basin, ed. W. L. D'Azevedo, 641–659. Washington, DC: Smithsonian Institution.

Lips, J. 1947. "Notes on Montagnais-Naskapi Economy (Lake St. John and Lake Mistassinibands)." Ethnos 12(1–2):1–78. https://doi.org/10.1080/00141844.1947.9980659.

Lorenzen, Eline D., D. Nogués-Bravo, L. Orlando, J. Weinstock, Jonas Binladen, Katharine A. Marske, Andrew Ugan, Michael K. Borregaard, M. Thomas P. Gilbert, Rasmus Nielsen, et al. 2011. "Species-Specific Responses of Late Quaternary Megafauna to Climate and Humans." Nature 479(7373):359–364. https://doi.org/10.1038/nature10574.

Lowie, R. H. 1923. "The Buffalo Drive and an Old-World Hunting Practice." Natural History 13: 280–282.

Manning, T. H. 1960. The Relationship of the Peary and Barren-Ground Caribou. Technical Paper No. 4. Calgary, AB: Arctic Institute North America.

McCabe, R. E., B. O'Gara, W. O'Gara, and H. M. Reeves. 2004. Prairie Ghost: Pronghorn and Human Interaction in Early America. Boulder: University Press of Colorado.

McClellan, C., and G. Denniston. 1981. "Environment and Culture in the Cordillera." In Handbook of North American Indians, Vol. 6, Subarctic, ed. J. Helm, 372–386. Washington DC: Smithsonian Institute.

McFee, Ron D. 1981. "Caribou Fence Facilities of the Historic Yukon." In *Megaliths to Medicine Wheels: Boulder Structures in Archaeology*, ed. Michael Wilson, Kathie L. Road, and Kenneth J. Hardy, 159–170. Proceedings of the Eleventh Annual Chacmool Conference. Archaeological Association. Calgary: University of Calgary.

Meldgaard, Morten. 1986. "The Greenland Caribou: Zoogeography, Taxonomy and Population Dynamics." *Meddelelser om Grønland. Bioscience* 20:1–88.

Morrison, David. 1981. "Chipewyan Drift Fences and Shooting-Blinds in the Central Barren Grounds." *In Megaliths to Medicine Wheels: Boulder Structures in Archaeology*, ed. M. Wilson, K. L. Road, and K. J. Hardy, 171–187. *Proceedings of the Eleventh Annual Chacmool Conference.* Calgary, AB: University of Calgary Archaeological Association.

Mowat, F. 1952. *People of the Deer*. Berlin, Germany: Seven Seas Publishers.

Nadel, D., G. Bar-Oz, U. Avner, D. Malkinson, and E. Boaretto. 2013. "Ramparts and Walls: Building Techniques of Kites in the Negev Highland." *Quaternary International* 297:147–154. https://doi.org/10.1016/j.quaint.2012.11.037.

Nellemann, George. 1970. "Caribou Hunting in West Greenland." *Folk (Kobenhavn)* 70(11–12):133–153.

Nowak, R. M. 1999. *Walker's Mammals of the World*. 6th ed. Baltimore: Johns Hopkins University Press.

O'Shea, John M. 2015a. "Constructed Features on the Alpena-Amberley Ridge." In *Caribou Hunting in the Upper Great Lakes: Archaeological, Ethnographic, and Paleoenvironmental Perspectives*, ed. E. Sonnenburg, A. K. Lemke, and J. O'Shea, 115–138. University of Michigan Museum of Anthropology Memoirs, No. 57. Ann Arbor: University of Michigan.

O'Shea, John M. 2015b. "Strategies and Techniques for the Discovery of Submerged Sites on the Alpena-Amberley Ridge." In *Caribou Hunting in the Upper Great Lakes: Archaeological, Ethnographic, and Paleoenvironmental Perspectives*, ed. E. Sonnenburg, A. K. Lemke, and J. O'Shea, 105–114. University of Michigan Museum of Anthropology Memoirs, No. 57. Ann Arbor: University of Michigan.

O'Shea, John M., Ashley Lemke, Robert Reynolds, Elizabeth Sonnenburg, and Guy Meadows. 2013. *Approaches to the Archaeology of Submerged Landscapes: Research on the Alpena-Amberley Ridge, Lake Huron*. Proceedings of the 2013 AAUS/ESDP Curaçao Joint International Scientific Diving Symposium, 211–215. American Academy of Underwater Sciences and European Scientific Diving Panel Joint International Scientific Diving Symposium, October 24–27, 2013, Curaçao. American Academy of Underwater Sciences, Dauphin Island, AL.

O'Shea, John M., Ashley K. Lemke, and Robert G. Reynolds. 2013. "'Nobody Knows the Way of the Caribou': *Rangifer* Hunting at 45° North Latitude." *Quaternary International* 297:36–44. https://doi.org/10.1016/j.quaint.2013.01.010.

O'Shea, John M., Ashley K. Lemke, Elisabeth Sonnenburg, Robert G. Reynolds, and Brian Abbott. 2014. "A 9,000-Year-Old Caribou Hunting Structure beneath Lake Huron." *Proceedings of the National Academy of Sciences of the United States of America* 111(19):6911–6915. https://doi.org/10.1073/pnas.1404404111.

O'Shea, John M., and Guy A. Meadows. 2009. "Evidence for Early Hunters beneath the Great Lakes." *Proceedings of the National Academy of Sciences of the United States of America* 106(25):10120–10123. https://doi.org/10.1073/pnas.0902785106.

Pelto, Pertti J. 1973. *Snowmobile Revolution: Technology and Social Change in the Arctic.* Long Grove, IL: Waveland Press.

Petersen, Robert. 2003. "Settlement, Kinship and Hunting Grounds in Traditional Greenland." *Meddelelser om Grønland (Man & Society)* 27. Copenhagen, Denmark: Danish Polar Center.

Reimers, E., and T. Ringberg. 1983. "Seasonal Changes in Body Weight of Svalbard Reindeer from Birth to Maturity." *Acta Zoologica Fennica* 175:69–72.

Rich, Edwin Ernest. 1967. *The Fur Trade and the Northwest to 1857.* Toronto, ON: Meclelland and Stewart.

Riches, D. 1982. *Northern Nomadic Hunter-Gatherers.* New York: Academic Press.

Rivals, F., S. Kacimi, and J. Moutoussamy. 2004. "Artiodactyls, Favourite Game of Prehistoric Hunters at the Caune de l'Arago Cave (Tautavel, France): Opportunistic or Selective Hunting Strategies?" *European Journal of Wildlife Research* 50(1):25–32. https://doi.org/10.1007/s10344-003-0030-z.

Rogers, E. S., and J.G.E. Smith. 1981. "Environment and Culture in the Shield and Mackenzie Borderlands." In *Handbook of North American Indians*, Vol. 6, *Subarctic*, ed. J. Helm, 130–145. Washington DC: Smithsonian Institute.

Semken, Holmes A., Jr., Russell W. Graham, and Thomas W. Stafford, Jr. 2010. "AMS [14]C Analysis of Late Pleistocene Non-Analog Faunal Components from 21 Cave Deposits in Southeastern North America." *Quaternary International* 217(1–2):240–255. https://doi.org/10.1016/j.quaint.2009.11.031.

Simchenko, Y. B. 1976. *The Culture of Reindeer Hunters of Northern Eurasia.* Moscow: Nauka.

Simeone, William E. 2007. "People of the River: The Subsistence Economy of the Han, Athabaskan People of the Upper Yukon River." In *International Handbook of Research on Indigenous Entrepreneurship*, ed. Léo-Paul Dana and Robert B. Anderson, 313–327. Cheltenham, UK: Edward Elgar. https://doi.org/10.4337/9781781952641.00036.

Smith, Bruce. 2013. "Modifying Landscapes and Mass Kills: Human Niche Construction and Communal Ungulate Harvests." *Quaternary International* 297:8–12. https://doi.org/10.1016/j.quaint.2012.12.006.

Smith, James G. E. 1981. "Chipewyan, Cree, and Inuit Relations West of Hudson Bay, 1714–1955." *Ethnohistory* (Columbus, Ohio) 28(2):133–156. https://doi.org/10.2307 /481115.

Smith, James G. E., and Ernest S. Burch, Jr. 1979. "Chipewyan and Inuit in the Central Canadian Subarctic, 1613–1977." *Arctic Anthropology* 16(2):76–101.

Sommer, R. S., and A. Nadachowski. 2006. "Glacial Refugia of Mammals in Europe: Evidence from Fossil Records." *Mammal Review* 36(4):251–265. https://doi.org/10 .1111/j.1365-2907.2006.00093.x.

Sonnenburg, Elizabeth. 2015. "Paleoenvironmental Reconstruction of the Alpena-Amberley Ridge Submerged Landscape during the Lake Stanley Lowstand (ca. 8.4–9 ka cal BP), Lake Huron." In *Caribou Hunting in the Upper Great Lakes: Archaeological, Ethnographic, and Paleoenvironmental Perspectives*, ed. E. Sonnenburg, A. K. Lemke, and J. O'Shea, 147–164. University of Michigan Museum of Anthropology Memoirs No. 57. Ann Arbor: University of Michigan.

Sonnenburg, Elizabeth, Ashley K. Lemke, and John M. O'Shea. 2015. *Caribou Hunting in the Upper Great Lakes: Archaeological, Ethnographic, and Paleoenvironmental Perspectives*. University of Michigan Museum of Anthropology Memoirs No. 57. Ann Arbor: University of Michigan.

Spencer, R. F. 1959. *The North Alaskan Eskimo: A Study in Ecology and Society*. Bulletin No. 171. Washington, DC: Bureau of American Ethnology, Smithsonian Institution.

Spiess, A. E. 1979. *Reindeer and Caribou Hunters: An Archaeological Study*. New York: Academic Press.

Stefansson, Vilhjalmur. 1919. "The Stefansson-Anderson Arctic Expedition of the American Museum, Preliminary Ethnological Report." Anthropological Papers of the American Museum of Natural History 16 (part 1). New York: American Museum of Natural History.

Stefansson, Vilhjalmur. 1951. *My Life with the Eskimo*. New York: Macmillan Company.

Sundstrom, L. 2000. "Cheyenne Pronghorn Procurement and Ceremony." In *Pronghorn Past and Present: Archaeology, Ethnography, and Biology*, vol. 32. ed. J. V. Pastor and P. M. Lubinski, 119–132. Plains Anthropologist Memoir 32. Abingdon, UK: Taylor and Francis on behalf of the Plains Anthropological Society.

Tester, Frank James, and Peter Kulchyski. 1994. *Tammarniit (Mistakes): Inuit Relocation in the Eastern Arctic, 1939–63*. Vancouver: University of Britich Columbia Press.

Thacker, P. T. 1997. "The Significance of *Rangifer* as a Human Prey Species during the Central European Upper Paleolithic." In *Caribou and Reindeer Hunters of the Northern Hemisphere*, ed. L. J. Jackson and P. T. Thacker, 82–104. Burlington, VT: Ashgate Publishing.

Wakelyn, Leslie. 1999. *The Qamanirjuaq Herd: An Arctic Enigma*. Iqaluit, Nunavut, Canada: The Beverly and Qamanirjuaq Caribou Management Board.

White, R., P. G. Bahn, J. Clottes, R. Cribb, F. Delpech, T. F. Kehoe, D. J. Olszewski, L. G. Straus, D. Sturdy, and J. Svoboda. 1989. "Husbandry and Herd Control in the Upper Paleolithic: A Critical Review of the Evidence [and Comments and Reply]." *Current Anthropology* 30(5):609–632. https://doi.org/10.1086/203789.

Wilke, P. J. 2013. "The Whiskey Flat Pronghorn Trap Complex, Mineral County, Nevada, Western United States: Preliminary Report." *Quaternary International* 297:79–92. https://doi.org/10.1016/j.quaint.2013.01.018.

Wobst, Martin. 1978. "The Archaeo-Ethnology of Hunter-Gatherers or the Tyranny of the Ethnographic Record in Archaeology." *American Antiquity* 43(2):303–309. https://doi.org/10.2307/279256.

4

Variation in the Occupation Intensity of Early Forager Sites of the Andean Puna

Implications for Settlement and Adaptation

Kurt Rademaker and Katherine Moore

We compare occupation intensity among early forager archaeological sites of the Andean *puna*, a high-elevation grass- and shrubland ecoregion spanning central Peru, Bolivia, and northern Chile and Argentina. The earliest sites in the Andean puna were established in the Terminal Pleistocene, and by the Early Holocene hunter-gatherers[1] were widespread. Despite the inherent challenges of high elevation, rapid and successful settlement of the puna was facilitated by favorable climatic conditions and similar resources throughout this "megapatch." Forager sites in the Andean puna exhibit striking similarities in campsite locations, hunted animals, stone raw material acquisition, and plant resource use. Similarities in stone-tool assemblages and projectile point styles suggest common activities and shared culture over vast, rugged landscapes. At a finer scale, forager sites in the Andean puna exhibit very different levels of occupation intensity and patterns of mobility. Some archaeologists interpret forager puna sites through a single, homogeneous evolutionary sequence of adaptation to high elevation. Using systematic comparisons, we show that differences in occupation intensity and mobility relate not to the constraints of elevation but to differences in primary productivity and congruity of critical resources in site habitats.

THE ANDEAN PUNA

The Andes are the longest continental mountain range in the world, spanning some 7,000 km of the

DOI: 10.5876/9781607327745.c004

76

tropics and subtropics through Colombia, Ecuador, Peru, Bolivia, Chile, and Argentina. This mountain region encompasses diverse environments due to variations in temperature, precipitation, elevation, and latitude. The extreme relief of the relatively narrow Andean cordillera compresses vertically stacked ecological zones into relatively short horizontal distances (Brush 1976). The grassland and montane shrubs of the Andean puna occur from approximately 10° to 30° S latitude and above 4,000 m above sea level (masl) in Peru and ~3,500 masl in Bolivia and northern Chile and Argentina (Olson et al. 2001). The lower limit of the puna ecoregion generally corresponds with the geographic boundaries of the Andean plateau, which, at an average elevation of 4,000 masl, is one of Earth's highest landscapes permanently inhabited by humans (Aldenderfer 2006).

Several features make the Andean puna an extreme environment. Mean annual temperatures throughout the puna are low. Although seasonal variation in temperature is minimal, diurnal temperature variation is considerable. Days are characterized by intense solar radiation, nights by below-freezing temperatures. The South American Summer Monsoon brings precipitation to the Andean puna in a pronounced wet season, with dry conditions predominating the rest of the year (Baker and Fritz 2015). The duration of the wet season decreases from north (October to April at 10° S) to south (December to March at ~30°S) (Vuille et al. 2003). Precipitation derives mainly from advection of tropical Atlantic moisture and prevailing easterly airflow over the Amazon Basin (Lenters and Cook 1997), with higher precipitation at the eastern edge of the Andes decreasing toward the Pacific. Year-round, dry, subsiding air masses in the southeast Pacific and persistent upwelling of the cold Humboldt Current maintain extremely dry conditions along the Pacific Coast and western Andean slope (Grosjean et al. 2007), most dramatically expressed in the hyperarid Atacama Desert of northern Chile.

Troll (1968) used gradients in precipitation and vegetation communities to divide the puna into wet puna, dry puna, and salt puna; this scheme continues to be used in biogeography (Olson et al. 2001) (figures 4.1, 4.2). Figure 4.3 shows the gradients in annual net primary production, from higher values in the wet puna to lower values in the salt puna (NASA LP DAAC 2016). At a continental scale, primary production of the puna appears low (Aldenderfer 1998), but at a finer spatial scale, the puna is a mosaic containing some extremely productive patches. The resource-rich patches of the salt puna are smaller and more localized relative to those in the dry puna and wet puna (Grosjean et al. 2007). All three puna divisions contain surface freshwater and resource-rich areas concentrated at lakes, along stream courses, and in

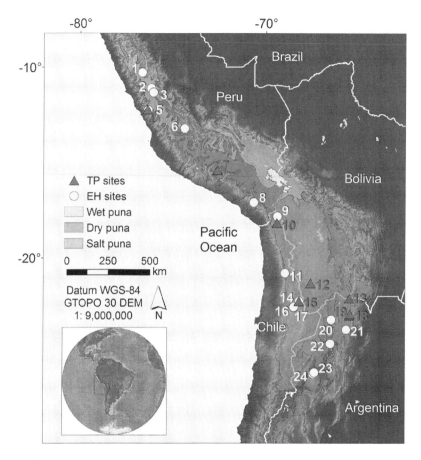

FIGURE 4.1. *Map of the Andes with archaeological sites ≥ 3,000 masl absolutely dated to the Terminal Pleistocene (triangles) and first millennium of the Early Holocene (circles). Sites include: (1) Lauricocha-2, (2) Pachamachay, (3) Panaulauca, (4) Tres Ventanas, (5) Quiqche-1, (6) Jaywamachay, (7) Cuncaicha, (8) Asana, (9) Hakenasa, (10) Las Cuevas-2, (11) Quebrada Blanca, (12) Cueva Bautista, (13) Cueva de Yavi, (14) Chulqui-1A, (15) El Pescador, (16) Tuina-1, (17) Tuina-5, (18) Pintoscayoc-1, (19) Inca Cueva-4, (20) Hornillos-2, (21) Huachichocana-3, (22) Alero Cuevas, (23) Peñas de las Trampas-1-1, (24) Quebrada Seca-3. Wet, dry, and salt puna divisions provided by World Wildlife Fund; Olson et al. 2001.*

bofedal, humedal, or *vega* wetlands. These areas tether the perennially territorial vicuña (Koford 1957; Franklin 1981) and the waterfowl that migrate along the Andean range. Permanent lakes are found from north-central Peru to

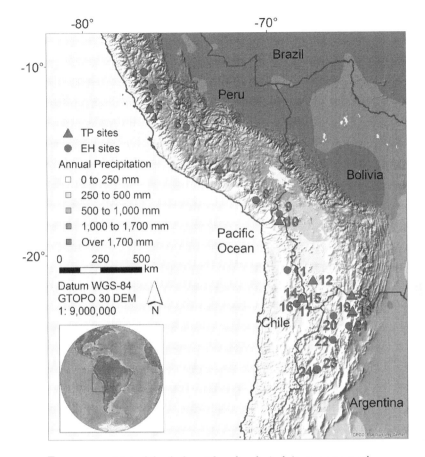

FIGURE 4.2. *Map of the Andes with archaeological sites ≥ 3,000 masl absolutely dated to the Terminal Pleistocene (triangles) and first millennium of the Early Holocene (circles). List of sites is the same as in figure 4.1. WorldClim BIO12 mean annual precipitation (mm) provided by Hijmans et al. (2005).*

northern Chile and Bolivia. In the more arid south and west are salt pans and shallow or seasonally dry endorheic basins (Stoertz and Ericksen 1974).

EARLY FORAGER ARCHAEOLOGY OF THE ANDEAN PUNA

Beyond temperature, precipitation, and resource distribution, the high elevation of the Andean puna poses numerous physiological challenges, including hypoxia (low-oxygen conditions) and high energetic costs of subsistence

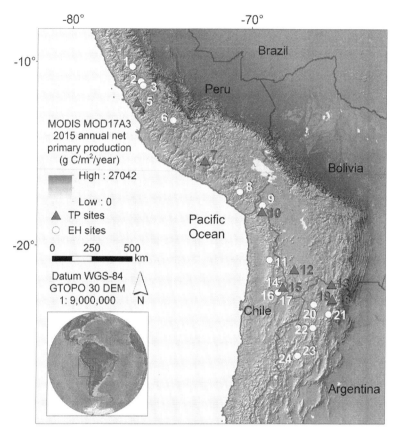

FIGURE 4.3. *Map of the Andes with archaeological sites ≥ 3,000 masl absolutely dated to the Terminal Pleistocene (triangles) and first millennium of the Early Holocene (circles). List of sites is the same as in figures 4.1 and 4.2. Terra/MODIS net primary production (g C/m²/year) (NASA LP DAAC).*

(Baker and Little 1976). Above 4,000 masl, oxygen partial pressure is less than 60 percent that at sea level and twice the caloric intake is needed to maintain normal metabolic function (Marriott and Newberry 1996). Given these stressors, it is remarkable that humans settled the Andean puna at all (Aldenderfer 2006). Yet, hunter-gatherers appeared in the high Andes of southern Peru, Bolivia, northern Chile, and northwest Argentina in the Terminal Pleistocene and were widespread throughout the puna by the Early Holocene (Rademaker et al. 2013a; Capriles and Albarracin-Jordan 2013; Méndez Melgar 2013; Prates et al. 2013). Despite the challenges of high-elevation life, the resources of the puna evidently were attractive enough for hunter-gatherers to explore and ultimately settle there.

The increase in frequency of archaeological sites in the Andean puna over time (figure 4.1) can be interpreted as resulting from initially low forager populations in the Terminal Pleistocene (Rick 1988) and larger forager populations by the end of the first millennium of the Early Holocene, in accord with summed radiocarbon probability studies (Muscio 2012; Muscio and López 2016; Gayo et al. 2015) and paleodemographic concepts (Surovell 2000). How did hunter-gatherers settle one of the planet's highest mountain regions so quickly? Archaeological sites throughout the high Andean puna share many similar characteristics—selection of caves and rockshelters proximal to streams and bofedal wetlands for camp sites, hunting a combination of large herbivores (the wild camelids *vicuña* and *guanaco* and the Andean deer *taruka*), large rodents (*vizcacha*), and birds, use of obsidian, andesite, and siliceous rocks for stone toolmaking, and collection of edible plants, such as *Chenopodium*, starchy roots and tubers, and *Opuntia* cactus.

These common characteristics led Osorio et al. (2016) to propose that the high Andes constituted a *megapatch* (after Kelly 2003). Once foragers initially learned how water and other critical resources were distributed in the Andean puna, they would have been able to use this experience to find the same resources elsewhere throughout the puna. Perhaps this concept partially explains the considerable cultural homogeneity in projectile-point forms and other material culture over large land areas.

From the beginning of archaeological research in the Andean puna, investigators recognized that puna sites probably were linked with each other and with lower-elevation sites in distinct ecological zones. Various seasonal residential mobility scenarios were suggested for different regions, depending on the structure of resources in site habitats and seasonal shifts in temperature and precipitation (Cardich 1964; Ravines 1967, 1972; Lynch 1971, 1980; Dauelsberg 1983; Santoro Vargas and Chacama Rodríguez 1984; Santoro and Núñez 1987; Núñez and Santoro 1988; Aldenderfer 1998). John Rick and his team (Rick 1980; Bocek and Rick 1982; Moore 1998; Rick and Moore 1999), working in the Junín basin of central Peru, suggested the possibility of sedentary occupation in resource-rich patches of the wet puna. The herds of vicuña that maintain year-round territories, the abundant siliceous rocks for stone toolmaking, and the variety of edible and combustible plants around extensive lakes could have made Junín attractive to foragers throughout the year, as long as camelid populations were not overhunted.

Others have viewed the Andean puna as a formidable barrier to hunter-gatherer settlement because of interannual variation in precipitation and challenges to physiology and reproduction posed by hypoxia. This argument was first formulated by Mark Aldenderfer (1998, 1999) to explain change through time in the occupation sequence at Asana, an open-air site at 3,435 masl in a montane valley in southern Peru. Aldenderfer's model of gradual physiological adaptation situated the process of settlement of the high Andes within an evolutionary framework. When this scenario was proposed, numerous Terminal Pleistocene sites were known from the South American lowlands, but none had been identified at very high elevation.[2] This evolutionary model therefore provided a much-needed explanation for the pattern of archaeological sites that existed at the time.

Luis Borrero (1995) had proposed a two-stage model for the initial settlement of empty and unfamiliar lands in Patagonia. This model described an exploratory stage of peopling, which would have left ephemeral traces in a landscape as knowledge was acquired, followed by a colonization stage, which created a more substantial archaeological footprint. Borrero's model was not formulated for the settlement of the Andean highlands, but considered in tandem with Aldenderfer's model, it was possible to define specific archaeological expectations for human adaptation to the puna. The earliest archaeological sites would be at lower elevations, with higher elevations settled progressively later as beneficial biological adaptations became frequent enough in forager populations to ensure demographic success (Aldenderfer 2006). Occupations associated with initial tentative explorations of the high puna would be of brief duration, involve men, and result from logistical resource-procuring rather than residential functions. Residential bases, where women and children would be stationed, would be at low-enough elevations to avoid the deleterious effects of hypoxia on reproduction and child-rearing. During a subsequent colonization stage, occupation of high elevations by biologically adapted foragers would be of greater duration (perhaps permanent) and involve residential functions. The sequence of settlement and adaptation should be reflected by increased occupation intensity through time (Aldenderfer 1998).

This model of progressive adaptation frequently has been the lens through which early Andean puna sites (and other sites) are viewed. For example, the acquisition of highland Alca obsidian ~13 ka at the Peruvian coastal Paleoindian site Quebrada Jaguay (Sandweiss et al. 1998), has been characterized as a logistical foray (Aldenderfer 2008; Jolie et al. 2011), despite a roundtrip distance of at least ~300 km. The material remains at Early Holocene sites in Chile and Argentina above 4,000 masl and a Terminal Pleistocene site in Bolivia at 3,933 masl are ephemeral because these sites must have been used briefly in exploratory, logistical visits (Osorio et al. 2011; Hoguin and Oxman 2015; Capriles et al. 2016a). The Terminal Pleistocene site of Guitarrero Cave (2,580 masl) and Early Holocene Asana (3435 m,asl) in Peru were ideal residential bases inhabited by the entire forager group because they were situated in warmer valleys below the puna (Jolie et al. 2011; Aldenderfer 1998, 2006). Cuncaicha, a Terminal Pleistocene rockshelter in Peru at 4,480 masl (Rademaker et al. 2014, 2016), could not have functioned as a residential base because the site is too early for people to have lived so high; rather, the site must result from brief, logistical exploration (Capriles et al. 2016b).

Despite the prevalence of the evolutionary model in interpretations of hunter-gatherer settlement of the Andean puna, the basic archaeological predictions of the model have not yet been evaluated using the larger body of archaeological data that has accumulated since the model was first proposed. Some of these predictions include:

1. At the regional scale, the earliest Andean puna forager sites should be at lower elevations, with progressively higher elevations of the puna settled later in time.
2. Andean puna site components resulting from initial, logistically organized explorations should contain ephemeral material evidence relative to the material amounts deposited later by colonizing foragers with residences on the puna.
3. At the scale of individual multicomponent puna sites, the earliest occupations should be ephemeral and subsequent occupations should be progressively richer in material remains through time, reflecting a process of landscape learning and adaptation.

To evaluate these three predictions of the progressive evolutionary model against empirical archaeological data, we developed a standardized quantitative measure for examining variation in occupation intensity among early Andean puna forager sites. We seek estimates of the most intense occupation in each region, and we assume that the largest sites in each region were discovered by archaeological surveys and selected for stratigraphic excavation. We set aside, for this purpose, the smaller and less visible sites that must also have been occupied across the puna.

METHODS FOR COMPARING OCCUPATION
INTENSITY IN EARLY FORAGER SITES

Table 4.1 lists all Andean forager sites above 3,000 masl and absolutely dated to the Terminal Pleistocene and first millennium of the Early Holocene.[3] These twenty-four sites are located from 10° S in north-central Peru to 26° S in Chile and Argentina (figure 4.1).

Archaeological components resulting from initial explorations should contain ephemeral material evidence (Aldenderfer 1998) relative to the materials deposited later in time by colonizing foragers. Multiple measures of occupation intensity are used to reveal specific behaviors that contribute to the formation of a component's material assemblages (Moore 1998), but the simplest measure of occupation intensity is the amount of deposited cultural material. We use this measure—material amount—for comparing the intensity-of-occupation components of various ages within individual sites and between sites of different ages and elevations. Intense occupation evidence can be created either by less frequent, longer-duration occupation and/or by many repeated, shorter-duration occupations, so these two modes of site use may be difficult to distinguish using only amounts of deposited materials in components.[4] However, the material evidence resulting from both of these types of site use should be readily distinguishable from that resulting from very brief site visits expected for tentative, initial puna exploration.

For the sites listed in table 4.1 we compiled published information on excavated area and recovery methods and a list of specific components with one or more radiocarbon ages. We tabulated the amounts of three of the most common and easily recognized artifact classes recovered from early forager sites—formal chipped-stone tools (count), chipped-stone debitage (weight, in g), and faunal remains (weight, in g). Within the limits of our literature review, counts of formal tools were common, while debitage counts and number of identified animal bone specimens (NISP) were more frequently reported than weights. Debitage counts and NISP cannot be used reliably to compare the amounts of materials between sites, because debitage counts are strongly affected by raw material characteristics and site formation history, while NISP reporting is influenced by taphonomy and research goals of the zooarchaeologist.

Site formation history and functional differences among sites being compared might cause the amounts of lithic tools or debitage or faunal remains to be over- or underrepresented relative to the other material classes. Our inferences therefore rely on the amounts of multiple material classes. Beyond the specific goals of our study, comparison of standardized amounts of different

TABLE 4.1. Summary data for Andean puna sites ≥3000 masl dated to the Terminal Pleistocene and first millennium of the Early Holocene.

Site name	Latitude	Longitude	Elevation (masl)	Level/ Stratum	Lab code	¹⁴C BP	SHCal13 95% cal BP	95% cal span	References
Lauricocha-2	−10.3	−76.7	4,050	R	I-107	9525 ± 260	11,616–9964	1652	Cardich 1964
Pachamachay	−11.1	−76.2	4,300	19	UCR-556	6100 ± 250	7432–6325	1107	Rick 1980
Pachamachay	−11.1	−76.2	4,300	25	UCR-557	6580 ± 255	7930–6810	1120	Rick 1980
Pachamachay	−11.1	−76.2	4,300	*19–25*	*mean, n = 2*	*6335 ± 179*	*7559–6754*	*805*	
Pachamachay	−11.1	−76.2	4,300	28	UCR-555	8125 ± 280	9577–8342	1235	Rick 1980
Pachamachay	−11.1	−76.2	4,300	31	UCR-554	9010 ± 285	11,067–9425	1642	Rick 1980
Panaulauca	−11.3	−76.1	4,150	Phase 4	WSU-2938	5135 ± 75	5990–5655	335	Moore 1998
Panaulauca	−11.3	−76.1	4,150	Phase 3	WSU-3002	5990 ± 90	7142–6510	632	Moore 1998
Panaulauca	−11.3	−76.1	4,150	Phase 2b	WSU-2939	7650 ± 95	8589–8201	388	Moore 1998
Panaulauca	−11.3	−76.1	4,150	Phase 2a	Beta-7724	8350 ± 140	9548–8810	738	Moore 1998
Panaulauca	−11.3	−76.1	4,150	Phase 1	WSU-2940	9650 ± 145	11,260–10,520	740	Moore 1998
Tres Ventanas	−12.2	−76.4	3,810	8	I-3091	10,030 ± 170	12,364–10,877	1487	Engel 1970
Quiqche-1	−12.2	−76.4	3,600	9	I-3160	9940 ± 200	12,044–10,720	1324	Engel 1970
Jaywamachay	−13.3	−74.4	3,400	J1	I-5275	9460 ± 145	11,127–10,277	850	MacNeish et al. 1981
Jaywamachay	−13.3	−74.4	3,400	I	I-5095	9560 ± 170	11,094–10,227	867	MacNeish et al. 1981
Jaywamachay	−13.3	−74.4	3,400		*mean, n = 2*	*9502 ± 110*	*11,156–10,423*	*733*	
Cuncaicha	−15.4	−72.6	4,480	Stratum 3	*mean, n = 3*	*4614 ± 36*	*5446–5050*	*396*	Rademaker et al. 2014
Cuncaicha	−15.4	−72.6	4,480	Stratum 3	*mean, n = 3*	*4867 ± 37*	*5646–5470*	*176*	Rademaker et al. 2014
Cuncaicha	−15.4	−72.6	4,480	Stratum 4	*mean, n = 6*	*8420 ± 34*	*9484–9296*	*188*	Rademaker et al. 2014
Cuncaicha	−15.4	−72.6	4,480	Stratum 5	*mean, n = 20*	*10,200 ± 14*	*11,990–11,710*	*280*	Rademaker et al. 2014
Cuncaicha	−15.4	−72.6	4,480	Feat. 12–4	*mean, n = 2*	*10,345 ± 71*	*12,411–11,822*	*589*	Rademaker et al. 2014

continued on next page

TABLE 4.1—*continued*

Site name	Latitude	Longitude	Elevation (masl)	Level/ Stratum	Lab code	^{14}C BP	SHCal13 95% cal BP	95% cal span	References
Asana	-17.1	-70.6	3,435	C13	Beta-24628	9580 ± 130	11,205–10,511	694	Aldenderfer 1998
Asana	-17.1	-70.6	3,435	P33	Beta-40063	9820 ± 150	11,713–10,702	1011	Aldenderfer 1998
Asana	*-17.1*	*-70.6*	*3,435*		*mean, n = 2*	*9683 ± 98*	*11,226–10,710*	*516*	
Hakenasa	-17.8	-69.4	4,100	7	Beta-187530	5140 ± 70	5989–5659	330	Osorio et al. 2011; LeFebvre 2004
Hakenasa	-17.8	-69.4	4,100	8/7	Beta-219700	6200 ± 80	7255–6803	452	Osorio et al. 2011
Hakenasa	-17.8	-69.4	4,100	10/9	Beta-219701	6960 ± 50	7923–7657	266	Osorio et al. 2011
Hakenasa	-17.8	-69.4	4,100	10	Beta-187531	8789 ± 60	10,119–9545	574	Osorio et al. 2011
Hakenasa	-17.8	-69.4	4,100	11a	Beta-187532	9170 ± 70	10,496–10,187	309	Osorio et al. 2011
Hakenasa	-17.8	-69.4	4,100	11b	Beta-187533	9260 ± 60	10,552–10,243	309	Osorio et al. 2011
Hakenasa	*-17.8*	*-69.4*	*4,100*	*11*	*mean, n = 2*	*9222 ± 46*	*10,493–10,237*	*256*	
Hakenasa	-17.8	-69.4	4,100	12	Beta-187534	9520 ± 70	11,089–10,559	530	Osorio et al. 2011
Hakenasa	-17.8	-69.4	4,100	13	Beta-187535	9580 ± 40	11,089–10,698	391	Osorio et al. 2011
Hakenasa	-17.8	-69.4	4,100	13	UCIAMS-77761	9830 ± 40	11,265–11,147	118	Osorio et al. 2011
Hakenasa	-17.8	-69.4	4,100	13	UCIAMS-77762	9975 ± 40	11,602–11,236	366	Osorio et al. 2011
Hakenasa	-17.8	-69.4	4,100	13	UGAMS-2953	9980 ± 40	11,603–11,238	365	Osorio et al. 2011
Hakenasa	*-17.8*	*-69.4*	*4,100*	*13*	*mean, n = 2*	*9978 ± 28*	*11,598–11,240*	*358*	
Las Cuevas-2	-18.2	-69.4	4,445	4A	I-13128	8270 ± 250	9698–8459	1239	Santoro Vargas and Chacama Rodríguez 1984
Las Cuevas-2	-18.2	-69.4	4,445	4A	—	9590 ± 70	11,159–10,660	499	Osorio 2013
Las Cuevas-2	-18.2	-69.4	4,445	4A	—	9630 ± 70	11,174–10,713	461	Osorio 2013

continued on next page

TABLE 4.1—*continued*

Site name	Latitude	Longitude	Elevation (masl)	Level/Stratum	Lab code	^{14}C BP	SHCal13 95% cal BP	95% cal span	References
Las Cuevas-2	−18.2	−69.4	4,445	4B	I-12835	9540 ± 160	11,214–10,301	913	Santoro and Núñez 1987
Las Cuevas-2	−18.2	−69.4	4,445	4C	—	9990 ± 70	11,707–11,223	484	Osorio 2013
Las Cuevas-2	−18.2	−69.4	4,445	4C	—	10,040 ± 70	11,761–11,246	515	Santoro et al. 2011
Las Cuevas-2	*−18.2*	*−69.4*	*4,445*	*4C*	*mean, n = 2*	*10,015 ± 49*	*11,700–11,246*	*454*	
Quebrada Blanca	−20.8	−68.9	4,500	3	Beta-139632	9610 ± 70	11,170–10,694	476	Osorio 2013
Cueva Bautista	*−21.3*	*−67.6*	*3,933*	*O*	*mean, n = 4*	*10,372 ± 28*	*12,390–11,967*	*423*	*Capriles et al. 2016a*
Cueva Bautista	*−21.3*	*−67.6*	*3,933*	*P*	*mean, n = 4*	*10,853 ± 26*	*12,746–12,687*	*59*	*Capriles et al. 2016a*
Cueva de Yavi	−22.1	−65.5	3,460	D (8a)	AC-1093	9480 ± 220	11,263–10,187	1076	Krapovickas 1987–1988
Cueva de Yavi	−22.1	−65.5	3,460	D (8b)	AC-1088	9760 ± 160	11,612–10,586	1026	Krapovickas 1987–1988
Cueva de Yavi	−22.1	−65.5	3,460	C	CSIC-1074	9790 ± 100	11,390–10,749	641	Kulemeyer et al. 1999
Cueva de Yavi	−22.1	−65.5	3,460	B	CSIC-1101	10,450 ± 55	12,541–12,021	520	Kulemeyer et al. 1999
Chulqui-1A	−22.3	−68.2	3,280	2	Beta-117558	9330 ± 140	11,070–10,192	878	DeSouza 2004
Chulqui-1A	−22.3	−68.2	3,280	6	Beta-6845	9590 ± 60	11,138–10,676	462	Sinclaire 1985
El Pescador	−22.3	−68.2	3,300	4 (6)	Beta-129877	9970 ± 60	11,619–11,215	404	DeSouza 2004
El Pescador	−22.3	−68.2	3,300	5	LP-503	10,310 ± 130	12,543–11,405	1138	DeSouza 2004
Tuina-1	−22.6	−68.5	3,160	—	—	9080 ± 130	10,515–9707	808	Núñez et al. 2002
Tuina-5	−22.6	−68.5	3,200	4	Beta-107121	9840 ± 70	11,398–10,872	526	Núñez et al. 2005
Tuina-5	−22.6	−68.5	3,200	4	Beta-107120	10,060 ± 70	11,803–11,254	549	Núñez et al. 2005
Tuina-5	*−22.6*	*−68.5*	*3,200*	*4*	*mean, n = 2*	*9905 ± 92*	*11,708–11,099*	*609*	

continued on next page

TABLE 4.1—continued

Site name	Latitude	Longitude	Elevation (masl)	Level/Stratum	Lab code	^{14}C BP	SHCal13 95% cal BP	95% cal span	References
Pintoscayoc-1	-22.9	-65.4	3,500	6 (2a)	LP-628	9190 ± 110	10,652–9943	709	Hernández Llosas 2000
Pintoscayoc-1	-22.9	-65.4	3,500	6 (6a)	LP-503	10,720 ± 150	12,838–12,057	781	Hernández Llosas 2000
Pintoscayoc-1	-22.9	-65.4	3,500	6 (9a)	Beta-79849	10,340 ± 70	12,410–11,817	593	Hernández Llosas 2000
Inca Cueva-4	-23.0	-65.5	3,730	2	CSIC-498	9230 ± 70	10,550–10,227	323	Aschero and Podestá 1986
Inca Cueva-4	-23.0	-65.5	3,730	2	LP-102	9650 ± 110	11,223–10,606	617	Aschero and Podestá 1986
Inca Cueva-4	-23.0	-65.5	3,730	2	AC-564	9900 ± 200	12,005–10,700	1305	Aschero and Podestá 1986
Inca Cueva-4	-23.0	-65.5	3,730	2	LP-137	10,620 ± 140	12,723–12,041	682	Aschero and Podestá 1986
Hornillos-2	-23.2	-66.5	4,020	2	Beta-111392	6190 ± 70	7246–6808	438	Yacobaccio et al. 2008
Hornillos-2	-23.2	-66.5	4,020	2	UGA-7829	6340 ± 110	7429–6942	487	Yacobaccio et al. 2008
Hornillos-2	*-23.2*	*-66.5*	*4,020*	*2*	*mean, n = 2*	*6233 ± 59*	*7255–6941*	*314*	Yacobaccio et al. 2008
Hornillos-2	-23.2	-66.5	4,020	3	UGA-7830	7430 ± 80	8365–8026	339	Yacobaccio et al. 2008
Hornillos-2	-23.2	-66.5	4,020	3	UGA-8722	7760 ± 160	8989–8203	786	Yacobaccio et al. 2008
Hornillos-2	*-23.2*	*-66.5*	*4,020*	*3*	*mean, n = 2*	*7496 ± 72*	*8407–8056*	*351*	Yacobaccio et al. 2008
Hornillos-2	-23.2	-66.5	4,020	4	LP-757	8280 ± 100	9467–9001	466	Yacobaccio et al. 2008
Hornillos-2	-23.2	-66.5	4,020	6	UGA-8723	9150 ± 50	10,415–10,186	229	Yacobaccio et al. 2008
Hornillos-2	-23.2	-66.5	4,020	6	UGA-8724	9590 ± 50	11,121–10,694	427	Yacobaccio et al. 2008

continued on next page

TABLE 4.1—*continued*

Site name	Latitude	Longitude	Elevation (masl)	Level/ Stratum	Lab code	^{14}C BP	SHCal13 95% cal BP	95% cal span	References
Hornillos-2	−23.2	−66.5	4,020	6d	UGA-13550	9710 ± 270	11,931–10,254	1677	Yacobaccio et al. 2008
Hornillos-2	*−23.2*	*−66.5*	*4,020*	*6-6d*	*mean, n = 2*	*9596 ± 49*	*11,121–10,701*	*420*	
Huachichocana-3	−23.8	−65.6	3,800	E₃	P-2236	9620 ± 130	11,229–10,566	663	Aguerre et al. 1975
Alero Cuevas	−24.5	−66.5	4,400	2	LP-1655	4210 ± 70	4854–4451	403	López 2013
Alero Cuevas	−24.5	−66.5	4,400	2	AA-90383	5106 ± 68	5938–5644	294	López 2013
Alero Cuevas	−24.5	−66.5	4,400	4	AA-71135	8504 ± 52	9543–9320	223	López 2013
Alero Cuevas	−24.5	−66.5	4,400	4	AA-71136	8838 ± 52	10,151–9603	548	López 2013
Alero Cuevas	−24.5	−66.5	4,400	4	LP-1736	9650 ± 100	11,213–10,672	541	López 2013
Peñas de las Trampas-1.1	−26.0	−67.4	3,580	1(1)	LP-1788	10,030 ± 100	11,926–11,217	709	Martínez 2014
Peñas de las Trampas-1.1	−26.0	−67.4	3,580	1(4)	UGA-1975	10,190 ± 90	12,061–11,331	730	Martínez 2014
Penas de las Trampas-1.1	*−26.0*	*−67.4*	*3,580*	*1*	*mean, n = 2*	*10,060 ± 90*	*11,932–11,241*	*691*	
Quebrada Seca-3	−26.1	−67.4	4,050	2b19	UGA-9257	9790 ± 50	11,254–10,877	377	Aschero and Martínez 2001
Quebrada Seca-3	−26.1	−67.4	4,050	2b25b	LP-895	9250 ± 100	10,652–10,200	452	Hocsman 2002
Quebrada Seca-3	−26.1	−67.4	4,050	2b25c	LP-881	9410 ± 120	11,075–10,249	826	Hocsman 2002
Quebrada Seca-3	*−26.1*	*−67.4*	*4,050*	*2b25*	*mean, n = 2*	*9316 ± 77*	*10,657–10,248*	*409*	

Note: Italics are used for the entries that are weighted mean ^{14}C ages.

material classes additionally may highlight differences among components resulting from site-formation processes, site functions, or shifts in hunter-gatherer behavior.

The amounts of the three artifact classes reported can depend on (1) the landform of the archaeological site, which influences whether artifacts will be concentrated (rockshelters and caves) or dispersed (open-air locations), (2) the original amounts of materials deposited prehistorically, (3) any postdepositional processes that altered the amounts of originally deposited material, (4) the amount of the archaeological deposit excavated (in m^2), (5) whether the sampled area was representative of the site as a whole, and (6) the recovery methods used.

All site components being compared are from the interior of stratified caves or rockshelters. None of these site components is known to have been affected by erosive events that would remove artifacts or sediments. We used the largest reported samples available. Recovery methods at all sites were similar, involving standard 2-mm, 3-mm, or 6-mm mesh screens. Moore (1998) determined experimentally that the fraction of recovered material between 3 mm and 6 mm contained an insignificant amount of cultural material by weight and count relative to the fraction of material larger than 6 mm. We suspect the 2–3-mm fraction is even less significant.

Amounts of materials recovered were standardized to the excavated area (in m^2) providing the sample. Because the components to be compared are not of equal duration, and we are interested in the intensity of site use, the amount per m^2 was standardized to the time in which the deposit was created. We calculated a maximum cumulative occupation span (*cal span*), determined as the 95% calibrated age range for the component,[5] to arrive at an (amount/m^2)/cal span. In most cases, only single radiocarbon ages were available for an occupation component. In cases where multiple radiocarbon ages were obtained for a component, we calculated weighted means for statistically indistinguishable[6] groups of ages and calibrated the means. Where χ^2 analysis indicated that radiocarbon ages from a site component should not be averaged, we used the maximum and minimum values encompassing the multiple distinct ages as the cal span for the component.

There is uncertainty in calculating a maximum cumulative occupation span from a single radiocarbon age, multiple statistically distinct ages, or a weighted mean of multiple statistically indistinguishable ages. A single radiocarbon age may not capture the entire true age range of a component. Were additional ages to be obtained from throughout a sediment package, these might capture greater variability, showing the component to be of longer duration than the estimate suggested by the single age. On the other hand, a single age may yield a wider calibrated range than multiple ages because calculating a weighted mean reduces the standard deviation. Regardless of how many radiocarbon ages are used to calculate the cal span, the true span of the component might have been far briefer than the 95% calibrated range of one or more radiocarbon ages. This is an inherent limitation of radiometric precision for all sites. Despite the uncertainties, which we have tried to acknowledge as transparently as possible, our approach allows the quantities of materials in archaeological sites to be compared using a standardized measure.

RESULTS

A simple prediction of the evolutionary model of Andean settlement is that foragers would have established the earliest puna archaeological sites at lower elevations, with progressively higher elevations of the puna settled later in time. To examine how well archaeological data from the Andean puna fit the model, we plot the oldest calibrated radiocarbon ages of sites dating to the Terminal Pleistocene and first millennium of the Early Holocene against elevation in figure 4.1, using weighted means of replicated oldest ages where possible for greater reliability (see table 4.1).[7] This plot includes all forager sites on the puna and adjacent ecological zones ≥ 3,000 masl in Peru, Bolivia, Chile, and Argentina.

Conservatively, we identify 12 archaeological sites ≥ 3,000 masl whose 95% calibrated median values are older than 11 ka. Twenty-two sites ≥ 3,000 masl have 95% calibrated age ranges that exceed 11 ka. Four puna sites have dates earlier than Cuncaicha rockshelter (4,480 masl) in southern Peru, the highest known Pleistocene site in the Andes. These include Inca Cueva-4 (Aschero 1980; Aschero and Podestá 1986), Cueva de Yavi (Krapovickas 1987–1988; Kulemeyer et al. 1999), and Pintoscayoc-1 (Hernández Llosas 2000) in Argentina. The earliest ages for these three sites are single, unreplicated conventional measurements, so these must be treated with caution. If these single ages are accurate, they are statistically indistinguishable from the earliest accelerator mass spectrometry (AMS) ages at Cuncaicha.

The Terminal Pleistocene component of Cueva Bautista in Bolivia, on the other hand, is well constrained by nine AMS ages on bone collagen and charcoal (Capriles et al. 2016a), and it is possible that this site predates Cuncaicha by about half a millennium. However, Cueva Bautista was a puma den prior to its use by humans, and the site's earliest four AMS ages (figure 4.4, older plotted weighted mean) are on bones of uncertain anthropogenic origin and on

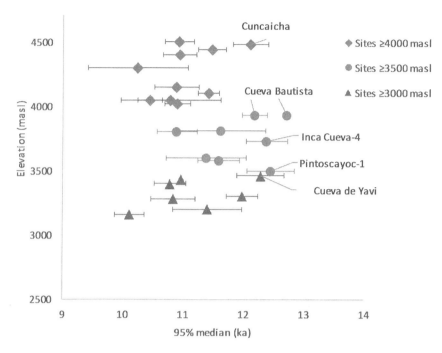

FIGURE 4.4. *Plot of Andean puna sites ≥ 3,000 masl, age (95% calibrated range median, in ka) versus elevation (masl).*

possible old wood. The next four oldest AMS ages at Cueva Bautista average 10,372 ± 28 ¹⁴C BP or ~12.4–12.0 ka (figure 4.4, younger plotted weighted mean), coeval with the earliest occupation of Cuncaicha. A progressive relationship between initial age of occupation and elevation is not evident for the early forager sites of the Andean puna.

A second prediction of the evolutionary model is that the earliest puna site components should have ephemeral materials because they result from brief, tentative, logistically organized explorations by a subset of the forager group, while later site components, associated with the entire forager group and residential behavior, should contain much richer material evidence. We tabulate material amounts (in count or weight/m²/cal span) for formal tools, debitage, and faunal remains in table 4.2 and plot component amounts by age in figures 4.5–4.7.

Formal tool comparisons were possible for 14 sites initially dating to the Terminal Pleistocene (*n* = 4) and Early Holocene (*n* = 10) (figure 4.5). Comparisons of debitage were possible for five sites (figure 4.6) and faunal

TABLE 4.2. Andean puna sites compared with occupation intensity information. *indicates an average obtained for a component using multiple level amounts drawn from different sampled areas (m²). Each component's average ct/m² and wt/m² was then divided by the cal span.

Site	Level/Phase/Stratum	95% cal range (ka)	¹⁴C n =	95% cal span	Tools count	Tools m²	Tools (count/m²)/cal span	Debitage weight (g)	m²	Debitage (g/m²)/cal span	Faunal weight (g)	m²	Faunal (g/m²)/cal span	References
Lauricocha-2	Level R	11.6–10.0	1	1,652	21	4.00	0.0032	n = 204	4.00	no data	—	4.00	—	Cardich 1964
Pachamachay	Levels 19–25	7.6–6.8	2	805	4928	6.1*	0.1241	153,000	6.1*	4.2741	—	6.10*	—	Rick 1980
Pachamachay	Level 28	9.6–8.3	1	1235	474	4.00	0.0960	11,960	4.00	2.4211	—	4.00	—	Rick 1980
Pachamachay	Level 31	11.1–9.4	1	1,642	76	4.00	0.0116	920	4.00	0.1401	—	4.00	—	Rick 1980
Panaulauca	Phase 4	6.0–5.7	1	335	3638	8.60*	0.1683	56,188	31.00*	3.2566	106,444	8.60*	13.5826	Rick and Moore 1999
Panaulauca	Phase 3	7.1–6.5	1	632	124	1.00	0.1962	4,019	1.00	6.3592	39,760	1.00	62.9114	Rick and Moore 1999
Panaulauca	Phase 2B	8.6–8.2	1	388	112	1.00	0.2887	2,588	1.00	6.6701	14,346	1.00	36.9742	Rick and Moore 1999
Panaulauca	Phase 2A	9.5–8.8	1	738	72	1.00	0.0976	2,317	1.00	3.1396	13,812	1.00	18.7154	Rick and Moore 1999
Panaulauca	Phase 1	11.3–10.5	1	740	4	1.00	0.0054	222	1.00	0.3000	1,507	1.00	2.0365	Rick and Moore 1999
Cuncaicha	Stratum 3	5.6–5.1	6	596	100	2.50	0.0671	2,020	2.50	1.3557	7,121	2.00	5.9739	Rademaker et al. 2014
Cuncaicha	Stratum 4	9.5–9.3	6	188	178	2.50	0.3787	2,470	2.50	5.2553	16,692	2.00	44.3939	Rademaker et al. 2014
Cuncaicha	Stratum 5	12.0–11.7	20	280	74	2.50	0.1057	1,030	2.50	1.4714	6,477	2.00	11.5664	Rademaker et al. 2014

continued on next page

TABLE 4.2—*continued*

Site	Level/Phase/Stratum	95% cal range (ka)	14C n =	95% cal span	Tools count	m²	Tools (count/m²)/cal span	Debitage weight (g)	m²	Debitage (g/m²)/cal span	Faunal weight (g)	m²	Faunal (g/m²)/cal span	References
Hakenasa	Levels 7, 8, 9	7.9–5.7	3	2,264	334	6.00	0.0246	1,594	6.00	0.1174	3,297	6.00	0.2427	Lefebvre 2004
Hakenasa	Level 10	10.1–9.5	1	574	71	6.00	0.0206	911	6.00	0.2645	768	6.00	0.2230	Lefebvre 2004
Hakenasa	Level 11	10.5–10.2	2	256	118	6.00	0.0768	1,866	6.00	1.2149	1,933	6.00	1.2585	Lefebvre 2004
Hakenasa	Levels 12, 13	11.6–10.6	5	1,044	71	6.00	0.0113	1,856	6.00	0.2963	4,964	6.00	0.7925	Lefebvre 2004
Hakenasa	Level 13	11.6–10.7	4	905	38	6.00	0.0070	$n = 1,246$	6.00	—	—	6.00	—	Osorio et al. 2011
Las Cuevas-2	Level 4c	11.7–10.2	2	454	3	2.00	0.0033	$n = 354$	2.00	—	2	2.00	0.0017	Osorio 2013
Quebrada Blanca	Level 3	11.2–10.7	1	476	1	4.00	0.0005	$n = 133$	4.00	—	47	4.00	0.0245	Osorio 2013
Cueva Bautista	Levels O-P	12.8–12.0	8	779	8	20.00	0.0005	$n = 376$	20.00	—	173	20.00	0.0111	Capriles et al. 2016a
Chulqui-1A	Strata 6, 6a	11.1–10.7	1	462	7	1.50	0.0101	$n = 98$	1.50	—	—	1.50	—	De Souza 2004
El Pescador	Level 5	12.5–11.4	1	1,138	3	2.50	0.0011	$n = 421$	2.50	—	—	2.50	—	De Souza 2004
Tuina-5	Stratum 4	11.7–11.1	2	609	268	13.00	0.0339	no data	13.00	—	2,595	13.00	0.3278	Nunez et al. 2005
Hornillos-2	Level 2	7.3–6.9	2	287	43	12.00	0.0125	$n = 2,800$	12.00	—	2,616	12.00	0.7596	Restifo and Hoguin 2012; Yacobaccio 2016 pers. comm.

continued on next page

TABLE 4.2—continued

Site	Level/ Phase/ Stratum	95% cal range (ka)	¹⁴C n =	95% cal span	Tools count	m²	Tools (count/ m²)/cal span	Debitage weight (g)	m²	Debitage (g/m²)/cal span	Faunal weight (g)	m²	Faunal (g/m²)/ cal span	References
Hornillos-2	Level 3	8.4–8.1	2	351	16	12.00	0.0038	n = 714	12.00	—	999	12.00	0.2372	Restifo and Hoguin 2012; Yacobaccio 2016 pers. comm.
Hornillos-2	Level 4	9.5–9.0	1	466	32	12.00	0.0057	n = 2,488	12.00	—	1,901	12.00	0.3399	Hoguin and Oxman, 2015; Yacobaccio 2016 pers. comm.
Hornillos-2	Levels 6, 6a–d	11.1–10.2	3	935	31	12.00	0.0028	n = 3,771	12.00	—	4,026	12.00	0.3588	Hoguin and Oxman, 2015; Yacobaccio 2016 pers. comm.
Alero Cuevas	Level 2	5.9–4.5	2	1,487	—	4.00	—	1,100	4.00	0.1849	4,480	4.00	0.7532	López 2016 pers. comm.
Alero Cuevas	Level 4	11.2–9.3	3	1,893	45	4.00	0.0059	995	4.00	0.1314	4,340	4.00	0.5732	López 2009, 2016 pers. comm.
Peñas de las Trampas-1.1	Levels 1–4	11.9–11.2	2	691	4	2.00	0.0029	n = 58	2.00	—	—	2.00	—	Martínez 2014

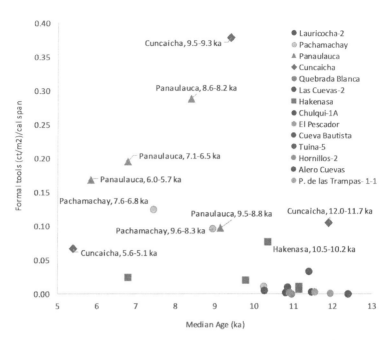

FIGURE 4.5. *Plot of Andean puna sites, formal tool amounts (count/m²)/cal span.*

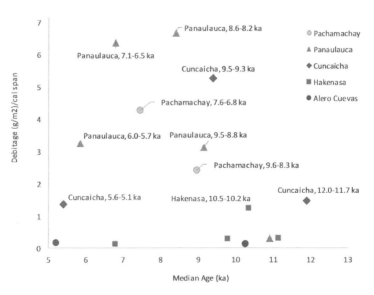

FIGURE 4.6. *Plot of Andean puna sites, debitage amounts (g/m²)/cal span.*

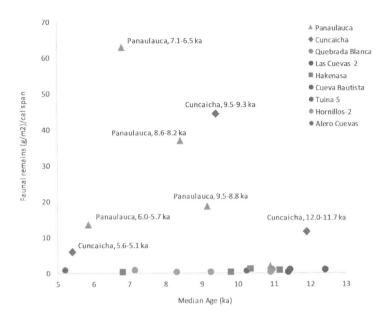

FIGURE 4.7. *Plot of Andean puna sites, faunal amounts (g/m²)/cal span.*

remains for nine sites (figure 4.7). Almost all puna site components predating ~10 ka have ephemeral amounts of formal tools, debitage, and faunal remains. The Early Holocene (~10.5–10.2 ka) component at Hakenasa (4,100 masl) in northern Chile and the Terminal Pleistocene (~12.0–11.7 ka) component at Cuncaicha are exceptions.

The earliest component at Cuncaicha contains more abundant formal tools and faunal remains compared with the other puna sites' earliest components. Cuncaicha's initial component has three times the formal tool amount as at Tuina-5 (~11.7–11.1 ka) but at least nine times that at any other initial component, for example, nine to 15 times that at Hakenasa (~11.6–10.6 ka), 20 times that at Panaulauca, and more than 200 times that at Cueva Bautista (~12.8–12.0 ka). The initial component at Cuncaicha contains an amount of faunal remains six times that at Panaulauca (~11.3–10.5 ka), 15 times that at Hakenasa (~11.6–10.6 ka), 32 times that at Hornillos-2 (~11.1–10.2 ka), and more than a thousand times that at Cueva Bautista. Cueva Bautista contains only eight tool fragments and ~174 g of faunal remains. If the earliest set of four Terminal Pleistocene AMS ages at this site really does reflect a human presence, this small amount of material would have been deposited over at least three distinct Terminal Pleistocene occupations (Capriles et al. 2016a).

To put these early data in perspective, we plotted amounts for additional Early to Late-Middle Holocene preceramic components from Junín wet puna sites Pachamachay (4,300 masl) and Panaulauca (4,150 masl), Cuncaicha, Hakenasa, Hornillos-2, and Alero Cuevas. Site cleaning behavior documented at Pachamachay removed faunal remains from the interior of the cave (Rick 1980), but the amounts of lithic formal tools and debitage at Pachamachay generally are similar to those at nearby Panaulauca. The highest amounts of formal tools of any components studied here are from the ~9.5–9.3 ka component at Cuncaicha and the ~8.6–8.2 ka component at Panaulauca, yet these components respectively contain only three and a half times and three times the higher formal tool amounts of Cuncaicha's ~12.0–11.7 ka component. Amounts of faunal remains tell a similar story. Cuncaicha's ~9.5–9.3 ka component contains four times the faunal amount as the ~12.0–11.7 ka component. Panaulauca's ~7.1–6.5 ka component, which contains the highest faunal amount of any puna component studied here, has five and a half times the amount at Terminal Pleistocene Cuncaicha.

It is clear that material amounts from the Terminal Pleistocene and Early Holocene Cuncaicha components are more similar to those from the Early to Middle Holocene Junín components than to those from other early components from the Andean puna studied here. These patterns of site intensity imply that Cuncaicha and the Junín sites had qualitatively different occupations from the sites to the south. Moreover, despite being from some of the highest-elevation sites in the comparative set, the Junín and Cuncaicha components contain strikingly abundant materials. Such high amounts in the early Cuncaicha components are contrary to expectations of the evolutionary model.

The Early to Middle Holocene components for Pachamachay and Panaulauca are interpreted as residential base camps with varying seasonality of occupation through time (Rick 1980; Bocek and Rick 1982; Moore 1998; Rick and Moore 1999). If this interpretation of the Junín sites is correct, similarity of site intensity between these components and Cuncaicha suggests that it also functioned as a residential base, at least in the Terminal Pleistocene and Early Holocene. Though seasonality data from Cuncaicha are not yet available, the material amounts of its Terminal Pleistocene component are similar to those at Panaulauca, where seasonality data are better developed. These include two of Panaulauca's Early Holocene (~9.5–8.8 ka and ~8.6–8.2 ka) components, where Moore (1998) identified wet-season occupation, and the ~6.0–5.7 ka component, where she inferred prolonged, non-seasonal occupation using a suite of paleobotanical and faunal evidence. Remains of six- to nine-month-old animals provide rare evidence for dry-season occupation, in contrast to numerous usable signals of resources collected in the wet, growing season.

Overall, quantitative comparisons of site intensity inferred from material amounts indicate considerable diversity among Terminal Pleistocene and Early Holocene occupations in the Andean puna. While Cuncaicha exhibits rich material remains from the beginning of its sequence, and the Junín sites contain dense assemblages by the Early to Middle Holocene, nearly all other plotted components for other puna sites have only ephemeral material remains. Why were Cuncaicha and the Junín sites so much richer in materials? We will address this question after examining data evaluating the third prediction of the evolutionary model.

The third prediction is that at the scale of individual multicomponent sites, the earliest occupations should be ephemeral and subsequent occupations should be progressively richer in material remains through time. We examine five site sequences in different areas of the puna—Pachamachay, Panaulauca, Cuncaicha, Hakenasa, and Hornillos-2.

At Pachamachay formal tool and debitage amounts did increase progressively through time. After initial ephemeral formal tool and debitage amounts ~11.1–9.4 ka, formal tools increased by eight times and debitage by 17 times during ~9.6–8.3 ka, and these amounts further increased by one to two times during ~7.6–6.8 ka.

Nearby, at Panaulauca the ~11.3–10.5 ka component also had ephemeral amounts of formal tools and debitage. Panaulauca's ~9.5–8.8 ka component had nearly identical formal tool and debitage amounts as the coeval component at Pachamachay. The amounts of tools and debitage at Panaulauca increased about two to three times during ~8.6–8.2 ka, then decreased at ~7.1–6.5 ka and ~6.0–5.7 ka.

The Terminal Pleistocene component at Cuncaicha had a similar amount of formal tools as some Early to Middle Holocene components at Junín sites understood to be residential bases. In the Early Holocene (~9.5–9.3 ka) this amount increased three and a half times, and Cuncaicha had more formal tools than any Andean puna component studied here. During ~5.6–5.1 ka, this amount decreased by five times. Fluctuations in debitage amounts at Cuncaicha closely tracked those of formal tools.

At Hakenasa the earliest component (~11.6–10.7) had ephemeral amounts of formal tools and debitage relative to the ~10.5–10.2 ka component. Osorio et al. (2011) interpreted the ~10.5–10.2 ka and subsequent two components as exhibiting residential base camp functions. However, only the ~10.5–10.2 ka component contained relatively high amounts of lithic tools and debitage.

At Hornillos-2 there was virtually no change in amounts of formal tools and faunal remains throughout its Early to Middle Holocene occupation (~11–7 ka). This is not to say that forager behavior at this site remained unchanged, only that occupation intensity, as indicated by the material amounts, was steady. Indeed, several investigators (Yacobaccio et al. 2008, 2013; Hoguin et al. 2012; Hoguin and Oxman 2015) have shown clear shifts over time at Hornillos-2 in intrasite spatial organization, lithic technology and raw-material acquisition, and subsistence behavior.

In summary, comparing formal tool amounts within five multicomponent sequences shows that initial occupations generally were followed by subsequent ones with richer material amounts. This progressive trend toward increasing intensity is consistent with Borrero's (1995) model for early settlement. However, when comparing components between sites, it is clear that there was no general relationship between age, elevation, and degree of site intensity registered by material amounts. Cuncaicha, one of the highest-elevation sites in the comparative set, contained rich material assemblages from the beginning of its occupation. In contrast, many puna sites lack any deposits with abundant materials.

Three multicomponent sites located in different areas of the Andean puna—Panaulauca, Cuncaicha, and Hakenasa—exhibited a peak in material amounts at different times in their sequences, followed by declines in amounts. The peaks occurred at ~10.5–10.2 ka at Hakenasa, ~9.5–9.3 ka at Cuncaicha, and ~8.6–6.5 ka at Panaulauca. There is striking similarity among coeval Early to Middle Holocene components in sites of the Junín basin, though sites do not exhibit identical occupational intensity patterns through time. Variations in site intensity reflect important differences in occupation histories likely influenced by local dynamics of environment and culture that can be explored with other measures.

ENVIRONMENT, SETTLEMENT, AND ADAPTATION IN THE ANDEAN PUNA

We now examine the new site-intensity data in the context of environmental change, initial settlement of the puna, and adaptation to high elevation, pointing to potential underlying causes of disparity in material amounts between sites. It would have been relevant to plot Middle and Late Holocene occupation components for all puna sites initially occupied in the Terminal Pleistocene or Early Holocene. However, many of these sites were not reoccupied following their initial use, essentially a shift from ephemeral to zero occupation intensity. Those sites that were abandoned and reoccupied only in the Late Holocene (or not at all) are in the most marginal regions of the puna, where various paleoenvironmental records indicate a major shift to more arid conditions after ~9 ka (Grosjean et al. 2007). Some, though not all, of these areas went archaeologically "silent" until ~3.5 ka, when agriculturalists arrived with a suite of new domesticates and irrigation technology (Grosjean and Núñez 1994; Grosjean et al. 2005; Núñez et al. 2002, 2005, 2013).

Why did hunter-gatherers settle these demanding environments of the high Andean puna to begin with? There are not so many Terminal Pleistocene and Early Holocene archaeological sites at lower elevations that would suggest population pressure pushed people from more comfortable lowlands into challenging highlands, in contrast to the situation in the Tibetan Plateau region (Brantingham and Xing 2006; Brantingham et al. 2007, 2013). Along the northern margin of the Tibetan Plateau below 4,000 masl, early foraging populations likely were concentrated along river valleys where resource abundance was highest, and these groups later explored and ultimately settled less-productive higher country (Madsen et al. 2006; Madsen 2016; Perreault et al. 2016). In the Andes, lands above 4,000 masl have *higher* resource abundance and productivity than the adjacent, lower ecological zones (Rick 1988), so the puna offered real incentives for groups exploring the plateau margins.

Paleoclimatic records from throughout the Central Andes are clear that ice and cold were never barriers to human exploration and settlement of high elevations (Borrero 2012; Rademaker et al. 2013a, 2014), and indeed the climate was warming from a late-glacial temperature minimum long before the earliest registered hunter-gatherer archaeological sites in the highlands (Bromley et al. 2016). Moreover, the initial entry of humans to the Andean puna coincided with favorable precipitation conditions, the Central Andean Pluvial Event (Quade et al. 2008). Between ~13 ka and 11.5 ka the intertropical convergence zone was displaced to the south by cold stadial conditions in northern latitudes (Peterson et al. 2000; Wang et al. 2001; Wang et al. 2004; Chiang and Bitz 2005). Enhanced monsoonal summer rainfall increased over much of the southern tropical Andes, indicated by elevated lake levels (Geyh et al. 1999; Baker et al. 2001a, 2001b; Grosjean et al. 2001; Placzek et al. 2006; Blard et al. 2011; Baker and Fritz 2015) and numerous other proxy records (Betancourt et al. 2000; Latorre et al. 2002, 2006; Nester et al. 2007; Quade et al. 2008). In the puna, precipitation may have increased by two and half to four times (Grosjean 1994; Grosjean et al. 1997, 2005), raising the levels of extant large lakes and creating many temporary lakes and wetlands.

The Central Andean Pluvial Event essentially primed the Andean puna for hunter-gatherer settlement. The abundance of archaeological sites throughout the puna and adjacent ecological zones during this period (Yacobaccio and Morales 2011), and even at low elevation in the presently hyperarid core of the Atacama Desert (Santoro et al. 2011; Latorre et al. 2013), demonstrates that hunter-gatherers took full advantage of hospitable conditions. Mean annual precipitation in the salt puna would have increased to levels typical of the dry puna today (figure 4.2), with an associated rise in primary production. It is likely that precipitation in the dry and wet puna also increased. Higher primary production in these relatively more productive zones would partly explain the high material amounts we document for ~12.0–11.7 ka at Cuncaicha, the peak in material amounts there at ~9.5–9.3 ka, and the peak in material amounts at Hakenasa ~10.5–10.2 ka. In several sites, the decoration of rockshelter walls with art and emplacement of human burials suggest that by the end of the Early Holocene, the puna landscape was not only useful for foragers but had become meaningful for cultural identity.

Following the end of the Central Andean Pluvial Event, hunter-gatherers ceased to use many of the salt and dry puna sites studied here. After ~9 ka some sites, such as Hakenasa and Hornillos–2, continued to be occupied, although at low intensity. The best-watered habitats were in the wet puna in the north. The Junín sites Panaulauca and Pachamachay not only continued to be occupied, they were used with increasing intensity through the Middle Holocene, just as areas to the south were becoming drier.

The presence or absence of sites shows which habitats and resources were desirable enough for hunter-gatherers to incorporate into the settlement and subsistence system. Hunter-gatherers must have settled the puna in the Terminal Pleistocene and Early Holocene for good reason, despite obvious challenges. When aridity rendered some areas of the puna less desirable, foragers simply made use of better-watered locations (Núñez et al. 2013). Increased occupation intensity in some puna sites shows the difference between perceptible human presence in an area and a substantial foraging footprint. Intense occupations show the potential of the Andean puna for supporting modes of foraging beyond the minimum of logistically organized exploration or resource extraction. Substantial forager footprints appear to have occurred in the dry puna only during the Terminal Pleistocene and Early Holocene, a time of increased precipitation (e.g., > 600–800 mm/year at Cuncaicha, modern value), and in the wet puna (~860 mm/year at Junín, modern value) under an Early to Mid-Holocene precipitation regime (figure 4.8).

These patterns suggest that the amount of surface freshwater and primary production are the important variables that influenced occupation intensity in forager sites of the Andean puna, pointing to a possible precipitation threshold

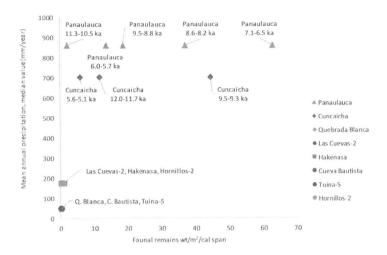

FIGURE 4.8. *Plot of Andean puna sites, faunal amounts (g/m²/cal span) versus mean annual precipitation (mm).*

of ~600–800 mm/year for supporting substantial puna occupations. We see such inferences not as environmental determinism but as environmental possibilism. The amount of freshwater and productivity may have set limits on how intensely some areas could be used, but hunter-gatherers made choices to avoid or use lightly more marginal areas. Where higher precipitation and primary production allowed it, foragers could use the puna more intensely, but all areas of higher primary production were not used the same way.

As two of the best examples of substantial hunter-gatherer occupations of the Andean puna, Cuncaicha and Panaulauca provide two contrasting views of early forager settlement and mobility configurations. There is an important similarity as well: both the Pucuncho and Junín basins contained the most critical resource (water) in abundance, but in addition, Cuncaicha and Panaulauca had congruous resource distributions, in which all resources critical for life were located within a local foraging range. A residential strategy is adaptive in situations of resource congruity; it is only when one or more necessary resources are not within a local foraging range that special logistical trips become advantageous (Binford 1980).

Cuncaicha is a small rockshelter situated on a low hill on the east side of the Pucuncho basin, a 132-km² highland depression ringed by three glaciated stratovolcanoes. The north-facing shelter overlooks a small perennial stream and offers a commanding view of rich wetland and grassland habitats. The interior of the main shelter is ~40 m²; a portion of this area contains early deposits to

~1.2 m depth. The complete remains of intensely butchered large and small herbivores and a complete lithic operational chain are present within the rockshelter. Alca obsidian constituted the primary raw material for Cuncaicha's diverse lithic industry, unsurprising given the site's location within one of South America's largest obsidian sources (Rademaker et al. 2013b). The obsidian likely was procured from an outcrop 25 m below the shelter. Most other stone tools were made from locally available andesite and jasper. Immediately available small woody shrubs and *Azorella compacta* were used for fuel (Rademaker et al. 2014). The reliance on local resources is expected, given that these resources are present within a short distance of the shelter, and the Pucuncho basin supports many thousands of domesticated and wild camelids, rodents, and waterfowl year-round. These resources are much more abundant within the basin than in the surrounding highland desert landscape, a classic situation of local abundance in a context of regional scarcity (Kelly 1995).

Not all materials at Cuncaicha originated in the Pucuncho basin. Charred fragments of parenchymous storage tissue are from starchy roots and/or tubers, likely gathered from lower elevations and brought to Cuncaicha for consumption. Some lithic tools and debitage are made from non-local silica rocks containing stream-polished cortex, suggesting that early plateau residents obtained these from high-energy river valleys below the plateau. Conversely, the presence of Alca obsidian artifacts at contemporary site Quebrada Jaguay-280, ~150 km south on the Pacific Coast, indicates either that a single group was moving between the Pacific Coast and the Pucuncho basin or that separate coast and highland groups were part of an exchange system (Sandweiss et al. 1998; Sandweiss and Rademaker 2013).

Given Cuncaicha's location ~40 to 50 km from elevations below 2,500 masl (a limit for detrimental effects of hypoxia) (Beall 2014), the reliance on local resources, and intense occupation suggested by suggested by rich deposits of materials, a logistical use of Cuncaicha to provision lower-elevation bases is unrealistic. The most parsimonious interpretation for Cuncaicha is a seasonal residential base camp, connected with contemporary settlements in other ecological zones spanning the Andes to the Pacific Coast (Rademaker et al. 2014, 2016), but inhabited by foragers familiar with puna resources and fully adapted to highland life. The substantial forager footprint exhibited in the Terminal Pleistocene at Cuncaicha suggests that high elevation was not a significant barrier for settlement of the Andean puna.

The site of Panaualuca consists of a narrow, south-facing cave with at least 3 m of dense cultural deposits within the main shelter. Approximately 50 m^2 of deposit is protected behind the drip line. Outside the drip line, coring and test trenches suggest that thick cultural deposits extend for several hundred additional m² within the protected area of limestone outcrops and boulders (Kaulicke 1980; Rick and Moore 1999). A perennial stream draining a bofedal and rolling hills (up to 4,500 masl) runs at the foot of the main cave. The region around Panaulauca is approximately 60 km from areas below 2,500 masl, even more remote from valley habitats than is Cuncaicha, but the heavy grass cover and abundant surface water mean that the area today is intensively used by pastoral villages raising sheep, cattle, and alpacas. Larger lakes such as Lake Junín are fringed by reed beds, which provide food, nesting sites for birds, and construction materials. Site survey and land-use traces indicate that the cultivation of *maca* tubers (*Lepidium meyenii*) was widespread in prehistoric times at these altitudes (Parsons et al. 2000).

Stone tools and debitage reflect procurement of high-quality cherts from local sources, with only traces of non-local obsidian and other materials. Similarly, the animal and plant remains from the site indicate local foraging in puna and wetland environments, with cactus fruits, tubers, and the seeds of wild herbs and legumes, the most ubiquitous plant foods in Early Holocene levels (Pearsall 1989). Intensively fragmented remains of vicuña, deer, and guanaco, along with large rodents and birds, also reflect the immediate local environment. For the Early Holocene, intense but seasonally restricted occupations gave way to occupation during the entire year by ~6 ka. Food-processing implements such as ground-stone objects are rare, but charred remains show preparation of food items in situ. Plant foods were clearly important to early foragers in the Junín puna, and carbohydrates from plant foods may have complemented animal foods more adequately than in the southern puna. This plant focus may confirm the essential role of water in foraging adaptations in these high altitudes. The wide extent of pasture in the Junín basin may have buffered foragers from having to seek alternative resources at lower altitude. Continuing research on the paleoethnobotany and stable isotope ecology of the Pucuncho basin should help us evaluate how important these differences in connections to lower valleys might have been.

CONCLUSIONS

Our comparisons of material accumulation as an indicator of occupation intensity, evaluated within a regional archaeological and paleoenvironmental context, suggest there is no need to resort to explanations of in situ biological change to explain hunter-gatherer colonization of the Andean puna. Indeed, viewing the settlement of the Andean puna within a single evolutionary sequence obscures important variation in paleogeography and human adaptation that can be better studied at the scale of individual habitats and situated within an interdisciplinary framework. Along with Borrero's (1995) model of landscape learning in the colonization process, differences in primary productivity and congruity of resources in site habitats offer a simple explanation for why some high Andean forager occupations were ephemeral and others were not. Beyond hypotheses about spatial and temporal patterns of Andean archaeological sites and their contents, there is as yet no empirical support for the notion that early Andean hunter-gatherers were severely challenged physiologically or reproductively by hypoxia.

Early forager sites of the Andean puna exhibit a spectrum of settlement and mobility configurations, which constitute responses to the structure of resources in their specific puna habitats and other ecological zones. Many puna sites demonstrate temporary occupations, not because foragers were incapable of permanent residence, but because, as demonstrated by many hunter-gatherers worldwide, mobility was an adaptive solution (Kelly 1995). Mobility must have been an especially useful strategy in the Andean puna, where critical resources were concentrated in widely dispersed patches and where vertically stacked ecological zones offered their own unique and seasonally complementary resources. Yet, in at least one highly productive puna basin—Junín—relatively sedentary occupation was possible as well. The early hunter-gatherer archaeology of the Andean puna thus exhibits a rich variety of adaptations about which we still have much to learn.

ACKNOWLEDGMENTS

Thanks to Gabriel López, Tom Lynch, César Méndez, Daniela Osorio, Elizabeth Pintar, Debbie Pearsall, Bonnie Pitblado, John Rick, Diego Salazar, Dan Sandweiss, Calogero Santoro, Hugo Yacobaccio, and many other colleagues for generously sharing data and valuable perspectives. We are especially grateful to volume editor Ashley Lemke and Brian Stewart at the University of Michigan Department of Anthropology for inviting us to contribute this manuscript. Finally, we would like to acknowledge Robert Kelly for his inspirational and enduring research on modern and archaeological hunter-gatherers.

NOTES

1. We use the terms *forager* and *hunter-gatherer* interchangeably, after Kelly (1995).

2. Single published Terminal Pleistocene dates from Peruvian sites Pachamachay (Rick 1980), Telarmachay (Lavallée et al. 1995), and PAn 12–58 (Lynch 1971) were

rejected by the investigators. Richardson (1992) suggested that these three ages may be evidence of earlier, failed attempts to settle the Andean puna, though in each case the sample material and/or lab procedures were problematic.

3. The first millennium of the Early Holocene corresponds to 10,000–9000 ^{14}C BP, or ~11.5–10.2 ka. Radiocarbon ages with one-sigma errors ≥300 ^{14}C BP were not included in this analysis, following procedures in Capriles and Albarracin-Jordan (2013), Méndez Melgar (2013), Prates et al. (2013), and Rademaker et al. (2013a).

4. Although we are interested in differentiating material amounts resulting from individual site *occupations*, the basic unit of analysis is the site *component*, a distinct package of sediment and artifacts that has been constrained by at least one radiocarbon age. A component may constitute an aggregate of evidence from multiple occupations, but the evidence resulting from individual occupations usually is not resolvable. Our inferences in this study do not require resolution beyond the aggregate component scale.

5. We used CALIB 7.0.4 (Stuiver et al. 2016) and SHCal13 (Hogg et al. 2013) to calibrate all radiocarbon ages

6. CALIB 7.0.4 reports the test statistic T for a series of uncalibrated ^{14}C ages from the same stratigraphic context (n) having a χ^2 distribution with $n - 1$ degrees of freedom (df) under the null hypothesis of no difference with respect to a threshold of $a = 0.05$ (Ward and Wilson 1978).

7. Calibrated radiocarbon age distributions are asymmetrical, and the true age may be older or younger than the plotted median value.

REFERENCES CITED

Aguerre, Ana M., Alicia A. Fernández Distel, and Carlos A. Aschero. 1975. "Comentarios Sobre Nuevas Fechas en la Cronología Arqueológica Precerámica de la Provincia de Jujuy." *Relaciones de la Sociedad Argentina de Antropología* 9:211–214.

Aldenderfer, Mark S. 1998. *Montane Foragers: Asana and the South-Central Andean Archaic.* Iowa City: University of Iowa Press. https://doi.org/10.2307/j.ctt20q1wq5.

Aldenderfer, Mark S. 1999. "The Pleistocene/Holocene Transition in Peru and its Effects upon Human Use of the Landscape." *Quaternary International* 53/54:11–19. https://doi.org/10.1016/S1040-6182(98)00004-4.

Aldenderfer, Mark S. 2006. "Modelling Plateau Peoples: The Early Human Use of the World's High Plateaux." *World Archaeology* 38 (3): 357–370. https://doi.org/10.1080/00438240600813285.

Aldenderfer, Mark S. 2008. "High Elevation Foraging Societies." In *Handbook of South American Archaeology*, ed. Helaine Silverman and William H. Isbell, 131–143. New York: Springer. https://doi.org/10.1007/978-0-387-74907-5_9.

Aschero, Carlos A. 1980. "Comentarios Acerca de un Fechado Radiocarbónico del Sitio Inca Cueva-4 (Departamento Humahuaca, Jujuy, Argentina)." *Relaciones de la Sociedad Argentina de Antropología* 14:165–168.

Aschero, Carlos A., and Jorge G. Martínez. 2001. "Técnicas de Caza en Antofagasta de la Sierra, Puna Meridional Argentina.". *Relaciones de la Sociedad Argentina de Antropología* 26:215–241.

Aschero, Carlos, and M. Mercedes Podestá. 1986. "El Arte Rupestre en Asentamientos Precerámicos de la Puna Argentina." *Runa* 16:29–57.

Baker, Paul A., and Sherilyn C. Fritz. 2015. "Nature and Causes of Quaternary Climate Variation of Tropical South America." *Quaternary Science Reviews* 124:31–47. https://doi.org/10.1016/j.quascirev.2015.06.011.

Baker, Paul T., and Michael A. Little. 1976. *Man in the Andes: Multidisciplinary Study of High-Altitude Quechua*. Stroudsberg, PA: Dowden, Hutchinson, and Ross.

Baker, Paul A., Catherine A. Rigsby, Geoffrey O. Seltzer, Sherilyn C. Fritz, Tim K. Lowenstein, Niklas P. Bacher, and Carlos Veliz. 2001a. "Tropical Climate Changes at Millennial and Orbital Timescales on the Bolivian Altiplano." *Nature* 409(6821):698–701. https://doi.org/10.1038/35055524.

Baker, Paul A., Geoffrey O. Seltzer, Sherilyn C. Fritz, Robert B. Dunbar, Matthew J. Grove, Pedro M. Tapia, Scott L. Cross, Harold D. Rowe, and James P. Broda. 2001b. "The History of South American Tropical Precipitation for the Past 25,000 Years." *Science* 291(5504):640–643. https://doi.org/10.1126/science.291.5504.640.

Beall, Cynthia M. 2014. "Adaptation to High Altitude: Phenotypes and Genotypes." *Annual Review of Anthropology* 43(1):251–272. https://doi.org/10.1146/annurev-anthro-102313-030000.

Betancourt, Julio L., Claudio Latorre, Jason A. Rech, Jay Quade, and Kate Aasen Rylander. 2000. "A 22,000-Year Record of Monsoonal Precipitation from Northern Chile's Atacama Desert." *Science* 289(5484):1542–1546. https://doi.org/10.1126/science.289.5484.1542.

Binford, Lewis R. 1980. "Willow Smoke and Dogs' Tails: Hunter-Gatherer Settlement Systems and Archaeological Site Formation." *American Antiquity* 45(1):4–20. https://doi.org/10.2307/279653.

Blard, P.-H., F. Sylvestre, A. K. Tripati, C. Claude, C. Causse, A. Coudrain, T. Condom, J.-L. Seidel, F. Vimeux, C. Moreau, et al. 2011. "Lake Highstands on the Altiplano (Tropical Andes) Contemporaneous with Heinrich 1 and the Younger Dryas: New Insights from ^{14}C, U-Th dating and δ^{18}O of Carbonates." *Quaternary Science Reviews* 30(27–28):3973–3989. https://doi.org/10.1016/j.quascirev.2011.11.001.

Bocek, Barbara, and John W. Rick. 1982. "La Época Precerámica en la Puna de Junín: Investigaciones en la Zona de Panaulauca." *Chungara (Arica)* 13:109–127.

Borrero, Luis A. 1995. "Arqueología de la Patagonia. Palimpsesto." *Revista de Arqueología* 4:9–69.

Borrero, Luis A. 2012. "The Human Colonization of the High Andes and Southern South America during the Cold Pulses of the Late Pleistocene." In *Hunter-Gatherer Behavior: Human Response during the Younger Dryas*, ed. Metin I. Eren, 57–77. Walnut Creek, CA: Left Coast Press.

Brantingham, P. Jeffrey, and Gao Xing. 2006. "Peopling of the Northern Tibetan Plateau." *World Archaeology* 38(3):387–414. https://doi.org/10.1080/00438240 600813301.

Brantingham, P. Jeffrey, Gao Xing, David B. Madsen, David Rhode, Charles Perreault, Jerome van der Woerd, and John W. Olsen. 2013. "Late Occupation of the High-Elevation Northern Tibetan Plateau Based on Cosmogenic, Luminescence, and Radiocarbon Ages." *Geoarchaeology: An International Journal* 28(5):413–431. https://doi.org/10.1002/gea.21448.

Brantingham, P. Jeffrey, Gao Xing., John W. Olsen, H. Ma, David Rhode, H. Zhang, and David B. Madsen. 2007. "A Short Chronology for the Peopling of the Tibetan Plateau." In *Human Adaptation to Climate Change in Arid China*, ed. David B. Madsen, F. H. Chen, Gao Xing, 129–150. Amsterdam: Elsevier. https://doi.org/10 .1016/S1571-0866(07)09010-0.

Bromley, Gordon R. M., Joerg M. Schaefer, Brenda A. Hall, Kurt M. Rademaker, Aaron E. Putnam, Claire E. Todd, Matthew Hegland, Gisela Winckler, Margaret S. Jackson, and Peter Strand. 2016. "A Cosmogenic [10]Be Chronology for the Local Last Glacial Maximum and Termination in the Cordillera Oriental, Southern Peruvian Andes: Implications for the Tropical Role in Global Climate." *Quaternary Science Reviews* 148:54–67. https://doi.org/10.1016/j.quascirev .2016.07.010.

Brush, Stephen B. 1976. "Man's Use of an Andean Ecosystem." *Human Ecology* 4(2):147–166. https://doi.org/10.1007/BF01531218.

Capriles, José M., and Juan Albarracin-Jordan. 2013. "The Earliest Human Occupations in Bolivia: A Review of the Archaeological Evidence." *Quaternary International* 301:46–59. https://doi.org/10.1016/j.quaint.2012.06.012.

Capriles, José M., Juan Albarracin-Jordan, Umberto Lombardo, Daniela Osorio, Blaine Maley, Steven T. Goldstein, Katherine A. Herrera, Michael D. Glascock, Alejandra I. Domic, Heinz Veit, et al. 2016a. "High-Altitude Adaptation and Late Pleistocene Foraging in the Bolivian Andes." *Journal of Archaeological Science Reports* 6:463–474. https://doi.org/10.1016/j.jasrep.2016.03.006.

Capriles, José M., Calogero M. Santoro, and Tom D. Dillehay. 2016b. "Harsh Environments and the Terminal Pleistocene Peopling of the Andean Highlands." *Current Anthropology* 57(1):99–100. https://doi.org/10.1086/684694.

Cardich, Augusto. 1964. *Lauricocha: Fundamentos para una Prehistoria de los Andes Centrales*. Buenos Aires: Studia Praehistorica III, Centro Argentino de Estudios Prehistóricos.

Chiang, John C. H., and Cecilia M. Bitz. 2005. "Influence of High Latitude Ice Cover on the Marine Intertropical Convergence Zone." *Climate Dynamics* 25(5):477–496. https://doi.org/10.1007/s00382-005-0040-5.

Dauelsberg, Percy. 1983. "Tojo-Tojone: Un Paradero de Cazadores Arcaicos en la Sierra de Arica." *Chungara (Arica)* 11:11–30.

DeSouza, H. Patricio. 2004. "Cazadores Recolectores del Arcaico Temprano y Medio en la Cuenca Superior del Rio Loa: Sitios, Conjuntos Líticos y Sistemas de Asentamiento." *Estudios Atacameños* 27:7–43.

Engel, Frederic. 1970. "Exploration of the Chilca Canyon, Peru." *Current Anthropology* 11(1):55–58. https://doi.org/10.1086/201093.

Franklin, William L. 1981. "Biology, Ecology, and Relationship to Man of the South American Camelids." In *Mammalian Biology in South America*, ed. Michael A. Mares and Hugh H. Genoways, 457–489. Special Publication Series, Volume 6. Pittsburgh, PA: Pymatuning Laboratory of Ecology, University of Pittsburgh.

Gayo, Eugenia M., Claudio Latorre, and Calogero M. Santoro. 2015. "Timing of Occupation and Regional Settlement Patterns Revealed by Time-Series Analyses of an Archaeological Radiocarbon Database for the South-Central Andes (16°–25°S)." *Quaternary International* 356:4–14. https://doi.org/10.1016/j.quaint.2014.09.076.

Geyh, Mebus A., Martin Grosjean, Lautaro Núñez, and Ulrich Schotterer. 1999. "Radiocarbon Reservoir Effect and the Timing of the Late-Glacial/ Early Holocene Humid Phase in the Atacama Desert (Northern Chile)." *Quaternary Research* 52(02):143–153. https://doi.org/10.1006/qres.1999.2060.

Grosjean, Martin. 1994. "Paleohydrology of the Laguna Lejía (North Chilean Altiplano) and Climatic Implications for Late-Glacial Times." *Palaeogeography, Palaeoclimatology, Palaeoecology* 109(1):89–100. https://doi.org/10.1016/0031-0182 (94)90119-8.

Grosjean, Martin, and Lautaro Núñez. 1994. "Lateglacial, Early and Middle Holocene Environments, Human Occupation, and Resource Use in the Atacama (Northern Chile)." *Geoarchaeology* 9(4):271–286. https://doi.org/10.1002/gea .3340090402.

Grosjean, Martin, Lautaro Núñez, and Isabel Cartajena. 2005. "Palaeoindian Occupation of the Atacama Desert, Northern Chile." *Journal of Quaternary Science* 20(7–8):643–653. https://doi.org/10.1002/jqs.969.

Grosjean, Martin, Lautaro Núñez, Isabel Cartajena, and Bruno Messerli. 1997. "Mid-Holocene Climate and Culture Change in the Atacama Desert, Northern Chile." *Quaternary Research* 48(02):239–246. https://doi.org/10.1006/qres.1997.1917.

Grosjean, Martin, Calogero M. Santoro, Lonnie G. Thompson, Lautaro Núñez, and Vivien Standen. 2007. "Mid-Holocene Climate and Culture Change in the South-Central Andes." In *Climate Change and Cultural Dynamics: A Global Perspective on Mid-Holocene Transitions*, ed. David G. Anderson, Kirk A. Maasch, and Daniel H. Sandweiss, 51–115. Burlington, MA: Academic Press. https://doi.org/10.1016/B978-012088390-5.50008-X.

Grosjean, Martin, J.F.N. van Leeuwen, W. O. van der Knaap, Mebus A. Geyh, B. Ammann, W. Tanner, Bruno Messerli, Lautaro A. Núñez, B. L. Valero-Garcés, and H. Veit. 2001. "A 22,000 ^{14}C yr B.P. Sediment and Pollen Record of Climate Change from Laguna Miscanti 23°S, Northern Chile." *Global and Planetary Change* 28(1–4):35–51. https://doi.org/10.1016/S0921-8181(00)00063-1.

Hernández Llosas, María Isabel. 2000. "Quebradas Altas de Humahuaca a Través del Tiempo: El Caso Pintoscayoc." *Estudios Sociales del NOA* 2:167–224.

Hijmans, Robert J., Susan E. Cameron, Juan L. Parra, Peter G. Jones, and Andy Jarvis. 2005. "Very High Resolution Interpolated Climate Surfaces for Global Land Areas." *International Journal of Climatology* 25(15):1965–1978. https://doi.org/10.1002/joc.1276.

Hocsman, Salomón. 2002. "Cazadores-Recolectores Complejos en la Puna Meridional Argentina? Entrelazando Evidencias del Registro Arqueológico de la Microrregión de Antofagasta de la Sierra, Catamarca." *Relaciones de la Sociedad Argentina de Antropología* (Buenos Aires, Argentina) 27:193–214.

Hogg, Alan G., Quan Hua, Paul G. Blackwell, Mu Niu, Caitlin E. Buck, Thomas P. Guilderson, Timothy J. Heaton, Jonathan G. Palmer, Paula J. Reimer, Ron W. Reimer, et al. 2013. "SHCal13 Southern Hemisphere Calibration, 0–50,000 years cal B.P." *Radiocarbon* 55(04):1889–1903. https://doi.org/10.2458/azu_js_rc.55.16783.

Hoguin, Rodolphe, María Paz Catá, Patricia Solá, and Hugo D. Yacobaccio. 2012. "The Spatial Organization in Hornillos 2 Rockshelter during the Middle Holocene (Jujuy Puna, Argentina)." *Quaternary International* 256:45–53. https://doi.org/10.1016/j.quaint.2011.08.026.

Hoguin, Rodolphe, and Brenda Oxman. 2015. "Palaeoenvironmental Scenarios and Lithic Technology of the First Human Occupations in the Argentine Dry Puna." *Quaternary International* 363:78–93. https://doi.org/10.1016/j.quaint.2014.04.010.

Jolie, Edward A., Thomas F. Lynch, Phil R. Geib, and James M. Adovasio. 2011. "Cordage, Textiles, and the Late Pleistocene Peopling of the Andes." *Current Anthropology* 52(2):285–296. https://doi.org/10.1086/659336.

Kaulicke, Peter. 1980. "Beitrage zur Kentniss der Lithischen Perioden in der Puna Junins." PhD dissertation: Rheiminschen Freidrich-Wilhelms-Universitet, Bonn, Germany.

Kelly, Robert L. 1995. *The Foraging Spectrum: Diversity in Hunter-Gatherer Lifeways.* Washington, DC: Smithsonian Institution.

Kelly, Robert L. 2003. "Colonization of New Land by Hunter-Gatherers: Expectations and Implications Based on Ethnographic Data." In *Colonization of Unfamiliar Landscapes: The Archaeology of Adaptation*, ed. Marcy Rockman and James Steele, 44–58. New York: Routledge.

Koford, Carl B. 1957. "The Vicuña and the Puna." *Ecological Monographs* 27(2):153–219. https://doi.org/10.2307/1948574.

Krapovickas, Pedro. 1987–1988. "Nuevos Fechados Radiocarbónicos para el Sector Oriental de la Puna y la Quebrada de Humahuaca." *Runa* 17–18:207–219.

Kulemeyer, Jorge A., Liliana C. Lupo, Julio J. Kulemeyer, and Julio R. Laguna. 1999. "Desarrollo Paleoecológico Durante las Ocupaciones Humanas del Precerámico del Norte de la Puna Argentina." In *Beiträge zur Quartären Landschaftsentwicklung Südamerikas*. Festschrift zum 65, ed. Karsten Garleff, 233–255. Bamberg, Germany: Bamberger Geographische Schriften 19.

Latorre, Claudio, Julio L. Betancourt, and Mary T. K. Arroyo. 2006. "Late Quaternary Vegetation and Climate History of a Perennial River Canyon in the Río Salado Basin (22°S) of Northern Chile." *Quaternary Research* 65(03):450–466. https://doi.org/10.1016/j.yqres.2006.02.002.

Latorre, Claudio, Julio L. Betancourt, Kate Aasen Rylander, and Jay Quade. 2002. "Vegetation Invasions into Absolute Desert: A 45 000 yr Rodent Midden Record from Calama–Salar de Atacama Basins, Northern Chile (Lat. 22°–24° S)." *Geological Society of America Bulletin* 114(3):349–366. https://doi.org/10.1130/0016-7606 (2002)114<0349:VIIADA>2.0.CO;2.

Latorre, Claudio, Calogero M. Santoro, Paula C. Ugalde, Eugenia M. Gayo, Daniela Osorio, Carolina Salas-Egaña, Ricardo De Pol-Holz, Delphine Joly, and Jason A. Rech. 2013. "Late Pleistocene Human Occupation of the Hyperarid Core in the Atacama Desert, Northern Chile." *Quaternary Science Reviews* 77:19–30. https://doi.org/10.1016/j.quascirev.2013.06.008.

Lavalée, Danièle, Michèle Julien, Jane Wheeler, and Claudine Karlin. 1995. *Telarmachay: Cazadores y Pastores Prehistóricos de los Andes*. Tomo 88. Lima: Travaux de l'Institut Francais d'Etudes Andines, Instituto Frances de Estudios Andinos.

Lefebvre, Raymond P. 2004. "Hakenasa: The Archaeology of a Rockshelter in the Altiplano of Northern Chile." PhD dissertation, Department of Anthropology, Rutgers-State University of New Jersey, New Brunswick.

Lenters, John D., and Kerry H. Cook. 1997. "On the Origin of the Bolivian High and Related Circulation Features of the South American Climate." *Journal of the Atmospheric Sciences* 54(5):656–677. https://doi.org/10.1175/1520-0469(1997)054<0656: OTOOTB>2.0.CO;2.

López, Gabriel E. J. 2009. "Arqueofaunas, Osteometría y Evidencia Artefactual en Pastos Grandes, Puna de Salta: Secuencia de Cambio a lo Largo del Holoceno

Temprano, Medio y Tardío en el Sitio Alero Cuevas." *Intersecciones en Antropología* 10:105–119.

López, Gabriel E. J. 2013. "Ocupaciones Humanas y Cambio a lo Largo del Holoceno en Abrigos Rocosos de la Puna de Salta, Argentina: Una Perspectiva Regional." *Chungara* (Arica) 45(3):411–426. https://doi.org/10.4067/S0717-73562013000300004.

Lynch, Thomas F. 1971. "Preceramic Transhumance in the Callejón de Huaylas, Peru." *American Antiquity* 36(2):139–148. https://doi.org/10.2307/278667.

Lynch, Thomas F. 1980. *Guitarrero Cave: Early Man in the Andes.* New York: Academic Press.

MacNeish, Richard S., Angel Garcia Cook, Luis G. Lumbreras, Robert K. Vierra, and Antoinette Nelken-Turner. 1981. *Excavations and Chronology,* vol. II, *Prehistory of the Ayacucho Basin, Peru.* Ann Arbor: University of Michigan Press.

Madsen, David B. 2016. "Conceptualizing the Tibetan Plateau: Environmental Constraints on the Peopling of the 'Third Pole.'" *Archaeological Research in Asia* 5:24–32. https://doi.org/10.1016/j.ara.2016.01.002.

Madsen, David B., Haizhou Ma, P. Jeffrey Brantingham, Gao Xing, David Rhode, Haiying Zhang, and John W. Olsen. 2006. "The Late Upper Paleolithic Occupation of the Northern Tibetan Plateau Margin." *Journal of Archaeological Science* 33(10):1433–1444. https://doi.org/10.1016/j.jas.2006.01.017.

Marriott, Bernadette M., and Sydne J. Newberry. 1996. *Nutritional Needs in Cold and High-Altitude Environments: Applications for Military Personnel in Field Operations.* Washington, DC: National Academy Press.

Martínez, Jorge G. 2014. "Contributions to the Knowledge of Natural History and Archaeology of Hunter-Gatherers of Antofagasta de la Sierra (Argentine Salt Puna): The Case of Peñas de las Trampas 1.1." In *Hunter-Gatherers from a High-Elevation Desert: People of the Salt Puna,* ed. Elizabeth Pintar, 71–94. British Archaeological Reports International Series, vol. 2641. Oxford, UK: Archaeopress.

Méndez Melgar, César. 2013. "Terminal Pleistocene/Early Holocene ^{14}C dates from Archaeological Sites in Chile: Critical Chronological Issues for the Initial Peopling of the Region." *Quaternary International* 301:60–73. https://doi.org/10.1016/j.quaint.2012.04.003.

Moore, Katherine M. 1998. "Measures of Mobility and Occupational Intensity in Highland Peru." In *Seasonality and Sedentism: Archaeological Perspectives from New World and Old World Archaeological Sites,* ed. Thomas R. Rocek and Ofer Bar-Josef, 181–197. Peabody Museum of Archaeology and Ethnology. Cambridge, MA: Harvard University.

Muscio, Hernán Juan. 2012. "Modelling Demographic Dynamics and Cultural Evolution: The Case of the Early and Mid-Holocene Archaeology in the Highlands

of South America." *Quaternary International* 256:19–26. https://doi.org/10.1016/j
.quaint.2011.10.021.

Muscio, Hernán Juan, and Gabriel E. J. López. 2016. "Radiocarbon Dates and
Anthropogenic Signal in the South-Central Andes (12,500–600 cal. years B.P.)."
Quaternary International 65:93–102.

NASA LP DAAC. 2016. "Terra/MODIS Net Primary Production Yearly L4 Global
1 km, GPP/NPP Project MOD17 A3. NASA EOSDIS Land Processes DAAC,
USGS Earth Resources Observation and Science (EROS) Center, Sioux Falls,
South Dakota." Accessed July, 4, 2016. ftp://ftp.ntsg.umt.edu/pub/MODIS
/NTSG_Products/MOD17/MOD17A3/Y2015/.

Nester, Peter L., Eugenia Gayó, Claudio Latorre, Teresa E. Jordan, and Nicolás
Blanco. 2007. "Perennial Stream Discharge in the Hyperarid Atacama Desert of
Northern Chile During the Latest Pleistocene." *Proceedings of the National Academy of Sciences of the United States of America* 104(50):19724–19729. https://doi.org/10
.1073/pnas.0705373104.

Núñez, Lautaro, Isabel Cartajena, and Martin Grosjean. 2013. "Archaeological Silence
and Ecorefuges: Arid Events in the Puna of Atacama During the Middle Holocene."
Quaternary International 307:5–13. https://doi.org/10.1016/j.quaint.2013.04.028.

Núñez, Lautaro, Martin Grosjean, and Isabel Cartajena. 2002. "Human Occupations
and Climate Change in the Puna de Atacama, Chile." *Science* 298(5594):821–824.
https://doi.org/10.1126/science.1076449.

Núñez, Lautaro, Martin Grosjean, and Isabel Cartajena. 2005. *Ocupaciones Humanas y
Paleoambientes en la Puna de Atacama.* Instituto de Investigaciones Arqueológicas y
Museo, Universidad Católica del Norte. Taraxacum: San Pedro de Atacama.

Núñez, Lautaro, and Calogero M. Santoro. 1988. "Cazadores de la Puna Seca y Sal-
ada del Área Centro-Sur Andina (Norte de Chile)." *Estudios Atacameños* 9:11–60.

Olson, David M., Eric Dinerstein, Erik D. Wikramanayake, Neil D. Burgess, George
V. N. Powell, Emma C. Underwood, Jennifer A. D'Amico, Illanga Itoua, Holly
E. Strand, John C. Morrison, et al. 2001. "Terrestrial Ecoregions of the World: A
New Map of Life on Earth." *Bioscience* 51(11):933–938. https://doi.org/10.1641/0006
-3568(2001)051[0933:TEOTWA]2.0.CO;2.

Osorio, Daniela. 2013. "Reevaluación del Arcaico Temprano de la Puna Seca:
(~12.000 años cal. AP–9.000 años cal. AP): Implicancias para el Poblamiento
Inicial del Altiplano del Norte Grande de Chile." Master's thesis, University of
Chile: Santiago.

Osorio, Daniela, Donald Jackson, Paula C. Ugalde, Claudio Latorre, Ricardo de Pol
Hoz, and Calogero M. Santoro. 2011. "Hakenasa Cave and Its Relevance for the
Peopling of the Southern Andean Altiplano." *Antiquity* 85(330):1194–1208. https://
doi.org/10.1017/S0003598X00062001.

Osorio, Daniela, Marcela Sepúlveda, José Capriles, Katherine Herrera, Paula Ugalde, Donald Jackson, Eugenia Gayo, Claudio Latorre, James Steele, and Calogero Santoro. 2016. "Early Occupation of the Highlands of Northernmost Chile: Technology, Activities and Mobility Routes." Paper presented at 81st Society for American Archaeology meeting, Orlando, FL.

Parsons, Jeffrey R., Charles M. Hastings, and Matos M. Ramiro. 2000. *Prehispanic Settlement Patterns in the Upper Mantaro and Tarmo Drainages, Junin, Peru*. University of Michigan Museum of Anthropology Memoir No. 34. Ann Arbor: University of Michigan.

Pearsall, Deborah M. 1989. "Adaptation of Prehistoric Hunter-Gatherers to the High Andes: The Changing Role of Plant Resources." In *Foraging and Farming: The Evolution of Plant Exploitation*, ed. David R. Harris and Gordon C. Hillman, 318–332. London: Unwin Hyman.

Perreault, Charles, Matthew T. Boulanger, Adam M. Hudson, David Rhode, David B. Madsen, John W. Olsen, Martina L. Steffen, Jay Quade, Michael D. Glascock, and P. Jeffrey Brantingham. 2016. "Characterization of Obsidian from the Tibetan Plateau by XRF and NAA." *Journal of Archaeological Science: Reports* 5:392–399. https://doi.org/10.1016/j.jasrep.2015.12.009.

Peterson, Larry C., Gerald H. Haug, Konrad A. Hughen, and Ursula Röhl. 2000. "Rapid Changes in the Hydrologic Cycle of the Tropical Atlantic during the Last Glacial." *Science* 290(5498):1947–1951. https://doi.org/10.1126/science.290.5498.1947.

Placzek, Crista, Jay Quade, and P. Jonathan Patchett. 2006. "Geochronology and Stratigraphy of Late Pleistocene Lake Cycles on the Southern Bolivian Altiplano: Implications for Causes of Tropical Climate Change." *Geological Society of America Bulletin* 118(5–6):515–532. https://doi.org/10.1130/B25770.1.

Prates, Luciano, Gustavo Politis, and James Steele. 2013. "Radiocarbon Chronology of the Early Human Occupation of Argentina." *Quaternary International* 301:104–122. https://doi.org/10.1016/j.quaint.2013.03.011.

Quade, Jay, Jason A. Rech, Julio L. Betancourt, Claudio Latorre, Barbra Quade, Kate Aasen Rylander, and Timothy Fisher. 2008. "Paleowetlands and Regional Climate Change in the Central Atacama Desert, Northern Chile." *Quaternary Research* 69(03):343–360. https://doi.org/10.1016/j.yqres.2008.01.003.

Rademaker, Kurt, Gordon R. M. Bromley, and Daniel H. Sandweiss. 2013a. "Peru Archaeological Radiocarbon Database, 13,000–7000 ^{14}C B.P." *Quaternary International* 301:34–45. https://doi.org/10.1016/j.quaint.2012.08.2052.

Rademaker, Kurt, Michael D. Glascock, Bruce Kaiser, David Gibson, Daniel R. Lux, and Martin G. Yates. 2013b. "Multi-Technique Geochemical Characterization of the Alca Obsidian Source, Peruvian Andes." *Geology* 41(7):779–782. https://doi.org/10.1130/G34313.1.

Rademaker, Kurt, Gregory Hodgins, Katherine Moore, Sonia Zarrillo, Christopher Miller, Gordon R. M. Bromley, Peter Leach, David A. Reid, Willy Yépez Álvarez, and Daniel H. Sandweiss. 2014. "Paleoindian Settlement of the High-Altitude Peruvian Andes." *Science* 346(6208):466–469. https://doi.org/10.1126/science .1258260.

Rademaker, Kurt, Gregory Hodgins, Katherine Moore, Sonia Zarrillo, Christopher Miller, Gordon R. M. Bromley, Peter Leach, David A. Reid, Willy Yépez Álvarez, and Daniel H. Sandweiss. 2016. "Cuncaicha Rockshelter, A Key Site for Understanding Colonization of the High Andes." *Current Anthropology* 57(1):101–103. https://doi.org/10.1086/684826.

Ravines, Rogger. 1967. "El Abrigo de Caru y sus Relaciones Cultures con Otros Sitios Tempranos del Sur del Perú." *Ñawpa Pacha* 5(1):39–57. https://doi.org/10.1179/naw .1967.5.1.003.

Ravines, Rogger. 1972. "Secuencia y Cambios en los Artefactos Líticos del Sur del Perú." Lima, Peru. *Revista del Museo Nacional (Lima)* 38:133–184.

Restifo, Federico, and Rodolphe Hoguin. 2012. "Risk and Technological Decision-Making During the Early to Mid-Holocene Transition: A Comparative Perspective in the Argentine Puna." *Quaternary International* 256:35–44. https://doi.org/10 .1016/j.quaint.2011.10.030.

Richardson, James B. 1992. "Early Hunters, Fishers, Farmers, and Herders: Diverse Economic Adaptations in Peru to 4500 B.P." *Revista de Arqueología Americana* 6:71–90.

Rick, John W. 1980. *Prehistoric Hunters of the High Andes*. New York: Academic Press.

Rick, John W. 1988. "The Character and Context of Highland Preceramic Society." In *Peruvian Prehistory*, ed. Richard W. Keatinge, 3–40. New York: Cambridge University Press.

Rick, John W., and Katherine M. Moore. 1999. "El Precerámico de las Punas de Junín: El Punto de Vista desde Panaulauca." Lima, Peru. *Boletín de Arqueología PUCP* 3:263–296.

Sandweiss, Daniel H., Heather McInnis, Richard L. Burger, Asunción Cano, Bernardino Ojeda, Rolando Paredes, Sandweiss María del Carmen, and Michael D. Glascock. 1998. "Quebrada Jaguay: Early Maritime Adaptations in South America." *Science* 281(5384):1830–1832. https://doi.org/10.1126/science.281.5384.1830.

Sandweiss, Daniel H., and Kurt M. Rademaker. 2013. "El Poblamiento del Sur Peruano: Costa y Sierra." Lima, Peru. *Boletín de Arqueología PUCP* 15:274–294.

Santoro Vargas, Calogero, and Juan Chacama Rodríguez. 1984. "Secuencia de Asentamientos Precerámicos del Extremo Norte de Chile." *Estudios Atacameños* 7:85–103.

Santoro, Calogero M., and Lautaro Núñez. 1987. "Hunters of the Dry Puna and the Salt Puna in Northern Chile." *Andean Past* 1:57–109.

Santoro, Calogero M., Daniela Osorio, Vivien G. Standen, Paula C. Ugalde, Katherine Herrera, Eugenia M. Gayó, Francisco Rothhammer, and Claudio Latorre. 2011. "Ocupaciones Humanas Tempranas y Condiciones Paleoambientales en el Desierto de Atacama Durante la Transición Pleistoceno-Holoceno." Lima, Peru. *Boletín de Arqueología PUCP* 215:295–314.

Sinclaire, Carol. 1985. "Dos Fechas Radiocarbónicas del Alero Chulqui, Río Toconce: Noticia y Comentario." *Chungara* (Arica) 14:71–79.

Stoertz, George E., and George E. Ericksen. 1974. "Geology of Salars in Northern Chile." *U.S. Geological Survey Professional Paper* 811:1–65.

Stuiver, Minze, Paula J. Reimer, and Ron W. Reimer. 2016. CALIB 7.0.4 [WWW program] at http://calib.org.

Surovell, Todd A. 2000. "Early Paleoindian Women, Children, Mobility, and Fertility." *American Antiquity* 65(3):493–508. https://doi.org/10.2307/2694532.

Troll, Carl. 1968. "The Cordilleras of the Tropical Americas: Aspects of Climatic, Phytogeographical and Agrarian Ecology." In *Geo-Ecology of the Mountainous Regions of the Tropical Americas*, ed. Carl Troll, 15–56. Bonn, Germany: Colloquium Geographicum 9, Geographischen Institut der Universitat Bonn.

Vuille, M. R. S., Bradley, R. Healy, M. Werner, D. R. Hardy, L. G. Thompson, and F. Keimig. 2003. "Modeling δ^18O in Precipitation over the Tropical Americas: 2. Simulation of the Stable Isotope Signal in Andean Ice Cores." *Journal of Geophysical Research* 108(D6):4174. https://doi.org/10.1029/2001JD002039.

Wang, Xianfeng, Augusto S. Auler, R. Lawrence Edwards, Hai Cheng, Patricia S. Cristalli, Peter L. Smart, David A. Richards, and Chuan-Chou Shen. 2004. "Wet Periods in Northeastern Brazil over the Past 210 kyr Linked to Distant Climate Anomalies." *Nature* 432(7018):740–743. https://doi.org/10.1038/nature 03067.

Wang, Y. J., H. Cheng, R. L. Edwards, Z. S. An, J. Y. Wu, C. C. Shen, and J. A. Dorale. 2001. "A High-Resolution Absolute-Dated Late Pleistocene Monsoon Record from Hulu Cave, China." *Science* 294(5550):2345–2348. https://doi.org/10.1126/science.1064618.

Ward, Graeme K., and S. R. Wilson. 1978. "Procedures for Comparing and Combining Radiocarbon Age Determinations: A Critique." *Archaeometry* 20(1):19–31. https://doi.org/10.1111/j.1475-4754.1978.tb00208.x.

Yacobaccio, Hugo, M. Paz Catá, Patricia Solá, and M. Susana Alonso. 2008. "Estudio Arqueológico y Físicoquímico de Pinturas Rupestres en Hornillos 2 (Puna de Jujuy)." *Estudios Atacameños* 36:5–28.

Yacobaccio, Hugo, and Marcelo R. Morales. 2011. "Ambientes Pleistocénicos y Ocupación Humana Temprana en la Puna Argentina." Lima, Peru. *Boletín de Arqueología PUCP* 15:337–356.

Yacobaccio, Hugo D., Marcelo R. Morales, Patricia Solá, Celeste T. Samec, Rodolphe Hoguin, and Brenda I. Oxman. 2013. "Mid-Holocene Occupation in the Dry Puna in NW Argentina: Evidence from the Hornillos 2 Rockshelter." *Quaternary International* 307:38–49. https://doi.org/10.1016/j.quaint.2012.09.028.

5

In the long history of investigation into the novel environmental challenges faced by hominin and human populations expanding throughout Africa and into Europe, the Middle East, Asia, and Sahul during the Late Pleistocene (Gamble et al. 2004; Rabett 2012), much attention has been focused on the climatic and environmental thresholds crossed by our own species, *Homo sapiens* (Mellars 2006; Rabett 2012; Boivin et al. 2013). Recent research into the desertic environments of Africa, the Middle East, and equatorial south Asia has suggested that landscapes previously assumed to have been barriers to human occupation, including large parts of the Arabian peninsula, were successfully adapted to and navigated at various points in time (Groucutt and Petraglia 2012; Blinkhorn et al. 2013; Boivin et al. 2013; Crassard et al. 2013). Like deserts, tropical rainforests have been argued to represent impenetrable obstacles for human migration and adaptation. One consequence of this bias is that less attention has been focused on Late Pleistocene and Holocene hunter-gatherer adaptations to these environments (but see Barker et al. 2007; Barton et al. 2012; Barker 2013; Roberts and Petraglia 2015; Roberts et al. 2017a, 2017b).

Tropical rainforests exist only in regions with very high precipitation and (mostly) low rainfall seasonality (Whitmore 1998). They contain over half of the world's existing plant and animal species (Wilson 1988) and thus arguably provide highly productive and stable

Hunting and Gathering in Prehistoric Rainforests

Insights from Stable Isotope Analysis

Patrick Roberts,
John Krigbaum, and
Julia Lee-Thorp

DOI: 10.5876/9781607327745.c005

settings for human hunter-gatherers, with plentiful access to freshwater. In the 1980s, however, anthropologists argued that tropical rainforests would have been an unattractive prospect for long-term human foraging because they are difficult to navigate, offer little in the way of reliable carbohydrate and protein resources, and require sophisticated extraction technologies for long-term subsistence and occupation to be feasible (Hutterer 1983; Hart and Hart 1986). Some went so far as to suggest that human rainforest foraging, in the absence of agricultural support, is both undocumented and inconceivable in the tropical rainforests of the modern world and the recent past (Bailey et al. 1989; Headland et al. 1989). Archaeologists have drawn on these perspectives to suggest that intensive rainforest occupation and exploitation by *Homo sapiens* likely began only at the start of the Holocene, with rainforests being significant ecological barriers for human migration and adaptation prior to this point (e.g., Gamble 1993).

The perception of rainforests as unwelcoming and unproductive environments for human foragers has been questioned from ecological, anthropological, and archaeological standpoints (Colinvaux and Bush 1991; Balée 1994; Willis et al. 2004; Barton et al. 2012). Rainforests have been increasingly demonstrated to have shaped, and been shaped by, our species and its hominin ancestors over considerable timescales (Willis et al. 2004; Roberts and Petraglia 2015). This history may stretch back to the movement of *Homo erectus* into the rainforest environments of Southeast Asia 1.2 mya (Sémah et al. 2002; Brumm et al. 2010; Sémah and Sémah 2012). Furthermore, archaeological and paleoenvironmental research in tropical forest regions of Africa (Mercader 2002a), Southeast Asia (Barker et al. 2007), South Asia (Perera et al. 2011; Roberts et al. 2015a) and Melanesia (Gosden 2010; Summerhayes et al. 2010) has suggested that *Homo sapiens* was able to exploit and manipulate a variety of faunal and floral taxa available in rainforest ecologies as early as at least 45,000 years ago, and, as argued by Mercader (2002a, 2002b), on the basis of indirect association between stone artifacts and palynological evidence for forest presence, perhaps even 200,000 years ago.

Yet, despite the establishment of this "rainforest prehistory" there remain a number of impediments to investigating past human subsistence strategies in tropical rainforests. Tropical rainforests are poor preservational environments, especially with respect to organic remains that are the most likely to provide insight about human subsistence or prevailing environmental conditions (Tappen 1994). Well-preserved stratigraphic archaeological sequences are limited, and usually confined to cave or rockshelter sites. This results in a biased archaeological record with snapshots of human subsistence practices gleaned from preserved organic remains (e.g., Mercader et al. 2000, 2003; Barker et al. 2007; Perera et al. 2011). Furthermore, the high water flow in rainforest ecosystems means that many of these site sequences are disturbed, making chronological and paleoenvironmental reconstruction difficult (Mercader et al. 2003), and necessitating detailed micromorphological study (Kourampas et al. 2009). Finally, landscape or satellite surveying data that provide useful knowledge about the spatial extent and diverse nature of human landscape use in many other landscapes, are rarely available in rainforest regions, in part due to incredibly low site visibility. This is especially the case for open-air sites. While LiDAR methodologies have shown promise in the discovery of ancient sedentary settlements (Evans 2016), it remains unclear to what extent this will facilitate the discovery of more ephemeral forager sites in dense forest contexts.

The last two decades have increasingly produced information regarding particular rainforest adaptations where multidisciplinary studies have been applied. At the West Mouth of the Niah Caves, Sarawak (East Malaysia), recovered fragments of fruits, nuts, plant tissue, and starch grains, indicate that the collection of rainforest plants may have occurred as early as 45 ka (Barker 2005; Barton 2005; Barker et al. 2007). Further archaeozoological insight into human rainforest adaptations is suggested by the presence of cuscus (*Phalanger orientalis*) at archaeological sites in New Ireland at 20 ka, apparently as a transplanted protein source (Allen et al. 1989; Gosden and Robertson 1991). Finally, systematic use-wear and residue analysis of bone and stone tools at Late Pleistocene-Holocene sites have provided some insights into hunting (Barton et al. 2009; O'Connor et al. 2014) and foraging (Rabett 2005) methods. Nevertheless, information from these methods cannot be used to determine whether human populations were specialized in the use of rainforest resources all year round, or were using them on a more seasonal or ephemeral basis.

One alternative methodology is the application of stable carbon and oxygen analysis to human and faunal tooth enamel. Stable carbon ($\delta13C$) and oxygen ($\delta18O$) isotope analysis can provide direct insight into long-term human forest reliance in tropical environments. Following application in archaeology for over 30 years, stable isotope analysis has proven itself to have huge temporal, geographical, and theoretical scope, including the reliable reconstruction of hominin diets (Lee-Thorp 1989; Lee-Thorp et al. 1989a; Nelson 2007; Levin et al. 2008; White et al. 2009; Sponheimer et al. 2013). Furthermore, Schoeninger et al. (1997) initiated the application of stable isotope analysis of modern forest primate tissues to provide direct information about niche position, dietary variability, and dietary seasonality (Crowley 2012; Sandberg et al. 2012). Systematic reconstruction of these modern and prehistoric stable isotope ecologies has revealed the potential detail accessible through the stable isotopic analysis of tissues in tropical forest ecologies. In particular, the time-depth and preservation properties accessible to the stable isotopic analysis of well-preserved tooth enamel make it an important, yet largely ignored, tool in the reconstruction of human rainforest adaptations.

In this chapter we provide an overview of stable carbon and oxygen isotope systematics in a tropical context, tracking their variability across different plant types, and ecological conditions, and into the tooth enamel of their consumers, with particular focus on the so-called canopy effect. We apply these principles to explore how stable carbon and oxygen isotope measurements of hominin and primate tissues have been used to investigate the forest niches of our closest ancestors. We discuss the importance of tooth enamel as a focal material of analysis, given the issues of preservation presented by tropical rainforest environments, as well as the necessary preservation considerations and protocols required when working on fossil enamel excavated from these settings. Based on its long history of application in the testing of hominin forest reliance, we highlight the potential of stable carbon and oxygen analysis of tooth enamel as a means of exploring rainforest reliance in the Late Pleistocene and Holocene rainforest prehistories of our own species, with particular focus on our ongoing work in South and Southeast Asia.

STABLE CARBON AND OXYGEN ISOTOPES IN TOOTH ENAMEL IN A TROPICAL FOREST CONTEXT

STABLE CARBON ISOTOPE DYNAMICS IN TROPICAL FOREST PLANTS

All plants take in CO_2 from the atmosphere from which they construct their discrimination tissues. This process of photosynthesis introduces strong isotopic fractionation of against ^{13}C, the degree of which depends on which of the three main photosynthetic pathways is used: C_3, C_4, or CAM (Crassulacean Acid Metabolism) (Craig 1953; Smith and Epstein 1971). Fractionation during photosynthesis causes a depletion of, on average, −5‰ in C_4 and −19‰ in C_3 plants, relative to atmospheric $\delta^{13}CO_2$ (c. −6.5‰ prior to the Industrial Era). C_3 $\delta^{13}C$ values vary from about −24 to −36‰ (global mean −26.5‰) while C_4 values range from approximately −9 to −17‰ (global mean −12‰ (Smith and Epstein 1971)). C_3 and C_4 plants therefore have distinct and non-overlapping $\delta^{13}C$ values (Tieszen 1991) (figure 5.1). CAM plants may either fix atmospheric carbon in the manner of C_3 plants (using the enzyme RUBISCO) or through a modified, diurnal C_4 sequence in which phosphor-enol-pyruvate is carboxylated, then reduced, at night to form malate. This variation leads to $\delta^{13}C$ values

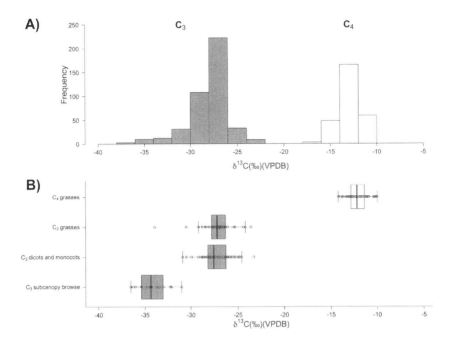

FIGURE 5.1. *(A) Histogram of δ¹³C values of East and Central African plants collected between 1997 and 2006 (data from Cerling et al. 2010), (B) δ¹³C values of plants from Mongolia, Argentina, Utah, Zaire, and Kenya collected between 1962 and 1997. Data from (Cerling and Harris 1999).*

that are within the range of either C_3 or C_4 plants, or intermediate between the two (O'Leary 1981). While these taxa are occasionally present in tropical forest environments (Whitmore 1998), they are unlikely to form significant parts of human diets (Krigbaum 2001).

In tropical and susbtropical contexts, the isotopic distinction between C_4 and C_3 biomass can be used to study the relative proportion of C_4 grassland to C_3 woodland or forest plants in faunal and hominin diets and their associated environments (Sponheimer et al. 2006a; Codron et al. 2014; Sponheimer et al. 2013; Crowley et al. 2014). Within forests there is a further influence on isotopic composition of plants. Vegetation growing under a closed-forest canopy is strongly depleted in ¹³C, due to low light (Farquhar et al. 1989) and large amounts of respired CO_2 (van der Merwe and Medina 1991). This *canopy effect* causes CO_2, soils, leaves, and fruits within a closed canopy to have low δ¹³C values that are also reflected in the tissues of animals feeding in the same

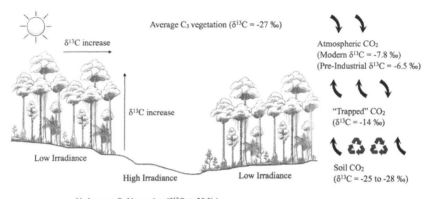

Average C₃ vegetation (δ¹³C = -27 ‰)

δ¹³C increase

δ¹³C increase

Low Irradiance

High Irradiance

Low Irradiance

Atmospheric CO₂
(Modern δ¹³C = -7.8 ‰)
(Pre-Industrial δ¹³C = -6.5 ‰)

"Trapped" CO₂
(δ¹³C = -14 ‰)

Soil CO₂
(δ¹³C = -25 to -28 ‰)

Understory C₃ Vegetation (δ¹³C ≤ -30 ‰)

FIGURE 5.2. *Diagram representing C_3 plant $\delta^{13}C$ variation in a tropical forest context. Low irradiance and recycled CO_2 result in lower $\delta^{13}C$ values in air, soil, and vegetation growing under a closed canopy, relative to more open areas. In closed areas, understory vegetation is significantly depleted in ^{13}C, and vegetation has more negative $\delta^{13}C$ values, compared to that growing higher in the canopy. Adapted from (Jackson et al. 1993) and (Krigbaum 2003).*

environments (van der Merwe and Medina 1991; Cerling et al. 2004). The canopy effect also works along a vertical gradient, with those animals living on the forest floor feeding on the most ^{13}C-depleted vegetation as a result of low light and respired CO_2 (Cerling et al. 2004). The effect has been demonstrated in temperate (Pearcy and Pfitsch 1991; Bonafini et al. 2013), subtropical (Ehleringer et al. 1986), and tropical forest formations (van der Merwe and Medina 1989, 1991; Ometto et al. 2006) (figure 5.2).

STABLE OXYGEN ISOTOPE DYNAMICS IN TROPICAL FOREST PLANTS

The $\delta^{18}O$ of environmental water in the tropics and subtropics largely reflects hydrological conditions through isotope effects on local precipitation and other sources of moisture (Dansgaard 1964; Gat 1980). Global patterns of $\delta^{18}O$ in precipitation are primarily structured by temperature-dependent processes of evaporation from the oceans and the movement of moisture masses over continents (Dansgaard 1964). Fractionation affecting precipitation $\delta^{18}O$ from these moisture sources is negatively influenced by temperature (cloud height and latitude), and a rain-out or Rayleigh distillation effect that impacts on distance from the oceanic source ("continental effect") and an "amount effect" related to heavy rain (Dansgaard 1964; Rozanski et al. 1993). Evaporation exerts a positive effect, so that continental water bodies and soils in areas with a water deficit are ^{18}O enriched. In the tropics, where precipitation $\delta^{18}O$ is primarily dictated by the "amount effect," lower rainfall $\delta^{18}O$ is recorded in months with more rainfall and during intense events.

The source water for plants is soil moisture, so the oxygen isotope composition of plants is partly governed by that of the precipitation. However, there are several potential fractionation effects before water isotopes become fixed in plant organic material. Given that there is no fractionation during plant-root water uptake (Wershaw et al. 1966), the critical site of fractionation is the leaf. Evaporation (transpiration) leads to a loss of lighter ^{16}O isotopes and, as a consequence, enrichment in ^{18}O (Gonfiantini et al. 1965). Leaf ^{18}O enrichment depends mainly on the difference between the isotopic compositions of the source water and the ambient moisture vapor, and on the ratio of vapor pressure inside to that outside of the leaf (Barbour 2007). As a result, the degree of $\delta^{18}O$ increase enrichment in the measurements of leaf water is negatively related to relative humidity, with decreasing humidity resulting in increased $\delta^{18}O$ values (Flanagan et al. 1991; Yakir et al. 1994; Sheshshayee et al. 2005).

In tropical regions, although there may be a dry season, relative humidity generally remains high throughout the year. This means that compared to more arid locations, evapotranspiration in plants is reduced, with only subtle linked $\delta^{18}O$ variation. However, the relationship between leaf $\delta^{18}O$ and evaporative potential can still be used to provide some insight into ecological variation in tropical forest contexts. First, plant matter growing in well-shaded, humid conditions will be more depleted in ^{18}O, and have lower $\delta^{18}O$ values, than those growing in more open, arid areas with high irradiance. As a result, the $\delta^{18}O$ of plant tissues, like $\delta^{13}C$, can be used to infer canopy density in a rainforest environment. Furthermore, a vertical stratification of $\delta^{18}O$ has been observed in tropical forests and is linked to gradients in stomatal conductance (da Silveira et al. 1989). Increased humidity on the forest floor results in low leaf $\delta^{18}O$ values, with enrichment of ^{18}O occurring along a vertical gradient with decreased humidity (da Silveira et al. 1989; Buchmann et al. 1997).

Stable carbon and oxygen isotopes in tropical tooth enamel

Modern studies have demonstrated that $\delta^{13}C$ measurements of faunal tooth enamel are reliable recorders of animal diet and behavior (Lee-Thorp and van der Merwe 1987; Cerling et al. 2003a, 2003b, 2004). In herbivores they have been shown to record the dietary proportion of C_3 closed canopy,

C$_3$, and C$_4$ resources, and thus provide a robust environmental indicator of the presence and prominence of these biomes. For example, Levin et al. (2008) used modern faunal tooth enamel from Central and East Africa to track environmental variation from the closed-canopy C$_3$ habitats of the Ituri Forest, Democratic Republic of Congo (−26.0 to −14.1‰) to the open C$_3$/C$_4$ grasslands of East Africa (−12.0 to 0.2‰) (figure 5.3). In pre-fossil-fuel faunal diets, tooth enamel with δ^{13}C lower than −14‰ represents reliance on dense or closed-canopy forest, while average values for C$_3$ and C$_4$ reliance are c. −12‰ and c. 0‰, respectively (Lee-Thorp et al. 1989a, 1989b; Levin et al. 2008).

It is important to note, however, that environmental factors, including temperature, precipitation, and atmospheric CO$_2$, mean that C$_3$ and C$_4$ plant δ^{13}C endpoints are necessarily context specific. Furthermore, the isotopic composition of the atmosphere has not been constant over geological or even recent human timescales. Modern atmospheric CO$_2$ δ^{13}C (−8‰) is more ^{13}C depleted than is the CO$_2$ in the pre-1850 atmosphere (Francey et al., 1999), with more minor changes visible further back into the Pliocene and Miocene (Zachos et al. 2001; Levin et al. 2008). Finally, different faunal taxa have different feeding behaviors and will therefore document different aspects of the environment in their tooth enamel δ^{13}C (figure 5.3). As a result, multispecies stable isotope ecologies are necessary to build up a reliable picture of the available vegetation and ecological contexts in a given region.

Variations in the δ^{18}O of tooth enamel are determined largely by the oxygen isotopic composition of ingested water, both from drinking water and plant/food water (Luz et al. 1984; Luz and Kolodny 1985). On this basis, and given the impacts of humidity on evapotranspiration and plant water and tissue δ^{18}O noted above, tooth enamel δ^{18}O has been used as a proxy for relative humidity (Longinelli 1984; Quade et al. 1995). However, physiological and behavioral variables have been shown to influence how faunal enamel δ^{18}O responds to changes in evaporative potential (Levin et al. 2006). Herbivores that obtain most of their water from plant sources (non-obligate drinkers) will have tooth enamel δ^{18}O that reflects not only local rain but also relative environmental humidity (the main source of fractionation in plant leaf water δ^{18}O). Obligate drinkers are not as sensitive to this environmental factor (Ayliffe et al. 1992; Levin et al. 2006). That said, obligate drinkers obtaining their water from open, highly irradiated water sources can be expected to show higher δ^{18}O than those drinking shaded standing water. Similarly, non-obligate drinkers feeding on plants living in open, evaporative regions will have higher δ^{18}O than those feeding in shaded, forest areas.

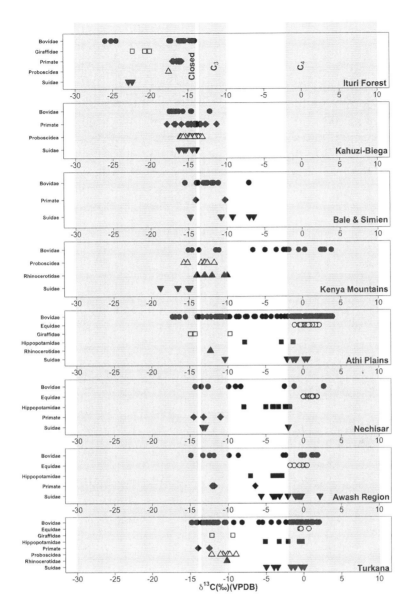

FIGURE 5.3. *Plot of faunal tooth enamel* $\delta^{13}C$ *from extant herbivores in East Africa plotted by location: Ituri Forest, Democratic Republic of Congo (Cerling et al. 2004); Kahuzi–Biega, Bale and Simien, Nechisar, Awash, and Turkana (Levin et al. 2008); Kenya Mountains and Athi Plains (Cerling et al. 1999; Harris and Cerling, 2002; Cerling et al. 2003a, 2003b).*

STABLE ISOTOPE ANALYSIS AND THE FOREST ADAPTATIONS OF OUR CLOSEST RELATIVES AND NEAREST ANCESTORS

WHY TOOTH ENAMEL?

A variety of tissues have been used to trace hominin, human, and faunal diets. Bone collagen and bone apatite provide the longest, averaged "adult" signature of an individual diet due to the continuous nature of bone turnover (Hedges et al. 2007). However, bone collagen degrades quickly in tropical zones that are hot and humid (Ambrose 1990; Krigbaum 2001, 2003) and bone mineral is highly susceptible to chemical alteration due to leaching and high water flow (Lee-Thorp 2000). By contrast, tooth enamel is primarily made up of an hydroxyapatite crystal lattice that is resistant to postmortem diagenetic substitution and degradation (Lee-Thorp et al. 1989a; Wang and Cerling 1994; Lee-Thorp 2000, 2008). The preserved, "biogenic" structural carbonate thus provides an accurate signature for the "bulk diet" of an individual during the period of enamel formation (Ambrose and Norr 1993; Lee-Thorp et al. 1989a).

This has made tooth enamel the material of choice in archaeological and paleontological stable isotope studies across temperate, arctic, subtropical, and tropical environments (Krigbaum 2001, 2003, 2005; Nelson 2007; Lee-Thorp 2008; White et al. 2009; Ecker et al. 2013; Roberts et al. 2017a, 2017b). Tooth enamel $\delta^{13}C$ and $\delta^{18}O$ represent a much shorter period of time than bone, and the enamel varies according to the timing of development of the particular tooth sampled. For humans, first-molar enamel mineralizes between birth and three years of age. The first-molar enamel forms, at least partly, prior to weaning and therefore in principle $\delta^{18}O$ measurements from this tooth will reflect milk rather than water or other food sources (Wright and Schwarcz 1998). Premolars mineralize between 2 and 6 years of age, and third molars mineralize during adolescence, between 7 and 13 years (Hillson 1996; AlQahtani et al. 2010).

The sequential nature of enamel mineralization and maturation allows the study of chronologically ordered, temporal isotopic changes (Balasse 2002; Sponheimer et al. 2006b), even though attenuation occurs as a result of ongoing mineralization beyond initial enamel deposition (Balasse 2002; Passey et al. 2005). The use of stable isotope sequences from human tooth enamel, alongside bulk data, enables testing of whether rainforest reliance was maintained throughout the period of enamel formation, or whether the diets fluctuated between deep forest and open-resource usage on a more seasonal basis. This approach is potentially useful, given ecological and anthropological questions regarding the sustainability of tropical rainforest use by human foragers, past and present (Bailey et al. 1989; Bailey and Headland 1991).

Robust data sets of $\delta^{13}C$ and $\delta^{18}O$ measurements from hominin and associated faunal tooth enamel now exist that have been used to track the changing diets and environments of our early ancestors in Africa. Particular focus in this regard has been on the proportion of C_3 closed canopy, C_3, and C_4 resources in hominin ecologies given that the development of "human" traits of bipedalism, tool use, and subsistence strategies in the hominin clade have been linked to the expansion of open, savannah ecosystems (Lee-Thorp et al. 1989b; Sponheimer et al. 2009; Lee-Thorp et al. 2010). It has been argued, on the basis of associated faunal assemblages and limb adaptations, that the earliest known hominins, including *Orrorin tugenensis* (*c.* 6 mya), *Ardipithecus kadabba* (*c.* 5.5 mya), and *Ardipithecus ramidus* (*c.* 4.4 mya), were forest adapted (WoldeGabriel et al. 1994, 2001; Pickford et al. 2004; White et al. 2006). By contrast, *Australopithecines* and the genus *Homo* post–*c.* 3 mya have been linked to more specialized bipedal movement, the procurement of medium to large mammalian resources, and the manufacture of the earliest stone-tool technologies at a time of expanding savannah ecosystems (Lee-Thorp et al. 1994; Sponheimer and Lee-Thorp 1999; Cerling et al. 2010; Lee-Thorp et al. 2010).

Direct testing of this theory using stable carbon and oxygen isotope analysis of hominin tooth enamel, however, has proved this picture to be too simplistic. Although a coarse trend from woodland use by *A. ramidus*, *Australopithecus anamensis*, and *Australopithecus afarensis* to more C_4 resources by *Australopithecus africanus*, *Homo habilis*, and *Paranthropus robustus* is broadly observed (Lee-Thorp et al. 2010), it is not straightforward and *H. habilis* shows less reliance on C_4 resources than *P. robustus*, and probably also *Au. africanus* (van der Merwe et al. 2008) (figure 5.4). Furthermore, direct isotopic work on *A. ramidus*, has suggested that it, and its associated fauna (giraffids, equids, bovids, hippotragines, primates, and rhinocerotids), are best associated with open-woodland conditions rather than dense forest (White et al. 2009) (figure 5.5). Indeed, additional work at a number of *A. ramidus*–bearing localities, as well as on *Australopithecus sediba*, have demonstrated more variable ecological preferences, including "open" values back to 3.8 mya (Levin et al. 2008, 2015), for early members of the hominin clade than had previously been indicated by indirect paleoenvironmental assumptions based on extant faunal preferences.

Sequential isotope analysis of hominin tooth enamel has also revealed intra-individual complexity in dietary reliance on C_3 and C_4 resources. Sponheimer et al. (2006b) used laser-ablation analysis of $\delta^{13}C$ on four *P. robustus* tooth crowns to demonstrate differences of up to 5‰ within a given tooth. These data suggest a considerable shift from a diet dominated by C_3 to a diet dominated by

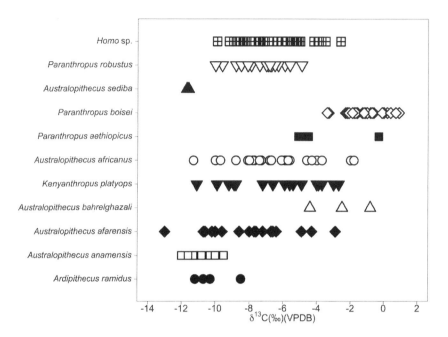

FIGURE 5.4. $\delta^{13}C$ *of hominin tooth enamel from southern, eastern, and central Africa plotted by genus/species (as per Levin et al. 2015). Hominin taxa are arranged from oldest (bottom) to youngest (top) (as per Levin et al. 2015). Data from Cerling et al. (2011, 2013); Henry et al. (2012); Lee-Thorp et al. (2012); Lee-Thorp, van der Merwe, and Brain (1994); Lee-Thorp, Thackeray, and van der Merwe (2000); Levin et al. (2015); Sponheimer and Lee-Thorp (1999); Sponheimer et al. 2005, 2006b, 2013; van der Merwe et al. 2003, (2008); White et al. (2009); Wynn et al. (2013).*

C_4 resources in certain individuals on both intra- and inter-annual scales. Lee-Thorp et al. (2010) performed similar analyses on three *Au. africanus* molar crowns from Sterkfontein Member 4. Variability in the reconstructed proportions of C_3 and C_4 resources between and within individuals was on a similar scale to that of *P. robustus*. One individual indicated a more or less uniform C_3 preference, while another showed variance of *c.* 6‰ through time. Although the precise timescales of this variation are hard to pinpoint given maturation complexities, the differences again demonstrate that C_4 resources formed an important, but highly variable, component of their diets.

To find an isotopic composition in our ancestors that unambiguously reflected tropical forest reliance we currently have to go back to the Miocene

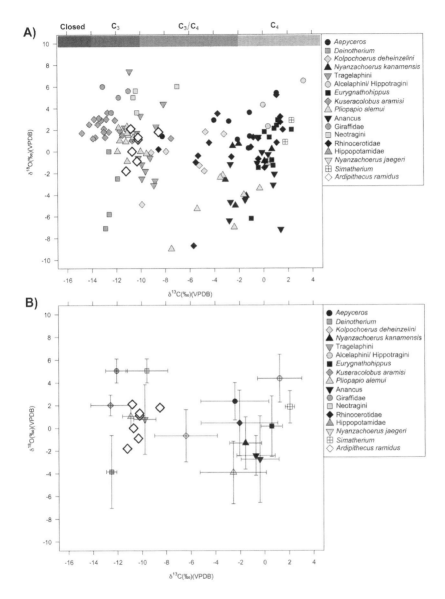

Figure 5.5. δ¹³C and δ¹⁸O composition of mammalian tooth enamel from the Lower Aramis Member of the Sagantole Formation in the Middle Awash Valley: (A) Individual δ¹³C and δ¹⁸O values plotted by taxon; (B) bivariate means ± 1 standard deviation. Data from White et al. (2009).

hominoid *Sivapithecus* from the Siwalik sediments of Pakistan (Nelson 2007). This hominoid has some of the lowest $\delta^{13}C$ values (between −13‰ to −14‰), and some of the highest $\delta^{18}O$ values (−2.6‰), of all associated fauna sampled from these sediments (dated to 9.3–9.2 mya) (Nelson 2003, 2007) (figure 5.6). $\delta^{13}C$ measurements from this hominoid overlap with those from the early Pleistocene ape *Gigantopithecus blacki* and modern chimpanzees from Uganda and the Democratic Republic of Congo, implying that it occupied closed humid tropical/subtropical, canopied forest. In sum, it therefore currently seems that *Homo sapiens* was the only member of the hominin clade that exhibits direct evidence for rainforest resource use (Roberts et al. 2016). However, stable carbon and oxygen isotope analysis of tooth enamel has rarely been applied to human remains recovered from rainforest contexts (Krigbaum 2001, 2003, 2005; Roberts and Petraglia 2015; Roberts et al. 2015b, 2017b).

RAINFOREST ADAPTATIONS OF HUMAN HUNTER-GATHERERS AND STABLE ISOTOPES

Enamel Preservation in a Tropical Rainforest Environment

Although reliable $\delta^{13}C$- and $\delta^{18}O$-based dietary signals and environmental distinctions have been demonstrated across millions of years (Lee-Thorp et al. 1989a), protocols to check the state of preservation of tooth enamel specimens, and the potential impacts this might have on the reliability of measured isotopic values, remain important. This is particularly the case in tropical forest environments that are home to ion-rich soils and are hydrologically very active. The primary source of concern is the origin of tooth enamel carbonate, from which stable carbon and oxygen isotope ratios are obtained. Postmortem recrystallization and addition of exogenous carbonates can introduce foreign carbonate ions into apatite crystal structures by various means: adsorption onto crystal surfaces (Rey et al. 1991), replacement of hydroxyl ions at external "A"-sites, and more fundamental structural replacement of phosphate ions at "B"-sites (LeGeros 1967; Poyart et al. 1975).

It is not inevitable that the original isotope composition is altered during this process, with rearrangement and incorporation often being internally constituted (Lee-Thorp 2008). Adsorbed secondary minerals, such as calcite, can be effectively removed by acid treatment (Lee-Thorp et al. 1989a). By contrast, recrystallization that introduces external carbonates *within* the crystal lattice are more problematic. Comparison of fauna with known dietary habits (e.g., C_3 or C_4 preferences) can provide some indication of the reliability of $\delta^{13}C$ measurements (Lee-Thorp et al. 1989a), though the reliability of $\delta^{18}O$ values is

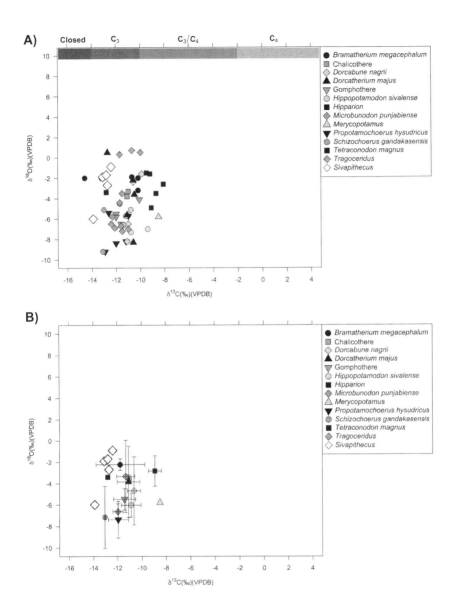

FIGURE 5.6. $\delta^{13}C$ and $\delta^{18}O$ values for the hominoid Sivapithecus and associated fauna within the S-Level (9.3–9.2 million years ago) of the Miocene Siwalik Group of Pakistan: (A) Individual $\delta^{13}C$ and $\delta^{18}O$ values plotted by taxon; (B) bivariate means ± 1 standard deviation Data from Nelson (2007).

more difficult to detect in this way (Zazzo et al. 2004; Lee-Thorp 2008). One means to check whether enamel is well preserved is the application of Fourier Transform Infrared spectroscopy (FTIR), which absorbs radiation at discrete vibrational frequencies related to the presence and exact crystallographic environment of the important functional groups such as CO_3^{2-} and PO_4^{3-}.

The polyatomic ions of interest are phosphates (PO_4^{3-}), carbonates (CO_3^{2-}), and hydroxyl groups (OH^-). The observed absorbance bands of enamel can be ascribed to the internal vibrations of these molecular groups (Farmer 1974; LeGeros 1991). The intensity of FTIR absorbance is proportional to the concentration of the absorbing molecule, enabling information on both the molecular species present and their concentrations in a sample. As a result, the infrared spectra of phosphate minerals with different structures such as enamel, dentine, and bone apatite are distinct, while biological apatites are also very different from carbonate minerals like calcite (Michel et al. 1996; Stuart-Williams et al. 1996; Sponheimer 1999). This methodology has now been used successfully in Sri Lanka back to 36,000 cal years BP to confirm adequate preservation of fossil *H. sapiens* tooth enamel in a tropical forest environment (Roberts et al. 2017b).

Human Rainforest Resource Reliance in Late Pleistocene Sri Lanka

Once such checks have been applied, stable carbon and oxygen isotope analysis of human and faunal tooth enamel can be applied to a variety of questions regarding prehistoric human-rainforest interactions. Sri Lanka has yielded some of the earliest dated fossil evidence for *H. sapiens* occupation (*c.* 38,000–36,000 cal years BP) in a modern rainforest context (Deraniyagala 1992; Perera et al. 2011; Roberts et al. 2015a), with the exception of Niah Cave in northern Borneo (c. 45,000 cal years BP) (Barker et al. 2007; Barker 2013). The well-preserved rockshelter sequences in Sri Lanka's Wet Zone tropical rainforest have yielded some of the earliest human remains, microlithic toolkits, bone technologies, and evidence for personal ornamentation anywhere in South Asia (Kennedy 2000; Perera et al. 2011). Significantly, this material culture record is directly associated with well-preserved floral, faunal, and micromorphological sequences at a series of rockshelter and cave sites (Deraniyagala 1992; Perera et al. 2011).

Vegetation models and pollen records suggest that the Wet Zone of Sri Lanka maintained tropical rainforest flora throughout the Late Pleistocene and into the Early Holocene (Premathilake and Risberg 2003; Premathilake

2012; Boivin et al. 2013), though the bearing of these records on locales of human relevance is debatable. Existing faunal records from Fa Hien-lena and Batadomba-lena indicate consistent human reliance on forest-dwelling, semi-arboreal and arboreal mammals, with primates making up 70–80 percent of the mammalian assemblages throughout the period of occupation (Perera, 2010; Perera et al. 2011). Botanical and molluscan records (Perera et al. 2011), as well as technological inferences (Perera et al. 2016), similarly support a rain-forest specialization for human hunter-gatherers at these sites. However, such evidence is unable to attest to the degree of prehistoric human rainforest reliance in Sri Lanka, especially on a relatively small island with climatic and ecological divisions, where human mobility could involve seasonal rainforest use.

Climate-driven precipitation and corresponding vegetation zones characterize the ecology of Sri Lanka today (Roberts et al. 2015a). The Wet Zone receives between 2,201 and 4,840 mm of annual rainfall and is home to Sri Lanka's wet deciduous and tropical evergreen rainforest (Ashton and Gunatilleke 1987; Gunatilleke et al. 2005; Roberts et al. 2015b), while the Intermediate Zone of the island receives 1,701–2,200 mm of rainfall and supports tropical moist deciduous and semi-evergreen "Intermediate" rainforest (Erdelen 1988; Roberts et al. 2015b). The remaining "Dry Zone" of the island is characterized by open, dry-adapted forest and large expanses of shrubs and grassland (Erdelen 1988; Somaratne and Dhanapala 1996). This transect—as well as the fact that Sri Lanka's archaeological sequences range from 36,000 cal years BP, through the climatically sensitive periods of the Last Glacial Maximum (LGM) (*c*. 20,000 years ago), to the Terminal Pleistocene/Holocene boundary (*c*. 12,000–8,000 years ago)—makes Sri Lanka particularly suited to stable isotopic ecological reconstruction.

Roberts et al. (2015b, 2017b) applied stable carbon and oxygen isotope analysis to human and faunal tooth enamel from four Late Pleistocene/Holocene archaeological sequences in Sri Lanka in order to directly test the extent of prehistoric human reliance on rainforest resources at different archaeological sites through time. Tooth enamel samples from a variety of fauna and humans from the Terminal Pleistocene/Holocene deposits (*c*. 12,000 to 3,000 cal years BP) of Fa Hien-lena, Balangoda Kuragala, and Bellan-bandi Palassa provided a suite of samples encompassing the full climatic and ecological spectrum of the island's modern climate and vegetation zones (Roberts et al. 2015b) (figure 5.7). Human specimens dated from *c*. 36,000 to 20,000–17,000 cal years BP from Batadomba-lena, with associated fauna, provided an earlier record of Wet Zone rainforest hunter-gatherer adaptations. Moreover, sequential analysis of Late Pleistocene and Terminal Pleistocene/Holocene tooth enamel

FIGURE 5.7. *(A) δ¹³C and δ¹⁸O measurements of fauna from the Terminal Pleistocene/ Holocene deposits of Fa Hien-lena, Balangoda Kuragala, and Bellan-bandi Palassa with 90% confidence ellipses, representing "Wet Zone" tropical forest, "Intermediate" tropical forest, and "open" environment; (B) Late Holocene human δ¹³C and δ¹⁸O measurements from Balangoda Kuragala; (C) Terminal Pleistocene/Early Holocene human δ¹³C and δ¹⁸O measurements from Balangoda Kuragala and Fa Hien-lena; (D) δ¹³C and δ¹⁸O values of human specimens from Layer 6 (dated to c. 20,000 cal years BP) at Batadomba-lena; (E) δ¹³C and δ¹⁸O values of human specimen from Layer 7c (dated to 36,000 cal years BP) at Batadomba-lena. Data from Roberts et al. (2015b, 2017b).*

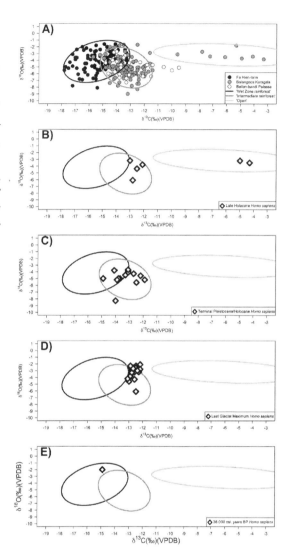

enabled seasonal or interannual changes in tropical forest resource reliance to be studied for a given individual (Roberts et al. 2015b).

The results demonstrated that the earliest human fossil in Sri Lanka, and indeed South Asia, was reliant on tropical forest resources c. 36,000 cal years BP (Roberts et al. 2017b), despite the Wet Zone rainforest of the island apparently being more open during this period. This adaptation was maintained throughout the LGM albeit with a preference for more open-forest resources

(Roberts et al. 2015b, 2017b). Isotopic evidence from associated fauna indicates that the Wet Zone rainforests of Sri Lanka were more open during the LGM than during the Terminal Pleistocene/Holocene, a pattern noted in tropical regions elsewhere (Colinvaux et al. 1996; Dupont et al. 2000; Haberle et al. 2012). Terminal Pleistocene and Holocene human hunter-gatherer $\delta^{13}C$ and $\delta^{18}O$ from Fa Hien-lena and Balangoda Kuragala demonstrates long-term reliance on closed canopy and more open resources (Roberts et al. 2015b) (figure 5.7), although there is apparently a distinct preference for Intermediate rainforest. No individuals showed any significant contribution from open-grassland resources apart from two individuals dated to 3,000 cal years BP whose $\delta^{13}C$ and $\delta^{18}O$ measurements were indicative of a reliance on open C_4 resources at a time when Iron Age farming likely expanded into the region (Deraniyagala 2007; Roberts et al. 2015b).

Stable carbon and oxygen analysis therefore demonstrated that hunter-gatherer dietary reliance on rainforest resources was both possible and preferable in Late Pleistocene and Holocene Sri Lanka, even when open, grassland resources were available, and throughout periods of climatic change. Tropical-forest foraging even persisted following the appearance of agriculture in the region (Roberts et al. 2015b, 2017b). Sequential $\delta^{13}C$ and $\delta^{18}O$ measurements from Late Pleistocene and Terminal Pleistocene/Holocene individuals also indicate that this reliance on tropical-forest resources was stable throughout the period of enamel formation (figure 5.8). As a result, Sri Lanka's early human foragers not only used tropical forest resources but also specialized in their acquisition for their subsistence. It is hoped that the application of bulk and sequential analysis of fossil human tooth enamel, and associated faunal tooth enamel, will provide useful comparative data sets regarding the environmental and ecological context of other potential examples of Late Pleistocene tropical forest foragers in Southeast Asia (Barker et al. 2007; Demeter et al. 2012) and Early and Middle Pleistocene members of the genus *Homo* in Southeast Asia whose status as tropical-forest foragers remains debated (Roberts et al. 2016).

TRANSITIONS FROM FORAGING TO FARMING IN RAINFORESTS OF SOUTHEAST ASIA

The onset of the Neolithic in the low latitudes of Southeast Asia (*c.* 4,000 cal years BP) has been characterized by complex demographic changes, technological and cultural innovations, and the introduction of agricultural foodstuffs in certain contexts (Spriggs 1989; Bellwood 1997). An increased frequency of archaeological sites, centered on cave and rockshelter habitation

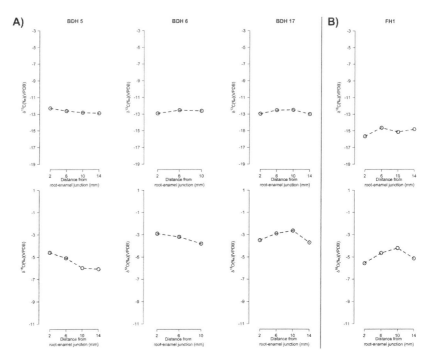

Figure 5.8. *Sequential human tooth enamel δ¹³C and δ¹⁸O measured in this study from (A) Layer 6b (dated to c. 20,000 cal years BP) from Batadomba-lena and (B) Layer 248 (dated to c. 12,000 cal years BP) from Fa Hien-lena. Data from Roberts et al. (2017b).*

sites, has also been documented at this time (Anderson 1997). However, surprisingly little "hard evidence" exists for transitions to farming despite renewed work at the Niah Cave complex (Barker 2013). These low-latitude contexts may have ebbed and flowed in terms of the distribution and density of rainforest, but rainforest biota were ostensibly maintained throughout the Terminal Pleistocene and Holocene contexts in the region after the Last Glacial Maximum (Bird et al. 2005).

Indeed the site of Gua Cha, situated in the rainforest of Peninsular Malaysia, was argued by Bailey and colleagues (1989) as discussed above, to be one of the few exceptions against their argument that rainforests could not have been inhabited by *Homo sapiens* prior to the Neolithic when foragers would have had contact with farmers (and carbohydrates). At Gua Cha in Kelantan (West Malaysia) and at the Niah Caves in northern Borneo (Sarawak, East Malaysia) there are clear pre-Neolithic and Neolithic stratigraphic sequences that have been excavated intact, and that recovered materials that have been meticulously analyzed (Bellwood 1997; Barker 2013), including analyses of recovered faunal remains and changing site contexts. Humans clearly occupied these rainforest areas, but in a very real sense, the overall archaeological record that exists to imply changes in subsistence in these contexts is principally focused on secondary evidence and associations with Neolithic material culture, such as pottery.

The lacunae in information regarding Late Pleistocene/Holocene transitions in human diet in Southeast Asia led Krigbaum (2001) to examine preserved human and faunal remains recovered from the Niah Caves' West Mouth, as well as several additional Neolithic sites from northern Borneo and human remains recovered from Gua Cha on the mainland (Bellwood 1997). All sites examined were situated in C_3-dominant lowland primary rainforest, and research focused on whether there was any noticeable diachronic shift in diet that might suggest that certain human groups may have increasingly relied on cultigens versus foraged rainforest resources by mid-Holocene times. Krigbaum (2001, 2003, 2005) applied stable carbon and oxygen isotope "bulk" analysis to human tooth enamel (third molars) from pre-Neolithic (N = 13) and Neolithic (N = 26) burials recovered West Mouth, Niah, and compared these results with Neolithic/Early Metal sites at Lubang Angin (N = 3), and at Gua Sireh (N = 5), the latter site with the earliest evidence for rice in island Southeast Asia at 4200 years BP (Bellwood et al. 1992). Pre-Neolithic Hoabinhian remains (N = 4) and Neolithic remains (N = 4) from Gua Cha in Peninsula Malaysia were sampled for comparative purposes.

Significant differences in $\delta^{13}C$, between sites and across time periods, highlighted different foraging strategies, from closed-forest resource gathering to open-forest horticulture (Krigbaum 2001, 2005). Lower $\delta^{13}C$ values (c. −16 to −14‰) in the pre-Neolithic individuals from Gua Cha and the Niah Caves suggested increased dependence on closed rainforest resources, while higher $\delta^{13}C$ values (c. −13 to −11‰) in most Neolithic individuals from the Niah Caves, Gua Cha, and Gua Sireh suggested access to ^{13}C-enriched food items and changes in resource procurement, such as open-forest horticulture with concomitant habitat modification (figure 5.9). The isotopic difference was quite marked for the Gua Cha sample, and its location in the middle of Peninsula Malaysia ruled out any potential marine dietary signals influencing $\delta^{13}C$ values. Interestingly, Neolithic/Early Metal individuals from Lubang Angin and some individuals interred in Neolithic contexts at the Niah Caves exhibited continued dependence on rainforest resources (lower $\delta^{13}C$ values), suggesting a more complex dynamic between foragers and potential "farmers" across the

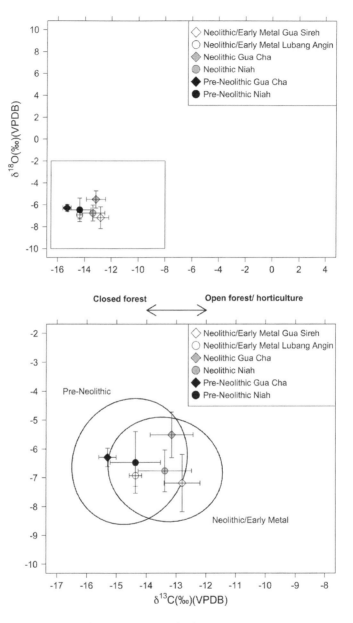

FIGURE 5.9. *(Top) δ¹⁸O and (bottom) δ¹³C values of tooth enamel from pre-Neolithic and Neolithic human skeletons from Gua Sireh, Lubang Angin, Gua Cha, and the Niah Caves, Sarawak. Data from Krigbaum (2001, 2003, 2005).*

Neolithic landscape of northern Borneo (Krigbaum 2003). Subsequent work with heavy-isotope ratios of lead and strontium, coupled with $\delta^{13}C$, demonstrate how complex albeit connected human interaction between people with different subsistence regimes was in this region of Southeast Asia during the mid-later Holocene (Valentine et al. 2008; Lloyd-Smith et al. 2015).

Faunal tooth enamel recovered from the Niah Caves was also analyzed (Krigbaum 2001) to establish an isotopic baseline and clarify patterns observed in human tooth enamel $\delta^{13}C$ and $\delta^{18}O$ values. Significant differences were observed across taxa, underscoring the role of the canopy effect on these systems. Samples analyzed included nonhuman primates (*Pongo, Hylobates, Macaca, Trachypithecus, Presbytis* spp.), artiodactyls (*Bos, Cervus, Muntiacus, Tragulus, Sus*), perissodactyls (*Rhinoceros* and *Tapirus*), and carnivores (*Arctictus, Lutra, Helarctos, Neofelis*). Isotopic data were interpreted against baseline plant isotope values derived from field studies and the published literature. For all fauna sampled, $\delta^{13}C$ values range from −21.6 to −9.9‰ and this variability was influenced by both "total" diet during tooth enamel formation and the "canopy effect." The $\delta^{18}O$ values also varied considerably, from −12.8 to 9.9‰, reflecting differential diets and evapotranspiration regimes based on species diet, in addition to potential climate-related (i.e., precipitation) changes over the course of Late Pleistocene/Holocene site occupation.

Like Sri Lanka (Roberts et al. 2017b), follow-up analysis of pre-Neolithic and Neolithic humans, and associated fauna, from the Niah Caves is now focused on isotopic analysis of incremental growth layers in tooth enamel to explore forager seasonality in a rainforest setting. Comparison of $\delta^{18}O$ and $\delta^{13}C$ will be made for "bulk" and serially sampled molars recovered from Holocene deposits at Niah Cave (northern Borneo). These data will then be coupled with "bulk" strontium and lead isotope ratios derived from the same tooth. Stable oxygen and carbon isotope data, respectively, reflect sequential events of seasonality and diet of each individual sampled, whereas lead and strontium reflect inferred dietary catchment. It is hoped that the combination of these data will reveal a complex pattern of life history for different individuals and groups of individuals interred at the site, and underscore diverse patterns of mobility and subsistence (Valentine et al. 2008; Lloyd-Smith et al. 2015). The results will also be examined against Holocene climate variables in the region. For example, it is hypothesized that stable oxygen and carbon isotope results of "Neolithic" individuals will show increased subannual variation, which may correlate with increased incidence of El Niño Southern Oscillation (ENSO) variability during and after the Holocene thermal maximum

CONCLUSION

The environmental flexibility of our species during the Late Pleistocene is being increasingly emphasized in discussions as to what it means to be human (Rabett 2012; Boivin et al. 2013). Yet, with this ecological plasticity established, it is now necessary to develop methodologies that can provide more in-depth analyses into specific human adaptations in these varied ecologies across time and space. Stable carbon and oxygen isotope analysis of human and faunal tooth enamel offers significant potential in this regard, providing direct insight into the extent of human reliance on rainforest resources in a way that other methods cannot. The time-depths and taphonomies covered by this methodology mean it can be applied on Late Pleistocene, Holocene, historical, and ethnographic timescales, and to questions ranging from the earliest human movement into rainforest environments to the relationship of rainforest hunter-gatherers with incoming agricultural populations and lifeways. While the limited application of stable isotope analysis of humans in rainforest ecologies thus far is almost certainly due in part to a lack of fossil preservation, it is hoped that future discoveries will bear in mind the considerable potential of this technique.

Sri Lankan botanical, faunal, molluscan, pollen, technological, and now isotopic records, imply sustained, specialized Late Pleistocene human rainforest occupation (Deraniyagala 1992; Perera et al. 2011; Roberts et al. 2015a, 2015b, 2017a, 2017b). However, other regions of the world where early rainforest adaptations have been suggested, including Southeast Asia, Melanesia, and Africa, frequently show evidence for mobile human groups (Pavlides 2004; Summerhayes et al. 2010), mosaic habitats (Barker et al. 2007; Blome et al. 2012), and early, sporadic occupation followed by more sustained rainforest colonization during the Terminal Pleistocene (Roberts and Petraglia 2015). Stable carbon and oxygen isotope analysis of human and faunal tooth enamel has much to offer in the context of comparing the nature of human rainforest colonization, adaptation, and reliance in these regions, both across space and time. The potential for early human fossil discoveries in these regions (Demeter et al. 2012), and the existence of other hominin fossils in these regions, namely *Homo erectus* and *Homo floresiensis* (Brumm et al. 2010), should, in time, provide interesting comparative data sets in this regard.

Advances in sampling techniques and measurable sample sizes mean that high-resolution, sectional analysis of the tooth enamel of rainforest hunter-gatherers is becoming an increasingly widespread possibility. This methodology makes it possible to investigate intra- and interannual shifts in hunter-gatherer diet, particularly useful in the context of suspected seasonal rainforest-resource use in a number of regions. In the context of the adoption of agricultural lifeways in rainforest habitats by hunter-gatherers (prehistoric, historic, and ethnographic), this enables the investigation of the seasonal role of agricultural versus wild, forest foodstuffs in subsistence strategies. Combination of inter- and intratooth $\delta^{13}C$ and $\delta^{18}O$ analyses with studies of human mobility using strontium and lead isotope analysis has the potential to provide increasingly resolved pictures of human rainforest forager subsistence strategies and mobility.

Further work using these tools should also explore more recent archaeological contexts and ethnohistoric/contemporary studies where plentiful contextual information is available. Froment and Ambrose (1995) examined recent human populations inhabiting equatorial rainforest in Cameroon, and demonstrated significant variation between different groups subsisting on different types of food, with hunter-gatherer populations less ^{13}C enriched than agriculturalists. This study demonstrates that novel approaches to isotopic analysis and potential access to different tissues may be useful in modern contexts, coupled with ethnoarchaeology and documentation of different dietary trends between groups. Such an approach is likely to be particularly revealing in studies of African pygmy groups for which complex demographic, genetic, and subsistence interactions with local Bantu farmers have been postulated (Patin et al. 2009; Verdu et al. 2009). Stable isotopic analysis of diets among contemporary tropical forest groups, in contexts of habitat change and loss, will likely demonstrate that this methodology can provide hard evidence for rainforest-forager diets in modern tropical habitats as well as prehistoric settings.

ACKNOWLEDGMENTS

We would like to thank Ashley Lemke for inviting us to contribute a chapter to this volume. We would also like to thank Thure Cerling and Naomi Levin for providing the data used in figures 5.1 and 5.3, and Thomas Roberts for his help with figure 5.2. P.R. is indebted to the Natural Environmental Research Council, UK, and the University of Oxford for funding support.

REFERENCES CITED

Allen, J., C. Gosden, and J. P. White. 1989. "Human Pleistocene Adaptations in the Tropical Island Pacific: Recent Evidence from New Ireland, a Greater Australian Outlier." *Antiquity* 63(240):548–561. https://doi.org/10.1017/S0003598X00076547.

AlQahtani, S. J., M. P. Hector, and H. M. Liversidge. 2010. "Brief Communication: The London Atlas of Human Tooth Development and Eruption." *American Journal of Physical Anthropology* 142(3):481–490. https://doi.org/10.1002/ajpa.21258.

Ambrose, S. H. 1990. "Preparation and Characterization of Bone and Tooth Collagen for Stable Carbon and Isotopic Analysis." *Journal of Archaeological Science* 17(4):431–451. https://doi.org/10.1016/0305-4403(90)90007-R.

Ambrose, S. H., and L. Norr. 1993. "Experimental Evidence for the Relationship of the Carbon Isotope Ratios of Whole Diet and Dietary Protein to Those of Bone Collagen and Carbonate." In *Prehistoric Human Bone: Archaeology at the Molecular Level*, ed. J. B. Lambert and G. Grupe, 1–37. Berlin: Springer-Verlag. https://doi.org/10.1007/978-3-662-02894-0_1.

Anderson, D. D. 1997. "Cave Archaeology in Southeast Asia." *Geoarchaeology: An International Journal* 12(6):607–638. https://doi.org/10.1002/(SICI)1520-6548(199709)12:6<607::AID-GEA5>3.0.CO;2-2.

Ashton, P. S., and C. V. S. Gunatilleke. 1987. "New Light on the Plant Geography of Ceylon I: Historical Plant Geography." *Journal of Biogeography* 14(3):249–285. https://doi.org/10.2307/2844895.

Ayliffe, L. K., A. M. Lister, and A. R. Chivas. 1992. "The Preservation of Glacial-Interglacial Climatic Signatures in the Oxygen Isotopes of Elephant Skeletal Phosphate." *Palaeogeography, Palaeoclimatology, Palaeoecology* 99(3–4):179–191. https://doi.org/10.1016/0031-0182(92)90014-V.

Bailey, R., G. Head, M. Jenike, B. Owen, R. Rechtman, and E. Zechenter. 1989. "Hunting and Gathering in Tropical Rain Forest: Is It Possible?" *American Anthropologist* 91(1):59–82. https://doi.org/10.1525/aa.1989.91.1.02a00040.

Bailey, R. C., and T. N. Headland. 1991. "The Tropical Rain Forest: Is It a Productive Environment for Human Foragers?" *Human Ecology* 19(2):261–285. https://doi.org/10.1007/BF00888748.

Balasse, M. 2002. "Reconstructing Dietary and Environmental History from Enamel Isotopic Analysis: Time Resolution of Intra-Tooth Sequential Sampling." *International Journal of Osteoarchaeology* 12(3):155–165. https://doi.org/10.1002/oa.601.

Balée, W. 1994. *Footprints of the Forest: Ka'apar Ethnobotany—The Historical Ecology of Plant Utilization by an Amazonian People*. New York: Columbia University Press.

Barbour, M. M. 2007. "Stable Oxygen Isotope Composition of Plant Tissue: A Review." *Functional Plant Biology* 34(2):83–94. https://doi.org/10.1071/FP06228.

Barker, G. 2005. "The Archaeology of Foraging and Farming at Niah Cave, Sarawak." *Asian Perspective* 44(1):90–106. https://doi.org/10.1353/asi.2005.0004.

Barker, G., ed. 2013. *The Archaeology of the Niah Caves, Sarawak*. McDonald Institute Monographs, Vol. 1, *Rainforest Foraging and Farming in Island Southeast Asia*. Cambridge, UK: McDonald Institute for Archaeological Research.

Barker, Graeme, Huw Barton, Michael Bird, Patrick Daly, Ipoi Datan, Alan Dykes, Lucy Farr, David Gilbertson, Barbara Harrisson, Chris Hunt, et al. 2007. "The 'Human Revolution' in Lowland Tropical Southeast Asia: The Antiquity and

Behaviour of Anatomically Modern Humans at Niah Cave (Sarawak, Borneo)." *Journal of Human Evolution* 52(3):243–261. https://doi.org/10.1016/j.jhevol.2006.08.011.

Barton, H. 2005. "The Case for Rainforest Foragers: The Starch Record at Niah Cave, Sarawak." *Asian Perspective* 44(1):56–72. https://doi.org/10.1353/asi.2005.0005.

Barton, H., T. Denham, K. Neumann, and M. Arroyo-Kalin. 2012. "Long-Term Perspectives on Human Occupation of Tropical Rainforests: An Introductory Overview." *Quaternary International* 249:1–3. https://doi.org/10.1016/j.quaint.2011.07.044.

Barton, H., P. J. Piper, R. Rabett, and I. Reeds. 2009. "Composite Hunting Technologies from the Terminal Pleistocene and Early Holocene, Niah Cave, Borneo." *Journal of Archaeological Science* 36(8):1708–1714. https://doi.org/10.1016/j.jas.2009.03.027.

Bellwood, P. 1997. *Prehistory of the Indo-Malaysian Archipelago*. 2nd ed. Honolulu: University of Hawai'i Press.

Bellwood, P., R. Gillespie, G. B. Thompson, J. S. Vogel, I. W. Ardika, and Ipoi Datan. 1992. "New Dates for Prehistoric Asian Rice." *Asian Perspective* 32:37–60.

Bird, M., D. Taylor, and C. Hunt. 2005. "Palaeoenvironments of Insular Southeast Asia during the Last Glacial Period: A Savanna Corridor in Sundaland?" *Quaternary Science Reviews* 24(20–21):2228–2242. https://doi.org/10.1016/j.quascirev.2005.04.004.

Blinkhorn, J., H. Achyuthan, M. Petraglia, and P. Ditchfield. 2013. "Middle Palaeolithic Occupation in the Thar Desert during the Upper Pleistocene: The Signature of a Modern Human Exit out of Africa." *Quaternary Science Reviews* 77:233–238. https://doi.org/10.1016/j.quascirev.2013.06.012.

Blome, M. W., A. S. Cohen, C. A. Tryon, A. S. Brooks, and J. Russell. 2012. "The Environmental Context for the Origins of Modern Human Diversity: A Synthesis of Regional Variability in African Climate 150,000–30,000 Years Ago." *Journal of Human Evolution* 62(5):563–592. https://doi.org/10.1016/j.jhevol.2012.01.011.

Boivin, N., D. Q. Fuller, R. Dennell, R. Allaby, and M. D. Petraglia. 2013. "Human Dispersal across Diverse Environments of Asia during the Upper Pleistocene." *Quaternary International* 300:32–47. https://doi.org/10.1016/j.quaint.2013.01.008.

Bonafini, M., M. Pellegrini, P. Ditchfield, and A. M. Pollard. 2013. "Investigation of the 'Canopy Effect' in the Isotope Ecology of Temperate Woodlands." *Journal of Archaeological Science* 40(11):3926–3935. https://doi.org/10.1016/j.jas.2013.03.028.

Brumm, A., G. M. Jensen, G. D. van den Bergh, M. J. Morwood, I. Kurniawan, F. Aziz, and M. Storey. 2010. "Hominins on Flores, Indonesia, by One Million Years Ago." *Nature* 464(7289):748–752. https://doi.org/10.1038/nature08844.

Buchmann, N., J.-M. Guehl, T. S. Barigah, and J. R. Ehleringer. 1997. "Interseasonal Comparison of CO_2 Concentrations, Isotopic Composition, and Carbon Dynamics in an Amazonian Rainforest (French Guiana)." *Oecologia* 110(1):120–131. https://doi.org/10.1007/s004420050140.

Cerling, T. E., and J. M. Harris. 1999. "Carbon Isotope Fractionation between Diet and Bioapatite in Ungulate Mammals and Implications for Ecological and Paleoecological Studies." *Oecologia* 120(3):347–363. https://doi.org/10.1007/s004420050868.

Cerling, T. E., J. M. Harris, M. G. Leakey, and N. Mudida. 2003a. "Stable Isotope Ecology of Northern Kenya with Emphasis on the Turkana Basin." In *Lothagam: The Dawn of Humanity*, ed. M. G. Leakey and J. M. Harris, 583–594. New York: Columbia University Press. https://doi.org/10.7312/leak11870-023.

Cerling, T. E., J. M. Harris, M. G. Leakey, B. H. Passey, and N. E. Levin. 2010. "Stable Carbon and Oxygen Isotopes in East African Mammals: Modern and Fossil." In *Cenozoic Mammals of Africa*, ed. L. Werdelin and W. J. Sanders, 941–952. Oakland: University of California Press. https://doi.org/10.1525/california/9780520257214.003.0048.

Cerling, Thure E., John M. Harris, and Meave G. Leakey. 1999. "Browsing and Grazing in Elephants: The Isotope Record of Modern and Fossil Proboscideans." *Oecologia* 120(3):364–374. https://doi.org/10.1007/s004420050869.

Cerling, T. E., J. M. Harris, and B. H. Passey. 2003b. "Diets of East African Bovidae Based on Stable Isotope Analysis." *Journal of Mammalogy* 84(2):456–470. https://doi.org/10.1644/1545-1542(2003)084<0456:DOEABB>2.0.CO;2.

Cerling, T. E., J. A. Hart, and T. B. Hart. 2004. "Isotope Ecology in the Ituri Forest." *Oecologia* 138(1):5–12. https://doi.org/10.1007/s00442-003-1375-4.

Cerling, T. E., F. K. Manthi, E. N. Mbua, L. N. Leakey, M. G. Leakey, R. E. Leakey, F. H. Brown, F. E. Grine, J. A. Hart, P. Kaleme, et al. 2013. "Stable Isotope-Based Diet Reconstructions of Turkana Basin Hominins." *Proceedings of the National Academy of Sciences of the United States of America* 110(26):10501–10506. https://doi.org/10.1073/pnas.1222568110.

Cerling, T. E., E. Mbua, F. M. Kirera, F. K. Manthi, F. E. Grine, M. G. Leakey, M. Sponheimer, and K. T. Uno. 2011. "Diet of *Paranthropus boisei* in the Early Pleistocene of East Africa." *Proceedings of the National Academy of Sciences of the United States of America* 108(23):9337–9341. https://doi.org/10.1073/pnas.1104627108.

Codron, J., D. Codron, M. Sponheimer, K. Kirkman, K. J. Duffy, E. J. Raubenheimer, J.-L. Melice, R. Grant, M. Clauss, and J. A. Lee-Thorp. 2014. "Stable Isotope Series from Elephant Ivory Reveal Lifetime Histories of a True Dietary Generalist." *Proceedings of the Royal Society B, Biological Sciences*. DOI:10.1098/rspb.2011.2472.

Colinvaux, P. A., and M. B. Bush. 1991. "The Rain-Forest Ecosystem as a Resource for Hunting and Gathering." *American Anthropologist* 93(1):153–160. https://doi.org/10.1525/aa.1991.93.1.02a00100.

Colinvaux, P., P. de Oliveira, E. Moreno, C. Miller, and M. Bush. 1996. "A Long Pollen Record from Lowland Amazonia: Forest and Cooling in Glacial Times." *Science* 274(5284):85–88. https://doi.org/10.1126/science.274.5284.85.

Craig, H. 1953. "The Geochemistry of the Stable Carbon Isotope." *Geochimica et Cosmochimica Acta* 3(2–3):53–92. https://doi.org/10.1016/0016-7037(53)90001-5.

Crassard, R., M. D. Petraglia, N. A. Drake, P. Breeze, B. Gratuze, A. Alsharekh, M. Arbach, H. S. Groucutt, L. Khalidi, N. Michelsen, et al. 2013. "Middle Palaeolithic and Neolithic Occupations around Mundafan Palaeolake, Saudi Arabia: Implications for Climate Change and Human Dispersals." *pLoS One* 8(7):69665. https://doi.org/10.1371/journal.pone.0069665.

Crowley, B. E. 2012. "Stable Isotope Techniques and Applications for Primatologists." *International Journal of Primatology* 33(3):673–701. https://doi.org/10.1007/s10764-012-9582-7.

Crowley, B. E., L. R. Godfrey, T. P. Guilderson, P. Zermeño, P. L. Koch, and N. J. Dominy. 2014. "Extinction and Ecology Retreat in a Community of Primates." *Proceedings of the Royal Society B, Biological Sciences.* DOI: 10.1098/rspb.2012.0727.

Dansgaard, W. 1964. "Stable Isotopes in Precipitation." *Tellus* 16(4):436–468. https://doi.org/10.3402/tellusa.v16i4.8993.

da Silveira, Leonel, Lobo Sternberg, Stephen S. Mulkey, and S. Joseph Wright. 1989. "Oxygen Isotope Ratio Stratification in a Tropical Moist Forest." *Oecologia* 81(1):51–56. https://doi.org/10.1007/BF00377009.

Demeter, F., L. L. Shackelford, A.-M. Bacon, P. Duringer, K. Westaway, T. Sayavongkhamdy, J. Braga, P. Sichanthongtip, P. Khamdalavong, J.-L. Ponche, et al. 2012. "Anatomically Modern Human in Southeast Asia (Laos) by 46 ka." *Proceedings of the National Academy of Sciences of the United States of America* 109(36):14375–14380. https://doi.org/10.1073/pnas.1208104109.

Deraniyagala, S. U. 1992. *The Prehistory of Sri Lanka: An Ecological Perspective.* 2nd ed. Colombo, Sri Lanka: Department of Archaeological Survey.

Deraniyagala, S. U. 2007. "The Prehistory and Protohistory of Sri Lanka." In *The Art and Archaeology of Sri Lanka, 1,* ed. P. L. Prematilleke, S. Bandaranayake, S. U. Deraniyagala, and R. Silva, 1–96. Colombo, Sri Lanka: Central Cultural Fund.

Dupont, L., S. Jahns, F. Marret, and S. Ning. 2000. "Vegetation Change in Equatorial West Africa: Time Slices for the 150ka." *Palaeogeography, Palaeoclimatology, Palaeoecology* 155(1–2):95–122. https://doi.org/10.1016/S0031-0182(99)00095-4.

Ecker, M., H. Bocherens, M.-A. Julien, F. Rivals, J.-P. Raynal, and M.-H. Moncel. 2013. "Middle Pleistocene Ecology and Neanderthal Subsistence: Insights from Stable Isotope Analyses in Payre (Ardèche, southeastern France)." *Journal of Human Evolution* 65(4):363–373. https://doi.org/10.1016/j.jhevol.2013.06.013.

Ehleringer, J. R., P. W. Rundel, and K. A. Nagy. 1986. "Stable Isotopes in Physiological Ecology and Food Web Research." *Trends in Ecology & Evolution* 1(2):42–45. https://doi.org/10.1016/0169-5347(86)90072-8.

Erdelen, W. 1988. "Forest Ecosystems and Nature Conservation in Sri Lanka." *Biological Conservation* 43(2):115–135. https://doi.org/10.1016/0006-3207(88)90086-9.

Evans, D. 2016. "Airborne Laser Scanning as a Method for Exploring Long-Term Socio-Ecological Dynamics in Cambodia." *Journal of Archaeological Science* 74:164–175. https://doi.org/10.1016/j.jas.2016.05.009.

Farmer, V. C. 1974. *The Infrared Spectra of Minerals*. London: The Mineralogical Society. https://doi.org/10.1180/mono-4.

Farquhar, G. D., J. R. Ehleringer, and K. T. Hubick. 1989. "Carbon Isotope Discrimination and Photosynthesis." *Annual Review of Plant Physiology and Plant Molecular Biology* 40(1):503–537. https://doi.org/10.1146/annurev.pp.40.060189.002443.

Flanagan, L. B., J. P. Comstock, and J. R. Ehleringer. 1991. "Comparison of Modelled and Observed Environmental Influences on the Stable Oxygen and Hydrogen Isotope Composition of Leaf Water in *Phaseolus vulgaris* L." *Plant Physiology* 96(2):588–596. https://doi.org/10.1104/pp.96.2.588.

Francey, R. J., C. E. Allison, D. M. Etheridge, C. M. Trudinger, I. G. Enting, M. Leuenberger, R. L. Langenfelds, E. Michel, and L. P. Steele. 1999. "A 1000-Year High Precision Record of δ^{13}C in Atmospheric CO_2." *Tellus* 51(2):170–193. https://doi.org/10.3402/tellusb.v51i2.16269.

Froment, A., and S. H. Ambrose. 1995. "Analyses tissulaires isotopiques et reconstruction du regime alimentaire en milieu tropical: Implications pour l'archeologie." *Bulletins et Memoires de la Société d'Anthropologie de Paris* 7(3):79–98. https://doi.org/10.3406/bmsap.1995.2412.

Gamble, C. 1993. *Timewalkers: The Prehistory of Global Colonization*. Stroud, UK: Alan Sutton.

Gamble, C., W. Davies, P. Pettitt, and M. Richards. 2004. "The Evolutionary Legacy of the Ice Ages." *Royal Society B, Biological Sciences* 359:243–254.

Gat, J. R. 1980. "The Isotopes of Oxygen and Hydrogen in Precipitation." In *Handbook of Environmental Isotope Geochemistry*, ed. P. Fritz and J. C. Fontes, 21–47. Amsterdam: Elsevier Scientific Publishing. https://doi.org/10.1016/B978-0-444-41780-0.50007-9.

Gonfiantini, R., S. Gratziu, and E. Tongiorgi. 1965. "Oxygen Isotopic Composition of Water in Leaves." In *Isotopes and Radiation in Soil Plant Nutrition Studies*, 405–410. Technical Report Series No. 206. Vienna: Isotope Atomic Energy Commission.

Gosden, C. 2010. "When Humans Arrived in the New Guinea Highlands." *Science* 330(6000):41–42. https://doi.org/10.1126/science.1195448.

Gosden, C., and N. Robertson. 1991. "Models for Matenkupkum: Interpreting a Late Pleistocene Site from Southern New Ireland, Papua New Guinea." In *Report of* the *Lapita Homeland Project*, ed. J. Allen, and C. Gosden, 20–91. Occasional Papers in Prehistory 20. Canberra: Department of Prehistory. Research School of Pacific Studies, The Australian National University.

Groucutt, H. S., and M. D. Petraglia. 2012. "The Prehistory of the Arabian Peninsula: Deserts, Dispersals, and Demography." *Evolutionary Anthropology* 21(3):113–125. https://doi.org/10.1002/evan.21308.

Gunatilleke, I.A.U.N., C.V.S. Gunatilleke, and M.A.A.B. Dilhan. 2005. "Plant Biogeography and Conservation of the South-Western Hill Forests of Sri Lanka." *Raffles Bulletin of Zoology* Supplement No. 12:9–22.

Haberle, S. G., C. Lentfer, S. O'Donnell, and T. Denham. 2012. "The Palaeoenvironments of Kuk Swamp from the Beginnings of Agriculture in the Highlands of Papua New Guinea." *Quaternary International* 249:129–139. https://doi.org/10.1016/j.quaint.2011.07.048.

Harris, J. M., and T. E. Cerling. 2002. "Dietary Adaptations of Extant and Neogene African Suids." *Journal of Zoology* 256(1):45–54. https://doi.org/10.1017/S0952836902000067.

Hart, T. B., and J. A. Hart. 1986. "The Ecological Basis of Hunter-Gatherer Subsistence in African Rain Forests." *Human Ecology* 14(1):29–55. https://doi.org/10.1007/BF00889209.

Headland, T. N., L. A. Reid, M. G. Bicchieri, Charles A. Bishop, Robert Blust, Nicholas E. Flanders, Peter M. Gardner, Karl L. Hutterer, Arkadiusz Marciniak, Robert F. Schroeder, et al. 1989. "Hunter-Gatherers and Their Neighbors from Prehistory to the Present." *Current Anthropology* 30(1):43–66. https://doi.org/10.1086/203710.

Hedges, R.E.M., J. G. Clement, C.D.L. Thomas, and T. C. O'Connell. 2007. "Collagen Turnover in the Adult Femoral Mid-Shaft: Modeled from Anthropogenic Radiocarbon Tracer Measurements." *American Journal of Physical Anthropology* 133(2):808–816. https://doi.org/10.1002/ajpa.20598.

Henry, A. G., P. S. Ungar, B. H. Passey, M. Sponheimer, L. Rossouw, M. Bamford, P. Sandberg, D. J. de Ruiter, and L. Berger. 2012. "The Diet of *Australopithecus sediba.*" *Nature* 48 (7405):90–93. https://doi.org/10.1038/nature11185.

Hillson, S. 1996. *Dental Anthropology.* Cambridge, UK: Cambridge University Press. https://doi.org/10.1017/CBO9781139170697.

Hutterer, K. L. 1983. "The Natural and Cultural History of Southeast Asian Agriculture." *Anthropos* 78:169–212.

Jackson, P. C., F. C. Meinzer, G. Goldstein, N. M. Holbrook, J. Cavelier, and F. Rada. 1993. "Environmental and Physiological Influences on Carbon Isotope Composition of Gap and Understory Plants in a Lowland Tropical Forest." In *Stable Isotopes and Plant Carbon-Water Relations*, ed. J. R. Ehleringer, A. E. Hall, and G. D.

Farquhar, 131–140. San Diego, CA: Academic Press. https://doi.org/10.1016/B978-0
-08-091801-3.50016-7.

Kennedy, K.A.R. 2000. *God-Apes and Fossil Men: Palaeoanthropology of South Asia.*
Ann Arbor: University of Michigan Press. https://doi.org/10.3998/mpub.16180.

Kourampas, N., I. A. Simpson, N. Perera, S. U. Deraniyagala, and W. H. Wijeya-
pala. 2009. "Rockshelter Sedimentation in a Dynamic Tropical Landscape: Late
Pleistocene–Early Holocene Archaeological Deposits in Kitulgala Beli-lena,
Southwestern Sri Lanka." *Geoarchaeology: An International Journal* 24(6):677–714.
https://doi.org/10.1002/gea.20287.

Krigbaum, J. 2001. "Human Paleodiet in Tropical Southeast Asia; Isotopic Evidence from Niah Cave and Gua Cha." PhD thesis, New York University, New
York.

Krigbaum, J. 2003. "Neolithic Subsistence Patterns in Northern Borneo Reconstructed with Stable Carbon Isotopes of Enamel." *Journal of Anthropological
Archaeology* 22(3):292–304. https://doi.org/10.1016/S0278-4165(03)00041-2.

Krigbaum, J. 2005. "Reconstructing Human Subsistence in the West Mouth (Niah
Cave) Sarawak) Burial Series Using Stable Isotopes of Carbon." *Asian Perspective*
44(1):73–89. https://doi.org/10.1353/asi.2005.0008.

Lee-Thorp, J. A. 1989. "Stable Carbon Isotopes in Deep Time: The Diets of Fossil
Fauna and Hominids." PhD thesis, University of Cape Town, Cape Town, South
Africa.

Lee-Thorp, J. A. 2000. "Preservation of Biogenic Carbon Isotopic Signals in Plio-
Pleistocene Bone and Tooth Mineral." In *Biogeochemical Approaches to Paleodietary
Analysis,* ed. S. H. Ambrose and M. A. Katzenberg, 89–115. New York: Kluwer
Academic/Plenum Publishers.

Lee-Thorp, J. A. 2008. "On Isotopes and Old Bones." *Archaeometry* 50(6):925–950.
https://doi.org/10.1111/j.1475-4754.2008.00441.x.

Lee-Thorp, J. A., A. Likius, H. T. Mackaye, P. Vignaud, M. Sponheimer, and M.
Brunet. 2012. "Isotopic Evidence for an Early Shift to C_4 Resources by Pliocene
Hominins in Chad." *Proceedings of the National Academy of Sciences of the United
States of America* 109(50):20369–20372. https://doi.org/10.1073/pnas.1204209109.

Lee-Thorp, J. A., J. C. Sealy, and N. J. van der Merwe. 1989b. "Stable Carbon Isotope
Ratio Differences between Bone Collagen and Bone Apatite, and Their Relationship to Diet." *Journal of Archaeological Science* 16(6):585–599. https://doi.org/10.1016
/0305-4403(89)90024-1.

Lee-Thorp, J. A., M. Sponheimer, B. H. Passey, D. J. de Ruiter, and T. E. Cerling. 2010.
"Stable Isotopes in Fossil Hominin Tooth Enamel Suggest a Fundamental Dietary
Shift in the Pliocene." *Philosophical Transactions of the Royal Society of London. Series
B, Biological Sciences* 365(1556):3389–3396. https://doi.org/10.1098/rstb.2010.0059.

Lee-Thorp, J. A., J. F. Thackeray, and N. J. van der Merwe. 2000. "The Hunters and the Hunted Revisited." *Journal of Human Evolution* 39(6):565–576. https://doi.org /10.1006/jhev.2000.0436.

Lee-Thorp, J. A., and N. J. van der Merwe. 1987. "Carbon Isotope Analysis of Fossil Bone Apatite." *South African Journal of Science* 83:712–715.

Lee-Thorp, J. A., N. J. van der Merwe, and C. K. Brain. 1989a. "Isotopic Evidence for Dietary Differences between Two Extinct Baboon Species from Swartkrans (South Africa)." *Journal of Human Evolution* 18(3):183–189. https://doi.org/10.1016 /0047-2484(89)90048-1.

Lee-Thorp, J. A., N. J. van der Merwe, and C. K. Brain. 1994. "Diet of *Australopithecus robustus* at Swartkrans Deduced from Stable Carbon Isotope Ratios." *Journal of Human Evolution* 27(4):361–372. https://doi.org/10.1006/jhev.1994.1050.

LeGeros, R. Z. 1967. "Crystallographic Studies of the Carbonate Substitution in the Apatite Structure." PhD thesis, New York University, New York.

LeGeros, R. Z. 1991. "Calcium Phosphates in Oral Biology and Medicine." *Monographs in Oral Science* 15:1–201. https://doi.org/10.1159/000419232.

Levin, N. E., T. E. Cerling, B. H. Passey, J. M. Harris, and J. R. Ehleringer. 2006. "A Stable Isotope Aridity Index for Terrestrial Environments." *Proceedings of the National Academy of Sciences of the United States of America* 103(30):11201–11205. https://doi.org/10.1073/pnas.0604719103.

Levin, N. E., Y. Haile-Selassie, S. R. Frost, and B. Z. Saylor. 2015. "Dietary Change among Hominins and Cercopithecids in Ethiopia during the Early Pliocene." *Proceedings of the National Academy of Sciences of the United States of America* 112(40):12304–12309. https://doi.org/10.1073/pnas.1424982112.

Levin, N. E., S. W. Simpson, J. Quade, T. E. Cerling, and S. R. Frost. 2008. "Herbivore Enamel Carbon Isotopic Composition and the Environmental Context of *Ardipithecus* at Gona, Ethiopia." In *The Geology of Early Humans in the Horn of Africa*, vol. 446. ed. J. Quade and J. G. Wynn, 215–234. Geological Society of America Special Paper. Boulder, CO: Geological Society of America.

Lloyd-Smith, L., J. Krigbaum, and B. Valentine. 2015. "Social Affiliation, Settlement Pattern Histories, and Subsistence Change in Neolithic Borneo." In *The Routledge Handbook of Bioarchaeology in Southeast Asia and the Pacific*, ed. M. Oxenham and H. Buckley, 257–288. London: Routledge.

Longinelli, A. 1984. "Oxygen Isotopes in Mammal Bone Phosphate: A New Tool for Paleohydrological and Paleoclimatological Research?" *Geochimica et Cosmochimica Acta* 48(2):385–390. https://doi.org/10.1016/0016-7037(84)90259-X.

Luz, B., and Y. Kolodny. 1985. "Oxygen Isotope Variations in Phosphate of Biogenic Apatites, IV: Mammal Teeth and Bones." *Earth and Planetary Science Letters* 75(1):29–36. https://doi.org/10.1016/0012-821X(85)90047-0.

Luz, B., Y. Kolodny, and M. Horowitz. 1984. "Fractionation of Oxygen Isotopes between Mammalian Bone Phosphate and Environmental Drinking Water." *Geochimica et Cosmochimica Acta* 48(8):1689–1693. https://doi.org/10.1016/0016-7037 (84)90338-7.

Mellars, P. 2006. "Why Did Modern Human Populations Disperse from Africa ca. 60,000 Years Ago? A New Model." *Proceedings of the National Academy of Sciences of the United States of America* 103(25):9381–9386. https://doi.org/10.1073/pnas .0510792103.

Mercader, J. 2002a. "Forest People: The Role of African Rainforests in Human Evolution and Dispersal." *Evolutionary Anthropology* 11(3):117–124. https://doi.org/10 .1002/evan.10022.

Mercader, J., ed. 2002b. *Under the Canopy: The Archaeology of Tropical Rainforests*. New Brunswick, NJ: Rutgers University Press.

Mercader, J., R. Martí, I. González, A. Sánchez, and P. García. 2003. "Archaeological Site Formation in Rain Forests: Insights from the Ituri Rock Shelters, Congo." *Journal of Archaeological Science* 30(1):45–65. https://doi.org/10.1006/jasc .2002.0810.

Mercader, J., F. Runge, L. Vrydaghs, H. Doutrelepont, Corneille E N. Ewango, and J. Juan-Tresseras. 2000. "Phytoliths from Archaeological Sites in the Tropical Forest of Ituri, Democratic Republic of Congo." *Quaternary Research* 54(01):102–112. https://doi.org/10.1006/qres.2000.2150.

Michel, V., P. Ildefonse, and G. Morin. 1996. "Assessment of Archaeological Bone and Dentine Preservation from Lazaret Cave (Middle Pleistocene) in France." *Palaeogeography, Palaeoclimatology, Palaeoecology* 126(1–2):109–119. https://doi.org/10 .1016/S0031-0182(96)00074-0.

Nelson, S. 2003. *The Extinction of Sivapithecus: Faunal and Environmental Changes Surrounding the Disappearance of a Miocene Hominoid in the Siwaliks of Pakistan*. American School of Prehistoric Research Monographs, vol. 1. Boston, MA: Brill Academic Publishers.

Nelson, S. 2007. "Isotopic Reconstructions of Habitation Change Surrounding the Extinction of *Sivapithecus*, a Miocene Hominoid, in the Siwalik Group of Pakistan." *Palaeogeography, Palaeoclimatology, Palaeoecology* 243(1–2):204–222. https://doi .org/10.1016/j.palaeo.2006.07.017.

O'Connor, S., G. Robertson, and K. P. Aplin. 2014. "Are Osseous Artefacts a Window to Perishable Material Culture? Implications of an Unusually Complex Bone Tool from the Late Pleistocene of East Timor." *Journal of Human Evolution* 67:108–119. https://doi.org/10.1016/j.jhevol.2013.12.002.

O'Leary, M. 1981. "Carbon Isotope Fractionation in Plants." *Phytochemistry* 20(4):553–567. https://doi.org/10.1016/0031-9422(81)85134-5.

Ometto, J.P.H.B., J. R. Ehleringer, T. F. Domingues, J. A. Berry, F. Y. Ishida, E. Mazzi, N. Higuchi, L. B. Flanagan, G. B. Nardoto, and L. A. Martinelli. 2006. "The Stable Carbon and Nitrogen Isotopic Composition of Vegetation in Tropical Forests of the Amazon Basin, Brazil." *Biogeochemistry* 79(1–2):251–274. https://doi.org/10.1007/s10533-006-9008-8.

Passey, B. H., T. E. Cerling, G. T. Schuster, T. F. Robinson, B. L. Roeder, and S. K. Krueger. 2005. "Inverse Methods for Estimating Primary Input Signals from Time-Averaged Isotope Profiles." *Geochimica et Cosmochimica Acta* 69(16):4101–4116. https://doi.org/10.1016/j.gca.2004.12.002.

Patin, E., L. Guillaume, L. B. Barreiro, A. Salas, O. Semino, S. Santachiara-Benerecetti, K. K. Kidd, J. R. Kidd, L. Van der Veen, J.-M. Hombert, et al. 2009. "Inferring the Demographic History of African Farmers and Pygmy Hunter-Gatherers Using a Multilocus Resequencing Data Set." *PLoS One*. https://doi.org/10.1371/journal.pgen.1000448.

Pavlides, C. 2004. "From Misisil Cave to Eliva Hamlet: Rediscovering the Pleistocene in Interior West New Britain." In *A Pacific Odyssey: Archaeology and Anthropology in the Western Pacific*. Papers in honour of Jim Specht, ed. V. Auenbrow, R. Fullager, 97–108. Records of the Australian Museum, Supplement 29. Sydney: Australian Museum.

Pearcy, R. W., and W. A. Pfitsch. 1991. "Influence of Sunflecks on the $\delta^{13}C$ of *Adenocaulon bicolor* Plants Occurring in Contrasting Forest Understory Microsites." *Oecologia* 86(4):457–462. https://doi.org/10.1007/BF00318310.

Perera, N. 2010. *Prehistoric Sri Lanka: Late Pleistocene Rockshelters and an Open Air Site.* BAR International Series. Oxford, UK: Archaeopress.

Perera, N., N. Kourampas, I. A. Simpson, S. U. Deraniyagala, D. Bulbeck, J. Kamminga, J. Perera, D. Q. Fuller, K. Szabo, and N. V. Oliveira. 2011. "People of the Ancient Rainforest: Late Pleistocene Foragers at the Batadomba-lena Rockshelter, Sri Lanka." *Journal of Human Evolution* 61(3):254–269. https://doi.org/10.1016/j.jhevol.2011.04.001.

Perera, N., P. Roberts, and M. Petraglia. 2016. "Bone Technology in South Asia from Late Pleistocene Rockshelter Deposits in Sri Lanka." In *Osseous Projectile Weaponry: Towards an Understanding of Pleistocene Cultural Variability*, ed. M. C. Langley. VERT Series. New York: Springer-Verlag. https://doi.org/10.1007/978-94-024-0899-7_12.

Pickford, M., B. Senut, and C. Mourer-Chauviré. 2004. "Early Pliocene Tragulidae and Peafowls in the Rift Valley, Kenya: Evidence for Rainforest in East Africa." *Comptes Rendus. Palévol* 3(3):179–189. https://doi.org/10.1016/j.crpv.2004.01.004.

Poyart, C. F., A. Freminet, and E. Bursaux. 1975. "The Exchange of Bone CO_2 in Vivo." *Respiration Physiology* 25(1):101–107. https://doi.org/10.1016/0034-5687(75)90054-7.

Premathilake, R. T. 2012. "Human Used Upper Montane Ecosystem in the Horton Plains, Central Sri Lanka: A Link to Late Glacial-Early Holocene Climate and Environmental Changes." *Quaternary Science Reviews* 50:23–42. https://doi.org/10.1016/j.quascirev.2012.07.002.

Premathilake, R., and J. Risberg. 2003. "Late Quaternary Climate History of the Horton Plains, Central Sri Lanka." *Quaternary Science Reviews* 22(14):1525–1541. https://doi.org/10.1016/S0277-3791(03)00128-8.

Quade, J., T. E. Cerling, P. Andrews, and B. Alpagut. 1995. "Paleodietary Reconstruction of Miocene Faunas from Paşalar, Turkey, Using Stable Carbon and Oxygen Isotopes of Fossil Tooth Enamel." *Journal of Human Evolution* 28(4):373–384. https://doi.org/10.1006/jhev.1995.1029.

Rabett, R. J. 2005. "The Early Exploitation of Southeast Asian Mangroves: Bone Technology from Caves and Open Sites." *Asian Perspective* 44(1):154–179. https://doi.org/10.1353/asi.2005.0013.

Rabett, R. J. 2012. *Human Adaptation in the Asian Palaeolithic.* Cambridge, UK: Cambridge University Press. https://doi.org/10.1017/CBO9781139087582.

Rey, C., V. Renugopalakrishnan, M. Shimizu, B. Collins, and M. J. Glimcher. 1991. "A Resolution Enhanced Fourier Transform Infrared Spectroscopic Study of the Environment of the CO_3 Ion in the Mineral Phase of Enamel during Its Formation and Maturation." *Calcified Tissue International* 49(4):259–268. https://doi.org/10.1007/BF02556215.

Roberts, P., N. Boivin, J. Lee-Thorp, M. Petraglia, and J. Stock. 2016. "Tropical Forests and the Genus *Homo*." *Evolutionary Anthropology* 25(6):306–317. https://doi.org/10.1002/evan.21508.

Roberts, P., N. Boivin, and M. D. Petraglia. 2015a. "The Sri Lankan 'Microlithic' Tradition c. 38,000 to 3000 Years Ago: Tropical Technologies and Adaptations of *Homo sapiens* at the Southern Edge of Asia." *Journal of World Prehistory* 28(2):69–112. https://doi.org/10.1007/s10963-015-9085-5.

Roberts, P., D. Gaffney, J. Lee-Thorp, and G. Summerhayes. 2017a. "Persistent Tropical Foraging in the Highlands of Terminal Pleistocene/Holocene New Guinea." *Nature Ecology & Evolution* 1 (3): 0044. https://doi.org/10.1038/s41559-016-0044.

Roberts, P., N. Perera, O. Wedage, S. Deraniyagala, J. Perera, S. Eregama, A. Gledhill, M. D. Petraglia, and J. A. Lee-Thorp. 2015b. "Direct Evidence for Human Reliance on Rainforest Resources in Late Pleistocene Sri Lanka." *Science* 347(6227):1246–1249. https://doi.org/10.1126/science.aaa1230.

Roberts, Patrick, Nimal Perera, Oshan Wedage, Siran Deraniyagala, Jude Perera, Saman Eregama, Michael D. Petraglia, and Julia A. Lee-Thorp. 2017b. "Fruits of the Forest: Human Stable Isotope Ecology and Rainforest Adaptations in Late

Pleistocene and Holocene (~ 36 to 3 ka) Sri Lanka." *Journal of Human Evolution* 106:102–118. https://doi.org/10.1016/j.jhevol.2017.01.015.

Roberts, P., and M. D. Petraglia. 2015. "Pleistocene Rainforests: Barriers or Attractive Environments for Early Human Foragers?" *World Archaeology* 47(5):718–739. https://doi.org/10.1080/00438243.2015.1073119.

Rozanski, K., L. Araguás-Araguás, and R. Gonfiantini. 1993. "Isotopic Patterns in Modern Global Precipitation." In *Climate Change in Continental Isotopic Records*, ed. P. K. Swart, K. C. Lohmann, J. McKenzie, and S. Savin, 1–35. Washington, DC: American Geophysical Union.

Sandberg, P. A., J. E. Loudon, and M. Sponheimer. 2012. "Stable Isotope Analysis in Primatology: A Critical Review." *American Journal of Primatology* 74(11):969–989. https://doi.org/10.1002/ajp.22053.

Schoeninger, M. J., U. T. Iwaniec, and K. E. Glander. 1997. "Stable Isotope Ratios Indicate Diet and Habitat Use in New World Monkeys." *American Journal of Physical Anthropology* 103(1):69–83. https://doi.org/10.1002/(SICI)1096-8644(199705)103:1<69::AID-AJPA5>3.0.CO;2-8.

Sémah, A.-M., and F. Sémah. 2012. "The Rain Forest in Java through the Quaternary and Its Relationships with Humans (Adaptation, Exploitation and Impact on the Forest)." *Quaternary International* 249:120–128. https://doi.org/10.1016/j.quaint.2011.06.013.

Sémah, F., A.-M. Sémah, and T. Simanjuntak. 2002. "More than a Million Years of Human Occupation in Insular Southeast Asia: The Early Archaeology of Eastern and Central Java." In *Under the Canopy: The Archaeology of Tropical Rain Forests*, ed. J. Mercader, 161–190. New Brunswick, NJ: Rutgers University Press.

Sheshshayee, M. S., H. Bindumadhava, R. Ramesh, T. G. Prasad, M. R. Lakshminarayana, and M. Udayakumar. 2005. "Oxygen Isotope Enrichment ($\Delta^{18}O$) as a Measure of Time-Averaged Transpiration Rate." *Journal of Experimental Botany* 56(422):3033–3039. https://doi.org/10.1093/jxb/eri300.

Smith, B. N., and S. Epstein. 1971. "Two Categories of $^{13}C/^{12}C$ Ratios for Higher Plants." *Plant Physiology* 47(3):380–384. https://doi.org/10.1104/pp.47.3.380.

Somaratne, S., and A. H. Dhanapala. 1996. "Potential Impact of Global Climate Change on Forest in Sri Lanka." In *Climate Change Variability and Adaptation in Asia and the Pacific*, ed. L. Erda, W. Bolhofer, S. Huq, S. Lenhart, S. K. Mukherjee, J. B. Smith, and J. Wisniewski, 129–135. Dordrecht, The Netherlands: Kluwer. https://doi.org/10.1007/978-94-017-1053-4_12.

Sponheimer, M. 1999. "Isotopic Paleoecology of the Makapansgat Limeworks Fauna." PhD thesis, the State University of New Jersey.

Sponheimer, M., Z. Alemseged, T. E. Cerling, F. E. Grine, W. H. Kibel, M. G. Leakey, and J. A. Lee-Thorp, F. K. Manthi, K. E. Reed, B. A. Wood, and J. G.

Wynn. 2013. "Isotopic Evidence of Early Hominin Diets." *Proceedings of the National Academy of Sciences of the United States of America* 110:10513–10518.

Sponheimer, M., D. Codron, B. H. Passey, D. J. de Ruiter, T. E. Cerling, and J. A. Lee-Thorp. 2009. "Using Carbon Isotopes to Track Dietary Change in Modern, Historical, and Ancient Primates." *American Journal of Physical Anthropology* 140(4):661–670. https://doi.org/10.1002/ajpa.21111.

Sponheimer, M., and J. A. Lee-Thorp. 1999. "Isotopic Evidence for the Diet of an Early Hominid, *Australopithecus africanus*." *Science* 283(5400):368–370. https://doi.org/10.1126/science.283.5400.368.

Sponheimer, M., J. Lee-Thorp, D. de Ruiter, D. Codron, J. Codron, A. T. Baugh, and F. Thackeray. 2005. "Hominins, Sedges, and Termites: New Carbon Isotope Data from the Sterkfontein Valley and Kruger National Park." *Journal of Human Evolution* 48(3):301–312. https://doi.org/10.1016/j.jhevol.2004.11.008.

Sponheimer, M., J. E. Loudon, D. Codron, M. E. Howells, J. D. Pruetz, J. Codron, D. J. de Ruiter, and J. A. Lee-Thorp. 2006a. "Do 'Savanna' Chimpanzees Consume C_4 Resources?" *Journal of Human Evolution* 51(2):128–133. https://doi.org/10.1016/j.jhevol.2006.02.002.

Sponheimer, M., B. H. Passey, D. J. de Ruiter, D. Guatelli-Steinberg, T. E. Cerling, and J. A. Lee-Thorp. 2006b. "Isotopic Evidence for Dietary Variability in the Early Hominin *Paranthropus robustus*." *Science* 314(5801):980–982. https://doi.org/10.1126/science.1133827.

Spriggs, M. 1989. "The Dating of the Island Southeast Asian Neolithic: An Attempt at Chronometric Hygiene and Linguistic Correlation." *Antiquity* 63(240):587–613. https://doi.org/10.1017/S0003598X00076560.

Stuart-Williams, H. L., H. P. Schwarcz, C. D. White, and M. W. Spence. 1996. "The Isotopic Composition and Diagenesis of Human Bone from Teotihuacan and Oaxaca, Mexico." *Palaeogeography, Palaeoclimatology, Palaeoecology* 126(1–2):1–14. https://doi.org/10.1016/S0031-0182(96)00066-1.

Summerhayes, G. R., M. Leavesley, A. Fairbairn, H. Mandui, J. Field, A. Ford, and R. Fullagar. 2010. "Human Adaptation and Plant Use in Highland New Guinea 49,000 to 44,000 Years Ago." *Science* 330(6000):78–81. https://doi.org/10.1126/science.1193130.

Tappen, M. 1994. "Bone Weathering in the Tropical Rain Forest." *Journal of Archaeological Science* 21(5):667–673. https://doi.org/10.1006/jasc.1994.1066.

Tieszen, L. L. 1991. "Natural Variations in the Carbon Isotope Values of Plants: Implications for Archaeology, Ecology, and Paleoecology." *Journal of Archaeological Science* 18(3):227–248. https://doi.org/10.1016/0305-4403(91)90063-U.

Valentine, B., G. D. Kamenov, and J. Krigbaum. 2008. "Reconstructing Neolithic Groups in Sarawak, Malaysia through Lead and Strontium Isotope Analysis."

Journal of Archaeological Science 35(6):1463–1473. https://doi.org/10.1016/j.jas.2007.10.016.

van der Merwe, N. J., F. T. Masao, and R. J. Bamford. 2008. "Isotopic Evidence for Contrasting Diets of Early Hominins *Homo habilis* and *Australopithecus boisei* of Tanzania." *South African Journal of Science* 104:153–155.

van der Merwe, N. J., and E. Medina. 1989. "Photosynthesis and $^{13}C/^{12}C$ Ratios in Amazonian Rainforests." *Geochimica et Cosmochimica Acta* 53(5):1091–1094. https://doi.org/10.1016/0016-7037(89)90213-5.

van der Merwe, N. J., and E. Medina. 1991. "The Canopy Effect, Carbon Isotope Ratios and Foodwebs in Amazonia." *Journal of Archaeological Science* 18(3):249–259. https://doi.org/10.1016/0305-4403(91)90064-V.

Van der Merwe, N. J., J. F. Thackeray, J. A. Lee-Thorp, and J. Luyt. 2003. "The Carbon Isotope Ecology and Diet of *Australopithecus africanus* at Sterkfontein, South Africa." *Journal of Human Evolution* 44(5):581–597. https://doi.org/10.1016/S0047-2484(03)00050-2.

Verdu, P., F. Austerlitz, A. Estoup, R. Vitalis, M. Georges, S. Théry, A. Froment, S. Le Bomin, A. Gessain, J. M. Hombert, et al. 2009. "Origins and Genetic Diversity of Pygmy Hunter-Gatherers from Western Central Africa." *Current Biology* 19(4):312–318. https://doi.org/10.1016/j.cub.2008.12.049.

Wang, Y., and T. E. Cerling. 1994. "A Model of Fossil Tooth and Bone Diagenesis: Implications for Paleodiet Reconstruction from Stable Isotopes." *Palaeogeography, Palaeoclimatology, Palaeoecology* 107(3–4):281–289. https://doi.org/10.1016/0031-0182(94)90100-7.

Wershaw, R. L., I. Friedman, S. J. Heller, and P. A. Frank. 1966. "Hydrogen Isotope Fractionation of Water Passing through Trees." In *Advances in Organic Geochemistry*, ed. G. D. Hobson, 55–67. Oxford, UK: Pergamon Press.

White, T. D., B. Asfaw, Y. Beyene, Y. Haile-Selassie, C. Owen Lovejoy, G. Suwa, and G. WoldeGabriel. 2009. "*Ardipithecus ramidus* and the Paleobiology of Early Hominids." *Science* 326(5949):64–86. https://doi.org/10.1126/science.1175802.

White, T. D., G. WoldeGabriel, B. Asfaw, S. Ambrose, Y. Beyene, R. L. Bernor, J.-R. Boisserie, B. Currie, H. Gilbert, Y. Haile-Selassie, et al. 2006. "Asa Issie, Aramis, and the Origin of *Australopithecus*." *Nature* 440(7086):883–889. https://doi.org/10.1038/nature04629.

Whitmore, T. C. 1998. *An Introduction to Tropical Rainforests.* 2nd ed. Oxford, UK: Oxford University Press.

Willis, K. J., L. Gillison, and T. M. Brncic. 2004. "How 'Virgin' Is Virgin Rainforest?" *Science* 304:402–403. https://doi.org/10.1126/science.1093991.

Wilson, E. O. 1988. "The Current State of Biological Diversity." In *Biodiversity*, ed. E. O. Wilson, 3–18. Washington, DC: Washington National Academic Press.

WoldeGabriel, G., Y. Haile-Selassie, P. R. Renne, W. K. Hart, S. H. Ambrose, B. Asfaw, G. Heiken, and T. White. 2001. "Geology and Palaeontology of the Late Miocene Middle Awash Valley, Afar Rift, Ethiopia." *Nature* 412(6843):175–178. https://doi.org/10.1038/35084058.

WoldeGabriel, G., T. D. White, G. Suwa, P. Renne, J. de Heinzelin, W. K. Hart, and G. Heiken. 1994. "Ecological and Temporal Placement of Early Pliocene Hominids at Aramis, Ethiopia." *Nature* 371(6495):330–333. https://doi.org/10.1038/371330a0.

Wright, L. E., and H. P. Schwarcz. 1998. "Stable Carbon and Oxygen Isotopes in Human Tooth Enamel: Identifying Breastfeeding and Weaning in Prehistory." *American Journal of Physical Anthropology* 106(1):1–18. https://doi.org/10.1002/(SICI)1096-8644(199805)106:1<1::AID-AJPA1>3.0.CO;2-W.

Wynn, J. G., M. Sponheimer, W. H. Kimbel, Z. Alemseged, K. Reed, Z. K. Bedaso, and J. N. Wilson. 2013. "Diet of *Australopithecus afarensis* from the Pliocene Hadar Formation, Ethiopia." *Proceedings of the National Academy of Sciences of the United States of America* 110(26):10495–10500. https://doi.org/10.1073/pnas.1222559110.

Yakir, D., J. A. Berry, L. Giles, and C. B. Osmond. 1994. "Isotopic Heterogeneity of Water in Transpiring Leaves: Identification of the Component that Controls the $\delta^{18}O$ of Atmospheric O_2 and CO_2." *Plant, Cell & Environment* 17(1):73–80. https://doi.org/10.1111/j.1365-3040.1994.tb00267.x.

Zachos, J., M. Pagani, L. Sloan, E. Thomas, and K. Billups. 2001. "Trends, Rhythms, and Aberrations in Global Climate 65 Ma to Present." *Science* 292(5517):686–693. https://doi.org/10.1126/science.1059412.

Zazzo, A., C. Lecuyer, S.M.F. Sheppard, P. Grandjean, and A. Mariotti. 2004. "Diagenesis and the Reconstruction of Paleoenvironments: A Method to Restore Original $\delta^{18}O$ Values of Carbonate and Phosphate from Fossil Tooth Enamel." *Geochimica et Cosmochimica Acta* 68(10):2245–2258. https://doi.org/10.1016/j.gca.2003.11.009.

6

The ethnography and archaeology of African hunter-gatherers are so intertwined it is sometimes difficult to discern where one ends and the other begins. This close convergence of the observable and the inferential can be traced to the 1960s, when a series of systematic studies to document several living African hunter-gatherer societies coincided with early attempts to discern the behavioral inputs structuring the archaeological record of deep human history. The relationship was, for the most part, symbiotic. Pioneering ethnographic field campaigns in the savannas of southern and East Africa (Heinz 1972; Lee and DeVore 1976; Lee 1968, 1969, 1972, 1979; Silberbauer 1965, 1981; Tanaka 1969, 1976, 1980; Woodburn 1968) were, for example, largely catalyzed by the discovery of Early Pleistocene "living floors" at sites like Olduvai Gorge (Leakey 1971) and Kalambo Falls (Clark 1969, 1974a, 1974b). The now-classic ethnographies that resulted—of groups including the Ju/'hoansi, G/wi, G//ana, !Xóõ, and Hadza—in turn fed directly into interpretive models for other major human origins projects (e.g., Isaac 1984). Paleolithic archaeologists even harnessed ethnographic research not conducted with an evolutionary bent. The adaptations of contemporary tropical foragers in central Africa (Turnbull 1961), for example, came to inform models of rainforest colonization during the Middle Pleistocene (Clark 1959). Similarly, most studies of Africa's more recent archaeological records of the Holocene and later Pleistocene, especially in southern Africa, have drawn

Beyond the Shadow of a Desert

Aquatic Resource Intensification on the Roof of Southern Africa

BRIAN A. STEWART AND
PETER MITCHELL

DOI: 10.5876/9781607327745.c006

heavily—and understandably—on its rich hunter-gatherer ethnographies, including considerations of mobility, aggregation-dispersal, domestic spatial organization, gender relations, *hxaro* gift-exchange, and shamanism (e.g., Hall and Binneman 1987; Lewis-Williams 1981, 1982; Parkington 1996; Parkington et al. 1992; Sampson 1988; Solomon 1992, 1994; Wadley 1987, 1998).

As a consequence, there is arguably no continent more susceptible to its own "ethnographic tyranny" (Wobst 1978). It is perhaps ironic, then, that analogies and inferences drawn from African hunter-gatherer ethnography have particularly severe limitations. A complex blend of historical contingency and resource structure has resulted in Africa's forager societies being some of the world's most encapsulated within, and entangled with, those of food producers. Binford (2001), for example, notes that, of all the continents, Africa has the highest percentage (65%) of hunter-gatherer groups whose economies were tied into those of neighboring food producers at the time of ethnographic documentation. The resulting changes to and dispersed distribution of African hunter-gatherer societies have profound implications for our ability to model past behaviors using ethnographic and ethnoarchaeological data, an issue whose contours were shaped during the Kalahari Debates of a quarter century ago (Schrire 1980, 1984; Solway and Lee 1990; Wilmsen 1989; Wilmsen and Denbow 1990). Moreover, Binford (2001) showed that strong relationships exist between *effective temperature* (ET) and a range of variables central to hunter-gatherer lifeways, including subsistence, settlement, mobility technology, and social and spatial organization (Kelly 1983, 1995, 2013; Oswalt 1976; Whitelaw 1991). Relative to other continents, ETs in present-day Africa are high, with all but a few regions exceeding 15.75°C. Across his global sample of 339 groups, Binford noted that foragers living in regions with comparable ETs subsist primarily on terrestrial plants, do not practice storage, and have no wealth differentiation or hierarchical ranking. They also typically have high residential mobility (Kelly 1983) and use relatively "simple" technologies (*sensu* Oswalt 1976). As far as the ethnographic record is concerned, therefore, Africa samples comparatively little latitudinally mediated diversity in hunter-gatherer lifeways.

These facts hinder the utility of the African ethnographic record as a prism for viewing the continent's past. The marginalization of surviving hunter-gatherer groups to Africa's ecological and sociopolitical fringes (Kent 1996) makes it certain that very different societal forms existed in the past, particularly in more productive environments. In relatively recent periods, rich, well-preserved archaeological records can mitigate this issue. Indeed, marked divergences between behaviors registered in such records and their ethnographic equivalents are often noted (for southern Africa, see Humphreys 2005;

Jerardino 1996, 2010; Sealy 2006; B. Stewart 2010, 2011). Much more challenging are the problems created in the temporal dimension, particularly across deep time. For example, it is now abundantly clear that Africa played host to our species' behavioral evolution (Barham and Mitchell 2008), and that this occurred during—and was at least partly fueled by—later Pleistocene climatic and environmental change (Jones and Stewart 2016). As many researchers have noted, the nature, scale, and pace of these changes have no parallels in the Holocene, including, of course, the ethnographic present. Beyond climatic flux, moreover, during the bulk of the later Pleistocene, Africa experienced ETs substantially lower than those of today. What forms did African hunter-gatherer societies take during periods of pronounced climatic instability or cooling—that is, when conditions differed most from those of the ethnographic present?

We address this question here by integrating later Pleistocene and Holocene paleoenvironmental and archaeological data to explore hunter-gatherer adaptive diversity in one of the continent's most temperate regions: the Maloti-Drakensberg Mountains of Lesotho (figure 6.1). Not only does this region fall well below Binford's "storage threshold" (ET ≤ 15.75°C), but, together with a strip of the interior Karoo dryland biome, it is also one of only two zones of the subcontinent with ETs approaching 12.75°C (figure 6.2). Binford's ethnographic data suggest that hunter-gatherers inhabiting regions with ETs colder than this latter value cannot rely on plants as their primary food base, but depend instead on terrestrial or aquatic animal resources, although only the latter represent a viable intensification option (Johnson 2014:15). If past episodes of climatic cooling pushed ETs in highland Lesotho below this "terrestrial plant dependence threshold" (ET ≤ 12.75°C), we anticipate expansions of subsistence regimes to incorporate greater quantities of freshwater fish at such times.

To explore this, we consider the fish assemblages from three archaeological sites: Sehonghong, Pitsaneng, and Likoaeng. Between them, they provide a history of highland fish exploitation over the past 30,000 years. We show that during glacial and stadial phases highland Lesotho sustained severe temperature depressions. At times, these shifts appear to have obliged humans to abandon the highland zone. At others our data make clear that people managed to adjust to ecological pressure by transforming their dietary base, with knock-on implications for settlement, technology, and perhaps sociopolitical structures. Cultural responses to highland Lesotho environments during such phases probably contrasted sharply with those developed by hunter-gatherer groups in the modern Kalahari from which many archaeologists derive behavioral models. Our analysis, therefore, furthers ongoing efforts (Pargeter et al. 2016) to move African hunter-gatherer archaeology beyond the shadow of the Kalahari Desert.

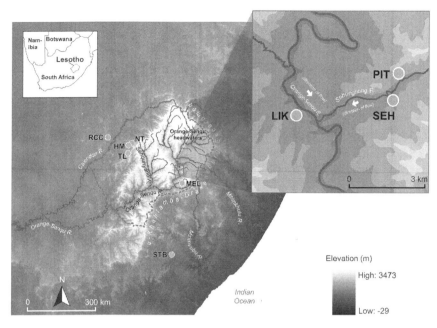

FIGURE 6.1. *Map showing sites mentioned in the text: HM, Ha Makotoko; LIK, Likoaeng; MEL, Melikane; NT, Ntloana Tšoana; PIT, Pitsaneng; RCC, Rose Cottage Cave; SEH, Sehonghong; STB, Strathalan B; TL, Tloutle.*

THE MALOTI-DRAKENSBERG MOUNTAINS: LANDSCAPE, CLIMATE AND VEGETATION

The Maloti-Drakensberg Mountains lie in the far southeastern corner of Africa and extend for some 55,000 km² over most of Lesotho and adjacent parts of South Africa's KwaZulu-Natal and Eastern Cape Provinces (figure 6.1). The highest peaks exceed 3,000 masl with Thabana Ntlenyana (3,482 masl) Africa's tallest south of Mount Kilimanjaro. The mountain system is a roughly quadrangular-shaped massif composed of three sub-parallel ranges. Drakensberg Group flood basalts cap several Karoo Supergroup sedimentary strata. One of these—the Clarens Formation—outcrops as cliffs up to 150 m high within which hundreds of rockshelters and overhangs have formed, many containing archaeological sequences and rock art. Intense fluvial erosion of these geological strata has produced an intricate network of drainages that deeply dissect the landscape. This fluvial system represents the most productive catchment area for southernmost Africa's largest river, the Orange, known in Lesotho as the Senqu.

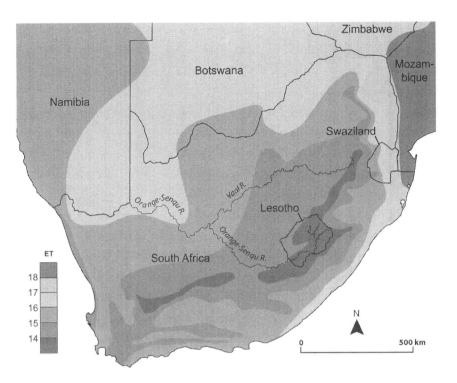

FIGURE 6.2. *Effective Temperature (ET) map of southern Africa (°C; modified after Stuckenberg 1969).*

The climate of the Maloti-Drakensberg Mountains is continental, with cold, dry winters and warm, humid summers. The region lies in southern Africa's summer rainfall zone and receives over 75 percent of its rainfall between October and March. Overall precipitation varies tremendously with altitude and locality, decreasing from north to south and from east to west because of the pronounced orographic rain-shadow cast by the uKhahlamba-Drakensberg Escarpment, which defines the eastern edge of the Mountains. Thus, while estimates of mean annual precipitation for the escarpment typically exceed 1,500 mm (Killick 1963; Schulze 1979), a mean of only 578 mm has been recorded in the upper Orange-Senqu Valley (Bawden and Carroll 1968). Temperatures also vary drastically by altitude, as well as seasonally and diurnally. Mean annual values range from ~15°C in lowland Lesotho to 6°C on the highest mountains (Grab 1994, 1997). The lowlands experience mean mid-summer maxima of 29°C and mid-winter minima 4.3°C, with respective values for the highlands of 17°C and −6.1°C (Grab and Nash 2010). Snow can fall at any time, but especially between May and September, after which it may persist on southern slopes for up to six months. Frost is also widespread (~31 days per year in the lowlands to ~150 days in the highlands; Schulze 2008) and ground freezing is estimated to occur in the high Maloti-Drakensberg up to two hundred days per year (Grab 1997).

As might be expected, vegetation is also strongly differentiated by altitude. Mucina and Rutherford (2006) distinguish three main units in the Lesotho highlands: (1) Senqu Montane Shrubland, (2) Lesotho Highland Basalt Grassland, and (3) Drakensberg Afroalpine Heathland. Senqu Montane Shrubland is found along the Orange-Senqu Valley and its tributaries at ~1,600–1,900 masl. Effectively an eastern intrusion of lowland Lesotho taxa into the highlands along the Orange-Senqu corridor, this is a *Cymbopogon-Themeda-Eragrostis* C_4 grassland with numerous tree and evergreen shrub species. Lesotho Highland Basalt Grassland occurs between ~1,900 and 2,900 masl. This is a dense, subalpine, C_4-dominated *Themeda-Festuca* grassland with patchy shrublands dominated by *Passerina montana* (Mucina and Rutherford 2006). Due to its large altitudinal range (~1,000 m), it contains several altitude-specific vegetation belts. At lower elevations (~1,900–2,100 masl on south-facing [cooler] slopes, but reaching up to ~2700 masl on north-facing [warmer] slopes) grasses are dominated by *Themeda triandra*, a C_4 species that provides excellent pasture (Jacot Guillarmod 1971). However, above these ranges and extending to ~2,900 masl, *Themeda* gives way to shorter, less palatable C_3 *Festuca-Merxmuellera* grasses. Although some ericaceous and composite taxa occur in this unit, trees are mostly absent. Above 2,900 masl, the Basalt Grassland gives way to Drakensberg Afroalpine Heathland, an afroalpine short shrubland with dwarf bushes and C_3 *Merxmuellera*-dominated grasses (Killick 1978; Mucina and Rutherford 2006). Embedded within it, numerous alpine bogs help regulate the flow of rainwater into the Orange-Senqu river system (van Zinderen Bakker and Werger 1974).

THE FISH FAUNA OF THE ORANGE-SENQU RIVER

The rivers of highland Lesotho currently support seven indigenous fish species (Ambrose et al. 2000), all adapted to a fairly hostile riverine environment in which temperature, precipitation, food supply, shelter, and levels of predation can vary widely during the year (Arthington et al. 1999). Neither the chubbyhead barb (*Barbus anoplus*) nor the endemic Maloti minnow (*Pseudobarbus quathlambae*) is large enough to attract human interest and a third taxon, the sharptooth catfish or barbel (*Clarias gariepinus*), is currently only documented archaeologically in the most minimal numbers. A fourth, the rock catfish (*Austroglanis sclateri*), is more in evidence, but it is three members of the Cyprinid family that dominate the samples we discuss: the largemouth yellowfish (*Labeobarbus kimberleyensis*), the smallmouth yellowfish (*Labeobarbus aeneus*), and the Orange River mudfish (*Labeo capensis*). Hobart (2003), Vinnicombe (2009), and Plug et al. (2010) discuss the procurement methods used to capture these species. These methods included angling with hooks and fish gorges, shooting with bow and arrow, spearing/harpooning, and trapping using baskets, weirs, and/or drag screens. The last two techniques (spearing/harpooning, typically from boats or rafts, and trapping) are depicted in surviving rock art in the region (figure 6.3).

It is impossible to estimate fish numbers in highland Lesotho before the onset of increased siltation brought about by human-induced soil erosion and overgrazing and of competition from invasive rainbow trout (*Oncorhynchus mykiss*) and brown trout (*Salmo trutta*), but they must have been considerably higher than today. Archaeological data (Plug and Mitchell 2008b; Plug et al. 2010) support this insofar as they include cyprinids bigger than those recorded recently in highland Lesotho (Arthington et al. 1999) and—by some margin—the southern African angling records reported by Skelton (2001).

Although we do not discuss the ecology of the fish species caught by past hunter-gatherers in Lesotho in detail here for reasons of space, one observation is worth stressing. To an even greater degree than other cyprinids, *Labeo capensis* is noted for its capacity to put on fat before breeding (Baird and Fourie 1978). The combination of increased fat content with an important source of protein probably made these fish especially attractive to people able to intercept them during their spawning runs in spring/early summer, since not only are these events predictable in location and—in a more general sense—time, but this is a season when game animals are still in poor condition following winter and few plant foods are yet available. An extensive literature documents the importance of fat-rich foods in such environments, as well as the relevance of accessing aquatic resources (including freshwater fish) for coping with this situation (Speth 2010; K. Stewart 1994).

MALOTI-DRAKENSBERG PALEOENVIRONMENTS SINCE EARLY MIS 2

Our current understanding of Maloti-Drakensberg paleoenvironments is patchy. Here we synthesize our current state of knowledge as it relates to the period since the start of marine isotope stage (MIS) 2 (~25 ka), with the caveat that spatiotemporal gaps in our comprehension remain considerable. All the ^{14}C dates and age estimates given have been calibrated using the most recent

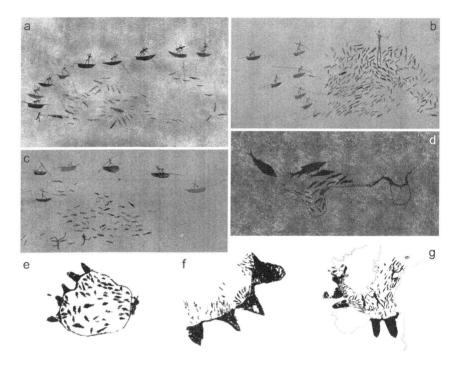

FIGURE 6.3. *Fishing (a–c) and fish mass-capture (d–g) scenes depicted in Lesotho's rock art. (a–d) After Vinnicombe (1976:figures 63, 206, 209; courtesy of the KwaZulu-Natal Museum); (e–g) after Smits (1967:figures 1–3).*

versions of OxCal (4.2.4) and the southern hemisphere calibration curve (Hogg et al. 2013).

Our most detailed evidence comes from Sehonghong and another highland rockshelter, Melikane, located some 40 km to its south. Their sequences stretch from the late Holocene back to early MIS 3 (~57 ka) and early MIS 5a (~83–80 ka), respectively, though human occupation at each was highly discontinuous (Jacobs et al. 2008; B. Stewart et al. 2012). Both sites register an occupational pulse centered on ~25–24 ka, in the early stages of the Last Glacial Maximum (LGM). At Melikane, soil organic matter (SOM) $\delta^{13}C$, phytolith, and charcoal records suggest cooler conditions than had prevailed previously during early and mid-MIS 3. Grassland cover with a strong C_3 component most likely derived from alpine sour grasses is present, along with a low C_4 component. However, the C_4 taxa probably reflect lower pCO_2 levels during the onset of the LGM rather than warmer temperatures. This is because the

sediments from this level comprise anthropogenic materials mixed with colluvial sediments and host bedrock attrition materials derived from roof fall
debris (B. Stewart et al. 2012). This supports the notion of colder and drier
conditions, with material derived from landscape erosion as well as freeze-
thaw and weathering processes. Moreover, tree cover is much reduced, with
trees and shrubs likely to have been tightly restricted to deeper river corridors
where there was sufficient shelter and surface water to support them. This is
supported by the presence in the immediately pre-LGM faunal assemblages
at Sehonghong of small antelope species that browse and/or require cover,
indicating that riverine shrubs and bushes were still available in sufficient density (Plug and Mitchell 2008a). In addition, cold- and frost-tolerant taxa are
present in the Melikane charcoal assemblage, including *Leucosidea sericea* and
Protea sp. At Rose Cottage Cave in the Caledon Valley just beyond the Maloti
Front Range to the west, late MIS 3 and early MIS 2 are also marked by the
presence of *Protea* sp. along with *Leucosidea sericea* and other heathland species
(Wadley et al. 1992). To the east, at a newly analyzed sedimentary exposure in
the high Drakensberg, a major organic-poor gravel layer suggesting colluvial
deposition under conditions of lowered temperatures and humidity is brack-
eted between ^{14}C dates of 27,410 and 23,055 cal BP (Grab and Mills 2011).

Humans abandoned Sehonghong and Melikane for the remainder of the
LGM. Hiatuses at both sites begin ~24 ka, when conditions throughout the
Maloti-Drakensberg seem to have deteriorated sharply. Geomorphological
indications of periglacial conditions along the high uKhahlamba-Drakensberg
Escarpment are extensive, accompanied by evidence at several locales of small
niche (cirque) glaciers (Mills et al. 2009a, 2009b). Comparable evidence comes
from the Eastern Cape Drakensberg immediately to the south of Lesotho
(Lewis 2008) and here too people abandoned the area shortly after 24 ka
(Opperman and Heydenrych 1990). People may have returned to this area only
as late as 11.8 ka (Opperman 1987), but in both highland and lowland Lesotho
sporadic human activity was underway long before this. At Ha Makotoko
and Ntloana Tšoana, for example, in western Lesotho's Phuthiatsana Valley,
occupation is evident at 15.1–13.5 ka (Mitchell and Arthur 2014), slightly later
than its resumption at Rose Cottage Cave in the Caledon Valley immediately to the west (Wadley 1996). Perhaps preceded by one or more earlier,
ephemeral visits (e.g., at 19.3–18.6 ka; Mitchell 1995), newly obtained dates
from Sehonghong register human presence there between ~16.0 and ~15.0 ka,
and again between ~14.8 and ~13.7 ka (Pargeter et al. 2017). The first of these
occupational pulses coincides with a ~3‰ positive shift in SOM δ^{13}C at the
site (to −19.8‰), suggesting a greater contribution of C_4 taxa under markedly

warmer temperatures relative to the previous (pre-LGM) occupation (Loftus et al. 2015). The subsequent pulse, however, records a negative shift (to −21.8‰), signaling a return to cooler temperatures. While Loftus et al. (2015) ascribed this cold reversal to the Younger Dryas (YD; ~12.7–11.5 ka) on the basis of previous dates from this portion of the Sehonghong sequence (Mitchell 1996a), the new chronology suggests that it more likely accords with the slightly earlier Antarctic Cold Reversal (ACR; ~14.7–13.0 ka). Interestingly, two of the seven ^{14}C dates for the above-mentioned high Drakensberg glacial moraines give ages of 14,700 and 13,820 cal BP (Mills et al. 2009a), indicating that some of these features likely formed during the ACR.

The YD itself may be registered slightly later in the Sehonghong sequence, since SOM δ^{13}C values (and thus temperatures) remain relatively depressed until ~11.0 ka. Thereafter, they increase once again by ~3‰ as temperatures warm into the mid-Holocene (Loftus et al. 2015). Higher temperatures, and probably higher rainfall too, are also signaled by increased numbers of small antelopes and ground game in Sehonghong's faunal assemblage by ~11.0 ka (Plug and Mitchell 2008a). More clearly than the Sehonghong sequence, multiple proxy records from western Lesotho and Rose Cottage Cave demonstrate sizable climatic oscillations across the Pleistocene-Holocene transition rather than a smooth, unidirectional sequence of change (Roberts et al. 2013 with references). In this they are broadly in line with similar evidence elsewhere in southern Africa (e.g., Abell and Plug 2000; Chase et al. 2011; Coetzee 1967; Quick et al. 2011; Scott and Lee Thorp 2004).

The higher temperatures that set in across the Maloti-Drakensberg ~9.5 ka have been argued to signal the start of the mid-Holocene altithermal (Smith et al. 2002). This phase of widespread warming between ~9 ka and ~4.5 ka is apparent in numerous archives throughout the subcontinent (Partridge et al. 1999). However, considerably more climatic variability exists within it than previously appreciated, particularly as regards moisture availability through time and space (e.g., Nash and Meadows 2012). The Maloti-Drakensberg likely witnessed fluctuations in both precipitation and temperature, even though records from the Lesotho highlands are poor at this time, compared to those along the Caledon and Phuthiatsana Valleys (e.g., Esterhuysen and Mitchell 1996; Smith et al. 2002). The onset of peat formation in the upper Mashai Valley to the northeast of Sehonghong ~8.2 ka (7280 ± 150 BP, Q–1165; Carter 1976) does, however, fit with other proxies, hinting at cooler, moister conditions around this time that may be local manifestations of the so-called 8200 cal yr BP event, a period of global-scale cooling triggered by mass glacial meltwater influx into the North Atlantic (Barber et al. 1999).

Thereafter, and beginning from at least ~7.5 ka, temperatures across the region appear to have remained relatively high until the start of the late Holocene Neoglacial (~3.5 ka), although moisture availability fluctuated. Dramatic habitat changes in the highlands that may have been associated with a warming climate are likely implicated in a major faunal turnover event registered at Sehonghong ~7–6 ka. While several medium and large grazing ungulates (springbok, *Antidorcas marsupialis*; bluebuck, *Hippotragus leucophaeus*; blesbok, *Damaliscus pygargus phillipsi*) that had been archaeologically present throughout the later Pleistocene disappear, others increase in frequency, among them the common reedbuck *Redunca arundinum*, which is restricted to this part of the site's sequence; its heavy water dependence signals a wetter landscape (Plug and Mitchell 2008a).

The later Holocene witnessed warm temperatures overall, punctuated by several cold reversals of variable duration and intensity. The longest such excursion was the Neoglacial, a period of widespread cooling and humidity registered across much of southern Africa, including the Maloti-Drakensberg region, between ~3.5 and 2.0 ka (Nash and Meadows 2012; but see Chase et al. 2009). A strong Neoglacial signature has been recorded at Likoaeng (1,725 masl), an open-air site near Sehonghong, the fish assemblages from which we consider below. Here, phytoliths and SOM δ^{13}C values from strata dated between c. 3000 and 2180 cal BP (Layers XIV–XI) suggest a distinct habitat change from preceding or subsequent periods. Whereas the bulk of this later Holocene sequence is dominated by C_4 phytolith morphotypes (Panicoids and Chloridoids) and high δ^{13}C values indicative of warm temperatures not dissimilar to today, these third millennium BP layers register a switch to C_3 Pooid grass dominance and correspondingly low δ^{13}C values (Parker et al. 2011); charcoal data corroborate this (Mitchell et al. 2011). As mentioned above, today C_3 alpine grasslands occur in the high Maloti-Drakensberg at altitudes above ~2,100 masl. Their dominance in the area surrounding Likoaeng thus indicates that, as with earlier cold events, the Neoglacial provoked a substantial lowering of vegetation belts in response to temperature depressions, in this case in the order of 2.5°C (Parker et al. 2011). The Neoglacial portion of the Likoaeng sequence also contains the highest counts of phytoliths laid down under very wet conditions, suggesting substantially increased moisture availability at this time. This agrees well with evidence from the Eastern Cape Drakensberg, where humid conditions in this time range are indicated by the formation of paleosols and overbank deposits at Kilchurn (~3.2–2.3 ka), and gully erosion at Tiffindell (~2.8–2.7 ka) (Lewis 2005).

Over parts of the past two millennia the Maloti-Drakensberg region experienced some of the warmest temperatures of the Holocene. At Likoaeng, the cool, humid Neoglacial was followed from around 2100 cal BP by enhanced drying and warmth, evidenced respectively by higher frequencies of C_4 phytoliths and SOM $\delta^{13}C$ values consistent with a mixed C_3/C_4 grassland. This was followed some four centuries later by a shift to markedly warmer and drier conditions in the site's uppermost levels, dated 1615–1066 cal BP (Parker et al. 2011). During this final pulse of human occupation SOM $\delta^{13}C$ values are the highest in the Likoaeng sequence, indicating an upper Orange-Senqu Valley heavily dominated by C_4 taxa, with frequencies of arid-adapted Chloridoid (C_4) phytoliths also peaking and the lowest counts of Pooid (C_3) grass phytoliths, which had peaked in the Neoglacial.

This is not, however, to suggest that conditions in the Maloti-Drakensberg were uniform over the last 2 ka. Two of the later Holocene's sharpest climatic swings—the Medieval Warm Epoch (1390–650 cal BP) and the ensuing Little Ice Age (650–150 cal BP)—register at several regional proxy archives, including peat deposits at Tlaeeng Pass in the high Drakensberg north of Sehonghong (Hanvey and Marker 1992), the pollen sequence at Craigrossie in the easternmost Free State (Scott 1989), and the SOM $\delta^{13}C$ values obtained from several open-air sampling locations near Sehonghong itself (Julia Lee-Thorp, personal communication 2016). The absence of zebra (*Equus quagga*) and extreme scarcity of black wildebeest (*Connochaetes gnou*) in archaeological faunas of the last two thousand years at Sehonghong, Likoaeng, Pitsaneng, and other highland sites also suggests a further impoverishment of the region's mammalian fauna, with roan antelope (*Hippotragus equinus*) too disappearing before the first literate observers arrived in the second half of the nineteenth century (Plug and Mitchell 2008a). Whether or not these losses were climatically instigated, they certainly imply a degree of ongoing ecological reorganization during the later Holocene.

In sum, far from the conventional picture of a cool, dry later Pleistocene and warm, wet Holocene, major changes in temperature and humidity are evident throughout the period under consideration. We wish to highlight the evidence presented above for at least three periods of sharply reduced temperatures during MIS 2 and the Holocene: ~24–18 ka (the LGM), 14.8–13.7 (the ACR), and ~3.5–2 ka (the Neoglacial). The paleoenvironmental evidence just summarized provides the requisite climatic backdrop against which we now frame and interpret the archaeological record of fishing in highland Lesotho.

THE ARCHAEOLOGY OF HIGHLAND FISH
EXPLOITATION AND ITS CLIMATIC CORRELATES

Three archaeological sites are especially important to understanding the pre-history of fishing in highland Lesotho: Sehonghong, Pitsaneng, and Likoaeng (figure 6.1). Sehonghong is one of five sites originally excavated by Pat Carter in 1971 as part of his and Patricia Vinnicombe's pioneering research of the region (Carter 1978; Vinnicombe 1976). A large sandstone rockshelter (fig-ure 6.4a) situated on the south side of the Sehonghong River, which flows into the Orange-Senqu about 3 km downstream, Sehonghong's sequence reaches back to early MIS 3 (Carter et al. 1988; Jacobs et al. 2008). Faunal remains, including fish, are variably well preserved throughout at least the upper 35,000 years of its sequence. Sehonghong has been excavated twice since 1971. In 1992 Mitchell investigated its Later Stone Age (LSA) deposits, including those dating to early in MIS 2 that appear to register a transition between Middle Stone Age (MSA) and LSA lithic technologies (Mitchell 1995). As already mentioned, the Pleistocene LSA and MSA/LSA transitional levels from Mitchell's excavation have recently been re-dated using AMS [14]C (Pargeter et al. 2017). In 2011, Stewart reopened Mitchell's trench to allow exploration of underlying MSA levels; this work continues. Approximately 1 km upstream from Sehonghong, Pitsaneng is a much smaller rockshelter (figure 6.4b) with a sequence that includes fish remains but is restricted to the second millennium AD (Hobart 2004). Likoaeng, located some 3 km to the northwest of Sehonghong on the west bank of the Orange-Senqu River, is a very different kind of site. Here, in 1995 and 1998, Mitchell explored a series of superimposed open-air occupations (figure 6.4c and d) dating to the late Holocene in which fish were exceptionally numerous and well preserved (Mitchell et al. 2011). The relevant radiometric dates for all three sites are listed in table 6.1.

Excavations at Sehonghong employed a 1.5-mm mesh (except in the upper-most layers, DC and SS, where a mesh of 3.0 mm was used) and those at the other two sites used a sieve with 2.0-mm mesh. All bone retrieved from Likoaeng, Pitsaneng, and the 1992 excavations at Sehonghong was analyzed by the same analyst, Ina Plug, at the Transvaal (now Ditsong) Museum, Pretoria, South Africa, using the comparative collections and procedures detailed else-where (Plug and Mitchell 2008b; Plug et al. 2010). All told, 14,333 identifiable specimens were recovered from Sehonghong, 918 from Pitsaneng, and 61,241 from Likoaeng. Collectively, this provides one of the largest concentrations of freshwater fish remains anywhere in sub-Saharan Africa. We are confident that the assemblages were accumulated by people, since many of the bones

FIGURE 6.4. *Views of the primary sites discussed in this chapter: (a) looking southeast into Sehonghong Rockshelter from the Sehonghong River bank; (b) a view south into Pitsaneng Rockshelter, also from the Sehonghong River bank; Likoaeng (c) before excavation, looking west from the Orange-Senqu River bank, and (d) during excavation, looking north up the Orange-Senqu River in the winter dry season.*

are burnt, none show any sign of gnawing or of carnivore digestive processes, and all occur in association with other residues of human activity, such as charcoal and lithic debitage. Leopards (*Panthera pardus*), water mongooses (*Atilax paludinosus*), and Cape clawless otters (*Aonyx capensis*) occur in the assemblages, but are rare. Only otters regularly eat fish, but they tend to do this in the water, and defecate along the water's edge, rarely moving as far from the riverbank as the Sehonghong or Likoaeng sites. These facts, and the virtual absence from the archaeological faunas of crabs, which dominate otter diets in the KwaZulu-Natal Drakensberg (Skinner and Chimimba 2005), reinforce our view that the fish remains we discuss are of human origin (Plug et al. 2010).

Tables 6.2 and 6.3 present the relative proportions of fish to mammalian Number of Identifiable Specimens (NISP) by layer for Sehonghong and Likoaeng. Figure 6.5 then graphs the frequencies of fish remains through the Sehonghong and Likoaeng sequences both as densities (NISP per cubic meter

TABLE 6.1. Published radiocarbon dates from Likoaeng, Pitsaneng, and Sehonghong from Marine Isotope Stages 1 and 2.

Site	Stratigraphic context	Cultural association	Laboratory number	Date BP	Calibrated BP		Material	Reference
Pitsaneng	Q2, spit 3	Ceramic Wilton	OXL-1314	AD 1580 ± 60	—	—	Pottery	Hobart (2004)
Pitsaneng	Burial	Ceramic Wilton	Pta-8360	810 ± 50	786	571	Human bone	Hobart (2004)
Pitsaneng	M4, spit 9	Ceramic Wilton	Pta-8491	840 ± 40	773	665	Charcoal	Hobart (2004)
Pitsaneng	M4, spit 18	Ceramic Wilton	OXL-1316	AD 1140 ± 80	—	—	Pottery	Hobart (2004)
Pitsaneng	Q2, spit 7	Ceramic Wilton	OXL-1315	AD 1040 ± 90	—	—	Pottery	Hobart (2004)
Sehonghong	DC	Ceramic Wilton	Wk-34785	1132 ± 25	1057	933	Mammal bone	Horsburgh et al. (2016)
Sehonghong	DC	Ceramic Wilton	Wk-34786	1132 ± 25	1057	933	Mammal bone	Horsburgh et al. (2016)
Sehonghong	DC	Ceramic Wilton	Wk-34784	1201 ± 25	1173	974	Mammal bone	Horsburgh et al. (2016)
Sehonghong	GAP	Ceramic Wilton	Pta-6084	1240 ± 50	1265	980	Charcoal	Mitchell and Vogel (1994)
Likoaeng	Layer I	Ceramic Wilton	GrA-23237	1285 ± 40	1269	1066	Sheep	Mitchell et al. (2011)
Likoaeng	Layer I	Ceramic Wilton	GrA-26831	1290 ± 30	1268	1071	Iron	Mitchell et al. (2011)
Likoaeng	Layer I	Ceramic Wilton	Pta-7877	1310 ± 80	1309	981	Charcoal	Mitchell et al. (2011)
Sehonghong	Layer IX, unit 6	Ceramic Wilton	Pta-885	1400 ± 50	1357	1180	Charcoal	Carter et al. (1988)
Sehonghong	GAP	Ceramic Wilton	Pta-6063	1710 ± 20	1691	1528	Charcoal	Mitchell and Vogel (1994)
Likoaeng	Layer III	Postclassic Wilton	Pta-7865	1830 ± 15	1784	1615	Charcoal	Mitchell et al. (2011)
Likoaeng	Layer III	Postclassic Wilton	Pta-7097	1850 ± 15	1811	1703	Charcoal	Mitchell et al. (2011)
Likoaeng	Layer V	Postclassic Wilton	Pta-7092	1850 ± 40	1834	1610	Charcoal	Mitchell et al. (2011)

continued on next page

TABLE 6.1—*continued*

Site	Stratigraphic context	Cultural association	Laboratory number	Date BP	Calibrated BP	Material	Reference
Likoaeng	Layer V	Postclassic Wilton	Pta-9048	2000 ± 70	2085	1734	Charcoal	Mitchell et al. (2011)
Likoaeng	Layer V	Postclassic Wilton	Pta-7870	2100 ± 80	2306	1836	Charcoal	Mitchell et al. (2011)
Likoaeng	Layer VII/IX	Postclassic Wilton	Pta-7876	2020 ± 60	2091	1749	Charcoal	Mitchell et al. (2011)
Likoaeng	Layer VII/IX	Postclassic Wilton	Pta-7098	2060 ± 45	2096	1843	Charcoal	Mitchell et al. (2011)
Likoaeng	Layer XI	Postclassic Wilton	Pta-7101	2390 ± 60	2703	2180	Charcoal	Mitchell et al. (2011)
Likoaeng	Layer XIII	Postclassic Wilton	GrA-23236	2555 ± 45	2749	2382	Mammal bone	Mitchell et al. (2011)
Likoaeng	Layer XIII	Postclassic Wilton	Pta-7093	2650 ± 60	2859	2490	Charcoal	Mitchell et al. (2011)
Likoaeng	Layer XIII	Postclassic Wilton	GrA-23239	2860 ± 45	3064	2793	Charcoal	Mitchell et al. (2011)
Likoaeng	Layer XIII	Postclassic Wilton	GrA-23233	2810 ± 45	2978	2761	Mammal bone	Mitchell et al. (2011)
Likoaeng	Layer XV	Postclassic Wilton	GrA-23232	3355 ± 45	3687	3411	Charcoal	Mitchell et al. (2011)
Likoaeng	Layer XVII	Postclassic Wilton	GrA-26178	2875 ± 35	3071	2845	Eland	Mitchell et al. (2011)
Likoaeng	Layer XVII	Postclassic Wilton	GrA-13535	3110 ± 50	3395	3081	Charcoal	Mitchell et al. (2011)
Sehonghong	DC (displaced upward from GWA)	Wilton	Wk-34787	5870 ± 25	6736	6537	Mammal bone	Horsburgh et al. (2016)
Sehonghong	GWA	Classic Wilton	Pta-6154	5950 ± 70	6931	6548	Charcoal	Mitchell and Vogel (1994)
Sehonghong	Layer IX, unit 28	Later Oakhurst	Q-3174	6870 ± 60	7818	7571	Charcoal	Carter et al. (1988)
Sehonghong	ALP	Later Oakhurst	Pta-6278	7290 ± 80	8297	7879	Charcoal	Mitchell and Vogel (1994)
Sehonghong	ALP	Later Oakhurst	Pta-6280	7090 ± 80	8007	7697	Charcoal	Mitchell and Vogel (1994)
Sehonghong	ALP	Later Oakhurst	Pta-6072	7210 ± 80	8173	7839	Charcoal	Mitchell and Vogel (1994)

continued on next page

TABLE 6.1—*continued*

Site	Stratigraphic context	Cultural association	Laboratory number	Date BP	Calibrated BP	Material	Reference
Sehonghong	ALP	Later Oakhurst	Pta-6083	7010 ± 70	7942	Charcoal	Mitchell and Vogel (1994)
Sehonghong	SA	Oakhurst	Pta-6368	9280 ± 45	10550	Charcoal	Mitchell and Vogel (1994)
Sehonghong	SA	Oakhurst	Pta-6057	9740 ± 140	11595	Charcoal	Mitchell and Vogel (1994)
Sehonghong	BARF	Robberg	Pta-6065	11090 ± 230	13395	Charcoal	Mitchell and Vogel (1994)
Sehonghong	RF	Robberg	OxA-39742	12010 ± 50	14018	Charcoal	Pargeter et al. (2017)
Sehonghong	RF	Robberg	Pta-6282	12180 ± 110	14467	Charcoal	Mitchell and Vogel (1994)
Sehonghong	Layer IX, unit 39	Robberg	Q-3175	12250 ± 300	15229	Bulk bone	Carter et al. (1988)
Sehonghong	Layer IX, unit 42	Robberg	Q-3176	12200 ± 250	15080	Bulk bone	Carter et al. (1988)
Sehonghong	RF	Robberg	OxA-39741	12355 ± 50	14712	Charcoal	Pargeter et al. (2017)
Sehonghong	RF	Robberg	OxA-39740	12420 ± 50	14877	Charcoal	Pargeter et al. (2017)
Sehonghong	RBL	Robberg	Pta-6062	12410 ± 45	14735	Charcoal	Mitchell and Vogel (1994)
Sehonghong	CLBRF	Robberg	Pta-6058	12470 ± 100	15040	Charcoal	Mitchell and Vogel (1994)
Sehonghong	Layer IX, unit 48	Robberg	Q-3174	12800 ± 250	15925	Charcoal	Carter et al. (1988)
Sehonghong	RBL	Robberg	OxA-39739	12870 ± 55	15601	Charcoal	Pargeter et al. (2017)
Sehonghong	RBL	Robberg	OxA-39738	12960 ± 55	15725	Charcoal	Pargeter et al. (2017)
Sehonghong	Layer IX, unit 50	Robberg	Pta-884	13000 ± 140	15948	Charcoal	Carter et al. (1988)
Sehonghong	Layer IX, unit 52	Robberg	Q-3172	13200 ± 150	16210	Charcoal	Carter et al. (1988)
Sehonghong	BAS	Robberg	Pta-6060	15700 ± 150	19298	Charcoal	Mitchell and Vogel (1994)
Sehonghong	Layer IX, unit 54	Robberg	Q-1452	17820 ± 270	22246	Charcoal	Carter et al. (1988)
Sehonghong	BAS	Robberg	Pta-6281	19400 ± 200	23853	Charcoal	Mitchell and Vogel (1994)

continued on next page

TABLE 6.1—*continued*

Site	Stratigraphic context	Cultural association	Laboratory number	Date BP	Calibrated BP		Material	Reference
Sehonghong	BAS	Robberg	Pta-6077	20200 ± 100	24495	23952	Charcoal	Mitchell and Vogel (1994)
Sehonghong	BAS	Robberg	OxA-39736	20270 ± 100	24648	24022	Charcoal	Pargeter et al. (2017)
Sehonghong	BAS	Robberg	OxA-39737	20600 ± 100	25178	24457	Charcoal	Pargeter et al. (2017)
Sehonghong	Layer IX, unit 60	Robberg	Pta-789	20900 ± 270	25735	24430	Charcoal	Carter et al. (1988)
Sehonghong	Layer IX, unit 72	Robberg	Pta-918	19860 ± 220	24401	23316	Charcoal	Carter et al. (1988)
Sehonghong	Layer VII (MOS)	Transitional MSA/LSA	Pta-919	20240 ± 230	25015	23745	Charcoal	Carter et al. (1988)
Sehonghong	MOS	Transitional MSA/LSA	OxA-39735	20290 ± 90	24656	24058	Charcoal	Pargeter et al. (2017)
Sehonghong	MOS	Transitional MSA/LSA	OxA-39734	20460 ± 100	25019	24287	Charcoal	Pargeter et al. (2017)
Sehonghong	MOS	Transitional MSA/LSA	Pta-6059	20500 ± 230	25272	24061	Charcoal	Mitchell and Vogel (1994)
Sehonghong	OS	Transitional MSA/LSA	OxA-39733	20100 ± 90	24420	23914	Charcoal	Pargeter et al. (2017)
Sehonghong	RFS	Transitional MSA/LSA	Pta-6271	25100 ± 300	29890	28466	Charcoal	Mitchell and Vogel (1994)
Sehonghong	RFS	Transitional MSA/LSA	OxA-39731	25510 ± 150	30191	29206	Charcoal	Pargeter et al. (2017)
Sehonghong	RFS	Transitional MSA/LSA	OxA-39730	25870 ± 160	30615	29595	Charcoal	Pargeter et al. (2017)
Sehonghong	RFS	Transitional MSA/LSA	Pta-6268	26000 ± 430	30983	29243	Charcoal	Mitchell and Vogel (1994)

continued on next page

TABLE 6.1—*continued*

Site	Stratigraphic context	Cultural association	Laboratory number	Date BP	Calibrated BP		Material	Reference
Sehonghong	162	MSA	OxA-27689	25330 ± 130	29706	28692	Charcoal	Loftus et al. (2015)
Sehonghong	163	MSA	OxA-27690	28650 ± 200	33148	31867	Charcoal	Loftus et al. (2015)
Sehonghong	167	MSA	OxA-27691	29120 ± 190	33737	32804	Charcoal	Loftus et al. (2015)
Sehonghong	169	MSA	OxA-27692	29170 ± 190	33769	32858	Charcoal	Loftus et al. (2015)
Sehonghong	1030	MSA	OxA-27693	29200 ± 200	33801	32870	Charcoal	Loftus et al. (2015)
Sehonghong	1031	MSA	OxA-27694	28800 ± 190	33517	32197	Charcoal	Loftus et al. (2015)
Sehonghong	1036	MSA	OxA-27695	30910 ± 250	35332	34273	Charcoal	Loftus et al. (2015)
Sehonghong	1037	MSA	OxA-27696	31030 ± 250	35482	34417	Charcoal	Loftus et al. (2015)
Sehonghong	1111A	MSA	OxA-27697	30710 ± 240	35063	34127	Charcoal	Loftus et al. (2015)
Sehonghong	Layer V, unit 88	MSA	Pta-787	30900 ± 550	35978	33916	Charcoal	Carter et al. (1988)
Sehonghong	Layer V, unit 93	MSA	Pta-785	32150 ± 770	38315	34695	Charcoal	Carter et al. (1988)
Sehonghong	Layer IV	MSA	SEH4	31600 ± 1400	—	—	Sediment	Jacobs et al. (2008)
Sehonghong	Layer III	MSA	SEH3	30300 ± 3400	—	—	Sediment	Jacobs et al. (2008)
Sehonghong	Layer III	MSA	SEH2	46500 ± 2500	—	—	Sediment	Jacobs et al. (2008)
Sehonghong	Layer II	MSA	SEH1	57600 ± 2300	—	—	Sediment	Jacobs et al. (2008)

Notes: All dates are conventional radiocarbon ages except for those prefixed by GrA-, OxA- and Wk. Dates prefixed by OXL- and SEH are OSL dates. Radiocarbon dates have been calibrated using OxCAl 4.2.4 and SHCal 13 (Hogg et al. 2013) and are presented at 95% CIs.

of deposit) and as ratios of fish to mammals. The latter are expressed using a fish/mammal index similar to those advocated by Broughton (1994):

$$\Sigma \text{ NISP fish} / \Sigma \text{ (NISP fish + NISP mammals)}$$

Values approaching 1 or 0 indicate diets with higher relative contributions of fish or mammals, respectively. For Likoaeng we also present a large ungulate/fish index:

$$\Sigma \text{ NISP large ungulates} / \Sigma \text{ (NISP large ungulates + NISP fish)}$$

In this index, values approaching 1 or 0 respectively indicate diets with higher relative contributions of large ungulates or fish, with large ungulates defined as size class 3 or above (Brain 1981). Tables 6.4 and 6.5 break down Sehonghong and Likoaeng's fish NISPs and Minimum Number of Individuals (MNI) by taxon. Pitsaneng is treated as a single assemblage for this comparison and is presented in table 6.6 (NISPs only). Note that a precise count for the total number of unidentifiable fish remains does not exist for Likoaeng, but that they are estimated to be on the order of ~1.3 million (Plug et al. 2010:3114).

Both the density of fish remains and their abundance relative to mammals are low in the oldest layer sampled at Sehonghong (RFS), which is now dated to between 30,615 and 29,206 cal BP (figure 6.5; table 6.2). Both measures of fish prevalence then increase, peaking in BAS, the oldest layer assigned to the late Pleistocene Robberg Industry; associated AMS radiocarbon dates fall between 25,178 and 24,022 cal BP. Fish remains decline sharply in the succeeding RBL/CLBRF layer, which is now dated to 15,725–15,163 cal BP, but pick up again in the two youngest Robberg-associated layers, RF and BARF, which have dates of between 14,877 and 12,559 cal BP. Their density and relative abundance then decline sharply once more in the early and middle Holocene parts of the sequence (Layers SA, ALP, and GWA, 11,595–6537 cal BP) (figure 6.5; table 6.2). The period from 6537 to 1691 cal BP is not represented at Sehonghong, but its second half is present at Likoaeng, where the basal excavated deposits date to c. 3400–3000 cal BP. Fish are relatively unimportant in these lowest horizons, but increase dramatically from Layer XIV onward (c. 3000 cal BP) both in absolute terms and relative to the frequency with which mammal remains were introduced to the site (figure 6.5; table 6.3). Overlapping with the end of the Likoaeng sequence, Layer GAP (1691–980 cal BP) at Sehonghong also registers a high incidence of fish. However, they are very rare in the latter part of this time range at Likoaeng (i.e., in Layer I, that site's youngest occupation). For the last thousand years, fish numbers are again high at Sehonghong (though not as high as in GAP), but a lack of stratigraphic resolution for these layers (DC/SS) precludes matching any part of them closely with the sample from Pitsaneng (Hobart 2004).

We have hypothesized that people will have intensified their use of fish during colder climatic episodes (after Binford 2001:368). On the whole our data appear to support this. For example, peaks of fishing activity occur in the Sehonghong sequence at 25,178 to 24,022 cal BP (Layer BAS) and between 14,877 and 12,559 cal BP (Layers RF and BARF) and at Likoaeng in layers dated to c. 3000–1749 cal BP (Layers XIV–VII/IX) (figure 6.5). The first of these episodes coincides with the LGM onset, the second with the ACR, which interrupted the last deglaciation (c. 14,700–13,000 cal BP) (Pedro et al. 2016), although its precise impact in southern Africa remains unclear (Chevalier and Chase 2015; Green et al. 2015; Pedro et al. 2016), and the third with the late Holocene Neoglacial (Parker et al. 2011). We suggest that enhanced fishing was part of a strategy to broaden diets as the descent of C_3-dominated alpine grasslands that today occur ≥ 2,100–2,700 masl reduced the abundance and availability of edible plants, as well as ungulate grazing capacity and biomass. Search costs for large game and edible plant foods would consequently have increased. A sharp decline in large ungulate hunting with the onset of the Neoglacial is especially apparent at Likoaeng (figure 6.5e). At the same time, higher winter snowfalls during these cold episodes would have generated greater spring/early summer river flow as snow melted (Mills et al. 2012), which should have benefited *Labeobarbus aeneus* and the size of its spawning runs. Conversely, during warmer periods immediately before the onset of the LGM and the ACR (represented at Sehonghong by Layers RFS and RBL/CLBRF respectively), in the early and middle Holocene (Sehonghong Layers SA, ALP, and GWA), and at the very base of the Likoaeng sequence (Layers XV–XVII) game and plant resources were probably more abundant and relatively little emphasis was placed upon fishing.

Our data do, however, show an interesting exception to this latter pattern. Whereas fishing declined as temperatures rose after the earlier two cold phases (LGM and ACR), this does not appear to have been the case following the Neoglacial at Likoaeng. There, the dietary emphasis on fish remained strong into the first millennium AD even if densities fell, before dropping off steeply in Likoaeng's uppermost stratum, Layer I (c. 1309–981 cal BP) (figure 6.5, table 6.3). The Neoglacial is not represented at Sehonghong, but the site's second highest stratum—Layer GAP (1691–980 cal BP)—overlaps with Likoaeng's immediately post-Neoglacial, first-millennium AD layers. Echoing the latter, Layer GAP contains the highest density and relative abundance of fish remains of the entire Sehonghong sequence (figure 6.5). We are

TABLE 6.2. Sehonghong and Pitsaneng: proportion of fish versus mammals, by layer, calculated using NISP

| Age cal BP | Layer | NISP | | Percentage ratio fish/mammal |
		Fish	Mammal	
SEHONGHONG				
≤ 1200	DC/SS	5,489	910	86/14
1691–980	GAP	4,042	170	96/04
6931–6548	GWA	107	933	10/90
8297–7697	ALP	726	1,855	28/72
11,595–10,255	SA	442	1,190	27/73
13,395–12,559	BARF	78	72	52/48
14,877–13,744	RF	1,473	757	66/34
15,725–15,163	RBL/CLBRF	208	921	18/82
25,178–24,022	BAS	1,626	653	71/29
24,420–23,914	OS	76	104	42/58
25,019–24,058	MOS	63	142	31/69
30,615–29,206	RFS	3	40	07/93
PITSANENG				
	All contexts	911	4,175	18/82

tempted to suggest that these fish-rich post-Neoglacial strata at Likoaeng and Sehonghong coincide with a cold, moist period indicated by the development of pronival ramparts in the high Drakensberg ^{14}C-dated to 1702–1602 cal. BP (Grab and Mills 2011:183). However, testing this would require better chronological control in this part of these sequences than we currently possess. Poorly resolved stratigraphy in Sehonghong's uppermost and only slightly less fish-rich Layer DC/SS (≤ 1200 cal BP) also means that we cannot say whether and how many fish there relate to any putative Little Ice Age occupation of the site. Newly obtained radiocarbon dates for a DNA-analyzed mammalian bone from Layer DC do, however, point to at least one focused occupation very close in time to the tail end of that represented by GAP, between 1173 and 933 cal BP (Horsburgh et al. 2016). Pitsaneng presents similar dating difficulties, though we know that it was occupied during both the Little Ice Age and the preceding Medieval Warm Epoch (Hobart 2004). If these late Holocene episodes of enhanced fishing buck the trend described in this chapter by not correlating to colder climatic intervals, future research should

TABLE 6.3. Likoaeng: proportion of fish *versus* mammals, by layer, calculated using NISP

| Age cal BP | Layer | NISP | | Percentage ratio |
		Fish	Mammal	fish/mammal
1309–980	I	96	45	68/32
	II	308	3	99/01
1811–1615	III	5,510	293	95/05
	IV	58	8	88/12
2085–1610	V	7,548	108	99/01
	VI	2,727	78	97/03
2096–1749	VII/IX	21,660	575	97/03
	X	62	1	98/02
2703–2180	XI	2,683	297	90/10
	XII	41	17	71/29
3064–2382	XIII	19,138	910	95/05
	XIV	808	188	81/19
3687–3411	XV	162	117	58/42
	XVI	89	45	66/34
3395–2845	XVII	324	107	75/25

pursue alternative hypotheses for their occurrence, perhaps rooted in more widespread indications of population increase at this time (Mitchell 2002).

In addition to the intensity with which fish were procured, changes are also apparent in the relative frequency of different fish species over time and between sites. At Sehonghong *Labeobarbus aeneus* dominates every sample at a percentage NISP frequency of ≥ 80 percent, while *Austroglanis sclateri* and *Labeo capensis* oscillate between second and third position but become more common overall in the mid- and late Holocene (Layers GWA, GAP, and DC/SS). The pattern at Likoaeng is quite different: *Labeobarbus aeneus* is more common than *Labeo capensis* in the small samples from Layers XVII (NISP = 74) and XVI (NISP = 31), but these positions are reversed in Layers XV, XIV, and lower XIII. *Labeobarbus aeneus* is then again the most common taxon in the middle of Layer XIII, but declines thereafter and is present in only trace amounts in the remainder of the sequence, which is wholly dominated by *Labeo capensis*. *Austroglanis sclateri* is almost entirely absent at Likoaeng. *Labeobarbus kimberleyensis*, the largemouth yellowfish, registers a minimal presence in all but the smallest samples, but is almost wholly absent from

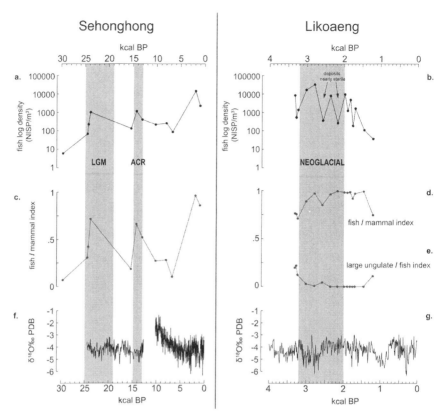

FIGURE 6.5. *Fluctuations in the densities of fish remains at (a) Sehonghong and (b) Likoaeng, expressed as Number of Identifiable Specimens (NISP) per cubic meter of deposit, and fluctuations in fish:mammal ratios for (c) Sehonghong and (d) Likoaeng as well as (e) large ungulate:fish ratios for Likoaeng (where large ungulates are defined as size class 3 and above; Brain 1981). Also shown is the semicontinuous δ¹⁸O speleothem record from Cold Air Cave (Makapansget Valley, South Africa; Holmgren et al. 2003) in (f) its full 25 kyr span and (g) only the past 4 kyr. The cold phases under discussion—the LGM, ACR and Neoglacial—are highlighted in gray.*

Sehonghong, while *Clarias gariepinus*, the sharptooth catfish, is extremely rare at both sites. Pitsaneng most closely resembles Layers DC/SS at Sehonghong, with which it is broadly contemporary.

Some of these intersite differences likely reflect differences in the season at which fish were taken, in the permanency of river flow and other water

TABLE 6.4. NISP and MNI frequencies of the fish taxa present at Sehonghong (by layer).

Taxon	DC/SS	GAP	GWA	ALP	SA	BARF	RF	RBL/CLBRF	BAS	OS	MOS	RFS
NISP												
Labeobarbus kimberleyensis	—	1	—	—	—	—	16	—	4	—	—	—
Labeobarbus cf. *kimberleyensis*	1	11	—	—	—	—	—	—	1	—	—	—
Labeobarbus aeneus	1,645	1,316	22	226	84	11	449	31	233	31	16	1
Labeobarbus cf. *aeneus*	—	—	—	—	—	—	—	—	140	—	—	—
Labeo capensis	140	70	3	13	12	—	23	—	6	1	—	—
Labeobarbus/Labeo	1	2,515	48	472	345	56	974	166	1,218	44	46	2
Austroglanis sclateri	259	129	3	15	1	—	11	3	1	—	1	—
cf. *Austroglanis sclateri*	9	—	—	—	—	—	—	2	—	—	—	—
Claris gariepinus	2	—	—	—	—	—	—	—	—	—	—	—
Not identified	3,432	—	31	—	—	11	—	6	23	—	—	—
Total	**5,489**	**4,042**	**107**	**726**	**442**	**78**	**1,473**	**208**	**1,626**	**76**	**63**	**3**
MNI												
Labeobarbus kimberleyensis	—	1	—	—	—	—	2	—	1	—	—	—
Labeobarbus cf. *kimberleyensis*	1	1	—	—	—	—	—	—	1	—	—	—
Labeobarbus aeneus	83	55	2	11	10	2	15	5	30	3	3	1

continued on next page

TABLE 6.4—continued

Taxon	DC/SS	GAP	GWA	ALP	SA	BARF	RF	RBL/ CLBRF	BAS	OS	MOS	RFS
Labeobarbus cf. aeneus	—	—	—	—	—	—	—	—	9	—	—	—
Labeo capensis	8	5	1	2	1	—	2	—	3	1	—	—
Labeobarbus/Labeo	—	17	3	4	6	3	8	3	22	2	6	1
Austroglanis sclateri	43	18	1	3	1	—	2	1	1	—	1	—
cf. Austroglanis sclateri	—	—	—	—	—	—	—	—	—	—	—	—
Claris gariepinus	1	—	—	—	—	—	—	—	—	—	—	—
Not identified	18	—	—	—	—	—	—	—	—	—	—	—
Total	154	97	7	20	18	5	29	9	67	6	10	2

Note: Columns are arranged in order from the youngest layer (DC/SS) at the left to the oldest (RFS) at the right.

TABLE 6.5. NISP and MNI frequencies of the fish taxa present at Likoaeng.

Taxon	I	II	III	IV	V	VI	VII/IX	X	XI	XII	XIII	XIV	XV	XVI	XVII
NISP															
Labeobarbus kimberleyensis	—	1	187	1	23	76	388	—	25	2	133	3	—	1	—
Labeobarbus cf. kimberleyensis	—	—	2	—	12	13	55	—	—	—	12	—	—	—	—
Labeobarbus aeneus	—	—	82	2	54	14	228	—	9	—	3,246	69	19	19	35
Labeobarbus cf. aeneus	1	5	5	—	20	25	36	—	—	—	11	2	1	—	—
Labeobarbus spp.	6	—	30	1	16	51	310	—	23	2	309	22	4	—	—

continued on next page

TABLE 6.5—*continued*

Taxon	I	II	III	IV	V	VI	VII/IX	X	XI	XII	XIII	XIV	XV	XVI	XVII
Labeo capensis	33	93	2,203	28	3,531	965	9,486	23	783	14	2,974	196	51	11	31
Labeobarbus/Labeo	55	209	2,993	25	3,889	1,583	11,152	39	1,842	23	12,447	516	87	58	247
Clarias gariepinus	1	—	8	1	—	—	2	—	1	—	5	—	—	—	8
Austroglanis sclateri	—	—	—	—	2	—	—	—	—	—	1	—	—	—	—
cf. *Austroglanis sclateri*	—	—	—	—	1	—	3	—	—	—	—	—	—	—	—
Total	**96**	**308**	**5,510**	**58**	**7,548**	**2,727**	**21,660**	**62**	**2,683**	**41**					
MNI															
Labeobarbus kimberleyensis	—	1	9	1	3	4	20	—	3	1	9	1	—	1	—
Labeobarbus cf. *kimberleyensis*	—	—	0	—	1	0	1	—	—	—	2	—	—	—	—
Labeobarbus aeneus	—	—	5	1	6	3	12	—	2	—	178	6	2	3	4
Labeobarbus cf. *aeneus*	1	2	0	—	1	0	0	—	—	—	1	0	0	—	—
Labeobarbus spp.	1	—	0	1	1	3	6	—	2	0	6	1	2	—	—
Labeo capensis	5	5	129	5	173	50	429	4	31	3	114	12	4	3	4
Labeobarbus/Labeo	1	1	9	0	9	12	10	1	2	0	26	7	1	1	8
Clarias gariepinus	1	—	1	1	—	—	1	—	1	—	2	—	—	—	1
Austroglanis sclateri	—	—	—	—	1	—	—	—	—	—	1	—	—	—	—
cf. *Austroglanis sclateri*	—	—	—	—	1	—	2	—	—	—	—	—	—	—	—
Total	**9**	**9**	**153**	**9**	**196**	**72**	**481**	**5**	**41**	**4**	**339**	**27**	**9**	**8**	**17**

Note: Columns are arranged in order from the youngest layer (I) at the left to the oldest (XVII) at the right.

TABLE 6.6. Pitsaneng: NISP frequencies of fish taxa (after Hobart 2004). Note that MNI frequencies could not be calculated at this site because of small sample size and the interdependence of the excavated samples.

Taxon	NISP
Labeobarbus cf. *kimberleyensis*	3
Labeobarbus cf. *aeneus*	79
Labeobarbus spp.	137
Cf. *Labeobarbus*	1
Labeobarbus/Labeo	1
Cf. *Labeo* sp.	1
Unidentified cyprinids	483
Austroglanis sclateri	52
Austroglanis sp.	2
Unidentified catfish	9
Unidentified fish	150
Total	**918**

conditions between the Senqu River and its Sehonghong tributary (on which both Sehonghong and Pitsaneng lie), and perhaps also in changes in fishing strategy or in the overall role of fishing within broader subsistence-settlement decisions. The enhanced representation of *Austroglanis sclateri* at Sehonghong and Pitsaneng, for example, likely reflects its preference for side streams over larger rivers, even though it occurs at the confluence of the Sehonghong and Senqu Rivers today (Arthington et al. 2003). At Likoaeng, in contrast, the high presence of *Labeo capensis* probably derives from the opportunity provided by the shallow rapids adjacent to this site for intercepting it when it spawns in spring to midsummer, with a most probable focus in November (Plug et al. 2010:3117). *Labeobarbus aeneus*, on the other hand, breeds slightly later, with a peak in spawning activity in January (Nthimo 2000). At those times when it dominates at Likoaeng (middle and lower Layer XIII) the site was therefore likely occupied rather later in summer; the greater number of very small—and thus immature—individuals identifiable only as *Labeobarbus/Labeo* found in these levels and in Layer XIV supports this (Plug et al. 2010:3117). The more equal presence of both *Labeo capensis* and *Labeobarbus aeneus* toward the base of the Likoaeng sequence may instead indicate a more extended fishing season c. 3400–2800 cal BP stretching from October (when *Labeo capensis* begins to spawn) to February (when *Labeobarbus aeneus* ceases to do so) (Plug et al.

2010:3117). Conversely, whether or not the smallmouth yellowfish recovered at Sehonghong were obtained from the Sehonghong River itself and/or the main Senqu channel, the consistent dominance of this species across the past 30,000 years at this site suggests that fishing—and perhaps other aspects of the site's occupation—were heavily focused on summer, rather than spring, as originally suggested by Carter (1978).

To explain why *Labeobarbus aeneus* was specifically targeted in preference to *Labeo capensis* during the occupation of Likoaeng Layers XIII and XIV we need to consider climate. As we have already noted, a range of paleoenvironmental evidence, including charcoal studies, phytolith samples, and SOM $\delta^{13}C$ analysis of the sediments from which they derive (Mitchell et al. 2011; Parker et al. 2011), indicates a pronounced shift toward a C_3-dominated grassland and generally cooler, wetter conditions around 3000 cal BP, equivalent to a ≥ 400-m lowering of high-elevation alpine grassland and a likely minimum temperature depression of 2.5°C (Parker et al. 2011:208). *Labeobarbus aeneus* requires water temperatures of 18–21.5°C for its eggs to incubate successfully, whereas *Labeo capensis* demands a temperature at the extreme upper end of this range (Arthington et al. 2003). The Neoglacial downturn registered by the Likoaeng sequence, and confirmed by multiple other data sets from the Maloti-Drakensberg Mountains (Lewis 2005, 2008; Rosen et al. 1999) and more broadly in southern Africa (Holmgren et al. 2003; Lee-Thorp et al. 2001) between 3200/2900 and 2400/2300 cal BP, may thus have favored the more cold-tolerant smallmouth yellowfish over the Orange River mudfish. In turn, this may have encouraged people to camp at Likoaeng later in the year when *Labeobarbus aeneus* migrated upstream past the site or spawned there on coarser gravel substrates in the main riverbed. At the same time, lower snowlines and thus increased flooding in spring/early summer may have enhanced the predictability and size of fish runs. When climatic conditions reversed and the Neoglacial came to an end we can expect that the constraints on *Labeo capensis* populations eased. As a result people shifted their exploitation focus toward it and an earlier point in the spring/summer, when the importance of fish as a substitute for other foods (especially those rich in fat) is likely to have been greater than later in the year.

These seasonal changes in site use serve to remind us that any understanding of fish exploitation must be situated within the broader context of hunter-gatherer settlement-subsistence strategies as a whole. With very few sites—especially smaller sites rather than large rockshelters—having yet been excavated in highland Lesotho and continuing difficulties in developing a robust chronology for open-air artifact scatters, we are still a long way from achieving this (Mitchell 1996b). Nevertheless, along with the likelihood that fish were particularly favored as a resource when conditions became colder, we need to acknowledge that their relative predictability in space and time could also have made them attractive at other times, especially given the paucity of other fat- (or carbohydrate-) rich resources available in this environment in spring/early summer. This may have made fish an appealing resource focus around which people could aggregate for several weeks or even a couple of months for purposes that were as much as social as they were economic (Carter 1970; Wadley 1987). However, we currently lack additional evidence from the Lesotho highlands for enhanced exploitation of aquatic resources in a broader context of social intensification as proposed by Hall (1990, 2000) in the Fish River Basin of South Africa's Eastern Cape Province.

DISCUSSION

Climatic cooling appears to have affected highland Lesotho in complex ways, simultaneously impoverishing terrestrial plant and animal resources while improving conditions for certain taxa of freshwater fish. Although a detailed understanding of highland paleoenvironments remains elusive, it is self-evident from the topography of the Maloti-Drakensberg Mountains that people can more easily travel along the main river valleys rather than directly across the mountain ranges and uplands between them (Stewart et al. 2016). Preliminary analysis of the likely distribution of resources (edible and non-edible) of interest to hunter-gatherers in the greater Sehonghong area (Mitchell 1996b) has indicated the importance of river valleys and the immediately adjacent plateaus up to about 2,000 masl. In contrast, higher areas may have been only infrequently visited—to hunt, to collect flakeable rock or geophytes (plants with edible underground storage organs), or while passing through en route elsewhere. The overall distribution of archaeological sites supports this (Mitchell 1996b: table 6.4). Under Neoglacial conditions the extensive (≥ 400 m) depression of vegetation belts inferred at Likoaeng can only have reinforced this pattern, something surely even truer of stadial episodes in the Pleistocene. The downslope movement of nutrient-poor alpine grasses at such times would have thinned local populations of grazing ungulates, substantially raising search costs for human hunters. Increased snowfall in spring, autumn, and winter (Mills et al. 2012) may have further impeded ungulate grazing and browsing opportunities and human mobility. As Pat Carter (1976, 1978) presciently argued four decades ago, we can infer from this that human use of the Lesotho highlands under stadial conditions was substantially—and perhaps quite narrowly—focused along the Senqu Valley and its lower tributaries relative to periods of greater warmth. People—and the plant, animal, and firewood resources on which they depended—will have become increasingly packed along these linear corridors as the attractions of using other parts of the landscape declined. Aquatic resources are predicted to have become more important in cool to cold environments under precisely such conditions (Binford 2001:368; Kelly 2013), and this is what our data show. The very restriction of fish to rivers will, moreover, have encouraged a degree of positive feedback here, and thus a yet more linear focus for human settlement and activity (Binford 2001:384).

In further support of this, we note other indications of people intensifying their use of river valley sites during cold phases. The Neoglacial levels at Likoaeng (Layers XV–XI) contain the highest densities of both lithic artifacts and bone of the sequence's four occupational pulses (Mitchell et al. 2011; Plug et al. 2003). At Sehonghong, Layer BAS, which dates to immediately before the LGM, sees a sharp increase in artifact densities relative to the underlying terminal MSA and transitional MSA/LSA strata (Mitchell 1994, 1995). When humans returned to the site after the height of the LGM, densities remain high. In contrast, higher-altitude zones of the Maloti-Drakensberg witness a complete absence of occupation at this time at Moshebi's Shelter and Ha Soloja in the Sehlabathebe Basin southeast of Sehonghong (Carter 1978). Excavations at sites on the South African side of the uKhahlamba-Drakensberg Escarpment have likewise failed to produce evidence of Pleistocene occupation (Mitchell 2009a). Conversely, Melikane, 40 km south of Sehonghong and, like it, situated on a tributary of the Senqu, *does* have evidence of occupation ~24,000 cal BP, contemporary with Layer BAS at Sehonghong, and again in the form of an as-yet-undated Robberg assemblage later in the Pleistocene (B. Stewart et al. 2012). Fish are, however, almost entirely absent here, a product perhaps of poor preservation, but also of this site's having been used principally in winter, when fish were probably less abundant and harder to catch (Carter 1978). Should archaeological deposits of Pleistocene age be located along the other major river system of highland Lesotho—the Senqunyane—where only very limited survey work and almost no excavation has yet taken place (Bousman 1988; Kaplan and Mitchell 2012), we predict that they too will show evidence for intensified use of fish coincident with the LGM, the ACR, and the late Holocene Neoglacial.

Regional dietary intensification and resultant shifts in settlement and demography can also be expected to have engendered changes to hunter-gatherer technologies. In addition to shifts in raw material procurement and reduction, the reconfiguration of highland groups into more packed, river valley–focused subsistence-settlement regimes could have impacted rates of technological innovation. At Sehonghong, the immediately pre-LGM-aged Layer BAS (25,178 to 24,022 cal BP) correlates with the region's earliest full-blown LSA technocomplex—the microlithic, bladelet-rich Robberg Industry (Mitchell 1995). In fact, Layer BAS at Sehonghong is currently the oldest occurrence anywhere in southern Africa of Robberg technology, which then persists until the cessation of the second cold phase registered in the ACR-aged Layers RF and BARF (14,877 to 12,559 cal BP). Various ideas have been advanced to explain the Robberg's origins, uses, and spatial distribution (Binneman 1997; Binneman and Mitchell 1997; Deacon 1984a, 1984b; Mitchell 1988, 2002; Parkington 1984, 1990), review of which is beyond the scope of this chapter. Here we note only that the early onset of such a major technological reorganization in a highland context as regional environments responded to climatic deterioration in early MIS 2 is striking. Whether such innovations originated in the Maloti-Drakensberg and spread to other regions, were imported into the mountains from elsewhere in southern Africa, or arose independently in multiple locations must await better chronological resolution for relevant Robberg assemblages across the subcontinent, work on which we are currently engaged. But we suspect that the industry's multicomponent tools, for which standardized bladelets likely functioned as replaceable parts (Mitchell 2002:122), offered highland foragers enhanced reliability in the face of heightened search costs such as those suggested by our data. Such tools may have served as essential gear, in the Maloti-Drakensberg at least, for logistical (upland?) extraction forays by late Pleistocene foragers whose primary resource base had become constrained to the Orange-Senqu River valley and its principal tributaries.

Changes to the lithic repertoire are less evident during the Neoglacial at Likoaeng, but the sheer quantities of fish taken at this site may suggest innovations in other technologies—specifically the employment of mass-capture techniques. Without doubt, a variety of fishing techniques were practiced at the site, including angling and spearing or killing with bow and arrow, as suggested by a single bone hook and several fish crania bearing punctures consistent in diameter with bone points, respectively (Plug et al. 2010). Both techniques are also documented ethnohistorically (Vinnicombe 2009) and spearing—using both barbed spears and leisters—is, as we have indicated, depicted in local rock art (figure 6.3). We imagine that some fish were probably also caught by hand. However, a more efficient method of intercepting fish spawning runs would have been to use baskets and/or fences and drag screens, methods that are also depicted in the region's rock art, including a panel directly adjacent to Likoaeng itself (Challis et al. 2008:figure 10). Though difficult to test, the dramatic change in subsistence emphasis from terrestrial to aquatic resources during the Neoglacial (Plug et al. 2003) may signal the development of new (or the reemployment of preexisting) mass-capture methods for maximizing fish returns during multiple, albeit brief, spawning runs (Arthington et al. 1999; Cambray 1985). Support for this comes from variation through the sequence in the size of fish taken, with the lower, Neoglacial-aged layers (particularly XIII and XIV) containing by far the highest number of small and very small individuals, many of which were immature (Plug et al. 2010). Although this may partly stem from the shift toward a more extended (spring to midsummer) occupation suggested by higher numbers of adult (spawning) *Labeobarbus aeneus* (Plug et al. 2010) that we discussed above, it could equally (also) reflect the more balanced age profile expected with nonselective mass capture, as argued for very similar changes in fish assemblages at LSA sequences in the Nile Valley (Sudan and Egypt) and northern Kenya (K. Stewart 1989:227–232).

The intensified use of aquatic resources during cold phases also raises the question of food storage. On the basis of his 339 ethnographic cases, Binford (2001) found that foragers living in regions with ET < 15.25°C are expected to practice food storage even at low densities, with investments in food storage increasing as ET reduces further and populations become more packed (Johnson 2014:15). Those living in areas with ETs of < 12.75°C are dependent on aquatic resources or, if unavailable, terrestrial animals, although in none of Binford's ethnographic cases was the latter a viable intensification option (Johnson 2014:15). Today, as mentioned above, the entirety of highland Lesotho has ETs below Binford's "storage threshold" (figure 6.2). While modeling past ETs is not currently possible, the evidence presented above for average annual temperature reductions of between −2.5°C (Neoglacial) and −5°C (later Pleistocene) makes it probable that these cold phases pushed the highlands below Binford's "terrestrial plant dependence threshold" as well. Our archaeological data support this; in cold phases the upper Orange-Senqu fluvial system appears to have offered foragers a good intensification option as terrestrial environments became more impoverished, plant and animal resources more costly to obtain, and people more tethered to deep river valleys. But did highland groups practice a delayed return economy? At Likoaeng, fishing ramps up in Layer XIV (c. 3000 cal. BP; NISP = 808) before increasing exponentially in the overlying Layer XIII (2978–2382 cal. BP), when fish remains (NISP = 19,138) massively outnumber those of mammalian fauna (NISP = 414). With such vast quantities, we may ask whether some or most of this meat was dried or smoked for later consumption in a leaner season (winter/early spring). Signs of fish being processed for storage are, however, absent at Likoaeng; vertebrae and especially intermuscular bones, which typically remain embedded in fish removed from the site, are well represented, and features consistent with fish smoking or drying absent (Plug et al. 2010:3121). Rather than signaling storage, therefore, the immense quantities of fish at the site have been interpreted as supporting spring/summertime aggregations of hunter-gatherers (Plug et al. 2003, 2010).

How, then, did foragers overwinter in highland Lesotho's continental climate without food storage, considering its improbability according to Binford's ethnographic data? The obvious question becomes whether people *did* overwinter in the highlands (Carter 1978), particularly during stadial and Neoglacial phases of heightened cold such as those we have highlighted here. Although continental, Lesotho is situated on the eastern edge of this interior climatic regime. Unlike hunter-gatherers living at higher latitudes, foragers regularly based in the Maloti-Drakensberg therefore had the option of overwintering in much more equable environments, such as the lower-altitude thornveld/bushveld of the midland regions of the Eastern Cape Province or KwaZulu-Natal (Carter 1970). The latter is a temperate zone below 35° S latitude that Binford's (2001:257) ethnographic data suggest hunter-gatherers can readily inhabit without food storage. Moreover, if relatively packed, cold-phase foragers were obliged to abandon the highlands during winter, this would have negated the need for storage and limited the potential for sedentism, thereby offsetting two major factors that typically underpin the kind of labor rearrangements leading to sociopolitical inequalities and ranking (Arnold 1996; Kelly 2013). The Maloti-Drakensberg has produced no archaeological evidence for hereditary social or political ranking, save perhaps for the last few centuries when hunter-gatherers entered into diverse relations with food producers (Blundell 2004; Campbell 1987; Challis 2012; Dowson 1994). Unfortunately, however, a firm understanding of seasonal mobility in the wider region remains stubbornly elusive despite considerable effort (Carter 1970, 1978; Cable 1984; Opperman 1987) and the occurrence in highland sites of items of personal adornment originating from the Indian Ocean (Mitchell 1996c), the frequency of which, incidentally, increases during warmer (early and mid-Holocene) rather than cooler (LGM, ACR or Neoglacial) climatic phases. Resolving patterns of hunter-gatherer seasonal mobility across the wider region should be a major priority for future research.

Finally, what of our argument that highland Lesotho bears out Binford's (2001:368, 385) expectation that hunter-gatherers with an aquatic intensification option should enhance their use of such resources when diminished terrestrial food resources raise the cost of maintaining high mobility? This might be countered by the fact that Lesotho is not alone in southern Africa in having produced evidence of late Pleistocene fishing activity, since Robbins et al. (1994, 2000) have documented a pulse of fish procurement focused on cichlids, most probably *Serranochromis* spp. and, more especially, sharptooth catfish (*Clarias gariepinus*) around 36–30 ka at White Paintings Shelter in the northwestern Kalahari (Robbins et al. 2012, 2016). The same authors have also shown that there is good evidence that fishing was important in this region during the Holocene (Robbins et al. 1998, 2000, 2009), while today and in the recent past Khoe-speaking Bushmen along Botswana's Botlele and Nata Rivers practice/ have practiced delayed return economies focused on fishing with heavy investment in nets, traps, and weirs (Cashdan 1986). However, what is significant about the northwestern Kalahari—a notoriously semiarid part of southern Africa—is that these activities depend either on *unearned* water—that is, on the inflow of rain falling hundreds of kilometers to the north in the highlands of Angola—or on significantly wetter conditions locally. The poor preservation of bone at Melikane and the still incomplete nature of excavations of the Pleistocene sequence at Sehonghong currently preclude comparing Lesotho with Botswana for MIS 3, but there is no evidence at present that people focused on fish in the Kalahari during MIS 2, even though conditions there were significantly wetter on several occasions at this time (see Burrough 2016).

CONCLUSION

Integrating archaeological and paleoenvironmental data, we have argued in this chapter for a connection between phases of heightened hunter-gatherer exploitation of freshwater fish and proxy data indicative of reduced temperatures in southern Africa's Maloti-Drakensberg Mountains. Such correlations have recently become clear to us because of fresh proxy paleoenvironmental analyses and significant new bodies of radiometric dates. We concentrated on three archaeological sites with well-preserved fish remains—Sehonghong, Likoaeng, and Pitsaneng—and particularly on the former two because of their larger assemblages and longer sequences. Two spikes in the frequencies of fish remains at Sehonghong and a third at Likoaeng coincide respectively with the early LGM and ACR in the late Pleistocene, and the late Holocene Neoglacial. Estimates of average annual temperature reductions during these phases range from −2.5°C (Neoglacial) to −5°C (early LGM). Reductions of this magnitude would likely have pushed the region's ET below Binford's terrestrial plant dependence threshold of 12.75°C, negating plants as a primary subsistence base let alone a viable intensification option. Multiple proxy data suggest that these cold phases triggered major descents of altitudinal vegetation belts, with nutrient-poor, C_3-dominated alpine grasses (that today live $\geq$ 2,100–2,700 masl, depending on aspect) descending hundreds of meters into the deeply incised Orange-Senqu fluvial system within which these sites are situated (~1,800 masl). These shifts would have lowered the highlands' overall carrying capacity for browsing and grazing ungulates, making these highly ranked terrestrial resources more costly to procure. Highland hunter-gatherers appear to have responded by diversifying their subsistence base to include much higher quantities of riverine fish.

We hypothesized that foragers also reoriented their settlement systems toward more constricted, linearly structured arrangements along the upper Orange-Senqu Valley and its main tributaries, with forays into higher altitudes probably occurring on a more logistical basis. The heavier emphasis on fishing and higher costs of hunting may have encouraged adoption of more specialized, efficient, and reliable technologies in the form of mass fish-capture facilities (e.g., weirs, baskets, and drag screens) and multicomponent hunting tools (e.g., spears with replaceable microlithic barbs), respectively. Such technological innovations may have been assisted by the spatial redistribution of highland populations into more packed concentrations within these fluvial corridors. There is currently no evidence, however, that increased yields of aquatic resources—whether by dispatching individuals or mass capture—translated into the practice of food storage, as would be expected on an ethnographic basis (Binford 2001). One plausible alternative, particularly during cold phases, is that foragers negated the need for this by overwintering at lower altitudes across the uKhahlamba-Drakensberg Escarpment in the more temperate climatic regimes of the Eastern Cape and/or KwaZulu-Natal midlands. However, seasonal mobility in the region remains very poorly understood for the whole sweep of hunter-gatherer history. This, and the still uneven nature of archaeological coverage through time, are weaknesses that must be remedied before determining whether and when the region may have encouraged delayed return systems and, by extension, incipient sociopolitical inequalities.

We began by noting the pivotal importance of Kalahari Bushman ethnography not only for the interpretation of the southern African LSA, but also for broader archaeological investigations of past hunter-gatherer (and hominin) behavior. Using insights derived from Binford's (2001) global comparative study of hunter-gatherers within the framework of variation in ET we have shown that, in at least one instance, that of highland Lesotho, LSA hunter-gatherers not only engaged in subsistence activities that are difficult, if not impossible, to parallel in the Kalahari ethnographic record, but did so in ways consistent with predictions derived from broader anthropological theory. This matters for at least two reasons. The first is because, despite several previous calls to "de-!Kung" the Later Stone Age (Parkington 1984; cf. Hall 1990; Humphreys 2005; Mitchell 2002) and explore a wider range of potentially relevant ethnographic comparanda, there has been little actual effort to do so, notwithstanding well-argued instances from coastal settings in the Western Cape Province for levels of sedentism and territoriality that cannot be matched by anthropological observations in the Kalahari (e.g., Jerardino 1996; Sealy 2006). Second, our choice of highland Lesotho adds weight to the realization that hunter-gatherer communities there did not remain unchanging over the past several thousand years (Mitchell 2009b; Pargeter et al. 2016) and to the caveat that this must be remembered when applying insights gleaned from late nineteenth/twentieth-century Maloti-Drakensberg Bushmen or their descendants to the explication and explanation of Bushman rock art (e.g., Lewis-Williams 2003). But above and beyond these specific contributions, we hope to have demonstrated that investigating southern Africa's archaeological record against a well-established body of predictive, anthropologically informed theory about hunter-gatherer behavior (e.g., Binford 2001) provides a robust means of learning more about its Stone Age populations.

ACKNOWLEDGMENTS

We thank Ashley Lemke for inviting us to contribute to this volume and to the SAA symposium from which it originates. The fieldwork on which our discussion is principally based took place in 1992 (Sehonghong) and 1995 and 1998 (Likoaeng), followed by John Hobart's excavations at Pitsaneng in 2000. All the excavations took place with the permission of Lesotho's Protection and Preservation Commission, now subsumed into the Department of Culture. We are grateful to the PPC's former chairman, the late 'Me Ntsema Khitšane for issuing the relevant permits, as well as to the chiefs and local communities at Sehonghong, Khomo-ea-Mollo, and Ha Mapola Letsatseng, and to all those who, having taken part in the excavations or facilitated them, have previously been acknowledged elsewhere. Fieldwork was supported by grants from the University of Cape Town, the University of Oxford (including the Boise, Meyerstein, and Swan Funds), the University of Wales, Lampeter, St Hugh's College, Oxford, the Arts and Humanities Research Board, the British Academy, the Prehistoric Society, the Sir Henry Strakosch Memorial Trust, and the Society of Antiquaries. Analysis of the faunal remains from Likoaeng was undertaken with the support of the Leverhulme Trust. During our revision of this essay we learned with sadness of the murder on his family farm of Gavin Carter, Pat Carter and Patricia Vinnicombe's son, who was present with them during their 1971 excavations at Sehonghong. We hope that, at some point, South Africa will cease to experience mindless violence of this kind.

REFERENCES CITED

Abell, P. I., and I. Plug. 2000. "The Pleistocene/Holocene Transition in South Africa: Evidence for the Younger Dryas Event." *Global and Planetary Change* 26 (1–3): 173–179. https://doi.org/10.1016/S0921-8181(00)00042-4.

Ambrose, D., S. Talukdar, and E. M. Pomela. 2000. *Biological Diversity in Lesotho.* Maseru, Lesotho: National Environmental Secretariat.

Arnold, J. E. 1996. "The Archaeology of Complex Hunter-Gatherers." *Journal of Archaeological Method and Theory* 3(1):77–126. https://doi.org/10.1007/BF02228931.

Arthington, A. H., J. L. Rall, and M. J. Kennard. 1999. "Specialist Report: Fish." Final Report to the Lesotho Highlands Development Authority.

Arthington, A. H., J. L. Rall, M. J. Kennard, and B. J. Pusey. 2003. "Environmental Flow Requirements of Fish in Lesotho Rivers Using the Drift Methodology." *River Research and Applications* 19(5–6):641–666. https://doi.org/10.1002/rra.728.

Baird, D. P., and S. Fourie. 1978. "The Length/Mass Relationship and Condition of *Labeo capensis* in the Caledon River." *Journal of the Limnological Society of South Africa* 4(1):53–58. https://doi.org/10.1080/03779688.1978.9633148.

Barber, D. C., A. Dyke, C. Hillaire-Marcel, A. E. Jennings, J. T. Andrews, M. W. Kerwin, G. Bilodeau, R. McNeely, J. Southon, M. D. Morehead, et al. 1999. "Forcing of the Cold Event of 8,200 Years Ago by Catastrophic Drainage of Laurentide Lakes." *Nature* 400(6742):344–348. https://doi.org/10.1038/22504.

Barham, L., and P. J. Mitchell. 2008. *The First Africans: African Archaeology from the Earliest Tool Makers to Most Recent Foragers.* Cambridge, UK: Cambridge University Press. https://doi.org/10.1017/CBO9780511817830.

Bawden, M. G., and D. M. Carroll. 1968. *The Land Resources of Lesotho.* London: United Kingdom Directorate of Overseas Surveys.

Binford, L. R. 2001. *Constructing Frames of Reference.* Berkeley: University of California Press.

Binneman, J.N.F. 1997. "Usewear Traces on Robberg Bladelets from Rose Cottage Cave." *South African Journal of Science* 93(10):479–481.

Binneman, J. N. F. and P. J. Mitchell. 1997. "Usewear Analysis of Robberg Bladelets from Sehonghong Shelter, Lesotho." *Southern African Field Archaeology* 6:42–49.

Blundell, G. 2004. *Nqabayo's Nomansland: San Rock Art and the Somatic Past.* Uppsala, Sweden: Uppsala University Press.

Bousman, C. B. 1988. "Prehistoric Settlement Patterns in the Senqunyane Valley, Lesotho." *South African Archaeological Bulletin* 43(147):33–37. https://doi.org/10.2307/3887611.

Brain, C. K. 1981. *The Hunters or the Hunted? An Introduction to Cave Taphonomy.* Chicago, IL: University of Chicago Press.

Broughton, J. M. 1994. "Late Holocene Resource Intensification in the Sacramento Valley, California: The Vertebrate Evidence." *Journal of Archaeological Science* 21(4):501–514. https://doi.org/10.1006/jasc.1994.1050.

Burrough, S. L. 2016. "Late Quaternary Environmental Change and Human Occupation of the Southern African Interior." In *Africa from MIS 6–2: Population Dynamics and Paleoenvironments*, ed. S. C. Jones and B. A. Stewart, 161–174. Dordrecht, Netherlands: Springer. https://doi.org/10.1007/978-94-017-7520-5_9.

Cable, J. H. C. 1984. *Economy and Technology in Late Stone Age Southern Natal.* vol. 201. BAR International Series. Oxford, UK: British Archaeological Reports.

Cambray, J. A. 1985. "Observations on Spawning of *Labeo capensis* and *Clarias gariepinus* in the Regulated Lower Orange River, South Africa." *South African Journal of Science* 81(6):318–321.

Campbell, C. 1987. "Art in Crisis: Contact Period Rock Art in the South-eastern Mountains of Southern Africa." Unpublished MSc thesis, University of the Witwatersrand.

Carter, P. L. 1970. "Late Stone Age Exploitation Patterns in Southern Natal." *South African Archaeological Bulletin* 25(98):55–58. https://doi.org/10.2307/3887948.

Carter, P. L. 1976. "The Effects of Climate Change on Settlement in Eastern Lesotho During the Middle and Later Stone Age." *World Archaeology* 8(2):197–206. https://doi.org/10.1080/00438243.1976.9979664.

Carter, P. L. 1978. "The Prehistory of Eastern Lesotho." PhD dissertation, Department of Archaeology, University of Cambridge, UK.

Carter, P. L., P. J. Mitchell, and P. Vinnicombe. 1988. *Sehonghong: The Middle and Later Stone Age Industrial Sequence at a Lesotho Rock-Shelter.* BAR International Series 406. Oxford: British Archaeological Reports.

Cashdan, E. 1986. "Hunter-Gatherers of the Northern Kalahari." In *Contemporary Studies on Khoisan I*, ed. R. Vossen and K. Keuthmann, 145–180. Hamburg, Germany: Helmut Buske Verlag.

Challis, S. 2012. "Creolisation on the Nineteenth-Century Frontiers of Southern Africa: A Case Study of the AmaTola 'Bushmen' in the Maloti-Drakensberg." *Journal of Southern African Studies* 38(2):265–280. https://doi.org/10.1080/03057070.2012.666905.

Challis, W., P. J. Mitchell, and J. D. Orton. 2008. "Fishing in the Rain: Control of Rain-making and Aquatic Resources at a Previously Undescribed Rock Art Site in Highland Lesotho." *Journal of African Archaeology* 6(2):203–218. https://doi.org/10.3213/1612-1651-10111.

Chase, B. M., M. E. Meadows, L. Scott, D.S.G. Thomas, E. Marais, J. Sealy, and P. J. Reimer. 2009. "A Record of Rapid Holocene Climate Change Preserved in Hyrax Middens from Southwestern Africa." *Geology* 37(8):703–706. https://doi.org/10 .1130/G30053A.1.

Chase, B. M., L. J. Quick, M. E. Meadows, L. Scott, D.S.G. Thomas, and P. J. Reimer. 2011. "Late Glacial Interhemispheric Climate Dynamics Revealed in South African Hyrax Middens." *Geology* 39(1):19–22. https://doi.org/10.1130/G31129.1.

Chevalier, M., and B. M. Chase. 2015. "Southeast African Records Reveal a Coherent Shift from High- to Low-Latitude Forcing Mechanisms along the East African Margin across Last Glacial-Interglacial Transition." *Quaternary Science Reviews* 125:117–130. https://doi.org/10.1016/j.quascirev.2015.07.009.

Clark, J. D. 1959. *The Prehistory of Southern Africa*. Harmondsworth, UK: Penguin.

Clark, J. D. 1969. *Kalambo Falls Prehistoric Site*, vol. 1, *The Geology, Palaeoecology and Detailed Stratigraphy of the Excavations*. Cambridge, UK: Cambridge University Press.

Clark, J. D. 1974a. *Kalambo Falls Prehistoric Site*, vol. 2, *The Later Prehistoric Cultures*. Cambridge UK: Cambridge University Press.

Clark, J. D., ed. 1974b. *Kalambo Falls Prehistoric Site*, vol. 3, *The Earlier Cultures: Middle and Earlier Stone Age*. Cambridge, UK: Cambridge University Press.

Coetzee, J. 1967. "Pollen Analytical Studies in East and Southern Africa." *Palaeoecology of Africa* 3:1–146.

Deacon, J. 1984a. *The Later Stone Age of Southernmost Africa*. vol. 213. BAR International Series. Oxford: British Archaeological Reports.

Deacon, J. 1984b. "Later Stone Age People and Their Descendants in Southern Africa." In *Southern African Prehistory and Paleoenvironments*, ed. R. G. Klein, 221–328. Rotterdam, Netherlands: Balkema.

Dowson, T. A. 1994. "Reading Art, Writing History: Rock Art and Social Change in Southern Africa." *World Archaeology* 25(3):332–345. https://doi.org/10.1080 /00438243.1994.9980249.

Esterhuysen, A. B., and P. J. Mitchell. 1996. "Palaeoenvironmental and Archaeological Implications of Charcoal Assemblages from Holocene Sites in Western Lesotho, Southern Africa." *Palaeoecology of Africa* 24:203–232.

Grab, S. W. 1994. "Thufur in the Mohlesi Valley, Lesotho, Southern Africa." *Permafrost and Periglacial Processes* 5(2):111–118. https://doi.org/10.1002/ppp.3430050205.

Grab, S. W. 1997. "Thermal Regime for a Thufa Apex and Its Adjoining Depression, Mashai Valley, Lesotho." *Permafrost and Periglacial Processes* 8 (4): 437–445. https:// doi.org/10.1002/(SICI)1099-1530(199710/12)8:4<437::AID-PPP264>3.0.CO;2-O.

Grab, S. W., and S. C. Mills. 2011. "Quaternary Slope Processes and Morphologies in the Upper Sehonghong Valley, Eastern Lesotho." *Proceedings of the Geologists' Association* 122:179–186. https://doi.org/10.1016/j.pgeola.2010.02.001.

Grab, S. W., and D. J. Nash. 2010. "Documentary Evidence of Climate Variability During Cold Seasons in Lesotho, Southern Africa, 1833–1900." *Climate Dynamics* 34(4):473–499. https://doi.org/10.1007/s00382-009-0598-4.

Green, H., R. Pickering, R. Drysdale, B. C. Johnson, J. Hellstrom, and M. Wallace. 2015. "Evidence for Global Teleconnections in a Late Pleistocene Speleothem Record of Water Balance and Vegetation Change at Sudwala Cave, South Africa." *Quaternary Science Reviews* 110:114–130. https://doi.org/10.1016/j.quascirev.2014.11.016.

Hall, S. L. 1990. "Hunter-Gatherer-Fishers of the Fish River Basin: A Contribution to the Holocene Prehistory of the Eastern Cape." D.Phil. dissertation, Department of Archaeology, University of Stellenbosch, South Africa.

Hall, S. L. 2000. "Burial Sequence in the Later Stone Age of the Eastern Cape Province, South Africa." *South African Archaeological Bulletin* 55(172):137–146. https://doi.org/10.2307/3888962.

Hall, S. L., and J. N. F. Binneman. 1987. "Later Stone Age Burial Variability in the Cape: A Social Interpretation." *South African Archaeological Bulletin* 42(146):140–152. https://doi.org/10.2307/3888740.

Hanvey, P. M., and M. E. Marker. 1992. "Present-Day Periglacial Microforms in the Lesotho Highlands: Implications for Present and Past Climatic Conditions." *Permafrost and Periglacial Processes* 3(4):353–361. https://doi.org/10.1002/ppp.3430030409.

Heinz, H. J. 1972. "Territoriality among the Bushmen in General and the !ko in Particular." *Anthropos* 67:405–416.

Hobart, J. H. 2003. "An Old Fashioned Approach to a Modern Hobby: Fishing in the Lesotho Highlands." In *Researching Africa's Past: New Contributions from British Archaeologists*, ed. P. J. Mitchell, A. Haour, and J. H. Hobart, 44–53. Oxford, UK: Oxford University School of Archaeology.

Hobart, J. H. 2004. "Pitsaneng: Evidence for a Neolithic Lesotho?" *Before Farming* 2:261–270.

Hogg, A., Q. Hua, P. Blackwell, M. Niu, C. Buck, T. Guilderson, T. Heaton, J. Palmer, P. Reimer, R. Reimer, C. Turney, S. Zimmerman. 2013. "SHCal13 Southern Hemisphere Calibration, 0–50,000 years cal BP." *Radiocarbon* 55(4):1889–1903.

Holmgren, K., J. A. Lee-Thorp, G.R.J. Cooper, K. Lundblad, T. C. Partridge, L. Scott, R. Sithaldeen, A. S. Talma, and P. D. Tyson. 2003. "Persistent Millennial-Scale Climatic Variability over the Past 25,000 Years in Southern Africa." *Quaternary Science Reviews* 22(21–22):2311–2326. https://doi.org/10.1016/S0277-3791(03)00204-X.

Horsburgh, A. K., J. V. Moreno-Mayar, and A. L. Gosling. 2016. "Revisiting the Kalahari Debate in the Highlands: Ancient DNA Provides New Faunal Identifications at Sehonghong, Lesotho." *Azania: Archaeological Research in Africa* 51(3):295–306. https://doi.org/10.1080/0067270X.2016.1169041.

Humphreys, A.J.B. 2005. "De-!Kunging the Later Stone Age of the Central Interior of South Africa." *Southern African Field Archaeology* 13:36–41.

Isaac, G. L. 1984. "The Archaeology of Human Origins: Studies of the Lower Pleistocene in East Africa 1971–1981." In *Advances in World Archaeology*, vol. 3. ed. F. Wendorf and A. Close, 1–87. New York: Academic Press.

Jacobs, Z., R. G. Roberts, R. F. Galbraith, H. J. Deacon, R. Grün, A. Mackay, P. J. Mitchell, R. Vogelsang, and L. Wadley. 2008. "Ages for the Middle Stone Age of Southern Africa: Implications for Human Behavior and Dispersal." *Science* 322(5902):733–735. https://doi.org/10.1126/science.1162219.

Jacot Guillarmod, A. 1971. *Flora of Lesotho (Basutoland)*. Lehre, Germany: Verlag Von Cramer.

Jerardino, A. 1996. "Changing Social Landscapes of the Western Cape Coast of Southern Africa over the Last 4500 Years." PhD dissertation, Department of Archaeology, University of Cape Town, South Africa.

Jerardino, A. 2010. "Large Shell Middens in Lamberts Bay, South Africa: A Case of Hunter-Gatherer Resource Intensification." *Journal of Archaeological Science* 37(9):2291–2302. https://doi.org/10.1016/j.jas.2010.04.002.

Johnson, A. L. 2014. "Exploring Adaptive Variation among Hunter-Gatherers with Binford's Frames of Reference." *Journal of Archaeological Research* 22(1):1–42. https://doi.org/10.1007/s10814-013-9068-y.

Jones, S. C., and B. A. Stewart, eds. 2016. *Africa from MIS 6–2: Population Dynamics and Paleoenvironments*. Dordrecht, Netherlands: Springer. https://doi.org/10.1007/978-94-017-7520-5.

Kaplan, J., and P. J. Mitchell. 2012. "The Archaeology of the Lesotho Highlands Water Project Phases IA and IB." *Southern African Humanities* 24:1–32.

Kelly, R. L. 1983. "Hunter-Gatherer Mobility Strategies." *Journal of Anthropological Research* 39(3):277–306. https://doi.org/10.1086/jar.39.3.3629672.

Kelly, R. L. 1995. *The Foraging Spectrum: Diversity in Hunter-Gatherer Lifeways*. Washington, DC: Smithsonian Institution Press.

Kelly, R. L. 2013. *The Lifeways of Hunter-Gatherers: The Foraging Spectrum*. Cambridge, UK: Cambridge University Press. https://doi.org/10.1017/CBO9781139176132.

Kent, S. 1996. *Cultural Diversity among Twentieth-Century Foragers: An African Perspective*. Cambridge, UK: Cambridge University Press.

Killick, D. J. B. 1963. "An Account of the Plant Ecology of the Cathedral Peak Area of the Natal Drakensberg." *Memoirs of the Botanical Survey of South Africa* 34:1–178.

Killick, D. J. B. 1978. "The Afro-Alpine Region." In *Biogeography and Ecology of Southern Africa*, ed. M.J.A. Werger, 515–560. The Hague, Netherlands: Junk. https://doi.org/10.1007/978-94-009-9951-0_12.

Leakey, M. D. 1971. *Olduvai Gorge: Excavations in Bed I and II: 1960–1963*. Cambridge, UK: Cambridge University Press.

Lee, R. B. 1968. "What Hunters Do for a Living, Or, How to Make Out on Scarce Resources." In *Man the Hunter*, ed. I. DeVore and R. B. Lee, 30–48. Chicago, IL: Aldine.

Lee, R. B. 1969. "!Kung Bushmen Subsistence: An Input-Output Analysis." In *Environment and Cultural Behavior: Ecological Studies in Cultural Anthropology*, ed. A. P. Vayda, 73–94. New York: Natural History Press.

Lee, R. B. 1972. "The !Kung Bushmen of Botswana." In *Hunters and Gatherers Today*, ed. M. G. Biccieri, 327–368. New York: Holt, Rinehart and Winston.

Lee, R. B. 1979. *The !Kung San: Men, Women, and Work in a Foraging Society*. Cambridge, UK: Cambridge University Press.

Lee, R. B., and I. DeVore. 1976. *Kalahari Hunter-Gatherers*. Cambridge, MA: Harvard University Press. https://doi.org/10.4159/harvard.9780674430600.

Lee-Thorp, J. A., K. Holmgren, S. E. Lauritzen, H. Linge, A. Moberg, T. C. Partridge, C. Stevenson, and P. D. Tyson. 2001. "Rapid Climate Shifts in the Southern African Interior through the Mid to Late Holocene." *Geophysical Research Letters* 28(23):4507–4510. https://doi.org/10.1029/2000GL012728.

Lewis, C. A. 2005. "Late Glacial and Holocene Palaeoclimatology of the Drakensberg of the Eastern Cape, South Africa." *Quaternary International* 129(1):33–48. https://doi.org/10.1016/j.quaint.2004.04.005.

Lewis, C. A. 2008. "Late Quaternary Climatic Changes, and Associated Human Responses during the last ~45,000 yr in the Eastern and Adjoining Western Cape, South Africa." *Earth-Science Reviews* 88(3–4):167–187. https://doi.org/10.1016/j.earscirev.2008.01.006.

Lewis-Williams, J. D. 1981. *Believing and Seeing: Symbolic Meanings in Southern San Rock Paintings*. London: Academic Press.

Lewis-Williams, J. D. 2003. *Images of Mystery*. Cape Town, South Africa: Double Storey.

Lewis-Williams, J. D. 1982. "The Economic and Social Context of Southern San Rock." *Current Anthropology* 23(4):429–449. https://doi.org/10.1086/202871.

Loftus, E., B. A. Stewart, G. Dewar, and J. A. Lee-Thorp. 2015. "Stable Isotope Evidence of Late MIS 3 to Middle Holocene Palaeoenvironments from Sehonghong Rockshelter, Eastern Lesotho." *Journal of Quaternary Science* 30(8):805–816. https://doi.org/10.1002/jqs.2817.

Mills, S. C., S. W. Grab, and S. J. Carr. 2009a. "Late Quaternary Moraines along the Sekhokong Range, Eastern Lesotho: Contrasting the Geomorphic History of North- and South-Facing Slopes." *Geografiska Annaler. Series A. Physical Geography* 91(2):121–140. https://doi.org/10.1111/j.1468-0459.2009.00359.x.

Mills, S. C., S. W. Grab, and S. J. Carr. 2009b. "Recognition and Palaeoclimatic Implications of Late Quaternary Niche Glaciation in Eastern Lesotho." *Journal of Quaternary Science* 24(7):647–663. https://doi.org/10.1002/jqs.1247.

Mills, S. C., S. W. Grab, B. R. Rea, S. J. Carr, and A. Farrow. 2012. "Shifting Westerlies and Precipitation Patterns during the Late Pleistocene in Southern Africa as Determined Using Glacier Reconstruction and Mass Balance Modelling." *Quaternary Science Reviews* 55:145–159. https://doi.org/10.1016/j.quascirev.2012.08.012.

Mitchell, P. J. 1988. "The Late Pleistocene Early Microlithic Assemblages of Southern Africa." *World Archaeology* 20(1):27–39. https://doi.org/10.1080/00438243.1988.9980054.

Mitchell, P. J. 1995. "Revisiting the Robberg: New Results and a Revision of Old Ideas at Sehonghong Rock Shelter, Lesotho." *South African Archaeological Bulletin* 50(161):28–38. https://doi.org/10.2307/3889272.

Mitchell, P. J. 1996a. "The Late Quaternary of the Lesotho Highlands, Southern Africa: Preliminary Results and Future Potential of Ongoing Research at Sehonghong Shelter." *Quaternary International* 33:35–43. https://doi.org/10.1016/1040-6182 (95)00097-6.

Mitchell, P. J. 1996b. "The Late Quaternary Landscape at Sehonghong in the Lesotho Highlands, Southern Africa." *Antiquity* 70(269):623–638. https://doi.org/10.1017/S0003598X00083757.

Mitchell, P. J. 1996c. "Prehistoric Exchange and Interaction in Southeastern Southern Africa: Marine Shells and Ostrich Eggshell." *African Archaeological Review* 13(1):35–76. https://doi.org/10.1007/BF01956132.

Mitchell, P. J. 2002. *The Archaeology of Southern Africa*. Cambridge, UK: Cambridge University Press.

Mitchell, P. J. 2009a. "Gathering Together a History of the *People of the Eland*: Towards an Archaeology of Maloti-Drakensberg Hunter-Gatherers." In *The Eland's People: New Perspectives in the Rock Art of the Maloti-Drakensberg Bushmen. Essays in Memory of Patricia Vinnicombe*, ed. P. J. Mitchell and B. W. Smith, 99–136. Johannesburg, South Africa: Wits University Press.

Mitchell, P. J. 2009b. "Hunter-Gatherers and Farmers: Some Implications of 1,800 Years of Interaction in the Maloti-Drakensberg Region of Southern Africa." *Senri Ethnological Studies* 73:15–46.

Mitchell, P. J., and C. Arthur. 2014. "Ha Makotoko: Later Stone Age Occupation across the Pleistocene/Holocene Transition in Western Lesotho." *Journal of African Archaeology* 12(2):205–232. https://doi.org/10.3213/2191-5784-10255.

Mitchell, P. J., I. Plug, G. N. Bailey, R. L. C. Charles, A. B. Esterhuysen, J. A. Lee-Thorp, A. G. Parker, and S. Woodborne. 2011. "Beyond the Drip-Line: A High-Resolution Open-Air Holocene Hunter-Gatherer Sequence from Highland Lesotho." *Antiquity* 85(330):1225–1242. https://doi.org/10.1017/S0003598X00062025.

Mitchell, P. J., and J. C. Vogel. 1994. "New Radiocarbon Dates from Sehonghong Rock-Shelter, Lesotho." *South African Journal of Science* 90:284–288.

Mucina, L., and M. C. Rutherford. 2006. *The Vegetation of South Africa, Lesotho and Swaziland. Strelitzia 19.* Pretoria, South Africa: South African National Biodiversity Institute.

Nash, D., and M. E. Meadows. 2012. "Africa." In *Quaternary Environmental Change in the Tropics*, ed. S. E. Metcalfe and D. Nash, 79–150. Oxford, UK: Wiley-Blackwell. https://doi.org/10.1002/9781118336311.ch4.

Nthimo, M. 2000. "The Biology of Commercially Important Fish Species and a Preliminary Assessment of the Fisheries Potential of the Katse Dam, Lesotho." M.Sc. thesis, Rhodes University, Grahamstown, South Africa.

Opperman, H. 1987. *The Later Stone Age of the Drakensberg Range and its Foothills.* vol. 339. BAR International Series. Oxford, UK: British Archaeological Reports.

Opperman, H., and B. Heydenrych. 1990. "A 22 000 Year-Old Middle Stone Age Camp Site with Plant Food Remains from the North-Eastern Cape." *South African Archaeological Bulletin* 45(152):93–99. https://doi.org/10.2307/3887967.

Oswalt, W. H. 1976. *An Anthropological Analysis of Food-Getting Technology.* New York: Wiley.

Pargeter, J., E. Loftus, and P. J. Mitchell. 2017. "New Ages from Sehonghong Rock-shelter: Implications for the Late Pleistocene Occupation of Highland Lesotho." *Journal of Archaeological Science: Reports* 12:307–315. https://doi.org/10.1016/j.jasrep.2017.01.027.

Pargeter, J., A. Mackay, P. J. Mitchell, J. Shea, and B. A. Stewart. 2016. "Primordialism and the 'Pleistocene San' of Southern Africa." *Antiquity* 90(352):1072–1079. https://doi.org/10.15184/aqy.2016.100.

Parker, A. G., J. A. Lee-Thorp, and P. J. Mitchell. 2011. "Late Holocene Neoglacial Conditions from the Lesotho Highlands, Southern Africa: Phytolith and Stable Carbon Isotope Evidence from the Archaeological Site of Likoaeng." *Proceedings of the Geologists' Association* 122:201–211. https://doi.org/10.1016/j.pgeola.2010.09.005.

Parkington, J. E. 1984. "Changing Views of the Later Stone Age of South Africa." *Advances in World Archaeology* 3:89–142.

Parkington, J. E. 1990. "A View from the South: Southern Africa Before, During, and After the Last Glacial Maximum." In *The World at 18,000 BP*, Volume 2, *Low Latitudes*, ed. O. Soffer and C. Gamble, 214–228. London: Unwin Hyman.

Parkington, J. E. 1996. "What Is an Eland? N!ao and the Politics of Age and Sex in the Paintings of the Western Cape." In *Miscast: Negotiating the Presence of the Bushmen*, ed. P. Skotnes, 281–289. Cape Town, South Africa: University of Cape Town Press.

Parkington, J. E., P. Nilssen, C. Reeler, and C. Henshilwood. 1992. "Making Sense of Space at Dunefield Midden Campsite, Western Cape, South Africa." *Southern African Field Archaeology* 1:63–70.

Partridge, T. C., L. Scott, and J. E. Hamilton. 1999. "Synthetic Reconstructions of Southern African Environments during the Last Glacial Maximum (21–18 kyr) and the Holocene Altithermal (8–6 kyr)." *Quaternary International* 57–58:207–214. https://doi.org/10.1016/S1040-6182(98)00061-5.

Pedro, J. B., H. C. Bostock, C.M.N. Bitz, F. He, M. J. Vandergoes, E. J. Steig, B. M. Chase, C. E. Krause, S. O. Rasmussen, B. R. Markle, et al. 2016. "The Spatial Extent and Dynamics of the Antarctic Cold Reversal." *Nature Geoscience* 9(1):51–55. https://doi.org/10.1038/ngeo2580.

Plug, I., and P. J. Mitchell. 2008a. "Sehonghong: Hunter-Gatherer Utilization of Animal Resources in the Highlands of Lesotho." *Annals of the Transvaal Museum* 45:31–53.

Plug, I., and P. J. Mitchell. 2008b. "Fishing in the Lesotho Highlands: 26,000 Years of Fish Exploitation, with Special Reference to Sehonghong Shelter." *Journal of African Archaeology* 6(1):33–55. https://doi.org/10.3213/1612-1651-10102.

Plug, I., P. J. Mitchell, and G. Bailey. 2003. "Animal Remains from Likoaeng, An Open-Air River Site, and Its Place in the Post-classic Wilton of Lesotho and Eastern Free State, South Africa: Research Articles." *South African Journal of Science* 99:143–152.

Plug, I., P. J. Mitchell, and H. N. Bailey. 2010. "Late Holocene Fishing Strategies in Southern Africa as Seen from Likoaeng, Highland Lesotho." *Journal of Archaeological Science* 37(12):3111–3123. https://doi.org/10.1016/j.jas.2010.07.012.

Quick, L. J., B. M. Chase, M. E. Meadows, L. Scott, and P. J. Reimer. 2011. "A 19.5 kyr Vegetation History from the Central Cederberg Mountains, South Africa: Palynological Evidence from Rock Hyrax Middens." *Palaeogeography, Palaeoclimatology, Palaeoecology* 309(3–4):253–270. https://doi.org/10.1016/j.palaeo.2011.06.008.

Robbins, L. H., G. A. Brook, M. L. Murphy, A. H. Ivester, and A. C. Campbell. 2016. "The Kalahari During MIS 6-2 (190-12 Ka): Archaeology, Paleoenvironment, and Population Dynamics." In *Africa from MIS 6–2: Population Dynamics and Paleoenvironments*, ed. S. C. Jones and B. A. Stewart, 175–193. Dordrecht, Netherlands: Springer. https://doi.org/10.1007/978-94-017-7520-5_10.

Robbins, L. H., A. C. Campbell, G. A. Brook, M. L. Murphy, and R. K. Hitchcock. 2012. "The Antiquity of the Bow and Arrow in the Kalahari Desert: Bone Points From White Paintings Rock Shelter, Botswana." *Journal of African Archaeology* 10(1):7–20. https://doi.org/10.3213/2191-5784-10211.

Robbins, L. H., A. C. Campbell, M. L. Murphy, G. A. Brook, A. A. Mabuse, R. K. Hitchcock, G. Babutsi, M. Mmolawa, K. M. Stewart, T. E. Steele, et al. 2009.

"Mogapelwa: Archaeology, Palaeoenvironment and Oral Traditions at Lake Ngami, Botswana." *South African Archaeological Bulletin* 64:13–32.

Robbins, L. H., M. L. Murphy, G. A. Brook, A. H. Ivester, A. C. Campbell, R. G. Klein, R. G. Milo, K. M. Stewart, W. S. Downey, and N. J. Stevens. 2000. "Archaeology, Palaeoenvironment and Chronology of the Tsodilo Hills White Paintings Rock Shelter, Northwest Kalahari Desert, Botswana." *Journal of Archaeological Science* 27(11):1085–1113. https://doi.org/10.1006/jasc.2000.0597.

Robbins, L. H., M. L. Murphy, A. C. Campbell, G. A. Brook, D. M. Reid, K. H. Haberyan, and W. S. Downey. 1998. "Test Excavation and Reconnaissance Palaeoenvironmental Work at Toteng, Botswana." *South African Archaeological Bulletin* 53(168):125–132. https://doi.org/10.2307/3889186.

Robbins, L. H., M. L. Murphy, K. M. Stewart, A. C. Campbell, and G. A. Brook. 1994. "Barbed Bone Points, Paleoenvironment and the Antiquity of Fish Exploitation in the Kalahari Desert, Botswana." *Journal of Field Archaeology* 21:257–264. https://doi.org/10.2307/529874.

Roberts, P., J. A. Lee-Thorp, P. J. Mitchell, and C. Arthur. 2013. "Stable Carbon Isotopic Evidence for Climate Change across the Late Pleistocene to Early Holocene from Lesotho, Southern Africa." *Journal of Quaternary Science* 28(4):360–369. https://doi.org/10.1002/jqs.2624.

Rosen, D. Z., C. A. Lewis, and P. M. Illgner. 1999. "Palaeoclimatic and Archaeological Implications of Organic-Rich Sediments at Tiffindell Ski Resort, Near Rhodes, Eastern Cape Province, South Africa." *Transactions of the Royal Society of South Africa* 54(2):311–321. https://doi.org/10.1080/00359199909520630.

Sampson, C. G. 1988. *Stylistic Boundaries among Mobile Hunter-Foragers*. Washington, DC: Smithsonian Institution Press.

Schrire, C. 1980. "An Inquiry into the Evolutionary Status and Apparent Identity of San Hunter-Gatherers." *Human Ecology* 8(1):9–32. https://doi.org/10.1007/BF01531466.

Schrire, C. 1984. "Wild Surmises on Savage Thoughts." In *Past and Present in Hunter Gatherer Studies*, ed. C. Schrire, 1–25. New York: Academic Press.

Schulze, R. E. 1979. *Hydrology and Water Resources of the Drakensberg*. Pietermaritzburg, South Africa: Natal Town and Regional Planning Commission.

Schulze, R. E. 2008. "South African Atlas of Climatology and Agrohydrology." WRC Report No. 1489/1/06. Pretoria, South Africa: Water Research Commission.

Scott, L. 1989. "Late Quaternary Vegetation History and Climatic Change in the Eastern Orange Free State, South Africa." *South African Journal of Botany* 55(1):107–116. https://doi.org/10.1016/S0254-6299(16)31238-8.

Scott, L., and J. A. Lee-Thorp. 2004. "Holocene Climatic Trends and Rhythms in Southern Africa." In *Past Climate Variability through Europe and Africa*, ed. R. W.

Battarbee, F. Gasse, and C. E. Stickley, 69–91. Dordrecht, Netherlands: Springer. https://doi.org/10.1007/978-1-4020-2121-3_5.

Sealy, J. C. 2006. "Diet, Mobility, and Settlement Pattern among Holocene Hunter-Gatherers in Southernmost Africa." Commentary. *Current Anthropology* 47(4):569–595. https://doi.org/10.1086/504163.

Silberbauer, G. B. 1965. *Report to the Government of Bechuanaland on the Bushman Survey*. Gaberone, Botswana: Bechuanaland Government.

Silberbauer, G. B. 1981. *Hunter and Habitat in the Central Kalahari Desert*. Cambridge, UK: Cambridge University Press.

Skelton, P. 2001. *The Freshwater Fishes of Southern Africa*. Cape Town, South Africa: Struik.

Skinner, J. D., and C. Chimimba. 2005. *The Mammals of the Southern African Sub-Region*. Cambridge, UK: Cambridge University Press. https://doi.org/10.1017/CBO9781107340992.

Smith, J. M., J. A. Lee-Thorp, and J. C. Sealy. 2002. "Stable Carbon and Oxygen Isotopic Evidence for Late Pleistocene to Middle Holocene Climatic Fluctuations in the Interior of Southern Africa." *Journal of Quaternary Science* 17(7):683–695. https://doi.org/10.1002/jqs.687.

Smits, L. G. A. 1967. "Fishing Scenes from Botsabelo, Lesotho." *South African Archaeological Bulletin* 22(86):60–67. https://doi.org/10.2307/3888087.

Solomon, A. C. 1992. "Gender, Representation, and Power in San Ethnography and Rock Art." *Journal of Anthropological Archaeology* 11(4):291–329. https://doi.org/10.1016/0278-4165(92)90011-Y.

Solomon, A. C. 1994. "'Mythic Women': A Study in Variability in San Rock Art and Narrative." In *Contested Images: Diversity in Southern African Rock Art Research*, ed. T. A. Dowson and J. D. Lewis-Williams, 331–371. Johannesburg, South Africa: University of the Witwatersrand Press.

Solway, J. S., and R. B. Lee. 1990. "Foragers, Genuine or Spurious?: Situating the Kalahari San in History." *Current Anthropology* 31(2):109–146. https://doi.org/10.1086/203816.

Speth, J. D. 2010. *The Palaeoanthropology and Archaeology of Big-Game Hunting: Protein, Fat or Politics?* New York: Springer. https://doi.org/10.1007/978-1-4419-6733-6.

Stewart, B. A. 2010. "Modifications on the Bovid Bone Assemblage from Dunefield Midden, South Africa: Stage One of a Multivariate Taphonomic Analysis." *Azania* 45(3):238–275. https://doi.org/10.1080/0067270X.2010.491951.

Stewart, B. A. 2011. "'Residues of Parts Unchewable': Stages Two and Three of a Multivariate Taphonomic Analysis of the Dunefield Midden Bovid Bones." *Azania* 46(2):141–168. https://doi.org/10.1080/0067270X.2011.580141.

Stewart, B. A., G. I. Dewar, M. W. Morley, R. H. Inglis, M. Wheeler, Z. Jacobs, and R. G. Roberts. 2012. "Afromontane Foragers of the Late Pleistocene: Site Formation, Chronology and Occupational Pulsing at Melikane Rockshelter, Lesotho." *Quaternary International* 270:40–60. https://doi.org/10.1016/j.quaint.2011.11.028.

Stewart, B. A., A. G. Parker, G. Dewar, M. W. Morley, and L. F. Allott. 2016. "Follow the Senqu: Maloti-Drakensberg Paleoenvironments and Implications for Early Human Dispersals into Mountain Systems." In *Africa from MIS 6–2: Population Dynamics and Paleoenvironments*, ed. S. C. Jones and B. A. Stewart, 247–271. Dordrecht, Netherlands: Springer. https://doi.org/10.1007/978-94-017-7520-5_14.

Stewart, K. M. 1989. *Fishing Sites of North and East Africa in the Late Pleistocene and Holocene: Environmental Change and Human Adaptation*. vol. 521. BAR International Series. Oxford, UK: British Archaeological Reports.

Stewart, K. M. 1994. "Early Hominid Utilisation of Fish Resources and Implications for Seasonality and Behaviour." *Journal of Human Evolution* 27(1–3):229–245. https://doi.org/10.1006/jhev.1994.1044.

Stuckenberg, B. R. 1969. "Effective Temperature as an Ecological Factor in Southern Africa." *Zoologica Africana* 4(2):145–197. https://doi.org/10.1080/00445096.1969.11447371.

Tanaka, J. 1969. "The Ecology and Social Structure of Central Kalahari Bushmen: A Preliminary Report." *Kyoto University African Studies* 3:1–26.

Tanaka, J. 1976. "Subsistence Ecology of Central Kalahari San." In *Kalahari Hunter-Gatherers: Studies of the !Kung San and Their Neighbors*, ed. R. B. Lee and I. DeVore, 98–119. Cambridge, MA: Harvard University Press. https://doi.org/10.4159/harvard.9780674430600.c7.

Tanaka, J. 1980. *The San, Hunter-Gatherers of the Kalahari: A Study in Ecological Anthropology*. Tokyo: University of Tokyo Press.

Turnbull, C. M. 1961. *The Forest People: A Study of the Pygmies of the Congo*. New York: Simon and Schuster.

van Zinderen Bakker, E. M., and M. J. Werger. 1974. "Environment, Vegetation and Phytogeography of the High-Altitude Bogs of Lesotho." *Plant Ecology* 29(1):37–49. https://doi.org/10.1007/BF02390894.

Vinnicombe, P. V. 1976. *People of the Eland: Rock Paintings of the Drakensberg Bushmen as a Reflection of Their Life and Thought*. Pietermaritzburg, South Africa: University of Natal Press.

Vinnicombe, P. V. 2009. "Basotho Oral Traditions: The Last Bushman Inhabitants of the Mashai District, Lesotho." In *The Eland's People: New Perspectives in the Rock Art of the Maloti-Drakensberg Bushmen. Essays in Memory of Patricia Vinnicombe*, ed. P. J. Mitchell and B. W. Smith, 165–191. Johannesburg, South Africa: Wits University Press.

Wadley, L. 1987. *Later Stone Age Hunters and Gatherers of the Southern Transvaal: Social and Ecological Interpretation*. vol. 380. BAR International Series. Oxford, UK: British Archaeological Reports.

Wadley, L. 1996. "The Robberg Industry of Rose Cottage Cave, Eastern Free State: The Technology, Spatial Patterns and Environment." *South African Archaeological Bulletin* 51(164):64–74. https://doi.org/10.2307/3888841.

Wadley, L. 1998. "The Invisible Meat Providers: Women in the Stone Age of South Africa." In *Gender in African Prehistory*, ed. S. Kent, 69–81. Walnut Creek, CA: AltaMira Press.

Wadley, L., A. Esterhuysen, and C. Jeannerat. 1992. "Vegetation Changes in the Eastern Orange Free State: The Holocene and Later Pleistocene Evidence from Charcoal Studies at Rose Cottage Cave." *South African Journal of Science* 88:558–563.

Whitelaw, T. 1991. "Some Dimensions of Variability in the Social Organization of Community Space among Foragers." In *Ethnoarchaeological Approaches to Mobile Campsites*, ed. C. S. Gamble and W. A. Boismier, 139–188. Ann Arbor, MI: International Monographs in Prehistory.

Wilmsen, E. N. 1989. *Land Filled with Flies: A Political Economy of the Kalahari*. Chicago, IL: University of Chicago Press.

Wilmsen, E. N., J. R. Denbow, M. G. Bicchieri, L. R. Binford, R. Gordon, M. Guenther, R. B. Lee, R. Ross, J. S. Solway, J. Tanaka, et al. "Paradigmatic History of San-Speaking Peoples and Current Attempts at Revision." *Current Anthropology* 31(5):489–524. https://doi.org/10.1086/203890.

Wobst, M. H. 1978. "The Archaeo-ethnology of Hunter-Gatherers or the Tyranny of the Ethnographic Record in Archaeology." *American Antiquity* 43(2):303–309. https://doi.org/10.2307/279256.

Woodburn, J. 1968. "An Introduction to Hadza Ecology." In *Man the Hunter*, ed. I. DeVore and R. B. Lee, 49–55. Chicago, IL: Aldine.

7

*Explaining Diachronic
Trends in Paleolithic
Subsistence in
Central Europe*

KEIKO KITAGAWA,
SUSANNE C. MÜNZEL,
PETRA KRÖNNECK,
BRITT M. STARKOVICH, AND
NICHOLAS J. CONARD

The study of extinct archaic hominins has been the main focal point for exploring the evolutionary history of humans. Recent advances enable us to examine the genetic markers (Castellano et al. 2014; Fu et al. 2014; Green et al. 2010; Prüfer et al. 2014) and paleoanthropological traits that distinguish Neanderthals and modern humans (Gunz et al. 2009; Harvati et al. 2010; Smith et al. 2010; Trinkaus 2006; Weaver 2011). However, the behavioral difference between extinct hominins and modern humans has become blurred as studies demonstrate that aspects of "behavioral modernity," which were previously assumed to be exclusive to *Homo sapiens*, are increasingly associated with Neanderthal and *Homo erectus* populations (Joordens et al. 2015; Morin and Laroulandie 2012; Radovčić et al. 2015; Romandini et al. 2014). Despite the large behavioral variability among different hominin groups, a simple presence/absence of traits for differentiating *Homo* is no longer tenable. Considering that the archaeological data, which support the concept of "modernity," is also regionally biased toward Europe and western Asia, some researchers question its use as an analytical construct to discuss the Paleolithic behavioral patterns (Henshilwood and Marean 2003; Shea 2011). The archaeological record of the transitional period between the Middle Paleolithic (MP) and the early Upper Paleolithic (eUP) is gaining greater importance as researchers attempt to redefine and understand the behavioral variability of *Homo sapiens* and their extinct relatives (McBrearty and Brooks 2000).

DOI: 10.5876/9781607327745.c007

Neanderthals have been one of the central topics in Paleolithic archaeology. Since their discovery, the study of Neanderthals was based on an assumption that they were evolutionarily less advanced compared to modern human populations (Mellars 1989, 1996; Speth 2004; Villa and Roebroeks 2014). This view, mostly supported by Mellars (1996), posits that modern humans were technologically and behaviorally more adept and served as a ground to explain the extinction of our closest relatives. This presumed cognitive explanation does not hold in the face of present data, as previous studies are often contradicted by new findings that validate Neanderthal's capability to hunt, adapt, and occasionally produce artifacts with social/symbolic values (Laroulandie et al. 2016; Romandini et al. 2014). Other possible explanations are discussed among scholars, including differences in the division of labor, demographic factors, climatic fluctuations, and sociality (Finlayson and Carrion 2007; Harrold 2009; Hill et al. 2009; Nowell 2010; Riel-Salvatore 2010; Stiner and Kuhn 2009). While the debate persists, models have shifted from that of ability to adaptation, exploring ecological and demographic factors, which is further complicated by the issue of possible contacts and interaction between Neanderthals and modern humans (Finlayson 2005; Finlayson and Carrion 2007; Golovanova et al. 2010).

In this frame of the debate, Paleolithic research has focused on regions where the archaeological record spans the cultural and biological transition between the MP and eUP. Western Europe, particularly in areas with large karstic systems such as southwestern France and northern Iberia, has been studied extensively and has shaped the definition of the Aurignacian, which is the first Europe-wide culture associated with modern humans and is dated to between 43 and 42 ka cal BP (Conard and Bolus 2006; Hahn 1977; Higham et al. 2014). Furthermore, interactions between Neanderthals and modern humans as well as the makers of the transitional industries remain a topic of debate, but we can better address these questions on a regional scale.

Here, we evaluate diachronic trends in the economic activities of Neanderthals and modern humans using the zooarchaeological data from multiple sites in the Swabian Jura that have yielded MP and eUP faunal remains. The aim of this chapter is to study the patterns of animal exploitation practiced by two hominin groups, reflecting both subsistence strategies and cultural practices on the landscape of southwestern Germany.

BACKGROUND

Recent studies of hominin fossils provide direct evidence of archaic and modern humans' diet. Microwear analyses on dental remains reveal that it was dominated by terrestrial animal resources but also supplemented with other foodstuffs (Henry et al. 2011, Salzar-García et al. 2013). Based on microwear analysis of Neanderthal and Upper Paleolithic human teeth (El Zaatari et al. 2011; El Zaatari and Hublin 2014), plant consumption was more evident among individuals who occupied mixed and wooden environments. The study of botanical remains in dental calculus further fills a gap in our understanding of plant use in the Paleolithic (Henry et al. 2011, 2014; Salazar-García et al. 2013). Phytolith and starch remains in calculi demonstrate plant consumption such as underground-storage-organ plants in the northern latitudes (Henry 2012; Henry et al. 2014).

Isotopic analyses on hominin fossils primarily reflect high levels of protein intake (Bocherens 2011; Lee-Thorp and Sponheimer 2006; Richards and Schmitz 2008). High $\delta^{15}N$ values of Neanderthals are interpreted as evidence for meat consumption comparable to other carnivores (Bocherens et al. 2005). Conversely, modern humans' isotopic signatures suggest resource diversification due to the greater range of $\delta^{15}N$, which may be attributed to the consumption of aquatic resources (Richards and Trinkaus 2009). However, subsequent works caution against a simple interpretation (Bocherens et al. 2014). Bocherens and colleagues note that meat consumption is better represented because plants contribute far less protein than meat to the general composition of collagens. Some studies suggest past fluctuations in the natural nitrogen of the environment, which can account for the high $\delta^{15}N$ values of Neanderthals (Bocherens et al. 2014). Therefore, it is not evident whether stable isotopic studies can be taken at face value to interpret dietary practices and breadth. Nonetheless, other lines of evidence support a normative view of Neanderthal subsistence practice, which is dominated by game animals.

The analysis of the faunal record is primarily used to reconstruct Paleolithic subsistence practices and prey acquisition (Adler et al. 2006; Discamps et al. 2011; Gaudzinski-Windheuser and Niven 2009; Grayson and Delpech 2006; Hoffecker 2009; Morin 2008; Starkovich 2014; Stiner and Munro 2011; Stiner et al. 2000). Furthermore, the nature of faunal remains is not solely determined by hominin activity but is influenced by additional factors, including the behavior of prey and their interaction with predators. As such, the taphonomic history relating to non-hominin behavior is as informative as that of hominins themselves. In the Swabian Jura, we see traces of human economic activities intermixed with those of carnivores, which reflect patterns of occupations in rockshelters and caves.

Archaeologists have conducted cross-site comparisons of economic behavior in areas with continuous archaeological records that span the Paleolithic.

This allows a systematic comparison of Neanderthal and modern human occupations and enables us to study the diachronic trends within geographically defined regions. One area with rich case studies of subsistence behavior is the Mediterranean Basin (Blasco et al. 2014; Brown et al. 2011; Starkovich 2012, 2014; Stiner and Munro 2002; Stiner et al. 2000). Many of the faunal assemblages demonstrate significant shifts in prey choices. The use of aquatic resources persists from the MP into the UP with changes in resources from shellfish to fish, which also coincides with the decrease of high-ranked animals and greater dominance of small game. Such patterns indicate greater pressure on the local resources and reflect changes in the population densities of hominins (Starkovich 2014; Stiner 2001). Hoffecker and colleagues (2009) also observe a notable diversification of resources in the Kostenki complex of the eUP. While the assemblages are dominated by large mammals such as horses, they documented an increased exploitation of small mammals, including hares, arctic fox, fish, and birds by modern humans.

On the other hand, many studies also show little difference associated with the dietary patterns of a specific *Homo* species (Adler et al. 2006; Hoffecker and Cleghorn 2000; Karavanić and Patou-Mathis 2009; Patou-Mathis 2000). This is particularly true when it comes to ungulate faunas. At Fumane cave, also known for the presence of the Uluzzian technocomplex, the mammalian remains demonstrate no significant changes in hunting strategies from the Late Mousterian to the Aurignacian; the authors attribute the faunal patterns to environmental changes (Tagliacozzo et al. 2013). Faunal data from the transitional periods in France are summarized in Grayson and Delpech's (2006) study. Their results argue for continuity in species selection with one exception. One significant trend is the increase of reindeer, but this shift correlates with a decrease in winter temperature and is not limited to the transition from the MP to the eUP. Thus, environmental changes were likely the primary driver of this shift. Similarly, recent overviews of northern Spain deposits show that the MP and eUP fauna are comparable without any significant differences (Straus 2013; Yravedra Sainz de los Terreros 2013). In all, the trend is marked by continuity in the prey selection between the Paleolithic periods. It is therefore worth expanding the study and considering temporal trends in Central Europe.

SWABIAN JURA

The Swabian Jura has yielded an extensive record of Neanderthal and modern human settlement in Central Europe (figure 7.1) (Conard 2009; Conard and Bolus 2003; Conard et al. 2006; Conard et al. 2009; Hahn 1988, 1995).

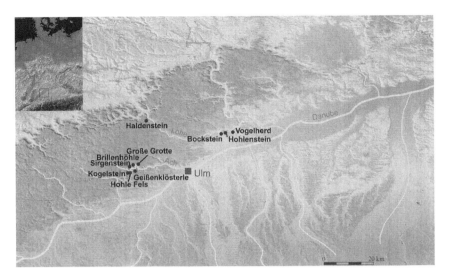

FIGURE 7.1. *Map of the Swabian Jura, southwestern Germany, with the principal sites mentioned in the text. Ach Valley: Hohle Fels (HF); Geißenklösterle (GK); Lone Valley: Bockstein (BS); Hohlenstein-Stadel (HS); Vogelherd (VH).*

Diachronic trends in the archaeological record of the Middle Paleolithic and Aurignacian enable us to better understand the continuity and differences in ways hominin groups adapted to the karstic landscape. The Swabian Jura is well known for the earliest evidence of musical instruments, figurative art, and ornaments that epitomize what we typically refer to as the Aurignacian culture, which spread with the dispersal of modern humans into Europe during MIS 3 (Bolus 2003; Conard et al. 2006; Floss and Rouquerol 2007).

The Swabian Jura represents the largest karst system consisting of calcareous massifs in Germany, forming part of the Jurassic limestone belt. Its topography is characterized by a dry upland plateau crossed by several tributaries of the Danube River and is bounded by the Upper Danube Valley that cuts through the Alpine Foreland to the south. The altitude of the plateau ranges from 450 to 1,000 masl. Due to tectonic activities, Jurassic chert is more common in the eastern area of the upland (Burkert and Floss 2005; Çep et al. 2011).

Researchers have radiometrically dated the late MP and Aurignacian, while the earlier MP occupations are temporally assigned based on climatic signals. The discovery of straight-tusk elephant at Vogelherd suggests an occupation in the interglacial period of MIS 5e (Niven 2006). Radiocarbon dates provide a minimum age of 50,000–45,000 cal BP in the MP horizons of Hohlenstein-Stadel (Beutelspacher et al. 2011) and late MP layers at Geißenklösterle date to a similar range (Richter et al. 2000). The Aurignacian begins with a small hiatus after the end of the MP around 43,000–41,000 cal BP, based on recent dating from Geißenklösterle (Conard and Bolus 2003, 2008; Higham et al. 2012). To date, a hiatus between the MP and eUP records argues against direct interaction between Neanderthals and modern humans (Conard et al. 2006, Miller 2015).

The archaeological deposits are concentrated in two valleys, Lone and Ach, which are ~15 km apart. Locales with evidence of hominin occupations are either caves or rockshelters with little evidence of open-air sites. While there are attempts to document settlements in open-air contexts, including test pits and geological investigations in the Ach and the Lone Valleys, intact, undisturbed artifact concentrations have not yet been documented, which is explained by the meandering of the tributaries as well as the large input of Holocene sediment (Bolus et al. 1999). The focus of our study is on the faunal material from Geißenklösterle (Hahn 1988) and Hohle Fels in the Ach Valley in addition to Hohlenstein-Stadel (Beck 1999; Wetzel 1961), Bockstein (Wetzel et al. 1969), and Vogelherd (Riek 1934) in the Lone Valley.

ENVIRONMENT

Paleoenvironmental records in the Swabian Jura give us a glimpse into past climatic conditions, which are particularly relevant for interpreting the regional faunal patterns. Palynological studies are not as abundant as in other regions, due to the glaciation and erosion that occurred periodically in this area of Central Europe (Heiri et al. 2014). Some of the few local pollen records include cores from the Füramoos Lake in the alpine foreland (Müller et al. 2003). The result of paleobotanical remains suggests mild climate from roughly 51,000 to 40,000 BP (> 50,000–41,500 cal BP), followed by a hiatus that lasted until the end of the glacial period (Müller et al. 2003). Another pollen record from the Bergsee in the Black Forest is under investigation for the period spanning 50,000 to 30,000 BP (> 50,000–32,000 cal BP) (Becker et al. 2006; Duprat-Oualid et al. 2017). The botanical record at Hohle Fels reveals that the area was dominated by open vegetation, which was characterized by shrub tundra around 44,200 cal BP (Riehl et al. 2015).

Microfauna and avian fauna document a fine-grained picture of the local climatic fluctuations. During the Late Pleistocene, the region is characterized by steppe tundra with fluctuating abundance of woodlands. Species such as *Dicrostonyx* (lemming) are scarce during the MP, corresponding to MIS 4 and the earlier stage of MIS 3 (60,000–50,000 BP), and the spectrum indicates that forests were more prominent in the milder climate of the MP periods leading up to the middle of the Aurignacian. After this, there is an increase in tundra elements. The avian assemblages are represented by taxa that prefer steppe-tundra, temperate steppe, and coniferous forest in the vicinity of lakes during the MP (Böttcher et al. 2000; Krönneck in press).

Micromorphological studies in the Ach Valley offer another picture of the past environment with some intersite variability (Conard et al. 2006; Goldberg et al. 2003; Miller 2015). At Geißenklösterle, the transitional period between the MP and Aurignacian is marked by an episode of erosion, pointing to an abrupt shift from a mild and moderately humid climate to a colder and drier climate evidenced by the abundance of phosphates (Miller 2015). On the other hand, the shift appears to be gradual at Hohle Fels, with a mild climate lasting through to the beginning of the Aurignacian, which is followed by a cooler climate. The onset of the harsher condition varies, depending on the employed methods of each site. Nonetheless, the current data suggest that there was a transition to a colder climate in the Aurignacian from the late MP period, but this abrupt climatic shift does not seem to coincide with the appearance of the Aurignacian culture.

MIDDLE PALEOLITHIC AND AURIGNACIAN CULTURE

The lithic raw material is dominated by Jurassic gray chert, found in the vicinity of the caves, and Bohnerz brown chert, found in the southern river deposits (Burkert and Floss 2005; Çep et al. 2011). Another important raw material of the region is radiolarite, which originated in the Alps and is found in the Danubian and moraine gravels (Floss and Kieselbach 2004).

Typical MP tools of Central Europe such as *Blattspitzen* or *Keilmesser* are not ubiquitous in the region (Bolus 2004; Conard et al. 2012). Instead, the lithic assemblage is referred to as the Swabian Mousterian (Conard et al. 2012). The assemblage shows little standardization with reduced Levallois components and is not defined by a particular tool type (Beck 1999; Conard 2011). Some diagnostic MP tools, *Keilmesser*, were recovered from Bockstein with other retouched tools (Çep and Krönneck 2015). While the use of organic artifacts for the MP is still debated with the exception of retouchers, there are a few examples of bone points from Vogelherd (Riek 1934), Große Grotte (Wagner 1983), and Bockstein (Krönneck 2012).

The emergence of the Aurignacian marks a clear break in the Swabian Jura. The lithic assemblages are characterized by scrapers and burins, and the production of artifacts is dominated by blade production with unidirectional knapping (Bolus 2003; Conard et al. 2006). The lithic technology, which lasts until 35,000–34,000 cal BP, remains consistent over time. Organic tools become incorporated into the artifact inventory, including antler tines with split bases (Conard and Bolus 2006; Liolios 2006). Furthermore, ivory was an important raw material, as people produced numerous organic artifacts from mammoth tusks, including personal ornaments, animal figurines, and musical instruments (Conard 2009; Conard et al. 2009; Wolf 2015).

Previous Work

Previous work on the fauna of the Swabian Jura touches on various archaeological and paleobiological interests (Boger et al. 2014; Krönneck 2012; Münzel in press; Münzel and Conard 2004; Niven 2006). Many have focused on the subsistence pattern and dietary practices of Neanderthals and modern humans, mostly based on large mammalian remains (Münzel in press; Münzel and Conard 2004; Niven 2006). In recent years, studies have explored the use of small game (Conard et al. 2013, Krönneck in press). Another line of research focused on cave bears, which are common in the local caves. Genetic analyses demonstrated the existence of two distinct populations (*Ursus spelaeus* and *Ursus ingressus*), which went regionally extinct around 29,757 ± 531 cal BP (Münzel et al. 2011). The co-occurrence of cave bear and hominin have led researchers to suggest a possible anthropogenic cause for their extinction (Münzel and Conard 2004; Stiller et al. 2010). Some studies have explored the role of carnivores and the interactions between hominins and other predators (Camarós et al. 2016; Kitagawa et al. 2012).

Sample

Assemblages that comprise this study originate from five deposits: Hohlenstein-Stadel (HS), Vogelherd (VH), and Bockstein (BS) in the Lone Valley, and Hohle Fels (HF) and Geißenklösterle (GK) in the Ach Valley (table 7.1). Some of the material was recovered in the first half of twentieth century, while the rest was excavated from the 1980s to the present. Data are based on studies conducted between the 1980s and 2014.

There are notable differences in the recovery method between the older excavations (BS, VH, and part of HS) and recent excavations (GK, HF, and part of HS), namely the use of screening, which creates a bias against small game and smaller skeletal elements. However, the piece-plotted remains from

TABLE 7.1. Sites in the Swabian Jura discussed in the text.

Site	Years of Excavation	Cultural Level		Sources
		MP	Aurignacian	
LONE VALLEY				
Hohlenstein-Stadel (HS)	1939–, 1950–1960	1939: VI–XI, 2009–2011: 3–8	1939: IV–Va, 2009–2011: 10–1u	Kitagawa 2014
Vogelherd (VH)	1931	VI–IX	IV–V	Niven 2006
Bockstein (BS)	1932–1936, 1953–1956	Törle X, Schmiede III–IV	Törle VII	Krönneck 2012
ACH VALLEY				
Hohle Fels (HF)	1977–1979, 1987–2014	VI–VIII	III–V	Münzel in press; Conard et al. 2013
Geißenklösterle (GK)	1974–1983, 2000–2002	IV–VIII	II–III	Münzel in press

GK and HF are the main focus of the study, so assemblages dominated by larger specimens (> 3 cm) in recent excavations is roughly comparable to the older collection. Thus, the data are limited to mammalian taxa larger than lagomorphs. Research on microfauna is ongoing at HF, GK, and HS.

No two caves are exactly alike and each deposit is formed through different taphonomic and post-depositional histories. The MP sequences are represented by several stratified deposits, with the exception of BS, where two separate chambers (Bocksteinschmiede and Törle), representing one MP component, make up the majority of the analyzed material. The MP occupations at VH, HS, and BS are represented by a longer sequence, but we only consider the upper MP layers here (Kitagawa 2014; Krönneck 2012; Niven 2006). The Aurignacian record is represented by two to three discrete layers at most of the sites (Conard and Bolus 2008; Higham et al. 2012). These layers are combined into broader MP and Aurignacian groups for adequate sample sizes and comparability. Results from HF are considered preliminary, as the excavation is ongoing, but the site should be representative of the MP and Aurignacian deposits.

METHODS

Faunal analyses follow the protocols employed in many zooarchaeological studies, with taxonomic and anatomical identification serving as the basis. The Number of Identified Specimens (NISP), referring to the count of specimens assigned to a taxon or body-size class, was employed (Grayson 1984). Bone weight was also employed in some analyses, which is based on the assumption that there is an allometric relationship between bone weight and body weight (Reitz et al. 1987; Uerpmann 1973). Weight was used as a proxy for species abundance and to establish anatomical profiles in some studies (Münzel 1988, 2009, in press). Here, we use bone weight for determining skeletal-part representation by comparing the weight of archaeological specimens to the weight of individual elements from modern animals.

Minimum Number of Elements (MNE) is used to quantify skeletal representation (Grayson 1984; Lyman 2008). Due to intersite differences in quantitative methods, MNE values are evaluated only for cranial remains. To quantify skeletal abundance based on bony remains, we use normed NISP (nNISP) following Grayson and Frey (2004) and Clark (2009), which is also referred to as relative skeletal abundance (RSA) (Broughton 1999). The value is derived from NISP divided by the frequency in which the part occurs in a complete skeleton for each body part (Clark 2009). This applies to whole, complete skeletal elements except for long bones, which are divided into proximal, shaft, and distal portions. The greatest difference between nNISP and MNE is that the former represents the maximum number of identified specimens per skeletal elements and could inflate the counts, while the latter accounts for the minimal count based on landmarks. NISP and other frequency measures often correlate, and these measures provide a valid estimate of anatomical parts that could be compared across sites (Grayson and Frey 2004).

RESULTS

Density mediated attrition

We first consider the degree of density-mediated attrition to estimate the bone loss that has affected the fauna pre- and post-depositionally (Binford 1978; Grayson 1984; Lyman 1984). We explore this for cave bears (*Ursus spelaeus*) by comparing the weight of the modern ursid skeleton and the weight of the archaeological materials by element for caves where the ursids are abundant (GK, HF, and HS; figures 7.2 and 7.3). In the MP, the weight of the cave bears shows a clear bias toward crania, pointing to the overrepresentation of the teeth. The fragile elements, including axial elements and scapula, are underrepresented. The skeletal element frequency of the Aurignacian is more even. The teeth decrease and vertebrae are more abundant compared to the MP. Vertebrae in HF assemblage are overrepresented, a pattern that may change with additional analyses. Spearman's correlation values between the modern ursid and cave bear

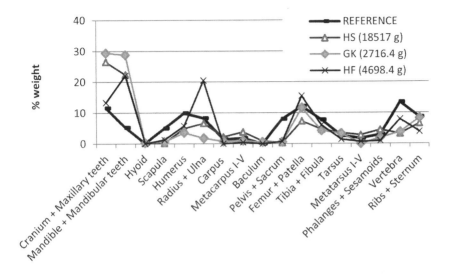

FIGURE 7.2. *PercentWeight of skeletal element for brown bear from reference skeleton (UR7) and cave bear assemblages from the MP. Hohle Fels (HF), Geißenklösterle (GK), Hohlenstein-Stadel (HS).*

remains demonstrate that the correlation is higher for HS and GK assemblages in the Aurignacian, indicating that the MP assemblages underwent a higher degree of attrition. HF is the exception in which the Rs^2 value is lower in the Aurignacian, but it is not at a significant level (p = 0.07).

We compared the MNE values of bony cranial elements and teeth for the most common tooth element of ursids (table 7.2). In the MP, the bony cranial element is extremely low, which demonstrates a heavy degree of in situ attrition. In the Aurignacian, the ratio between bone-based cranial MNE values and tooth-based MNE becomes more even, but the assemblage remains dominated by teeth. Cave bear remains are less likely to be affected by anthropogenic modification, so the factors that lead to the loss of bony material are mechanical and chemical, as well as biological.

We use another method to assess density-mediated attrition for abundant prey animals. The correlation between bone mineral density (BMD) and nNISP is considered for horses (*Equus ferus*) and reindeer (*Rangifer tarandus*) from GK, VH, and HF in the Aurignacian (Lam et al. 1999). The nNISP of long bones correlates with the scan sites and is employed here to assess bone survivorship in a manner that most researchers use MNE and MAU values.

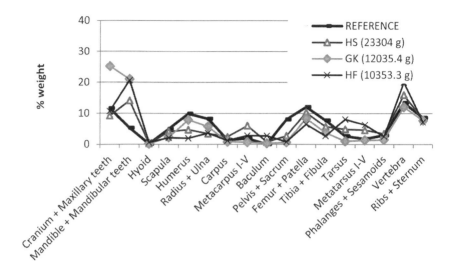

FIGURE 7.3. *PercentWeight of skeletal element for brown bear from reference skeleton (UR7) and cave bear assemblages from the Aurignacian. Hohle Fels (HF), Geißenklösterle (GK), Hohlenstein-Stadel (HS).*

The Spearman's correlation between bone density and skeletal representation of horse is low but significant at GK (Rs^2 = 0.36, p = 0.04) and HF (Rs^2 = 0.22, p = 0.05). The correlation is slightly higher in VH at a significant level, (Rs^2 = 0.44, p < 0.001) but still accounts for less than half of the variation. Reindeer show a similar degree of correlation between BMD and nNISP at a significant level, with VH exhibiting higher correlation (Rs^2 = 0.45, p < 0.001) compared to GK (Rs^2 = 0.31, p < 0.001) and HF (Rs^2 = 0.30, p < 0.001). For both species, robust elements are more abundant than the rest of skeletal elements, which drives the results of the Spearman's correlation. However, attrition does not solely account for the nature of the horse and reindeer assemblages. Such findings confirm Niven's results, although the methodology varies slightly and the difference between horses and reindeer is less pronounced in this study (Niven 2006). Overall, there is some attritional loss, but not to a high degree, and the assemblages provide valuable information on the exploitation of prey during the Aurignacian.

Carnivore modification

We now consider the role of carnivores in all the faunal assemblages. Based on the counts of specimens with modification (figure 7.4), carnivore damage

TABLE 7.2. MNE of cranial elements for cave bears at the respective sites during the Middle Paleolithic (MP) and Aurignacian (A). Hohle Fels (HF), Geißenklösterle (GK), Hohlenstein-Stadel (HS).

Ursid	GK		HF		HS	
	MP	A	MP	A	MP	A
Cranium	2	23	8	11	15	7
Maxillary teeth	12	33	22	11	67	21
Mandible	7	19	3	2	4	3
Mandibular teeth	16	44	18	34	73	27

is most frequently encountered at VH during the MP. Over 20 percent of remains exhibit carnivore modification, a high proportion for an archaeological assemblage. In one MP layer (level VII), over 79 percent of remains have gnawing marks from middle- to large-sized carnivores (Niven 2006). Many of the faunal remains appear to be affected by the activities of non-hominin predators. The low encounter rate of carnivore damage at BS (5.2%) is possibly due to the exclusion of material in Krönneck's study that was corroded by chemical processes or carnivore digestion (2014). When these specimens are included, the proportion rises to 16.4 percent. Other sites exhibit a comparable degree of carnivore damage ranging from 5.2 percent to 8.7 percent and are less disturbed by carnivores than at VH.

During the Aurignacian, the frequency of carnivore damage decreases considerably. The highest proportion is observed at HF while GK and VH assemblages have a low percentage of carnivore damage. Carnivore modification diminishes significantly ($p < .0001$) at all sites except HF, where there is a slight decline. VH reveals the greatest shift, from 22 percent to 2 percent. This is likely a result of decreasing carnivore activity in the Swabian Jura. The degree of modification suggests that humans are the main agent that contributed to the accumulation and modification of exogenous fauna in the Aurignacian, while carnivores were more active in the MP and were partially responsible for the higher degree of density-mediated attrition.

Species representation: herbivores

The MP is marked by the dominance of wild horse (*Equus ferus*) across the deposits with little intersite variability (figure 7.5). To date, European ass (*Equus hydruntinus*) remains rare in the Swabian Jura. They have only been identified at BS and two species are grouped together. The second most common herbivore varies, but woolly mammoth (*Mammuthus primigenius*) (excluding ivory

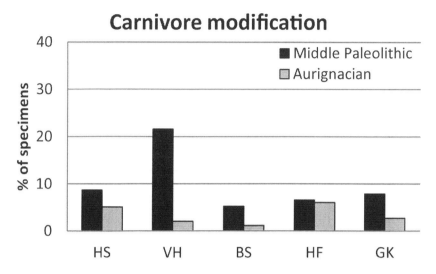

Carnivore modification

■ Middle Paleolithic
□ Aurignacian

% of specimens (y-axis: 0, 10, 20, 30, 40)

x-axis: HS, VH, BS, HF, GK

FIGURE 7.4. *Number of specimens with carnivore modification per site. Hohlenstein-Stadel (HS), Vogelherd (VH), Bockstein (BS), Hohle Fels (HF), Geißenklösterle (GK).*

remains) is abundant at HS and woolly rhinoceros (*Coelodonta antiquitatis*) is common in the Lone Valley (VH, HS, BS), more so than in the Ach Valley (GK, HF). Reindeer are important, following horses at BS and aurochs/bison (*Bos/Bison*) at VH and BS. Lagomorphs (*Lepus* sp.) remain scarce across all sites.

During the Aurignacian, horses continue to be the most abundant prey, but reindeer (excluding antler) gain greater significance (figure 7.6). At HF, reindeer are more abundant than horses and both species equally contribute to the VH assemblage. At HS, horses and reindeer make up the majority in a comparatively small pool of herbivore remains. The mammoths (excluding ivory) are also important at VH and GK, while they are far less abundant at other sites. Other prey animals include aurochs/bison, ibex, and woolly rhinoceros. Another difference lies in the abundance of bovids. Ibexes (*Capra ibex*) are frequent in the Ach Valley while small/middle-sized bovid remains are scarce in the Lone Valley. Red deer (*Cervus elaphus*), elk (*Alces alces*), roe deer (*Capreolus capreolus*), and chamois (*Rupicapra rupicapra*) are rare in the region, suggesting occasional exploitation of these animals. Overall, prey animals are largely dominated by horses and reindeer, followed by mammoths. Equids are the most common herbivore throughout the Pleistocene of the Swabian Jura.

Some temporal trends in the abundance of herbivores in the Swabian Jura concur among assemblages, but intersite variability also exists. The χ^2 and

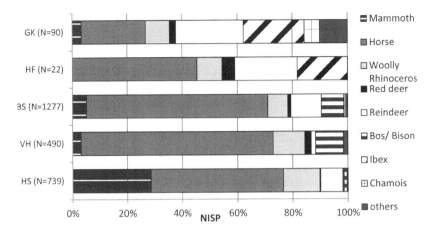

FIGURE 7.5. *NISP of herbivores by species for the MP. (Others includes elephant, wild boar, giant deer, roe deer, elk, and muskox.) Hohle Fels (HF), Geißenklösterle (GK), Bockstein (BS), Hohlenstein-Stadel (HS), Vogelherd (VH).*

standardized adjusted residual values of the overall species composition in the MP and Aurignacian reveal significant changes in the species abundance (table 7.3, p = < 0.05). The abundance of horses varies across the two valleys: there is a rise in the Ach Valley but a decrease in the Lone Valley. Woolly rhinoceroses also decrease significantly in the Lone Valley whereas little change is observed in the Ach Valley. Both patterns are influenced by small sample sizes from the Ach Valley in the MP. Therefore, we observe an overall decline of woolly rhinoceros and a slight decrease of horse during the Aurignacian.

Reindeer increase across most deposits, providing a clear regional trend at a significant level (p < 0.001). HS is an exception, where there is a slight increase, but earlier analyses suggest that the increase in reindeer is significant, based on Gamble's larger sample (Gamble 1979). We also observe increased abundance of mammoths at VH, GK, and HF (VH and GK at p = < 0.001 level). The frequency of woolly mammoth increases in assemblages with abundant herbivore remains. Hares increase at all sites with the exception of VH, which is most likely due to the recovery methods. The recent excavation of backdirt in VH has yielded a greater frequency of hare and confirms the general trend of their increased exploitation in the Aurignacian (Boger et al. 2014). Compared to the MP, we observe changes from hunting dominated by horses to continued exploitation of horses but with increased hunting of reindeer.

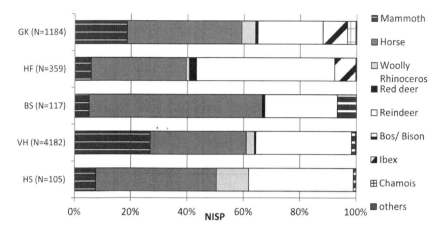

Figure 7.6. *NISP of herbivores by species for the Aurignacian. (Others includes wild boar, giant deer, roe deer, and elk.) Hohle Fels (HF), Geißenklösterle (GK), Bockstein (BS), Hohlenstein-Stadel (HS), Vogelherd (VH).*

Herbivores

HORSES

The sample size of horse and reindeer permits a more detailed analysis across the Ach Valley and VH (table 7.4). The skeletal representation of equids based on nNISP varies across sites, but the assemblage is characterized by the strong presence of the humerus as well as the hind limbs, femur, and tibia. Mandibles (excluding teeth) are also well represented at GK, where it is the most common element, and also scored high at HF. Due to the exclusion of teeth, the interpretation slightly differs from that of Niven (2006). Niven (2006) discusses the economic utility of skulls for their high nutritional values, due mostly to the brain (Lupo 1998), despite a low general utility (Outram and Rowley-Conwy 1998). However, we find no strong bias toward crania, although tooth elements are abundant and Minimum Animal Units (MAU) values were used instead of nNISP previously (Niven 2006). Tibia and upper forelimb are overrepresented when teeth are excluded. It is possible that the difference in the results lies in the use of different measures, but it seems likely that preservation bias accounts for the pattern, and the importance of crania may not be so pronounced.

Marrow and Standardized Food Utility indices (SFUI) rank the economic utility of body parts based on the quantity of meat and marrow. Here, we assess the correlation between nNISP and the indices for major skeletal

TABLE 7.3. Adjusted residual values (AR) and χ^2 value for species, between the MP and the Aurignacian, by site. (*italic* = $p < .05$; **bold** = $p < .01$.)

MP/A	Lone Valley			Ach Valley	
	HS	VH	BS	HF	GK
Hare	**4.04**	0.67	**5.75**	**4.20**	**4.44**
Wolf	**3.40**	−1.46	−0.19	1.35	−0.91
Fox	1.85	1.55	1.64	2.29	0.18
Bear	**11.87**	−2.57	**7.13**	**−12.09**	**−8.97**
Cave lion	1.65	−1.79	−1.03	1.20	**−3.53**
Hyena	**−7.79**	**−4.43**	−0.28	0.56	**−3.21**
Mammoth	**−9.35**	**11.74**	−0.56	2.79	**5.54**
Horse	**−9.51**	**−14.64**	**−3.80**	**5.12**	**6.62**
Woolly rhinoceros	**−4.75**	**−9.19**	**−3.39**	−0.36	0.42
Red deer	−0.98	**−4.60**	−0.55	1.20	−0.28
Reindeer	1.67	**14.72**	**3.22**	**7.65**	**3.27**
Aurochs/ Bison	*−2.15*	**−11.58**	−1.15	—	0.40
Ibex	—	—	−0.48	1.76	−0.77
χ^2	325.65	665.00	113.36	153.62	149.98
p value	< .001	< .001	< .001	< .001	< .001

elements using the values from Outram and Rowley-Conwy (1998). The overall patterns indicate no correlation between the SFUI index and nNISP values. The relative skeletal abundance, characterized by the abundance of tibia or humerus, cannot be explained by an overrepresentation of high-utility skeletal portions, especially when we consider the axial elements. However, as discussed above, if brains were included in the calculation of SFUI index on Outram and Rowley-Conwy (1998), as some have suggested, this interpretation may need reconsideration (Lupo 1998). There is also a high and significant correlation between nNISP and marrow index at HF (Rs^2 = 0.724, p = 0.03). We interpret this as preferential transport to HF based on marrow yields, though further analyses are needed to verify this hypothesis.

The age structure of horses based on the tooth crown height is considered from HS, VH, and BS in the MP using the program of Weaver and colleagues (figure 7.7a and 7.7b) (Fernandez 2009; Levine 1982; Stiner 1990; Weaver et al. 2011). A 95-percent CI based on the sample size determines the possible range in the age cohort expressed in a triangular plot. Here, we determine the age

TABLE 7.4. Relative abundance of skeletal elements in nNISP for horses in GK, HF, and VH in the Aurignacian.

nNISP of Horses	GK/A	HF/A	VH/A
Skull	1	2	6
Mandible	29	4	25.5
Atlas	—	—	1
Axis	1	—	—
Cervical vertebra	0.2	—	1.2
Thoracic vertebra	—	0.17	0.06
Lumber vertebra	0.33	—	0.33
Sacrum	—	1	1
Caudal vertebra	—	—	—
Pelvis	6	1.5	8
Rib	2.56	1.36	1.61
Scapula	2.17	1.22	0.58
Humerus	21.5	5.5	37
Radioulna	11	4	28.5
Carpals/Carpus	0.07	0.14	0.57
Metacarpal	2	0.5	7.5
Femur	14.5	4.5	29.5
Tibia	22	3	53
Metatarsal	1.5	0.5	8.5
Astralagus	—	—	1.5
Calcaneus	—	—	1
Phalanx 1	—	—	1.25
Phalanx 2	—	—	1
Phalanx 3	—	—	0.5

of individuals in broad categories including juveniles, adults, and old adults to avoid problems of accuracy, specifically regarding the underestimation of ages among adult groups (Greenfield et al. 2015). Prime adults outnumber other age groups in VH and HS assemblages, followed by juveniles and old adults. The BS assemblage is characterized by a large number of juveniles despite a considerable overlap with the neighboring caves and the overall pattern is close to a living age structure. These results do not conform to a well-documented pattern common for hominin hunters who targeted prime-aged individuals,

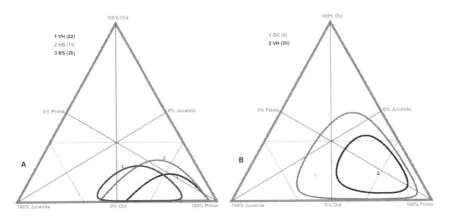

FIGURE 7.7. *Age group of horses based on MNE for (a) the MP assemblage (VH, HS, and BS) and (b) the Aurignacian assemblage (VH, GK). Geißenklösterle (GK), Bockstein (BS), Hohlenstein-Stadel (HS), Vogelherd (VH).*

but certainly differ from the patterns created by cursorial carnivores that preferentially hunt vulnerable individuals (juvenile and old adults) (Stiner 2005, 2009). Thus, the age structure of the horse populations is probably indicative of opportunistic hunting targeting local herds.

The taphonomic data suggest that unlike, HS and BS, VH assemblages are characterized by a greater number of bones bearing carnivore damage in the MP, but the age structure of horses from VH overlaps with the other two sites. It is possible that the accumulation of prey resulted from both carnivore and Neanderthal hunting, leading to a mixed signal of activities by multiple agents. Based on the degree and kinds of taphonomic damage, taxonomic representation of carnivores, and overlap with attritional mortality profiles most likely caused by cursorial predators or scavenging (Steele 2005; Stiner 1990, 2009), the other significant accumulator of faunal remains was most likely hyenas.

The horse assemblage of VH during the Aurignacian is the largest in the region. At VH, prime adults dominate and juveniles and old adults are underrepresented (Niven 2006). The assemblage fits the model of a living age structure, with the majority of the population represented by prime adults. Niven's (2006) analysis of each age group further reveals that individuals between 5 and 8 years old are underrepresented, which is related to the demographic changes in the herd structure, in which young male horses form groups of bachelors and separate from the rest of the herds. While the sample size is small, prime adults outnumber juveniles and old individuals at GK. Older adults are better represented compared to the MP, but the age profile does not alter significantly, all representing a living age structure. This pattern can be attributed to multiple factors, but the hallmark of hominin hunting—prime-adult-dominated assemblages—is not evident in the Swabian Jura.

REINDEER

The skeletal representation of reindeer differs from horses (table 7.5). The pattern of skeletal elements is similar among the three Aurignacian assemblages (HF, GK, and VH). There is a bias toward the hindlimbs, specifically toward the metatarsal and tibia. At VH, other long-bone elements are more evenly represented, with a greater presence of forelimbs, such as metacarpal, humerus, and radioulna. The general anatomical representation of HF and VH shows closer similarity based on the Spearman's correlation (Rs^2 = 0.68, p = < 0.001), while GK differs from the other assemblages. Compared to horses, there is a clear dominance of hindlimbs, while the forelimbs and mandible are underrepresented.

The unsaturated marrow values correlate significantly with the skeletal abundance from HF (Rs^2 = 0.69, p = < 0.04) and VH (Rs^2 = 0.78, p = < 0.03) (Morin 2007), which is roughly similar to what was found by Niven (2006), although she used marrow volume. This supports Niven's claim that during the Aurignacian humans preferentially transported elements based on their marrow yields (2006), but this interpretation must be regarded with caution since tibia and metatarsal have high bone-mineral density and are easier to identify. Nonetheless, the high correlation occurs at two sites, which strengthens the claim. In contrast, the correlation of skeletal abundance and SFUI is not significant. An alternative explanation is put forth by Münzel (in press), who suggests that the metatarsals are abundant due to their utility for tool production. It is therefore possible that multiple factors contributed to a high abundance of metatarsals.

The sample of aged teeth from VH in the Aurignacian suggests that adults (3–11 years) dominate other age groups (Niven 2006). Similar to horses, prime adults are common, but due to a relatively small sample size, the age profile cannot be used to distinguish living age structure from prime-adult-dominated assemblages. The sample from GK is small, but suggests that all age groups are equally represented, which does not fit a catastrophic or living age-structure model.

MAMMOTH

The relationship between mammoths and Neanderthals is more ambiguous, as ivory present at sites such as HS reveals no clear evidence of modification,

TABLE 7.5. Relative abundance of skeletal elements in nNISP for reindeer in GK, HF, and VH in the Aurignacian.

nNISP of Reindeer	GK/A	HF/A	VH/A
Skull	2	2	10
Mandible	6.5	0.5	11
Cervical vertebrae	0.2	—	0.4
Thoracic vertebrae	0.15	0.15	0.38
Lumber vertebrae	0.33	0.17	0.5
Pelvis	0.5	0.5	10
Rib	0.08	0.19	0.62
Scapula	—	0.5	9
Humerus	4.5	3.5	47.5
Radioulna	5	6	77
Metacarpal	0.65	4.5	48.5
Femur	3	5	57
Patella	—	1	2
Tibia	20	11.5	141
Astragalus	0.13	0.5	13
Calcaneus	0.13	0.5	23
Metatarsal	39.2	37.5	136
Phalanx 1	1.13	0.88	5.88
Phalanx 2	0.13	0.13	3.13
Phalanx 3	0.75	0.13	1.75

and the evidence for mammoth butchery is sparse (Kitagawa 2014). Mammoth gains considerable significance in the Aurignacian and correlates with an increase in human occupation. At most sites, the remains are largely represented by cranial elements, including teeth and ivory fragments, in addition to ribs (Kitagawa 2014; Münzel in press). In contrast, VH's mammoth assemblage is marked by greater frequency of postcranial remains (Niven 2006). The upper-limb elements, scapula, and humerus are the most common among the postcranial elements. The teeth demonstrate an age profile dominated by juveniles and old individuals, which reflects an attritional mortality and points to an opportunistic exploitation of the megafauna.

The limited evidence of butchery marks and the lack of anthropogenic modification of ivory does not rule out the active hunting of mammoths by humans. Niven's (2006) interpretation suggests varying modes of mammoth procurement that include active hunting, in addition to possible scavenging of hard tissues for architectural purposes, tool production, or fuel. In any case, the mammoth remains have led researchers to suggest that VH served as an aggregation site that saw visits by large groups and was an ideal spot for active hunting and for other purposes (Niven 2006). Ivory is a prominent part of the artifact and debitage assemblages during the Aurignacian across the Swabian Jura (Münzel in press; Wolf 2015). While the skeletal representation is uneven, providing few clues into the utility of postcranial elements, mammoths gain greater importance in the assemblage that is unequivocally related to artifact production and possibly linked to the exploitation of soft tissues.

DISCUSSION AND CONCLUSION

The faunal record of the Swabian Jura spanning from the MP to the Aurignacian reflects regional patterns as well as intersite variability. In this study, notable diachronic trends are observed in the species spectrum. Horse is the most abundant herbivorous taxon exploited by Neanderthals and modern humans alike, which is consistent with the previous studies (Krönneck et al. 2004; Münzel and Conard 2004; Niven 2006). Relative to the MP, the abundance of reindeer increases during the Aurignacian. In terms of biomass, a horse is ~60 percent heavier than a reindeer, making horses the preferred prey over reindeer in terms of energetic return (Broughton et al. 2011). The continued presence of the equids during the eUP argues against a decline in their population.

The rise in the abundance of reindeer likely corresponds with cooler climates in the Aurignacian. This cooling is evidenced by micromorphological (Miller 2015), microfaunal (Ziegler in press), and archaeobotanical (Riehl et al. 2015) studies, which may have spurred the growth of the local reindeer population. Studies in western Europe link climatic fluctuations in MIS 3 with an increased abundance of reindeer (Grayson and Delpech 2005; Morin 2008, 2012) and the signal of the Swabian Jura fits the pan-regional pattern during the Aurignacian. Münzel (in press) further suggests that selected remains, namely metatarsals and antlers, were regularly used as raw material for organic tools, which may account for their abundance in these faunal assemblages.

The abundance of mammoth shows intersite variability. Their contribution to the faunal assemblage increases significantly at VH, GK, and HF, which parallels the abundance of organic artifacts made from mammoth bones and ivory. Based on the paleoecological data, Drucker and colleagues argue for the stability of mammoth population during the Aurignacian and Gravettian (Drucker et al. 2015). Instead, such a trend appears to track human activity, increasing where there are greater artifact density and anthropogenic signatures (Conard et al. 2012). Thus, the roles of mammoths in the archaeological record may deviate from the conventional understanding of faunal exploitation that is largely driven by subsistence priorities. This pattern indicates that the faunal patterns reflect the exploitation of hard tissues, including antlers, ivory, and long bones in addition to the energetic return obtained from soft tissues (Münzel 2009, in press).

Many reconstructions of Paleolithic diets, including this study, are based on large game, but dietary diversification of Neanderthals and modern humans is also reflected by the inclusion of small game, fish, and birds. While small game is considered as a low-ranked resource in optimal foraging models, they make up a considerable part of the faunal record outside of the Swabian Jura (Colonese et al. 2011; Finlayson et al. 2012; Hockett and Haws 2003, 2005; Stiner et al. 2000). Since such resources usually rank low on scales of caloric values, they may have been exploited for nutritional and cultural reasons, which cannot be quantified in nutritional terms (Hockett and Haws 2005).

The question of species diversity is currently explored in the Swabian Jura (Conard et al. 2013; Krönneck in press; Owen 2013). There is a significant rise in the exploitation of lagomorphs, ptarmigan, and fish in the Upper Paleolithic (Conard et al. 2013). At the same time, studies suggest that small-sized animals underwent density-mediated attrition, which complicates this interpretation (Boger et al. 2014). To fully explore the dietary spectrum of Neanderthals and modern humans, the analysis of screened material, which was beyond the scope of this study, will complement the existing faunal data on small mammal, avian, and fish remains. If future studies confirm the trend in small game exploitation, we can consider the extent of dietary diversification in the eUP.

The current data on large game do not support differences in the subsistence behavior of Neanderthals and modern humans. It is no surprise that both hominin groups were adept hunter-gatherers who effectively exploited their environment and resources based on similar economic principles. Considering these findings, we argue that the hunting decisions of archaic and modern humans based on nutritional needs are mostly continuous without major shifts and do little to address the question of human uniqueness in the framework of behavioral modernity.

This case study of the Swabian Jura indicates that faunal patterns, in particular during the Aurignacian, are not solely driven by caloric yields but are also related to tool manufacture and symbolic activities. This makes for a complicated view in the reconstruction of the dietary practices, but contributes to the understanding of behavioral patterns that potentially reveal the important differences between Neanderthals and modern humans. This study highlights how alternative systems may be concurrently at work and shape behaviors of foragers in the past and the present. Economic models such as optimal foraging theory are a starting point for understanding human behaviors, but the deviations from the models form the basis on which we can build alternative hypotheses about cultural patterns in the MP and eUP.

Understanding "behavioral modernity" through the faunal record requires researchers to consider multiple layers of cultural and economic choices. In this regard, we hope that the debates of modern humans and Neanderthals will continue to provide us with analytical tools, in combination with other models and approaches, to evaluate and assess the material culture of the Middle and early Upper Paleolithic in Central Europe and beyond.

ACKNOWLEDGMENTS

We thank all of the organizations that have funded this work including Deutsche Forschungsgemeinschaft, Heidelberger Akademie der Wissenschaften, Heidelberger Cement, Voith Corporation, Alb-Donau-Kreis, Kreis Heidenheim, Gesellschaft für Urgeschichte, Museumsgesellschaft Schelklingen, Landesamt für Denkmalpflege Baden-Württemberg, and the cities of Blaubeuren, Niederstotzingen, and Förderverein Eiszeitkunst im Lonetal. We also thank our colleagues in the Institut für Naturwissenschaftliche Archäologie, and the Institut für Ur- und Frühgeschichte und Archäologie des Mittelalters at the Universität Tübingen for their continual support. Special thanks to Ashley Lemke for organizing the special session for Bob Kelly at the 2015 SAA meeting in San Francisco.

REFERENCES CITED

Adler, Daniel S., Guy Bar-Oz, Anna Belfer-Cohen, and Ofer Bar-Yosef. 2006. "Ahead of the Game: Middle and Upper Palaeolithic Hunting Behaviors in the Southern Caucasus." *Current Anthropology* 47(1):89–118. https://doi.org/10.1086/432455.

Beck, Dunja. 1999. *Das Mittelpaläolithikum des Hohlenstein, Städel und Bärenhöhle im Lonetal.* Bonn, Germany: R. Habelt.

Becker, Arnfried, Brigitta Ammann, Flavio S. Anselmetti, Ann Marie Hirt, Michel Magny, Laurent Millet, Anne-Marie Rachoud, Giuseppe Sampietro, and

Christoph Wüthrich. 2006. "Paleoenvironmental Studies on Lake Bergsee, Black Forest, Germany." *Neues Jahrbuch für Geologie und Paläontologie* 240(3):405–445.

Beutelspacher, Thomas. N. Ebinger-Rist, and Claus J. Kind. 2011. "Neue Funde aus der Stadelhöhle im Hohlenstein." In *Archäologische Ausgrabungen in Baden-Württemberg 2010*, 65–70. Stuttgart, Germany: Konrad Theiss Verlag.

Binford, Lewis R. 1978. *Nunamiut Ethnoarchaeology*. New York: Academic Press.

Blasco, Ruth, Clive Finlayson, Jordi Rosell, Antonio Sánchez Marco, Stewart Finlayson, Geraldine Finlayson, Juan José Negro, Francisco Giles Pacheco, and Joaquín Rodríguez Vidal. 2014. "The Earliest Pigeon Fanciers." *Scientific Reports* 4(1):5971. https://doi.org/10.1038/srep05971.

Bocherens, Hervé. 2011. "Diet and Ecology of Neanderthals: Implications from C and N Isotopes." In *Neanderthal Lifeways, Subsistence and Technology*, ed. N. J. Conard and J. Richter, 73–85. Vertebrate Paleobiology and Paleoanthropology Series. Dordrecht, Netherlands: Springer. https://doi.org/10.1007/978-94-007-0415-2_8.

Bocherens, Hervé, Dorothée G. Drucker, Daniel Billiou, Marylène Patou-Mathis, and Bernard Vandermeersch. 2005. "Isotopic Evidence for Diet and Subsistence Pattern of the Saint-Césaire I Neanderthal: Review and Use of a Multi-Source Mixing Model." *Journal of Human Evolution* 49:71–87. https://doi.org/10.1016/j.jhevol.2005.03.003.

Bocherens, Hervé, Dorothée G. Drucker, and Stéphane Madelaine. 2014. "Evidence for a 15N Positive Excursion in Terrestrial Foodwebs at the Middle to Upper Palaeolithic Transition in South-Western France: Implications for Early Modern Human Palaeodiet and Palaeoenvironment." *Journal of Human Evolution* 69(1):31–43. https://doi.org/10.1016/j.jhevol.2013.12.015.

Boger, Ulf, Britt Starkovich, and Nicholas J. Conard. 2014. "New Insights Gained from the Faunal Material Recovered during the Latest Excavations at Vogelherd Cave." *Mitteilungen der Gesellschaft für Urgeschichte* 23:57–81.

Bolus, Michael. 2003. "The Cultural Context of the Aurignacian of the Swabian Jura." In *The Chronology of the Aurignacian and of the Transitional Technocomplexes: Dating, Stratigraphies, Cultural Implications*, ed. J. Zilhão and F. d'Errico, *Proceedings of Symposium 6.1 of the XIVth Congress of the UISPP* 33: 152–163. Lisboa, Portugal: Instituto Português de Arqueologia.

Bolus, Michael. 2004. *"Settlement Analysis of Sites of the Blattspitzen Complex in Central Europe." Settlement Dynamics of the Middle Paleolithic and Middle Stone Age II.* Tübingen Publications in Prehistory., 201–226. Tübingen, Germany: Kerns Verlag.

Bolus, Michael, Nicholas J. Conard, and Andrew W. Kandel. 1999. "Grabungen vor dem Hohlenstein im Lonetal, Gemeinden Bissingen und Asselfingen, Alb-Donau-Kreis." *Archäologische Ausgrabungen in Baden-Württemberg* 1998:40–47.

Böttcher, R., Berrin Cep, Claus J. Kind, D. Mörike, Alfred F. Pawlik, W. Rähle, K. Steppan, R. Torke, W. Torke, and Reinhard Ziegler. 2000. "Kogelstein—eine mittelpaläolithische Fundstelle bei Schelklingen-Schmiechen." *Fundberichte aus Baden-Württemberg* 24:7–176.

Broughton, Jack M. 1999. *Resource Depression and Intensification during the Late Holocene, San Francisco Bay: Evidence from the Emeryville Shellmound Vertebrate Fauna,* University of California Publications 32. Berkeley: University of California Press.

Broughton, Jack M., Michael Cannon, Frank Bayham, and David Byers. 2011. "Prey Body Size and Ranking in Zooarchaeology: Theory, Empirical Evidence, and Applications from the Northern Great Basin." *American Antiquity* 76(3):403–428. https://doi.org/10.7183/0002-7316.76.3.403.

Brown, Kimberly, Darren A. Fa, Geraldine Finlayson, and Clive Finlayson. 2011. "Small Game and Marine Resource Exploitation by Neanderthals: The Evidence from Gibraltar." In *Trekking the Shore,* ed. N. F. Bicho, J. A. Haws and L. G. Davis, 247–272. Interdisciplinary Contributions to Archaeology. New York: Springer. https://doi.org/10.1007/978-1-4419-8219-3_10.

Burkert, Wolfgang, and Harald Floss. 2005. "Lithic Exploitation Areas in the Upper Palaeolithic of West and Southwest Germany—A Comparative Study." In *Stone Age-Mining Age,* ed. G. Körlin and G. Weisgerber, 35–49. Der Anschnitt, Beiheft. 19 vols. Bochum, Germany: Deutsches Bergbau-Museum.

Camarós, Edgard, Susanne C. Münzel, Marián Cueto, Florent Rivals, and Nicholas J. Conard. 2016. "The Evolution of Paleolithic Hominin–Carnivore Interaction Written in Teeth: Stories from the Swabian Jura (Germany)." *Journal of Archaeological Science: Reports* 6:798–809.

Castellano, Sergi, Genís Parra, Federico A. Sánchez-Quinto, Fernando Racimo, Martin Kuhlwilm, Martin Kircher, Susanna Sawyer, Qiaomei Fu, Anja Heinze, Birgit Nickel, et al. 2014. "Patterns of Coding Variation in the Complete Exomes of Three Neandertals." *Proceedings of the National Academy of Sciences of the United States of America* 111(18):6666–6671. https://doi.org/10.1073/pnas.1405138111.

Çep, Berrin, Wolfgang Burkert, and Harald Floss. 2011. "Zur mittelpaläolithischen Rohmaterialversorgung im Bockstein (Schwäbische Alb)." *Mitteilungen der Gesellschaft für Urgeschichte* 20:33–52.

Çep, Berrin, and Petra Krönneck. 2015. "Landscape and Cave Use in the Middle Paleolithic of Bockstein: New Results from the Lithic and Fauna Analysis." In *Settlement Dynamics of the Middle Paleolithic and Middle Stone Age,* vol. IV. ed. N. J. Conard and A. Delagnes, 227–243. Tübingen, Germany: Kerns Verlag.

Clark, Jamie L. 2009. *Testing Models on the Emergence and Nature of Modern Human Behavior: Middle Stone Age Fauna from Sibudu Cave (South Africa).* PhD thesis, University of Michigan, Ann Arbor: ProQuest.

Colonese, A. C., M. A. Mannino, D. E. Bar-Yosef Mayer, D. A. Fa, J. C. Finlayson, D. Lubell, and Mary C. Stiner. 2011. "Marine Mollusc Exploitation in Mediterranean Prehistory: An Overview." *Quaternary International* 239(1–2) 86–103. https://doi.org/10.1016/j.quaint.2010.09.001.

Conard, Nicholas J. 2009. "A Female Figurine from the Basal Aurignacian of Hohle Fels Cave in Southwestern Germany." *Nature* 459(7244):248–252. https://doi.org/10.1038/nature07995.

Conard, Nicholas J. 2011. "The Demise of the Neanderthal Cultural Niche and the Beginning of the Upper Paleolithic in Southwestern Germany." In *Neanderthal Lifeways, Subsistence and Technology: One Hundred Fifty Years of Neanderthal Study*, ed. N. J. Conard and J. Richter, 223–240. Vertebrate Paleobiology and Paleoanthropology. Dordrecht, Netherlands: Springer.

Conard, Nicholas J., and Michael Bolus. 2003. "Radiocarbon Dating the Appearance of Modern Humans and Timing of Cultural Innovations in Europe: New Results and New Challenges." *Journal of Human Evolution* 44(3):331–373. https://doi.org/10.1016/S0047-2484(02)00202-6.

Conard, Nicholas J., and Michael Bolus. 2006. ""The Swabian Aurignacian and Its Place in European Prehistory." *Towards a Definition of the Aurignacian*, Trabalhos de Arqueologia 45, ed. O. Bar-Yosef and J. Zilhão, 211–239. Lisbon: Portugal: Instituto Português de Arqueologia.

Conard, Nicholas J., and Michael Bolus. 2008. "Radiocarbon Dating the Late Middle Paleolithic and the Aurignacian of the Swabian Jura." *Journal of Human Evolution* 55(5):886–897. https://doi.org/10.1016/j.jhevol.2008.08.006.

Conard, Nicholas J., Michael Bolus, Paul Goldberg, and Susanne C. Münzel. 2006. "The Last Neanderthals and First Modern Humans in the Swabian Jura." In *When Neanderthals and Modern Humans Met*, ed. N. J. Conard, 305–341. Tübingen, Germany: Kerns.

Conard, Nicholas J., Michael Bolus, and Susanne C. Münzel. 2012. "Middle Paleolithic Land Use, Spatial Organization and Settlement Intensity in the Swabian Jura, Southwestern Germany." *Quaternary International* 247:236–245. https://doi.org/10.1016/j.quaint.2011.05.043.

Conard, Nicholas J., Keiko Kitagawa, Petra Krönneck, Madelaine Böhme, and Susanne C. Münzel. 2013. "The Importance of Fish, Fowl and Small Mammals in the Paleolithic Diet of the Swabian Jura, Southwestern Germany." In *Zooarchaeology and Modern Human Origins*, ed. J. L. Clark and J. D. Speth, 173–190. Vertebrate Paleobiology and Paleoanthropology. Dordrecht, Netherlands: Springer. https://doi.org/10.1007/978-94-007-6766-9_11.

Conard, Nicholas J., Maria Malina, and Susanne C. Münzel. 2009. "New Flutes Document the Earliest Musical Tradition in Southwestern Germany." *Nature* 460(7256):737.

Discamps, Emmanuel, Jacques Jaubert, and François Bachellerie. 2011. "Human Choices and Environmental Constraints: Deciphering the Variability of Large Game Procurement from Mousterian to Aurignacian times (MIS 5-3) in Southwestern France." *Quaternary Science Reviews* 30(19–20):2755–2775. https://doi.org /10.1016/j.quascirev.2011.06.009.

Drucker, Dorothée G., Carole Vercoutère, Laurent Chiotti, Roland Nespoulet, Laurent Crépin, Nicholas J. Conard, Susanne C. Münzel, Thomas Higham, Johannes van der Plicht, Martina Lázničková-Galetová, et al. 2015. "Tracking Possible Decline of Woolly Mammoth during the Gravettian in Dordogne (France) and the Ach Valley (Germany) Using Multi-Isotope Tracking (13C, 14C, 15N, 34S, 18O)." *Quaternary International* 359–360:304–317. https://doi.org/10.1016/j.quaint.2014.11.028.

Duprat-Oualid, Fanny, Damien Rius, Carole Bégeot, Michel Magny, Laurent Millet, Sabine Wulf, and Oona Appelt. 2017. "Vegetation Response to Abrupt Climate Changes in Western Europe from 45 to 14.7k cal a BP: The Bergsee Lacustrine Record (Black Forest, Germany)." *Journal of Quaternary Science* 32: 1008–1021.

El Zaatari, Sireen, Frederick E. Grine, Peter S. Ungar, and Jean-Jacques Hublin. 2011. "Ecogeographic Variation in Neandertal Dietary Habits: Evidence from Occlusal Molar Microwear Texture Analysis." *Journal of Human Evolution* 61(4):411–424. https://doi.org/10.1016/j.jhevol.2011.05.004.

El Zaatari, Sireen, and Jean-Jacques Hublin. 2014. "Diet of Upper Paleolithic Modern Humans: Evidence from Microwear Texture Analysis." *American Journal of Physical Anthropology* 153(4):570–581. https://doi.org/10.1002/ajpa.22457.

Fernandez, Philippe. 2009. "De l'estimation de l'âge individuel dentaire au modèle descriptif des structures d'âge des cohortes fossiles: l'exemple des 'Equidae' et du time-specific model en contextes paléobiologiques pléistocenes." *Bulletin de la Société Préhistorique Française* 106(1):5–14. https://doi.org/10.3406/bspf.2009.13826.

Finlayson, Clive. 2005. "Biogeography and Evolution of the Genus *Homo*." *Trends in Ecology & Evolution* 20(8):457–463. https://doi.org/10.1016/j.tree.2005.05.019.

Finlayson, Clive, Kimberly Brown, Ruth Blasco, Jordi Rosell, Juan José Negro, Gary R. Bortolotti, Geraldine Finlayson, Antonio Sánchez Marco, Francisco Giles Pacheco, Joaquín Rodríguez Vidal, et al. 2012. "Birds of a Feather: Neanderthal Exploitation of Raptors and Corvids." *PLoS One* 7(9):e45927. https://doi.org/10 .1371/journal.pone.0045927.

Finlayson, Clive, and J. S. Carrion. 2007. "Rapid Ecological Turnover and Its Impact on Neanderthal and Other Human Populations." *Trends in Ecology and Evolution* 22(4):213–222. https://doi.org/10.1016/j.tree.2007.02.001.

Floss, Harald, and Petra Kieselbach. 2004. "The Danube Corridor after 29,000 BP: New Results on Raw Material Procurement Patterns in the Gravettian of Southwestern Germany." *Mitteilungen der Gesellschaft für Urgeschichte* 13:61–78.

Floss, Harald, and Nathalie Rouquerol, eds. 2007. *Les chemins de l'art Aurignacien en Europe/Das Aurignacien und die Anfänge der Kunst in Europa.* Aurignac, France: Éditions Musée-Forum Aurignac.

Fu, Qiaomei, Heng Li, Priya Moorjani, Flora Jay, Sergey M. Slepchenko, Aleksei A. Bondarev, Philip L. F. Johnson, Ayinuer Aximu-Petri, Kay Prufer, Cesare de Filippo, et al. 2014. "Genome Sequence of a 45,000-Year-Old Modern Human from Western Siberia." *Nature* 514(7523):445–449. https://doi.org/10.1038/nature13810.

Gamble, Clive. 1979. "Hunting Strategies in the Central European Palaeolithic." *Proceedings of the Prehistoric Society* 45:35–52. https://doi.org/10.1017/S0079497X000 09646.

Gaudzinski-Windheuser, Sabine, and Laura Niven. 2009. "Hominin Subsistence Patterns During the Middle and Late Paleolithic in Northwestern Europe." In *The Evolution of Hominin Diets*, ed. J.-J. Hublin and M. Richards, 99–111. Vertebrate Paleobiology and Paleoanthropology. Dordrecht, Netherlands: Springer. https://doi.org/10.1007/978-1-4020-9699-0_7.

Goldberg, Paul, Solveig Schiegl, Karen Meligne, Chris Dayton, and Nicholas J. Conard. 2003. "Micromorphology and Site Formation at Hohle Fels Cave, Schwabian Jura, Germany." *Eiszeitalter und Gegenwart* 53(1):1–25.

Golovanova, Liubov V., Vladimir B. Doronichev, Naomi E. Cleghorn, Marianna Al. Koulkova, Tatiana V. Sapelko, and M. Steven Shackley. 2010. "Significance of Ecological Factors in the Middle to Upper Paleolithic Transition." *Current Anthropology* 51(5):655–691. https://doi.org/10.1086/656185.

Grayson, Donald K. 1984. *Quantitative Zooarchaeology: Topics in the Analysis of Archaeological Faunas.* Orlando, FL: Academic Press.

Grayson, Donald K., and Françoise Delpech. 2005. "Pleistocene Reindeer and Global Warming." *Conservation Biology* 19(2):557–562.

Grayson, Donald K., and Françoise Delpech. 2006. "Was There Increasing Dietary Specialization across the Middle-to-Upper Paleolithic Transition in France." In *When Neanderthals and Modern Humans Met*, ed. N. J. Conard, 377–417. Tübingen, Germany: Kerns Verlag.

Grayson, Donald K., and Carol J. Frey. 2004. "Measuring Skeletal Part Reptresentation in Archaeological Faunas." *Journal of Taphonomy* 2:27–42.

Green, Richard E., Johannes Krause, Adrian W. Briggs, Tomislav Maricic, Udo Stenzel, Martin Kircher, Nick Patterson, Heng Li, Weiwei Zhai, Markus Hsi-Yang Fritz, et al. 2010. "A Draft Sequence of the Neandertal Genome." *Science* 328(5979):710–722. https://doi.org/10.1126/science.1188021.

Greenfield, Haskel, N. Collin Moore, and Karlheinz Steppan. 2015. "Estimating the Age- and Season-of-Death for Wild Equids: A Comparison of Techniques Utilising a Sample from the Late Neolithic Site of Bad Buchau-Dullenried, Germany." *Open Quaternary* 1(1). https://doi.org/10.5334/oq.ac

Gunz, Philipp, Fred L. Bookstein, Philipp Mitteroecker, Andrea Stadlmayr, Horst Seidler, and Gerhard W. Weber. 2009. "Early Modern Human Diversity Suggests Subdivided Population Structure and a Complex Out-of-Africa Scenario." *Proceedings of the National Academy of Sciences of the United States of America* 106(15):6094–6098. https://doi.org/10.1073/pnas.0808160106.

Hahn, Joachim. 1977. *Aurignacien, das ältere Jungpaläolithikum in Mittel- und Osteuropa*. Köln/Wien, Germany: Böhlau.

Hahn, Joachim. 1988. *Fundhorizontbildung und Besiedlung im Mittelpaläolithikum und im Aurignacien*. Stuttgart, Germany: Theiss.

Hahn, Joachim. 1995. "Neue Beschleuniger–14C-Daten zum Jungpaläolithikum in Südwestdeutschland." *Eiszeitalter und Gegenwart* 45:86–92.

Harrold, Francis B. 2009. "Historical Perspectives on the European Transition from Middle to Upper Paleolithic." In *Sourcebook of Paleolithic Transitions*, ed. M. Camps and P. Chauhan, 283–299. New York: Springer. https://doi.org/10.1007/978-0-387-76487-0_19.

Harvati, Katerina, Jean-Jacques Hublin, and Philipp Gunz. 2010. "Evolution of Middle-Late Pleistocene Human Cranio-Facial Form: A 3-D Approach." *Journal of Human Evolution* 59(5):445–464. https://doi.org/10.1016/j.jhevol.2010.06.005.

Heiri, Oliver, Karin A. Koinig, Christoph Spötl, Sam Barrett, Achim Brauer, Ruth Drescher-Schneider, Dorian Gaar, Susan Ivy-Ochs, Hanns Kerschner, Marc Luetscher, et al. 2014. "Palaeoclimate Records 60–8 ka in the Austrian and Swiss Alps and Their Forelands." *Quaternary Science Reviews* 106:186–205. https://doi.org/10.1016/j.quascirev.2014.05.021.

Henry, Amanda G. 2012. "Recovering Dietary Information from Extant and Extinct Primates Using Plant Microremains." *International Journal of Primatology* 33(3):702–715. https://doi.org/10.1007/s10764-011-9556-1.

Henry, Amanda G., Alison S. Brooks, and Dolores R. Piperno. 2011. ""Microfossils in Calculus Demonstrate Consumption of Plants and Cooked Foods in Neanderthal Diets (Shanidar III, Iraq; Spy I and II, Belgium)." *Proceedings of the National Academy of Sciences of the United States of America* 108(2):486–491. https://doi.org/10.1073/pnas.1016868108.

Henry, Amanda G., Alison S. Brooks, and Dolores R. Piperno. 2014. "Plant Foods and the Dietary Ecology of Neanderthals and Early Modern Humans." *Journal of Human Evolution* 69:44–54. https://doi.org/10.1016/j.jhevol.2013.12.014.

Henshilwood, Christopher S., and Curtis W. Marean. 2003. "The Origin of Modern Human Behavior: Critique of the Models and Their Test Implications." *Current Anthropology* 44(5):627–651. https://doi.org/10.1086/377665.

Higham, Thomas, Laura Basell, Roger Jacobi, Rachel Wood, Christopher B. Ramsey, and Nicholas J. Conard. 2012. "Testing Models for the Beginnings of the Aurignacian and the Advent of Figurative Art and Music: The Radiocarbon Chronology of Geißenklösterle." *Journal of Human Evolution* 62(6):664–676. https://doi.org/10.1016/j.jhevol.2012.03.003.

Higham, Thomas, Katerina Douka, Rachel Wood, Christopher B. Ramsey, Fiona Brock, Laura Basell, Marta Camps, Alvaro Arrizabalaga, Javier Baena, Cecillio Barroso-Ruiz, et al. 2014. "The Timing and Spatiotemporal Patterning of Neanderthal Disappearance." *Nature* 512(7514):306–309. https://doi.org/10.1038/nature13621.

Hill, Kim, Michael Barton, and A. Magdalena Hurtado. 2009. "The Emergence of Human Uniqueness: Characters Underlying Behavioral Modernity." *Evolutionary Anthropology* 18(5):187–200. https://doi.org/10.1002/evan.20224.

Hockett, Bryan, and Jonathan A. Haws. 2003. "Nutritional Ecology and Diachronic Trends in Paleolithic Diet and Health." *Evolutionary Anthropology* 12(5):211–216. https://doi.org/10.1002/evan.10116.

Hockett, Bryan, and Jonathan A. Haws. 2005. "Nutritional Ecology and the Human Demography of Neandertal Extinction." *Quaternary International* 137(1):21–34. https://doi.org/10.1016/j.quaint.2004.11.017.

Hoffecker, John F. 2009. "Neanderthal and Modern Human Diet in Eastern Europe." In *The Evolution of Hominin Diets*, ed. J.-J. Hublin and M. Richards, 87–98. Vertebrate Paleobiology and Paleoanthropology. Dordrecht, Netherlands: Springer. https://doi.org/10.1007/978-1-4020-9699-0_6.

Hoffecker, John F., and Naomi Cleghorn. 2000. "Mousterian Hunting Patterns in the Northwestern Caucasus and the Ecology of the Neanderthals." *International Journal of Osteoarchaeology* 10(5):368–378. https://doi.org/10.1002/1099-1212(200009/10)10:5<368::AID-OA555>3.0.CO;2-H.

Joordens, Josephine C. A., Francesco d'Errico, Frank P. Wesselingh, Stephen Munro, John de Vos, Jakob Wallinga, Christina Ankjaergaard, Tony Reimann, Jan R. Wijbrans, Klaudia F. Kuiper, Herman J. Mucher, Helene Coqueugniot, Vincent Prie, Ineke Joosten, Bertil van Os, Anne S. Schulp, Michel Panuel, Victoria van der Haas, Wim Lustenhouwer, John J. G. Reijmer, and Wil Roebroeks. 2015. "*Homo Erectus* at Trinil on Java Used Shells for Tool Production and Engraving." *Nature* 518:228–231.

Karavanić, Ivor, and Marylène Patou-Mathis. 2009. "Middle/Upper Paleolithic Interface in Vindija Cave (Croatia): New Results and Interpretations." In *Sourcebook of Paleolithic Transitions*, ed. M. Camps and P. Chauhan, 397–405. New York: Springer. https://doi.org/10.1007/978-0-387-76487-0_26.

Kitagawa, Keiko. 2014. *Exploring Hominins and Animals in the Swabian Jura: Study of the Paleolithic Fauna from Hohlenstein-Stadel.* Tübingen, Germany: University of Tübingen.

Kitagawa, Keiko, Petra Krönneck, Nicholas J. Conard, and Susanne C. Münzel. 2012. "Exploring Cave Use and Exploitation among Cave Bears, Carnivores and Hominins in the Swabian Jura, Germany." *Journal of Taphonomy* 10(3–4):439–461.

Krönneck, Petra. 2012. "Die pleistozäne Makrofauna des Bocksteins (Lonetal-Schwäbische Alb): Ein neuer Ansatz zur Rekonstruktion der Paläoumwelt." PhD thesis, University of Tübingen, Tübingen, Germany.

Krönneck, Petra. in press. "Die Vogelknochen vom Geißenklösterle." In *Geißenklösterle II: Fauna, Flora und Umweltverhältnisse im Mittel- und Jungpaläolithikum*, ed. N. J. Conard, M. Bolus, and S. C. Münzel. Tübingen, Germany: Kerns.

Krönneck, P., L. Niven, H.-P. Uerpmann. 2004. "Middle Palaeolithic Subsistence in the Lone Valley (Swabian Alb, Southern Germany)." *International Journal of Osteoarchaeology* 14: (3–4) 212–224.

Lam, Y. M., Xingbin Chen, and Osbjorn Pearson. 1999. "Intertaxonomic Variability in Patterns of Bone Density and the Differential Representation of Bovid, Cervid, and Equid Elements in the Archaeological Record." *American Antiquity* 64(2):343–362. https://doi.org/10.2307/2694283.

Laroulandie, Véronique, Jean-Philippe Faivre, Magali Gerbe, and Vincent Mourre. 2016. "Who Brought the Bird Remains to the Middle Palaeolithic Site of Les Fieux (Southwestern, France)? Direct Evidence of a Complex Taphonomic Story." *Quaternary International.* 421:116–133.

Lee-Thorp, Julia, and Matt Sponheimer. 2006. "Contributions of Biogeochemistry to Understanding Hominin Dietary Ecology." *American Journal of Physical Anthropology* 131(S43) 131–148. https://doi.org/10.1002/ajpa.20519.

Levine, Marsha Ann. 1982. "The Use of Crown Height Measurements and Eruption-Wear Sequences to Age Horse Teeth." In *Ageing and Sexing Animal Bones from Archaeological Sites*, vol. 109. ed. B. Wilson, C. Grigson, and S. Payne, 223–250. Oxford, UK: Archaeopress.

Liolios, Despina. 2006. "Reflections on the Role of Bone Tools in the Definition of the Early Aurignacian." In *Towards a Definition of the Aurignacian*, Trabalhos de Arqueologia 45, ed. O. Bar-Yosef and J. Zilhão, 37–51. Lisboa, Portugal: Instituto Português de Arqueologia.

Lupo, Karen D. 1998. "Experimentally Derived Extraction Rates for Marrow: Implications for Body Part Exploitation Strategies of Plio-Pleistocene Hominid Scavengers." *Journal of Archaeological Science* 25(7):657–675. https://doi.org/10.1006/jasc.1997.0261.

Lyman, R. Lee. 1984. "Bone Density and Differential Survivorship of Fossil Classes." *Journal of Anthropological Archaeology* 3(4):259–299. https://doi.org/10.1016/0278-4165(84)90004-7.

Lyman, R. Lee. 2008. *Quantitative Paleozoology*. Cambridge, UK: Cambridge University Press.

McBrearty, Sally, and Alison S. Brooks. 2000. "The Revolution That Wasn't: A New Interpretation of the Origin of Modern Human Behavior." *Journal of Human Evolution* 39(5):453–563. https://doi.org/10.1006/jhev.2000.0435.

Mellars, Paul. 1989. "Major Issues in the Emergence of Modern Humans." *Current Anthropology* 30(3):349–385. https://doi.org/10.1086/203755.

Mellars, Paul. 1996. *The Neanderthal Legacy: An Archaeological Perspective from Western Europe*. Princeton, NJ: Princeton University Press. https://doi.org/10.1515/9781400843602.

Miller, Christopher E. 2015. *A Tale of Two Swabian Caves: Geoarchaeological Investigations at Hohle Fels and Geißenklösterle*. Tübingen, Germany: Kerns Verlag.

Morin, Eugène. 2007. "Fat Composition and Nunamiut Decision-Making: A New Look at the Marrow and Bone Grease Indices." *Journal of Archaeological Science* 34(1):69–82. https://doi.org/10.1016/j.jas.2006.03.015.

Morin, Eugène. 2008. "Evidence for Declines in Human Population Densities during the Early Upper Paleolithic in Western Europe." *Proceedings of the National Academy of Sciences of the United States of America* 105(1):48–53. https://doi.org/10.1073/pnas.0709372104.

Morin, Eugène. 2012. *Reassessing Paleolithic Subsistence: The Neandertal and Modern Human Foragers of Saint-Césaire*. Cambridge, UK: Cambridge University Press. https://doi.org/10.1017/CBO9781139150972.

Morin, Eugène, and Véronique Laroulandie. 2012. "Presumed Symbolic Use of Diurnal Raptors by Neanderthals." *PLoS One* 7(3):e32856. https://doi.org/10.1371/journal.pone.0032856.

Müller, Ulrich C., Jörg Pross, and Erhard Bibus. 2003. "Vegetation Response to Rapid Climate Change in Central Europe during the Past 140,000 yr Based on Evidence from the Füramoos Pollen Record." *Quaternary Research* 59(2):235–245. https://doi.org/10.1016/S0033-5894(03)00005-X.

Münzel, Susanne C. 1988. "Quantitative Analysis and Archaeological Site Interpretation." *Archaeozoologia* 2(1.2):93–110.

Münzel, Susanne C. 2009. "Der Mensch lebt nicht vom Brot allein . . ." (Matthäus 4,4) Taphonomische Anmerkungen zum Subsistenzverhalten von Neandertalern und modernen Menschen am Beispiel der Geißenklösterle-Höhle bei Blaubeuren, Schwäbische Alb." In *Knochen pflastern ihren Weg: Festschrift für Margarethe und Hans-Peter Uerpmann*, ed. R. de Beauclair, S. Münzel and H. Napierala, 169–180. Rahden, Germany: Verlag Marie Leidorf.

Münzel, Susanne C. In press. "Die jungpleistozäne Großsäugerfauna aus dem Geißenklösterle." In *Geißenklösterle II: Fauna, Flora und Umweltverhältnisse im*

Mittel- und Jungpaläolithikum, ed. N. J. Conard, M. Bolus, and S. C. Münzel. Tübingen, Germany: Kerns.

Münzel, Susanne C., and Nicholas J. Conard. 2004. "Change and Continuity in Subsistence during the Middle and Upper Palaeolithic in the Ach Valley of Swabia (South-West Germany)." *International Journal of Osteoarchaeology* 14(3–4):225–243. https://doi.org/10.1002/oa.758.

Münzel, Susanne C., Mathias Stiller, Michael Hofreiter, Alissa Mittnik, Nicholas J. Conard, and Hervé Bocherens. 2011. "Pleistocene Bears in the Swabian Jura (Germany): Genetic Replacement, Ecological Displacement, Extinctions and Survival." *Quaternary International* 245(2):225–237. https://doi.org/10.1016/j.quaint.2011.03.060.

Niven, Laura. 2006. *The Palaeolithic Occupation of Vogelherd Cave: Implications for the Subsistence Behavior of Late Neanderthals and Early Modern Humans*. Tübingen, Germany: Kerns Verlag.

Nowell, April. 2010. "Defining Behavioral Modernity in the Context of Neandertal and Anatomically Modern Human Populations." *Annual Review of Anthropology* 39(1):437–452. https://doi.org/10.1146/annurev.anthro.012809.105113.

Outram, Alan, and Peter Rowley-Conwy. 1998. "Meat and Marrow Utility Indices for Horse (*Equus*)." *Journal of Archaeological Science* 25(9):839–849. https://doi.org/10.1006/jasc.1997.0229.

Owen, Linda. 2013. "Fish in the Magdalenian of Southwest Germany. Emergency Food or Important Resource?" In *Plesitocene Foragers: Their Culture and Environment*, ed. A. Pastoors and B. Auffermann, 85–100. Mettmann, Germany: Neanderthal Museum.

Patou-Mathis, Marylène. 2000. "Neanderthal Subsistence Behaviours in Europe." *International Journal of Osteoarchaeology* 10(5):379–395. https://doi.org/10.1002/1099-1212(200009/10)10:5<379::AID-OA558>3.0.CO;2-4.

Prüfer, Kay, Fernando Racimo, Nick Patterson, Flora Jay, Sriram Sankararaman, Susanna Sawyer, Anja Heinze, Gabriel Renaud, Peter H. Sudmant, Cesare de Filippo, et al. 2014. "The Complete Genome Sequence of a Neanderthal from the Altai Mountains." *Nature* 505(7481):43–49. https://doi.org/10.1038/nature12886.

Radovčić, Davorka, Ankica Oros Sršen, Jakov Radovčić, and David W. Frayer. 2015. "Evidence for Neandertal Jewelry: Modified White-Tailed Eagle Claws at Krapina." *PLoS One* 10(3):e0119802. https://doi.org/10.1371/journal.pone.0119802.

Reitz, Elizabeth J., Irvy R. Quitmyer, H. Stephen Hale, Sylvia J. Scudder, and Elizabeth S. Wing. 1987. "Application of Allometry to Zooarchaeology." *American Antiquity* 52(2):304–317. https://doi.org/10.2307/281782.

Richards, Michael P., and Ralf W. Schmitz. 2008. "Isotope Evidence for the Diet of the Neanderthal Type Specimen." *Antiquity* 82(317):553–559. https://doi.org/10.1017/S0003598X00097210.

Richards, Michael P., and Erik Trinkaus. 2009. "Isotopic Evidence for the Diets of European Neanderthals and Early Modern Humans." *Proceedings of the National Academy of Sciences of the United States of America* 106(38):16034–16039. https://doi.org/10.1073/pnas.0903821106.

Richter, Daniel, J. Waiblinger, W. J. Rink, and G. A. Wagner. 2000. "Thermoluminescence, Electron Spin Resonance and ^{14}C-Dating of the Late Middle and Early Upper Palaeolithic Site of Geißenklösterle Cave in Southern Germany." *Journal of Archaeological Science* 27(1):71–89. https://doi.org/10.1006/jasc.1999.0458.

Riehl, Simone, Elena Marinova, Katleen Deckers, Maria Malina, and Nicholas J. Conard. 2015. "Plant Use and Local Vegetation Patterns during the Second Half of the Late Pleistocene in Southwestern Germany." *Archaeological and Anthropological Sciences* 7:151–167.

Riek, Gustav. 1934. *Die Eiszeitjägerstation am Vogelherd im Lonetal 1: Die Kulturen.* Tübingen, Germany: Akademische Buchhandlung Franz F. Heine.

Riel-Salvatore, Julien. 2010. "A Niche Construction Perspective on the Middle–Upper Paleolithic Transition in Italy." *Journal of Archaeological Method and Theory* 17(4):323–355. https://doi.org/10.1007/s10816-010-9093-9.

Romandini, Matteo, Marco Peresani, Véronique Laroulandie, Laure Metz, Andreas Pastoors, Manuel Vaquero, and Ludovic Slimak. 2014. "Convergent Evidence of Eagle Talons Used by Late Neanderthals in Europe: A Further Assessment on Symbolism." *PLoS One* 9 7):e101278. https://doi.org/10.1371/journal.pone.0101278.

Salazar-García, Domingo C., Robert C. Power, Alfred Sanchis Serra, Valentín Villaverde, Michael J. Walker, and Amanda G. Henry. 2013. "Neanderthal Diets in Central and Southeastern Mediterranean Iberia." *Quaternary International* 318:3–18. https://doi.org/10.1016/j.quaint.2013.06.007.

Shea, John J. 2011. "*Homo sapiens* Is as *Homo sapiens* Was." *Current Anthropology* 52(1):1–35. https://doi.org/10.1086/658067.

Smith, Tanya M., Paul Tafforeau, Donald J. Reid, Joane Pouech, Vincent Lazzari, John P. Zermeno, Debbie Guatelli-Steinberg, Anthony J. Olejniczak, Almut Hoffman, Jakov Radovčić, et al. 2010. "Dental Evidence for Ontogenetic Differences between Modern Humans and Neanderthals." *Proceedings of the National Academy of Sciences of the United States of America* 107(49):20923–20928. https://doi.org/10.1073/pnas.1010906107.

Speth, John. 2004. "News Flash: Negative Evidence Convicts Neanderthals of Gross Mental Incompetence." *World Archaeology* 36(4):519–526. https://doi.org/10.1080/0043824042000303692.

Starkovich, Britt M. 2012. "Intensification of Small Game Resources at Klissoura Cave 1 (Peloponnese, Greece) from the Middle Paleolithic to Mesolithic." *Quaternary International* 264:17–31. https://doi.org/10.1016/j.quaint.2011.10.019.

Starkovich, Britt M. 2014. "Optimal Foraging, Dietary Change, and Site Use during the Paleolithic at Klissoura Cave 1 (Southern Greece)." *Journal of Archaeological Science* 52:39–55. https://doi.org/10.1016/j.jas.2014.08.026.

Steele, Teresa E. 2005. "Comparing Methods for Analysing Mortality Profiles in Zooarchaeological and Palaeontological Samples." *International Journal of Osteoarchaeology* 15(6):404–420. https://doi.org/10.1002/oa.795.

Stiller, M., M. Hofreiter, M. Knapp, G. Baryshnikov, H. Bocherens, A. Grandal D'Anglade, B. Hilpert, Susanne C. Münzel, R. Pinhasi, G. Rabeder, et al. 2010. "Withering Away–25,000 Years of Genetic Decline Preceded Cave Bear Extinction." *Molecular Biology and Evolution* 27(5):975–978. https://doi.org/10.1093/molbev/msq083.

Stiner, Mary C. 1990. "The Use of Mortality Patterns in Archaeological Studies of Hominid Predatory Adaptations." *Journal of Anthropological Archaeology* 9(4):305–351. https://doi.org/10.1016/0278-4165(90)90010-B.

Stiner, Mary C. 2001. "Thirty Years on the 'Broad Spectrum Revolution' and Paleolithic Demography." *Proceedings of the National Academy of Sciences of the United States of America* 98(13):6993–6996. https://doi.org/10.1073/pnas.121176198.

Stiner, Mary C. 2005. *The Faunas of Hayonim Cave (Israel)*. Cambridge, MA: Peabody Museum of Archaeology and Ethnology, Harvard University.

Stiner, Mary C. 2009. "The Antiquity of Large Game Hunting in the Mediterranean Paleolithic: Evidence from Mortality Patterns." In *Transitions in Prehistory: Essays in Honor of Ofer Bar-Yosef*, ed. J. J. Shea and D. Lieberman, 103–123. Oxford, UK: Oxbow Books.

Stiner, Mary C., and Steven L. Kuhn. 2009. "Paleolithic Diet and the Division of Labor in Mediterranean Eurasia." In *The Evolution of Hominin Diets*, ed. J.-J. Hublin and M. P. Richards, 157–169. Vertebrate Paleobiology and Paleoanthropology. Dordrecht, Netherlands: Springer. https://doi.org/10.1007/978-1-4020-9699-0_11.

Stiner, Mary C., and Natalie D. Munro. 2002. "Approaches to Prehistoric Diet Breadth, Demography, and Prey Ranking Systems in Time and Space." *Journal of Archaeological Method and Theory* 9(2):181–214. https://doi.org/10.1023/A:1016530308865.

Stiner, Mary C., and Natalie D. Munro. 2011. "On the Evolution of Diet and Landscape during the Upper Paleolithic through Mesolithic at Franchthi Cave (Peloponnese, Greece)." *Journal of Human Evolution* 60(5):618–636. https://doi.org/10.1016/j.jhevol.2010.12.005.

Stiner, Mary C., Natalie D. Munro, and Todd A. Surovell. 2000. "The Tortoise and the Hare: Small-Game Use, the Broad-Spectrum Revolution, and Paleolithic Demography." *Current Anthropology* 41(1):39–73.

Straus, Lawrence Guy. 2013. "Iberian Archaeofaunas and Hominin Subsistence during Marine Isotope Stages 4 and 3." In *Zooarchaeology and Modern Human Origins*, ed. J. L. Clark and J. D. Speth, 97–128. Vertebrate Paleobiology and Paleoanthropology. Dordrecht, Netherlands: Springer. https://doi.org/10.1007/978-94-007-6766-9_7.

Tagliacozzo, Antonio, Matteo Romandini, Ivana Fiore, Monica Gala, and Marco Peresani. 2013. "Animal Exploitation Strategies during the Uluzzian at Grotta di Fumane (Verona, Italy)." In *Zooarchaeology and Modern Human Origins*, ed. J. L. Clark and J. D. Speth, 129–150. Vertebrate Paleobiology and Paleoanthropology. Dordrecht, Netherlands: Springer. https://doi.org/10.1007/978-94-007-6766-9_8.

Trinkaus, Erik. 2006. "Modern Human versus Neandertal Evolutionary Distinctiveness." *Current Anthropology* 47(4):597–620. https://doi.org/10.1086/504165.

Uerpmann, Hans-Peter. 1973. "Ein Beitrag zur Methodik der wirtschaftshistorischen Auswertung von Tierfunden aus Siedlungen." *Proceedings of the Domestikationsforschung und Geschichte der Haustiere Inteernationales Symposium in Budapest*: 391–395. Budapest, Hungary.

Villa, Paola, and Wil Roebroeks. 2014. "Neandertal Demise: An Archaeological Analysis of the Modern Human Superiority Complex." *PLoS One* 9(4):e96424. https://doi.org/10.1371/journal.pone.0096424.

Wagner, Eberhard. 1983. *Das Mittelpaläolithikum der Grossen Grotte bei Blaubeuren (Alb-Donau-Kreis)*. Stuttgart, Germany: Theiss.

Weaver, Timothy D. 2011. "Rates of Cranial Evolution in Neandertals and Modern Humans." In *Computational Paleontology*, ed. A. M. T. Elewa, 165–178. Berlin/Heidelberg, Germany: Springer. https://doi.org/10.1007/978-3-642-16271-8_9.

Weaver, Timothy D., Ryan H. Boyko, and Teresa E. Steele. 2011. "Cross-Platform Program for Likelihood-Based Statistical Comparisons of Mortality Profiles on a Triangular Graph." *Journal of Archaeological Science* 38(9):2420–2423. https://doi.org/10.1016/j.jas.2011.05.009.

Wetzel, Robert. 1961. "Der Hohlestein im Lonetal: Dokumente alteuropäischer Kulturen vom Eiszeitalter bis zur Völkerwanderung." *Mitteilungen des Vereins für Naturwissenschaft und Mathematik in Ulm (Donau)* 27:21–75.

Wetzel, Robert, Gerhard Bosinski, and Paul Filzer. 1969. *Die Bocksteinschmiede im Lonetal:(Markung Rammingen, Kreis Ulm)*. Stuttgart, Germany: Müller & Gräff.

Wolf, Sibylle. 2015. *Schmuckstücke: die Elfenbeinbearbeitung im Schwäbischen Aurignacien*. Tübingen, Germany: Kerns.

Yravedra Sainz de los Terreros,. José. 2013. "New Contributions on Subsistence Practices during the Middle-Upper Paleolithic in Northern Spain." In *Zooarchaeology and Modern Human Origins*, ed. J. L. Clark and J. D. Speth, 77–95. Vertebrate

Paleobiology and Paleoanthropology. Dordrecht, Netherlands: Springer. https://
doi.org/10.1007/978-94-007-6766-9_6.

Ziegler, Reinhard. In press. "Die Kleinsäugerfauna aus dem Geißenklösterle." In
*Geißenklösterle II: Fauna, Flora und Umweltverhältnisse im Mittel- und Jungpaläo-
lithikum*, ed. N. J. Conard, M. Bolus, and S. C. Münzel. Tübingen, Germany:
Kerns.

8

The Antiquity of
Hunter-Gatherers Revisited

Steven L. Kuhn and
Mary C. Stiner

In the late 1990s we had the opportunity to participate in an immensely instructive workshop on hunting and gathering societies of the past and present. The workshop was organized by Robert Layton, Peter Rowley-Conwy, and Julia Panter-Brick at Durham University. It brought together sociocultural anthropologists, human biologists, demographers, linguists, and archaeologists to discuss and debate salient issues in thinking about hunter-gatherers. Our particular role in the proceedings was to discuss "the antiquity of hunter-gatherers," which was also the title of our chapter in the book that came out of the conference: *Hunter-Gatherers: An Interdisciplinary Perspective* (Panter-Brick et al. 2001). Whether from naiveté or hubris (or a little bit of both) we decided to take the assignment literally. Anthropologists are fond of saying that human beings have lived as hunter-gatherers for 99.99 percent of their existence on earth. The question we asked was whether that assertion was anything more than a platitude. There is no disputing that before about 10,000 years ago all hominins depended exclusively on wild foods for their survival. However, the unanswered question is how much of what we understand about hunter-gatherers springs directly from the simple fact that they rely on non-domesticated plants and animals. Were all humans and early human ancestors just versions of hunter-gatherers of the recent past, or were there fundamental differences in how earlier humans dealt with the challenges of making a living from wild foods?

DOI: 10.5876/9781607327745.c008

Our 2001 paper focused on the more recent end of the time range, from the time of the Neanderthals and the Middle Paleolithic to the historic era, because that was (and is) where the data are most plentiful. We concluded that Middle Paleolithic foragers in fact looked very much like historically documented foragers in many important respects. Yet there were also anomalies: aspects of the Middle Paleolithic evidence as it stood that simply didn't fit with expectations based on hunter-gatherers of the last two centuries, or on archaeological knowledge of late Upper Paleolithic hunter-gatherers from ca. 20,000 years ago. We attributed some of these differences to the sizes and densities of human groups during various periods, rather than to differences in the capacities of the hominin taxa involved.

It has been more than 15 years since the "Antiquity of Hunter-Gatherers" (Kuhn and Stiner 2001) was published. Because our thinking about hunter-gatherers and their relevance for the study of Paleolithic foragers was and still is strongly influenced by the synthetic work of Bob Kelly (e.g., Kelly 2013) and our mutual mentor, Lewis Binford (2001), we thought this volume presented an excellent opportunity to assess what had changed in the last decade and a half, and perhaps reconsider our characterization of the Neanderthals and of Upper Paleolithic people. Hundreds of field and laboratory studies, combined with the application of methods that either didn't exist or were poorly developed back in the late twentieth century, have added immensely to what we know about the Neanderthals and early modern humans. Thanks in part to advances in the study of ancient and modern DNA, the ways we think about demography and the sizes and structures of Paleolithic populations have changed as well. Yet other observations have remained stable in spite of new data.

WHAT WE CLAIMED IN 2001

The 2001 paper began from a few simple premises. Most fundamentally, following the lead of Kelly, Binford, and others, we argued that a useful understanding of behavioral change over time must concentrate on behavior as a plastic phenotypic response. Simply enumerating the presence or absence of features such as bone tools, personal ornaments, or parietal art was an inadequate and indeed inappropriate approach to understanding evolutionary processes. The habit of gauging evolutionary change using trait lists derives from an antiquated progressivist view of evolution that visualized human societal improvement as a series of stages marked by major technical or social milestones. In other words, carved statuettes or blades do not define truly "modern behavior" any more than alphabets, iron smelting, or the waterwheel mark a true "civilization."

Instead of the checklist approach, we argued that understanding culture as a plastic system requires paleoanthropologsts to focus on variation in the frequencies of behaviors. A good place to start is by considering the ways in which the observed behavioral variation relates to those extrinsic factors that are also known to influence behavioral diversity among modern foragers. For example, the presence or absence of elaborate, multipart hunting weapons in Paleolithic sites of a given period does not by itself tell us about the nature of hominin culture or cognition. Such artifacts and attendant methods of production were not ubiquitous among recent foraging populations. One can push the discovery process further by using theories that predict the circumstances in which ancient foragers should invest more in manufacturing weapons. A conspicuous absence of such material culture where other factors lead us to expect it is therefore likely to be an anomaly of evolutionary significance.

A second supposition of our 2001 paper was that ethnographic and archaeological data on recent hunter-gatherers, as synthesized by Kelly (2013), Binford (2001), Hayden (1981), and others, provide an essential background for evaluating plastic response in earlier time periods. Theory is not sufficiently well developed to predict precisely how foragers might respond to a particular set of conditions from first principles alone. On the other hand, the historical and ethnographic records can tell us what is possible or even most reasonable. These data can be used to construct useful "frames of reference" (*sensu* Binford 2001) for evaluating past behavioral variation.

We recognized of course that recent foragers are influenced by unique histories, that they are not fossilized Paleolithic relics, and that they have existed in a very different world from Pleistocene hunter-gatherers, ecologically, demographically and culturally. Thus we did not expect ancient human populations to respond in identical ways to those of recent people. What we did expect, however, were similar *gradients* of response to the same external influences. For example, for obvious ecological reasons the caloric contribution of vegetable foods to hunter-gatherer diets declines with latitude (Hayden 1981; Keeley 1995; Kelly 2013; Cordain et al. 2000; Johnson 2014). It is reasonable to expect that this gradient in plant dependence would also have appeared thousands or tens of thousands of years ago. On the other hand, it is misguided to assume that forager diets would have been identical at a particular latitude 100 years ago and 50,000 years ago. Environmental and demographic conditions are simply too different to expect identical human responses based on latitude alone. The gradient serves more as a floating or relative standard, though it is no less valuable for being so.

With behavioral gradients in mind, we compared evidence of dietary and technological variation among the Neanderthals and other Middle Paleolithic hominins to the archaeological record of late Upper Paleolithic (LUP) *Homo sapiens*. Although these populations were not contemporaries, LUP hunter-gatherers show clear archaeological manifestations of the kinds of gradients of response that knowledge of recent hunter-gatherers leads us to predict. We also felt at the time that the record of early Upper Paleolithic foraging and technology was too thin and incomplete for effective comparison to Middle Paleolithic Neanderthals. Fifteen years of discovery and publication have changed this situation. What has changed most, however, is not so much our understanding of the early Upper Paleolithic but our understanding of the Neanderthals and Middle Paleolithic culture.

Our review of the evidence up to 2001 indicated that Neanderthals fit many—but not all—expectations derived from recent hunter-gatherers. Their diets shifted with climate and latitude, in response to variation in the composition of plant and animal communities. For example, the use of small game such as tortoises and legless lizards was confined to the Mediterranean region (Stiner 2001), whereas in high latitudes and during full glacial periods the meat diet was almost exclusively composed of large terrestrial herbivorous mammals (Gaudzinski-Windheuser and Niven 2009). Technological evidence showed similar levels of behavioral plasticity and strategic response to environmental conditions. Strategies of raw material use and artifact production and maintenance were very sensitive to raw material availability and mobility, consistent with what has been documented among *Homo sapiens* foragers of the late Pleistocene and Holocene.

At the same time there were some important points of difference between the Middle Paleolithic record and fundamental expectations based on modern foragers. First, while Neanderthal diets did vary across habitats and ecosystems, environmentally linked variation was attenuated overall. Middle Paleolithic hominins seldom engaged in very intensive exploitation and processing of their staple foods, whether big game or plants. These hominins seldom expanded their diets to include relatively costly, low-return foods such as elusive small game and plant foods that required a lot of processing to render them edible (Stiner 2001; Stiner et al. 2000). In regard to meat that is, while Middle Paleolithic hominins readily adjusted their diets to what was available within certain prey classes, but they stuck mainly to the most "profitable" animal foods: medium and large terrestrial herbivores. Later Upper Paleolithic foragers exploited these same large prey animals, but they routinely included a greater range of dietary choices and processing technologies overall.

Technological variability of the Middle Paleolithic appeared similarly attenuated. While Middle Paleolithic stone technology is characterized by a remarkable diversity of methods for producing blanks for stone tools (Kuhn 2013a), there is little evidence for variation in technological diversity on a larger scale or in their investment in artifact production. Seminal work by Oswalt (1976), Torrence (1983, 2001), and others shows that recent hunter-gatherer toolkits tend to be more diverse and complex with increasing latitude. This complexity has been attributed by various authors to higher levels of time stress or dependence on difficult-to-procure terrestrial and aquatic game. In contrast Middle Paleolithic toolkits are surprising for their lack of responsiveness to latitudinal differences. These technologies were composed of very similar ranges of elements regardless of latitude or global climate cycles. Possible hunting weapons of the Middle Paleolithic, which should have been sensitive to variation in the type of game hunted and the strategies of procurement, instead seemed quite uniform across the vast latitudinal and climatic range. In contrast, the much shorter period of the late Upper Paleolithic showed at least some latitudinal variation in the diversity, complexity, and composition of foraging toolkits: part of this diversity is manifest through the inclusion of artifact components of materials other than stone, such as bone, antler, and ivory. One could argue, rightly, that much—probably most—of the material culture of Paleolithic peoples was made up of perishable organic material and that archaeologists are missing out on much past technological variety. We would not dispute this point. However, there is also no reason to think that perishable material culture would behave in a fundamentally different way than durable artifacts. In other words, it is not unreasonable to use artifacts of stone and bone as a proxy for much larger inventories of material culture.

There are other complications that stand in the way of the environmental comparisons discussed above. One could claim that the apparently constricted variability in Middle Paleolithic technology and foraging was nothing more than a consequence of the geographical limits of the hominin species compared. The ethnographic and historical records of hunter-gatherers extend from the tropics to the high arctic, whereas the Middle Paleolithic record spans the subtropics to the subarctic. There are two reasons to dismiss this notion. First, the Middle Paleolithic record also spans a series of climate cycles over a very long period of around 200,000 years. While there are no Middle Paleolithic sites in the high arctic or near the equator, there are high-latitude sites occupied during very cold periods and there are sites at the southern end of the geographic range that correspond to warm interglacial conditions. In other words, while Middle Paleolithic sites do not cover an identical latitudinal range as ethnographically documented hunter-gatherers, Middle Paleolithic sites span a range of paleoenvironments that is nearly as broad. Such great geographic and temporal spans should increase the possibilities for archaeologists to find variation in economic responses if it existed. Second, the faunal and artifact assemblages from LUP archaeological sites within same the latitudinal range of the Middle Paleolithic do in fact show the kinds of variation that we see among recent hunter-gatherers (Kuhn and Stiner 2001), proving that the environmental range is sufficient to produce a response.

Finally, we followed many other scholars in noting that evidence for symbolic expression through material culture was very limited in the Middle Paleolithic. While pigments are frequently recovered from Middle Paleolithic sites (an important and interesting observation in its own right), durable objects such as beads and pendants were not regularly encountered. We have written about the significance of choices in media for body ornamentation in other contexts (Kuhn 2014; Kuhn and Stiner 2007; Stiner et al. 2013), but the lack of durable body ornamentation was what pointed us more strongly to social and demographic explanations for the seemingly anomalous features of Middle Paleolithic economies and technologies.

HOW HAVE KNOWLEDGE AND THINKING CHANGED SINCE 2001?

One obvious change over the past 15 years has been a growing recognition that a "trait list" approach to describing behavioral evolution is at best inadequate and sometimes even misleading. This realization comes from many sources, and we do not claim credit for it. A number of researchers have advocated greater attention to behavioral variation or flexibility (see for example Shea 2011) in comparing periods or hominin species. Many, however, continue to cling to the notion that the simple presence of shared archaeological characteristics demonstrates similar underlying behaviors and propensities (Hayden 2012). We also have a much broader range and quantity of evidence about Neanderthal diet and economies now than we did 15 years ago. Some of this new evidence derives from novel analytical methods, but much of it comes from discoveries that have accompanied the inevitable expansion of research. More data on any given theme in Middle Paleolithic studies better allows us to evaluate the full gamut of variation, its amplitude and periodicity.

Whereas large and medium-sized terrestrial herbivores were very clearly the mainstay of Middle Paleolithic diets across Eurasia, there is a growing body of evidence pertaining to the use of plant foods and small game animals.

Shellfish and reptiles were regular components of Middle Paleolithic diets where available, and evidence for their use is by now fairly non-controversial. In a number of cases, careful taphonomic studies have also documented hominin exploitation of birds and lagomorphs in some contexts (Aura et al. 2002; Blasco and Fernández Peris 2012; Cochard et al. 2012; Hardy et al. 2013). Because cases of the latter are scattered and comparatively rare, they cannot be argued to represent habitual behavior, in contrast to the situation for later Paleolithic foragers. Still other studies remind us that taphonomic evidence and ambiguities of context cannot be ignored; not every bird or rabbit in a Middle Paleolithic site got there through human actions (Lloveras et al. 2011). To date, claims for use of freshwater or marine fish by Middle Paleolithic hominins are patchy (e.g., Hardy and Moncel 2011) or wholly circumstantial (e.g., Bocherens et al. 2014).

More novel findings concern evidence for use of vegetable foods, from nuts and seeds to tubers. While no one expects macroscopic plant remains to be abundant or ubiquitous across Pleistocene sites, certain other kinds of scientifically based evidence help to fill in some of the gaps. Stable isotopes in hominin enamel (Bocherens and Drucker 2003; Richards and Trinkaus 2009; Wißing et al. 2016) and fecal sterols (Sistiaga et al. 2014) suggest a more generalized diet among Middle Paleolithic humans than some expected, although the majority of protein came (not surprisingly) from terrestrial mammals. Starch grains and phytoliths trapped in dental calculus provide fascinating evidence of the range of plant taxa consumed by Neanderthals (Henry et al. 2011, 2014), even if these data say nothing about the quantities consumed relative to other classes of foods. There is still little artifactual or other evidence for intensive processing of vegetable or animal foods through grinding or heat-in-liquid techniques. The tools that typically accompany heavy reliance on seeds and nuts as staples among recent foragers (Keeley 1995) can be highly durable, so we must take the paucity of milling tools in the Middle Paleolithic seriously. Such tools are known in some phases of the African MSA, though their frequencies are still poorly quantified, but we see few if any of these kinds of instruments in the Middle Paleolithic.

These new findings have certainly provided a better picture of the overall breadth of Middle Paleolithic diets, and sometimes of the range of foods consumed by individual Neanderthals in the months or years before their deaths. But while we have greater appreciation of the full range of foods targeted by Middle Paleolithic foragers, the real issue is not simply variety but proportions of different food classes. Observations about dietary variation among recent foragers highlight differences in relative quantities of foods consumed, not the simple number of food types. The emphasis on different foods also plays an important role in structuring labor and the modes of cooperation among members of the foraging society. Recent foragers living in the subarctic and the tropics consume fruits as well as meat from large game. The difference is in the contributions of these resources to the diets, as fruits are available during many months of the year in tropical areas but only during very short windows in the subarctic. Due to differential preservation, evidence of animal exploitation is incommensurate to that for plants, making it difficult to assess the dietary importance of the different resources on the same scale. Vertebrate and mollusk remains preserve well in many contexts because they have durable components, but they only provide us with information about animal foods.

Stable isotope data suggest which resources contributed the most dietary protein, but they tell us little about calories or other nutrient contributions to the diet. The emerging evidence from plant remains trapped in dental calculus, as well as rare examples of preserved macrobotanical fossils (e.g., charred nut hulls, Barton et al. 1999), may speak to taxonomic diversity but they cannot be translated into quantities consumed. It should not be surprising to anyone that Middle Paleolithic foragers were omnivorous. What we really need to know more about is the extent of the vegetable contribution relative to animal foods, and whether high-calorie plant foods (e.g., seeds, nuts) were an important part of the overall plant intake. The technological evidence remains the most important window on this particular question, because technological systems speak to differential investments in the food quest and in food processing.

The evidence for other dimensions of technology has also expanded in the last 15 years, though perhaps not as markedly as data on hominin diet and foraging. A number of researchers had long argued that Middle Paleolithic hominins hafted pointed stone tools to make hunting spears, but back in the late 1990s there remained some skepticism. In the intervening years a series of publications have presented powerful evidence of Middle Paleolithic weaponry and attendant manufacture processes. Data on point morphology (Shea 2006), traces of impact damage (Villa and Lenoir 2008; Villa et al. 2009), evidence of hafting (Rotts 2009; Pawlik and Thissen 2011), and even fragments of points embedded in animal bones (Boëda et al. 1999) demonstrate that Middle Paleolithic toolmakers regularly affixed pointed stone elements to handles of thrusting or hand-thrown spears. Not all Mousterian or Levallois points were used in this way (Plisson and Beyries 1998), but the evidence is common enough to show that the practice was widespread.

Even more intriguing is the evidence for mastics, binders, and other components in the manufacture of weapons with hafted stone points. All claims for hafted points in the Middle Paleolithic presuppose the use of some sort of natural adhesive, but advances in archaeological science have revealed what they were and how they were produced. Adhesive materials ranging from bitumen (Boëda et al. 2008; Mazza et al. 2006) to plant-based resins (Cârciumaru et al. 2012; Grünberg 2002) have been found adhering to the bases of stone artifacts. Though less showy than large, symmetrical stone points, the natural adhesives are important in that they reveal some of the diversity in materials and technological procedures for making even a "simple" stone-tipped spear.

We have also learned more over the past 15 years about possible body decoration in the Middle Paleolithic. It is still the case that pigments are the most ubiquitous material that could be related to decorative traditions and personal ornamentation (see d'Errico 2007, 2008). A number of other provocative cases indicate that Middle Paleolithic hominins sometimes may have employed other materials too. Distinctive butchery marks on wing bones of large raptors from Middle Paleolithic sites in Italy and elsewhere (Peresani et al. 2011; Morin and Laroulandie 2012) have been advanced as evidence for the use of feathers as decorative materials. Rare finds of raptor claws with traces of human manipulation (Radovčić et al. 2015), and modified marine shells (Bar-Yosef Mayer et al. 2009; Zilhão et al. 2010) are interpreted as possible evidence for deployment of these objects as beads, pendants, or other items of personal adornment. Again, the evidence is geographically dispersed and such objects are by no means as ubiquitous as they are in later periods, but it cannot be ignored. It is now safer to argue that the Middle Paleolithic is very poor in durable art forms. On the other hand the widespread evidence of the use of manganese and iron oxides suggests that nondurable arts were almost everywhere part of the Neanderthal repertoire.

HOW DOES THE NEW EVIDENCE AFFECT OUR EARLIER CONCLUSIONS ABOUT THE "ANTIQUITY OF HUNTER-GATHERERS"?

Recently acquired evidence about Neanderthal/Middle Paleolithic technology, foraging, and ornamentation provides novel perspectives on many of the topics that our 2001 paper addressed. First and foremost, the new evidence confirms that Middle Paleolithic hominins were *capable* of many behaviors that some archaeologists use as markers of behavioral modernity. The fact that Neanderthals and their immediate antecedents sometimes hunted lagomorphs and birds, and gathered roots, seeds, and leafy plants tells us that they recognized these species as food and knew how to render them edible.

The sporadic nature of some of these so-called modern behaviors among the Neanderthals is not a reflection of cognitive deficiency or excessive cognitive modularity. The fact that Middle Paleolithic hominins regularly joined distinct materials, including stone, wood, and natural mastics, together into composite artifacts shows that they were capable of executing quite complex, multicomponent technological procedures. They seemed to possess structured, "grammatical" mental models of final products (see Ambrose 2010). Similarly, probable evidence for use of feathers and raptor claws for non-nutritional purposes suggests that Middle Paleolithic hominins concepts of body decoration sometimes extended beyond the pigments that had already been in use since the Middle Pleistocene. In sum, results from the decade and a half since our paper was published in 2001 serve to move a number of behavioral elements out of the exclusive realm of modern *Homo sapiens* and into the domain of traits shared by both Neanderthals and modern humans.

We stand by our original proposition that presence or absence of specific elements of behavior is much less informative than are observations about variation in the frequency of these behaviors. While we can rule out innate capacities as explanations for the scarcity of certain behaviors, the simple fact that capturing birds, eating plants, or creating durable body ornaments were within the *range* of behaviors of Middle Paleolithic hominins does not mean that the patterns of behavioral variation are the same as for later humans. In our view, certain aspects of variation in the Middle Paleolithic record are still attenuated compared with what we know about more recent hunter-gatherers and Upper Paleolithic foragers before them. We briefly discuss three such aspects here.

RELIANCE ON PLANTS AND SMALL ANIMALS

Consistent with our observations back in 2001, we still do not see the same level of dietary variation with latitude and climate that is known for recent foragers. The relative contributions of plant foods and meat to Middle Paleolithic diets are difficult to quantify due to differential preservation, but the situation with small game (well represented by skeletal remains) continues to be anomalous. Very seldom if ever was small game more important than large game in the Middle Paleolithic meat diet, whether based on specimen counts or estimated meat weight, and regardless of environment (Stiner 2001; Stiner and Kuhn 2006). The fact that any hominin ate plant foods does not promise a broad diet, since dietary breadth is really about levels of time or labor investment. It would be a peculiar turn of logic, therefore to assume plant use was extensive while Middle Paleolithic foragers ignored difficult-to-capture small animals (quick species that run, fly, or swim), because the average foraging returns for these small animals have been shown to be intermediate to most plant foods and most large game (Kuhn and Stiner 2001; Kelly 2005, 81–82). In terminal Pleistocene and Holocene forager contexts, broad plant-food diets are usually accompanied by intensive foraging for a wide range of small animals, many of which require considerable technological investments to exploit in quantity. Possible evidence for cooking plant foods notwithstanding, there is still little or no evidence for the sorts of intensive processing (grinding and pounding) typically seen when plant foods become the caloric mainstays of the diet (Keeley 1995). The extreme rarity of grindstones in Middle Paleolithic sites is certainly not a matter of poor preservation.

Attenuated Technological Investment and Complexity

Technological variation is similarly attenuated across the Middle Paleolithic range. Rigorous quantitative studies of ethnographic and archeological evidence from Holocene foragers (Collard et al. 2011, 2012, 2013a, 2013b) have confirmed patterns of variation in technology according to latitude and climate first suggested by Oswalt (1976) and others. The diversity and complexity of foraging tools really do increase along a south-to-north gradient. Moreover, the recent work clearly attributes the trend to time stress or risk in sparse, seasonal habitats in high latitudes. Middle Paleolithic artisans commanded most of the basic technological procedures used by LUP toolmakers (Stiner and Kuhn 2009); they carved and shaped wood, flaked stone in sophisticated ways, created or collected natural adhesives, and sometimes even worked bone into specific forms (Soressi et al. 2013). They also had the capacity to assemble composite tools with elements of different materials. Despite these abilities in the Middle Paleolithic period, variation in technological investment and complexity of the sort documented among Holocene hunter-gatherers, or LUP peoples for that matter, is not found. Middle Paleolithic groups from the Syrian Desert to central Europe hafted stone points using a variety of mastics, but the artifacts used in foraging at high latitudes or during cold periods are no more elaborate than the ones produced in warmer climes. One could argue that this apparent homogeneity is due to the fact that Middle Paleolithic deposits may sample longer spans of time and more environmental variation than deposits in later sites, or than ethnographic observations. Sampling larger spans of time could result in less variation among assemblages because each assemblage included more of the full range of variation. However, it is not just a matter of the average condition remaining constant—the total range of variation is also quite restricted. The Middle Paleolithic record for investment in any sort of technology remains highly attenuated compared to more recent periods. Recent reviews suggest that while Upper Paleolithic groups responded to climate change technologically, Neanderthals responded by simply altering their target foods (within narrow limits) (El Zaatari et al. 2016), or by going locally extinct (Finlayson and Carrión 2007; Jiménez-Espejo et al. 2007).

Limited Use of Durable Body Ornamentation

Colorful mineral oxides, assumed to be pigments, were used widely across Middle Paleolithic populations. Isolated cases strongly suggest that these people also sometimes ornamented themselves with durable objects. But this was not a common behavior, nor do we see much in the way of repeated forms. Decorative traditions of the Middle Paleolithic, whatever they were, tended to take non-durable forms. We do not see ubiquitous use of beads, pendants, or other decorative items that are so characteristic of many early Upper Paleolithic and late Middle Stone Age populations (e.g., Bar-Yosef 1989; Bouzouggar et al. 2007; Fernández and Jöris 2008; Hahn 1972; Kuhn et al. 2001; Stiner 2010; Taborin 1993; Vanhaeren and d'Errico 2006; White 2007).

DISCUSSION

In our first attempt to evaluate the antiquity of hunter-gatherers, we argued that some of the differences between Middle Paleolithic and later hominins could be attributed to differences in the sizes of social groups. We still believe that group sizes played an important role in conditioning behavior, but along with many other researchers, we also look to broader demographic factors to explain many of the seemingly anomalous features of the Middle Paleolithic. Diverse results from genetics and archaeology suggest that Neanderthals were very thinly distributed across the Pleistocene landscapes of Eurasia, and that demes were small and demographically fragile (Mellars and French 2011; Bocquet-Appel and Degioanni, 2013; Lalueza-Fox 2013; Prüfer et al. 2014). Small, locally unstable populations would explain why Middle Paleolithic peoples did not permanently broaden their diets, invest in costly technology for procuring large animals, or engage in energetically expensive processing of plant foods (Stiner and Kuhn 2006). If populations were thinly distributed, local groups would have more options to move on to places where they could continue to exploit the high-return animal and plant foods rather than staying where they were and working harder to find and prepare food. In other words, people could mediate local subsistence risk simply by moving to places where risks were lower. Only when options to pack up and go were restricted should foragers have begun investing in costly technologies to mediate risk or engage in demanding processing procedures. These conditions seldom if ever occurred in the Middle Paleolithic. If, as we and many others have argued, body ornamentation was a means for transmitting social messages beyond a small coterie of intimate friends and relatives (Kuhn and Stiner 2007), the scarcity of durable materials in the Middle Paleolithic palette for body ornamentation would be entirely consistent with small groups and social networks. The kinds of social information broadcast by such items were relatively unimportant.

Of course, to any generalization there surely will be exceptions. Middle Paleolithic people did sometimes exploit small and quick game animals, and they may have sometimes engaged in more elaborate social signals using ornaments made from durable materials. These kinds of observations qualify the generalizations we make above but they do not eclipse them. It is time to abandon progressivist notions of evolution that equate the appearance of a new behavioral trait with the crossing of broad cognitive thresholds. Doing so puts rare cases in a very different evolutionary light that recognizes the fundamental difference between raw capability and necessity, and between behavioral ranges and behavioral tendencies. Middle Paleolithic populations did occasionally experience the same kinds of pressures hypothesized for later populations, encouraging expansion of the diet, intensification of social signaling, and perhaps greater investment in technological aids to food procurement and processing. Population "hot spots" could have resulted from rapid demic growth under particularly good conditions or from circumscription due to deterioration of surrounding habits: the effects would have been similar. An important contrast to conditions in the later Pleistocene and Holocene, however, is that these "hot spots" seem to have been transitory, and the associated behavioral responses were never widely adopted.

Models founded on notions of small, thinly distributed populations help to explain why some basic patterns of behavioral variation in the Middle Paleolithic differ from those of later time periods (Kuhn 2012, 2013a, 2013b; Villa and Roebroeks 2014). However, demographic models do not answer all of our questions: in fact, like any good hypothesis, this explanatory device forces us to ask yet other, challenging questions. For example, why did Middle Paleolithic hominin populations stay small for so long? How, over an existence of 200,000 years or so, did they not grow to fill up space the way late Pleistocene and early Holocene hunter-gather populations did over a much shorter period of time? By all indications, entrenched Neanderthal populations were swamped genetically by what must have been initially a small corps of intruding modern *Homo sapiens* over a few thousand years. This fact alone suggests that Eurasian Middle Paleolithic populations were not just small, but were somehow not able to grow as fast as exogenous populations of *Homo sapiens*.

The explanatory power of demographic explanations for major features of Middle Paleolithic culture is not without its problems and limitations. This viewpoint nonetheless offers a richer and potentially more enlightening mode of explanation than simply assuming cognitive superiority of invading modern humans. We believe that multiple, historically contingent factors interacted to keep Middle Paleolithic groups on locally optimal plateaus but a globally suboptimal plateau. Foraging strategies focused on high-return resources such as large game animals, and involving generalized cooperation in foraging rather than investment in high-efficiency weapons (Kuhn 2009), could discourage individuals from experimenting with other solutions. If a few individuals were to begin foraging on their own rather than cooperating fully, it would reduce both individual and group foraging efficiency. At the same time, diets very high in lean animal protein might reduce female fecundity/fertility (Hockett and Haws 2003; Chavarro et al. 2008). This sort of explanation is not based on some hypothetical deficiency in Middle Paleolithic hominins. Rather, it would be a form of "generative entrenchment," path-dependent fixation of particular alternatives in an uneven fitness landscape. Whatever these groups were doing, it was more successful than any "easy" alternative prior to the appearance of another hominin species in Eurasian landscapes. There could well have been more efficient strategies out there than the ones Neanderthals emphasized, but transitions to such alternatives would have involved loss of fitness over the short term, making transitions evolutionarily difficult. Indeed the Middle Paleolithic system would be quite stable and sufficient in the absence of competing populations with more efficient strategies. Once such a competitor appeared on the scene, however, Middle Paleolithic humans would either have undergone rapid socioeconomic reorganization or been swamped reproductively and genetically.

REFERENCES CITED

Ambrose, S. 2010. "Coevolution of Composite-Tool Technology, Constructive Memory, and Language: Implications for the Evolution of Modern Human Behavior." *Current Anthropology* 51(special issue):S135–S147. https://doi.org/10.1086/650296.

Aura, J. E., V. B. Villaverde, M. Perez Ripoll, R. Martinez Valle, and P. Calatayud Guillem. 2002. "Big Game and Small Prey: Palaeolithic and Epipaleolithic

Economy from Valencia (Spain)." *Journal of Archaeological Method and Theory* 9(3):215–268. https://doi.org/10.1023/A:1019578013408.

Bar-Yosef, D. E. 1989. "Late Paleolithic and Neolithic Marine Shells in the Southern Levant as Cultural Markers." In *Proceedings of the 1986 Shell Bead Conference, Selected Papers*, ed. C. F. Hayes, L. Ceci, and C. Cox Bodner, 169–174. Research Records no. 20. Rochester, NY: Rochester Museum and Science Center.

Bar-Yosef Mayer, D., B. Vandermeersch, and O. Bar-Yosef. 2009. "Shells and Ochre in Middle Paleolithic Qafzeh Cave, Israel: Indications for Modern Behavior." *Journal of Human Evolution* 56(3):307–314. https://doi.org/10.1016/j.jhevol.2008.10.005.

Barton, R.N.E., A. P. Currant, Y. Fernandez-Jalvo, J. C. Finlayson, P. Goldberg, R. Macphail, P. Pettitt, and C. B. Stringer. 1999. "Gibraltar Neanderthals and Results of Recent Excavations in Gorham's, Vanguard and Ibex Caves." *Antiquity* 73(279):13–23. https://doi.org/10.1017/S0003598X00087809.

Binford, L. R. 2001. *Constructing Frames of Reference: An Analytical Method for Archaeological Theory Building Using Ethnographic and Environmental Data Sets.* Berkeley: University of California Press.

Blasco, R., and J. Fernández Peris. 2012. "A Uniquely Broad Spectrum Diet during the Middle Pleistocene at Bolomor Cave (Valencia, Spain)." *Quaternary International* 252:16–31. https://doi.org/10.1016/j.quaint.2011.03.019.

Bocherens, H., A. Baryshnikov, and W. Van Neer. 2014. "Were Bears or Lions Involved in Salmon Accumulation in the Middle Palaeolithic of the Caucasus? An Isotopic Investigation in Kudaro 3 Cave." *Quaternary International* 339–340:112–118. https://doi.org/10.1016/j.quaint.2013.06.026.

Bocherens, H., and D. E. Drucker. 2003. "Reconstructing Neandertal Diet from 120,000 to 30,000 BP Using Carbon and Nitrogen Stable Isotopic Abundances." In *Le Rôle de l'Envireonnement dans le Comportements des Chasseurs-Cuillieur sPréhistoriques*, vol. 1105. ed. M. Patou-Mathis and H. Bocherens, 1–8. BAR International Series. Oxford, UK: British Archaeological Reports.

Bocquet-Appel, J.-P., and A. Degioanni. 2013. "Neanderthal Demographic Estimates." *Current Anthropology* 8(special issue):S202–S213. https://doi.org/10.1086/673725.

Boëda, E., S. Bonilauri, J. Connan, D. Jarvie, N. Mercier, M. Tobey, H. Valladas, H. al Sakhel, and S. Muhesen. 2008. "Middle Palaeolithic Bitumen Use at Umm el Tlel around 70 000 BP." *Antiquity* 82(318):853–861. https://doi.org/10.1017/S0003598X00097623.

Boëda, E., J.-M. Geneste, C. Griggo, N. Mercier, S. Muhesen, J.-L. Reyss, A. Taha, and H. Valladas. 1999. "A Levallois Point Embedded in the Vertebra of a Wild Ass (*Equus africanus*): Hafting, Projectiles and Mousterian Hunting Weapons." *Antiquity* 73(280):394–402. https://doi.org/10.1017/S0003598X00088335.

Bouzouggar, A., R.N.E. Barton, M. Vanhaeren, F. d'Errico, S. Collcutt, T. Higham, E. Hodge, S. Parfitt, E. Rhodes, J.-L. Schwenninger, et al., E., S. Ward, A. Moutmir, and A. Stambouli. 2007. "82,000-Year-Old Shell Beads from North Africa and Implications for the Origins of Modern Human Behavior." *Proceedings of the National Academy of Sciences (USA)* 104(24):9964–9969. https://doi.org/10.1073/pnas.0703877104.

Cârciumaru, M., I. Radica-Mariana, E. C. Nițu, and R. Ștefănescu. 2012. "New Evidence of Adhesive as Hafting Material on Middle and Upper Palaeolithic Artefacts from Gura Cheii-Râșnov Cave (Romania)." *Journal of Archaeological Science* 39(7):1942–1950. https://doi.org/10.1016/j.jas.2012.02.016.

Chavarro, J. E., J. W. Rich-Edwards, B. A. Rosner, and W. C. Willett. 2008. "Protein Intake and Ovulatory Infertility." *American Journal of Obstetrics and Gynecology* 198(2):210.e1–210.e7. https://doi.org/10.1016/j.ajog.2007.06.057.

Cochard, D., J.-P. Brugal, E. Morin, and L. Meignen. 2012. "Evidence of Small Fast Game Exploitation in the Middle Paleolithic of Les Canalettes, Aveyron, France." *Quaternary International* 264:32–51. https://doi.org/10.1016/j.quaint.2012.02.014.

Collard, M., B. Buchanan, J. Morin, and A. Costopoulos. 2011. "What Drives the Evolution of Hunter-Gatherer Subsistence Technology? A Reanalysis of the Risk Hypothesis with Data from the Pacific Northwest." *Philosophical Transactions of the Royal Society of London. Series B, Biological Sciences* 366:1129–1138. https://doi.org/10.1098/rstb.2010.0366.

Collard, M., A. Ruttle, B. Buchanan, and M. J. O'Brien. 2012. "Risk of Resource Failure and Toolkit Variation in Small-Scale Farmers and Herders." *PloS One* 7(7):1–8. https://doi.org/10.1371/journal.pone.0040975.

Collard, M., B. Buchanan, and M. J. O'Brien. 2013a. "Population Size as an Explanation for Patterns in the Paleolithic Archaeological Record: More Caution Is Needed." *Current Anthropology* 54(Supplement 8):388–396. https://doi.org/10.1086/673881.

Collard, M., B. Buchanan, M. J. O'Brien, and J. Scholnick. 2013b. "Risk, Mobility or Population Size? Drivers of Technological Richness among Contact-Period Western North American Hunter-Gatherers." *Philosophical Transactions of the Royal Society of London. Series B, Biological Sciences* 368(1630):20120412. https://doi.org/10.1098/rstb.2012.0412.

Cordain, L., J. B. Miller, S. B. Eaton, N. Mann, S.H.A. Holt, and J. D. Speth. 2000. "Plant-Animal Subsistence Ratios and Macronutrient Energy Estimations in Worldwide Hunter-Gatherer Diets." *American Journal of Clinical Nutrition* 71(3):682–692. https://doi.org/10.1093/ajcn/71.3.682.

d'Errico, F. 2007. "The Origin of Humanity and Modern Cultures: Archaeology's View." *Diogenes* 54(2):122–133. https://doi.org/10.1177/0392192107077652.

d'Errico, F. 2008. "The Rouge et le Noir: Implications of Early Pigment Use in Africa, the Near East and Europe for the Origin of Cultural Modernity." In *Current Themes in Middle Stone Age Research*, South African Archaeological Society Goodwin Series 10, ed. M. Lombard, C. Sievers, and V. Ward, 168–174.

Fernández, E. A., and O. Jöris. 2008. "Personal Ornaments in the Early Upper Paleolithic of Western Eurasia: An Evaluation of the Record." *Eurasian Prehistory* 5(2):31–44.

Finlayson, C., and J. S. Carrión. 2007. "Rapid Ecological Turnover and Its Impact on Neanderthal and Other Human Populations." *Trends in Ecology and Evolution* 22(4):213–222. https://doi.org/10.1016/j.tree.2007.02.001.

Gaudzinski-Windheuser, S., and L. Niven. 2009. "Hominid Subsistence Patterns During the Middle and Late Paleolithic in Northwestern Europe." In *The Evolution of Hominin Diets*, ed. J.-J. Hublin and M. Richards, 99–111. Dordrecht, Netherlands: Springer. https://doi.org/10.1007/978-1-4020-9699-0_7.

Grünberg, J. 2002. "Middle Palaeolithic Birch-Bark Pitch." *Antiquity* 76(291):15–16. https://doi.org/10.1017/S0003598X00089638.

Hahn, J. 1972. "Aurignacian Signs, Pendants, and Art Objects in Central and Eastern Europe." *World Archaeology* 3(3):252–266. https://doi.org/10.1080/00438243.1972.9979508.

Hardy, B. L., and M.-H. Moncel. 2011. "Neanderthal Use of Fish, Mammals, Birds, Starchy Plants and Wood 125–250,000 Years Ago." *PloS One* 6(8):e23768. https://doi.org/10.1371/journal.pone.0023768.

Hardy, B. L., M.-H. Moncel, C. Daujeard, P. Fernandes, P. Béarez, E. Descleaux, M. G. Chacon Navarro, S. Puaud, and R. Gallotti. 2013. "Impossible Neanderthals? Making String, Throwing Projectiles and Catching Small Game During Marine Isotope Stage 4 (Abri du Maras, France)." *Quaternary Science Reviews* 82:23–40. https://doi.org/10.1016/j.quascirev.2013.09.028.

Hayden, B. 1981. "Subsistence and Ecological Adaptations of Modern Hunter/Gatherers." In *Omnivorous Primates: Gathering and Hunting in Human Evolution*, ed. R. Harding and G. Teleki, 344–421. New York: Columbia University Press.

Hayden, B. 2012. "Neandertal Social Structure?" *Oxford Journal of Archaeology* 31(1):1–26. https://doi.org/10.1111/j.1468-0092.2011.00376.x.

Henry, A. G., A. S. Brooks, and D. Piperno. 2011. "Microfossils in Calculus Demonstrate Consumption of Plants and Cooked Foods in Neanderthal Diets (Shanidar III, Iraq; Spy I and II, Belgium)." *Proceedings of the National Academy of Sciences of the United States of America* 108(2):486–491. https://doi.org/10.1073/pnas.1016868108.

Henry, A. G., A. S. Brooks, and D. R. Piperno. 2014. "Plant Foods and the Dietary Ecology of Neanderthals and Early Modern Humans." *Journal of Human Evolution* 69:44–54. https://doi.org/10.1016/j.jhevol.2013.12.014.

Hockett, B., and J. Haws. 2003. "Nutritional Ecology and Diachronic Trends in Paleolithic Diet and Health." *Evolutionary Anthropology* 12(5):211–216. https://doi.org/10.1002/evan.10116.

Jiménez-Espejo, F. J., F. Martínez-Ruiz, C. Finlayson, A. Paytan, T. Sakamoto, M. Ortega-Huertas, G. Finlayson, K. Iijima, D. Gallego-Torres, and D. Fa. 2007. "Climate Forcing and Neanderthal Extinction in Southern Iberia: Insights from a Multiproxy Marine Record." *Quaternary Science Reviews* 26(7–8):836–852. https://doi.org/10.1016/j.quascirev.2006.12.013.

Johnson, A. 2014. "Exploring Adaptive Variation among Hunter-Gatherers with Binford's *Frames of Reference*." *Journal of Archaeological Research* 22(1):1–42. https://doi.org/10.1007/s10814-013-9068-y.

Keeley, L. 1995. "Protoagricultural Practices among Hunter-Gatherers: A Cross-Cultural Survey." In *Last Hunters, First Farmers*, ed. T. D. Price and A. B. Grebauer, 243–272. Santa Fe, NM: School of American Research.

Kelly, R. 2005. *The Foraging Spectrum: Diversity in Hunter-Gatherer Lifeways*. Washington, DC: Smithsonian Institution Press.

Kelly, R. 2013. *Diversity in Hunter-Gatherer Lifeways: The Foraging Spectrum*. Cambridge, UK: Cambridge University Press. https://doi.org/10.1017/CBO9781139176132.

Kuhn, S. 2009. "The Paradox of Diet and Technology in the Middle Paleolithic." In *Transitions in Prehistory Essays in Honor of Prof. Ofer Bar-Yosef*, ed. D. Lieberman and J. J. Shea, 57–70. Oxford, UK: American School of Prehistoric Research, Oxbow Books.

Kuhn, S. 2012. "Emergent Patterns of Creativity and Innovation in Early Technologies." In *Creativity, Innovation and Human Evolution*, ed. S. Elias, 69–87. Amsterdam, Netherlands: Elsevier. https://doi.org/10.1016/B978-0-444-53821-5.00006-3.

Kuhn, S. 2013a. "Roots of the Middle Paleolithic in Eurasia." *Current Anthropology* 54(8s):S255–S268. https://doi.org/10.1086/673529.

Kuhn, S. 2013b. "Cultural Transmission, Institutional Continuity and the Persistence of the Mousterian." In *Dynamics of Learning in Neanderthals and Modern Humans*, vol. 1. ed. T. Akazawa, Y. Nishiaki, and K. Aoki, 105–113. New York: Springer. https://doi.org/10.1007/978-4-431-54511-8_6.

Kuhn, S. 2014. "Signaling Theory and Technologies of Communication in the Paleolithic." *Biological Theory* 9(1):42–50. https://doi.org/10.1007/s13752-013-0156-5.

Kuhn, S., and M. C. Stiner. 2001. "The Antiquity of Hunter-Gatherers." In *Hunter-Gatherers: An Interdisciplinary Perspective*, ed. J. Panter-Brick, R. H. Layton, and P. A. Rowley-Conwy, 99–142. Cambridge, UK: Cambridge University Press.

Kuhn, S., and M. C. Stiner. 2007. "Body Ornamentation as Information Technology: Towards an Understanding of the Significance of Early Beads." In *Rethinking the*

Human Revolution: New Behavioural and Biological and Perspectives on the Origins and Dispersal of Modern Humans, ed. P. Mellars, K. Boyle, O. Bar-Yosef, and C. Stringer, 45–54. Cambridge, UK: MacDonald Institute of Archaeology.

Kuhn, S. L., M. C. Stiner, D. S. Reese, and E. Güleç. 2001. "Ornaments of the Earliest Upper Paleolithic: New Results from the Levant." *Proceedings of the National Academy of Sciences of the United States of America* 98(13):7641–7646. https://doi.org/10.1073/pnas.121590798.

Lalueza-Fox, C. 2013. "Agreements and Misunderstandings among Three Scientific Fields: Paleogenomics, Archaeology, and Human Paleontology." *Current Anthropology* 54(8s):S214–S220. https://doi.org/10.1086/673387.

Lloveras, L., M. Moreno-García, J. Nadal, and J. Zilhão. 2011. "Who Brought in the Rabbits? Taphonomical Analysis of Mousterian and Solutrean Leporid Accumulations from Gruta do Caldeirão (Tomar, Portugal)." *Journal of Archaeological Science* 38(9):2434–2449. https://doi.org/10.1016/j.jas.2011.05.012.

Mazza, P.P.A., F. Martini, B. Sala, M. Magi, M. P. Colombini, G. Giachi, F. Landucci, C. Lemorini, F. Modugno, and E. Ribechini. 2006. "A New Palaeolithic Discovery: Tar-Hafted Stone Tools in a European Mid-Pleistocene Bone-Bearing Bed." *Journal of Archaeological Science* 33(9):1310–1318. https://doi.org/10.1016/j.jas.2006.01.006.

Mellars, P., and J. C. French. 2011. "Tenfold Population Increase in Western Europe at the Neandertal-Modern Human Transition." *Science* 333(6042):623–627. https://doi.org/10.1126/science.1206930.

Morin, E., and V. Laroulandie. 2012. "Presumed Symbolic Use of Diurnal Raptors by Neanderthals." *PloS One* 7(3):e32856. https://doi.org/10.1371/journal.pone.0032856.

Oswalt, W. H. 1976. *An Anthropological Analysis of Food-Getting Technology*. New York: Wiley.

Peresani, M., I. Fiore, M. Gala, M. Romandini, and A. Tagliacozzo. 2011. "Late Neandertals and the Intentional Removal of Feathers as Evidenced from Bird Bone Taphonomy at Fumane Cave 44 ky B.P., Italy." *Proceedings of the National Academy of Sciences of the United States of America* 108(10):3888–3893. https://doi.org/10.1073/pnas.1016212108.

Panter-Brick, C., R. Layton, and P. A. Rowley-Conwy, eds. 2001. *Hunter-Gatherers: An Interdisciplinary Perspective*. Cambridge, UK: Cambridge University Press.

Pawlik, A., and J. Thissen. 2011. "Hafted Armatures and Multi-Component Tool Design at the Micoquian Site of Inden-Altdorf, Germany." *Journal of Archaeological Science* 38(7):1699–1708. https://doi.org/10.1016/j.jas.2011.03.001.

Plisson, H., and S. Beyries. 1998. "Pointes ou Outils Triangulaires? Données Functionnelles dans le Moustérien Levantin." *Paléorient* 24(1):5–16. https://doi.org/10.3406/paleo.1998.4666.

Prüfer, K., F. Racimo, N. Patterson, F. Jay, S. Sankararaman, A. Sawyer, A. Heinze, G. Renaud, C. H. Sudmant, C. de Filippo, et al. 2014. "The Complete Genome Sequence of a Neanderthal from the Altai Mountains." *Nature* 505(7481):43–49. https://doi.org/10.1038/nature12886.

Radovčić, D., A. O. Sršen, J. Radovčić, and D. W. Frayer. 2015. "Evidence for Neandertal Jewelry: Modified White-Tailed Eagle Claws at Krapina." *PloS One* 10(3):e0119802. https://doi.org/10.1371/journal.pone.0119802.

Richards, M., and E. Trinkaus. 2009. "Isotopic Evidence for the Diets of European Neanderthals and Early Modern Humans." *Proceedings of the National Academy of Sciences of the United States of America* 106(38):16034–16039. https://doi.org/10.1073/pnas.0903821106.

Rotts, V. 2009. "The Functional Analysis of the Mousterian and Micoquian Assemblages of Sesselfelsgrotte, Germany: Aspects of Tool Use and Hafting in the European Late Middle Palaeolithic." *Quartär* 56:37–66.

Shea, J. J. 2006. "The Origins of Lithic Projectile Point Technology: Evidence from Africa, the Levant and Europe." *Journal of Archaeological Science* 33(6):823–846. https://doi.org/10.1016/j.jas.2005.10.015.

Shea, J. J. 2011. "*Homo Sapiens* Is as *Homo Sapiens* Was." *Current Anthropology* 52(1):1–35. https://doi.org/10.1086/658067.

Sistiaga, A., C. Mallol, B. Galván, and R. E. Summons. 2014. "The Neanderthal Meal: A New Perspective Using Faecal Biomarkers." *PloS One* 9(6):e101045. https://doi.org/10.1371/journal.pone.0101045.

Soressi, S., S. P. McPherron, M. Lenoir, T. Dogandžić, P. Goldberg, Z. Jacobs, Y. Maigrot, N. L. Martisius, C. T. Miller, W. Rendu, et al. 2013. "Neandertals Made the First Specialized Bone Tools in Europe." *Proceedings of the National Academy of Sciences of the United States of America* 110(35):14186–14190. https://doi.org/10.1073/pnas.1302730110.

Stiner, M. C. 2001. "Thirty Years on the 'Broad Spectrum Revolution' and Paleolithic Demography." *Proceedings of the National Academy of Sciences of the United States of America* 98(13):6993–6996. https://doi.org/10.1073/pnas.121176198.

Stiner, M. C. 2010. "Shell Ornaments from the Upper Paleolithic and Mesolithic Layers of Klissoura Cave 1, Prosymnia, Greece." *Eurasian Prehistory* 7(2):287–308.

Stiner, M. C., and S. L. Kuhn. 2006. "Changes in the 'Connectedness' and Resilience of Paleolithic Societies in Mediterranean Ecosystems." *Human Ecology* 34(5):693–712. https://doi.org/10.1007/s10745-006-9041-1.

Stiner, M. C., and S. Kuhn. 2009. "Paleolithic Diet and Division of Labor in Mediterranean Eurasia." In *The Evolution of Hominid Diets: Integrating Approaches to the Study of Paleolithic Subsistence*, ed. M. Richards and J.-J. Hublin, 157–167. New York: Springer. https://doi.org/10.1007/978-1-4020-9699-0_11.

Stiner, M. C., S. Kuhn, and E. Güleç. 2013. "Early Upper Paleolithic Shell Beads at Üçagizli Cave I (Turkey): Technology and the Socioeconomic Context of Ornament Life-Histories." *Journal of Human Evolution* 64(5):380–398. https://doi.org/10.1016/j.jhevol.2013.01.008.

Stiner, M. C., N. D. Munro, and T. A. Surovell. 2000. "The Tortoise and the Hare: Small Game Use, the Broad Spectrum Revolution, and Paleolithic Demography." *Current Anthropology* 41:39–73.

Taborin, Y. 1993. *La Parure en Coquillage au Paléolithique. XXIXe supplément à Gallia Préhistoire.* Paris: C.N.R.S. Éditions.

Torrence, R. 1983. "Time Budgeting and Hunter-Gatherer Technology." In *Hunter-Gatherer Economy in Prehistory*, ed. G. Bailey, 11–22. Cambridge, UK: Cambridge University Press.

Torrence, R. 2001. "Hunter-Gatherer Technology: Macro- and Microscale Approaches." In *Hunter-Gatherers, an Interdisciplinary Perspective*, ed. J. Panter-Brick, R. H. Layton, and P. A. Rowley-Conwy, 73–98. Cambridge, UK: Cambridge University Press.

Vanhaeren, M., and F. d'Errico. 2006. "Aurignacian Ethno-Linguistic Geography of Europe Revealed by Personal Ornaments." *Journal of Archaeological Science* 33(8):1105–1128. https://doi.org/10.1016/j.jas.2005.11.017.

Villa, P., P. Boscato, F. Ranaldo, and A. Ronchitelli. 2009. "Stone Tools for the Hunt: Points with Impact Scars from a Middle Paleolithic Site in Southern Italy." *Journal of Archaeological Science* 36(3):850–859. https://doi.org/10.1016/j.jas.2008.11.012.

Villa, P., and M. Lenoir. 2008. "Hunting and Hunting Weapons of the Lower and Middle Paleolithic of Europe." In *The Evolution of Hominid Diets: Integrating Approaches to the Study of Paleolithic Subsistence*, ed. M. Richards and J.-J. Hublin, 59–87. New York: Springer.

Villa, P., and W. Roebroeks. 2014. "Neandertal Demise: An Archaeological Analysis of the Modern Human Superiority Complex." *PLoS One* 9(4):e96424. https://doi.org/10.1371/journal.pone.0096424.

White, R. 2007. "Systems of Personal Ornamentation in the Early Upper Paleolithic." In *Rethinking the Human Revolution: Eurasian and African Perspectives*, ed. P. Mellars, 287–303. Cambridge, UK: MacDonald Institute, Cambridge University.

Wißing, C., H. Rougier, I. Crevecoeur, M. Germonpré, Y. I. Naito, P. Semal, and H. Bocherens. 2016. "Isotopic Evidence for Dietary Ecology of Late Neandertals in North-Western Europe." *Quaternary International* 411(Part A):327–345. https://doi.org/10.1016/j.quaint.2015.09.091.

Zilhão, J., D. E. Angelucci, E. Badal-García, F. d'Errico, F. Daniel, L. Dayet, K. Douka, T. F. G. Higham, M. J. Martínez-Sánchez, R. Montes-Bernárdez, et al. V., R. Wood, and J. Zapata. 2010. "Symbolic Use of Marine Shells and Mineral

Pigments by Iberian Neandertals." *Proceedings of the National Academy of Sciences* 107(3):1023–1028.

El Zaatari, S., F. E. Grine, P. S. Ungar, and J.-J. Hublin. 2016. "Neandertal versus Modern Human Dietary Responses to Climatic Fluctuations." *PLoS One* 11(4):e0153277. https://doi.org/10.1371/journal.pone.0153277.

Contributors

NICHOLAS J. CONARD
Department of Early Prehistory and Quaternary Ecology
Senckenberg Center for Human Evolution and Paleoenvironment
Institute for Archaeological Sciences
University of Tübingen, Germany

RAVEN GARVEY
Department of Anthropology
Museum of Anthropological Archaeology
University of Michigan, Ann Arbor, USA

KEIKO KITAGAWA
Department of Early Prehistory and Quaternary Ecology
Institute for Archaeological Sciences
University of Tübingen, Germany
SFB 1070 RessourcenKulturen

UMR 7194 Histoire Naturelle de l'Homme Préhistorique, CNRS
Muséum national d'Histoire naturelle, UPVD, Paris, France

JOHN KRIGBAUM
Department of Anthropology
University of Florida, Gainesville, USA

PETRA KRÖNNECK
Institute for Archaeological Sciences
University of Tübingen, Germany

STEVEN L. KUHN
School of Anthropology
University of Arizona, Tucson, USA

JULIA LEE-THORP
Research Laboratory for Archaeology and the History of Art
University of Oxford, United Kingdom

ASHLEY K. LEMKE
Department of Sociology and Anthropology
University of Texas at Arlington, USA

PETER MITCHELL
School of Archaeology
University of Oxford, United Kingdom

School of Geography
Archaeology and Environmental Studies
University of Witwatersrand, South Africa

KATHERINE MOORE
Museum of Archaeology and Anthropology
University of Pennsylvania, USA

SUSANNE C. MÜNZEL
Institute for Archaeological Sciences
University of Tübingen, Germany

KURT RADEMAKER
Department of Anthropology
Northern Illinois University, USA

PATRICK ROBERTS
Group Leader of the Stable Isotope Laboratory
Department of Archaeology
Max Planck Institute for the Science of Human History, Germany

BRITT M. STARKOVICH
Senckenberg Center for Human Evolution and Paleoenvironment
Institute for Archaeological Sciences
University of Tübingen, Germany

School of Anthropology
University of Arizona, Tucson, USA

BRIAN A. STEWART

Department of Anthropology
Museum of Anthropological Archaeology
University of Michigan, Ann Arbor, USA

Rock Art Research Institute
University of Witwatersrand, South Africa

MARY C. STINER

School of Anthropology
University of Arizona, Tucson, USA

Ethnographic analogy, xv, 3, 5, 9–10, 63
Ethnographic record: of Africa, 160, 195; limitations of, xv, 4–5, 7, 9, 11, 19; moving beyond, 50; use of, 249
Exchange, 6, 104, 160

F
Fertility, 20, 25, 27, 34–35, 37, 40, 260
Firewood, 12, 189

G
Gender, 4, 160
G/wi people, 159
G//ana people, 159

H
Hadza people, 5, 159
Homo erectus, 7, 120, 142, 209
Homo floresiensis, 142
Homo sapiens: "behavioral modernity," 209; late Upper Paleolithic, 250; and Neanderthals, 256, 260; occupation of rainforests, 119–120, 132, 134, 138; tooth enamel, 134
Human behavioral ecology, 4, 11, 24
Hxaro, 160

I
Information, sharing of, 37, 259
Inuit peoples, 64
Ivory (mammoth), 216, 221–222, 228–231, 251

J
Ju/'honsi people, 159

K
Kinship, 3, 4

L
Later Stone Age (LSA) (time period), 171, 195
Logistical (mobility): in the Andes, 82–83, 92, 102–104; general, 11; in southern Africa, 190, 194

M
Mediterranean, 8, 212, 250
Megapatch, 76, 81
Microblade, 29, 40

Middle Stone Age (MSA) (time period), 171, 258
Middle Paleolithic: archaeology, 209, 213; culture, 250; demography, 15, 259–260; diets, 250, 252–254, 256–257; foragers, 248, 250; symbolic expression, 252, 255, 258; technology, 14–15, 251, 255–257
Migration: animal, 59–60, 63, 64; human, 27, 40, 119, 120
Mobility: and clothing, 35; forager, 4, 11, 12–13, 21, 31, 66; high, 192; historic, 63, 160; human, 188; and isotopes, 143; Neanderthal, 250; prey species, 23; regimes, 62, 76, 103, 106, 141; seasonal, 135, 192, 194; technology, 160. *See also* Residential mobility
Molars, 128, 139, 141

N
Naskapi people, 64
Neanderthal: clothing, 34; cultural/cognitive capacities, 14, 210, 256; demography, 258, 260; diet, 211, 216, 231, 252–255, 258; genetics, 209; hunting, 227, 230; occupation, 212; technology, 15, 250; teeth, 211; and Paleolithic archaeology, 210; populations, 14
Nunamiut people, 5, 63, 64

O
Optimal Foraging Theory, 23, 232
Ornament, 134, 213, 216, 248, 252, 255, 256, 258–259

P
Paleoindian (time period), 82
Patagonia, 30, 38, 39, 82
Plant foods: in the Andes, 105; gathering, 7; in hominin diets, 250, 252, 254, 256–258; in southern Africa, 165, 179
Preceramic (time period), 98
Premolars, 128

R
Raw material: acquisition/procurement, 76, 100, 189; characteristics, 84, 104, 215–216, 230; use, 52, 250
Residential mobility, 22, 81, 160
Resources: access, 22; aquatic/marine, 23, 28–31, 33, 64, 165, 188, 191, 212; C_3 and C_4,